U1009692

应用型系列法学教材

知识产权法

Intellectual Property Law

（汉英双语教程）

李正华 李珊 编著

微课版

WUHAN UNIVERSITY PRESS
武汉大学出版社

图书在版编目(CIP)数据

知识产权法:汉英双语教程:微课版/李正华,李珊编著. —武汉: 武汉大学出版社,2017.8

应用型系列法学教材

ISBN 978-7-307-19617-9

Ⅰ.知… Ⅱ.①李… ②李… Ⅲ.知识产权法—中国—双语教学—高等学校—教材—汉、英 Ⅳ.D923.4

中国版本图书馆 CIP 数据核字(2017)第 201055 号

责任编辑:胡　荣　　责任校对:李孟潇　　版式设计:马　佳

出版发行: **武汉大学出版社** (430072 武昌 珞珈山)

(电子邮件: cbs22@ whu. edu. cn 网址: www. wdp. com. cn)

印刷:武汉鑫佳捷印务有限公司

开本: 787×1092 1/16　印张:22　字数:519 千字　插页:1

版次:2017 年 8 月第 1 版　2017 年 8 月第 1 次印刷

ISBN 978-7-307-19617-9　定价:58.00 元

版权所有,不得翻印;凡购我社的图书,如有质量问题,请与当地图书销售部门联系调换。

前　言

知识产权制度最早出现在英国。英国于1623年就颁布了《垄断法规》。20世纪80年代以来我国开始制定知识产权法律、法规并根据需要进行了修改，还陆续加入了相应的知识产权国际公约及组织。

知识经济时代，知识产品已经成为了一种不可替代的生产要素。社会的法制化进程，也使得体现知识经济与法制结合的知识产权法在整个法学体系中更显出其重要的地位。

知识产权贸易与货物贸易、服务贸易成为了世界贸易的三大支柱。近年来，知识产权问题成为了对外贸易谈判的一个重要问题。"一带一路"①的建设，体现了"共商、共建、共享"，从而推动建立人类命运共同体，实现共同发展、共同安全和共同富裕。在"一带一路"建设中需要更多的懂外语、掌握专业技术的复合型人才。

根据教育部制定的《全国高等学校法学专业核心课程教学基本要求》，在法学专业的课程体系中，知识产权法成为16门核心课程之一。双语教学是适应我国高等教育国际化发展趋势，培养具有国际合作意识、国际交流与竞争能力的外向型和复合型人才的重要手段。因此，不少高校的法学院、知识产权学院开始为法学、知识产权专业的学生开设了一些全英文(如国际法等)或汉英双语的课程。知识产权法汉英双语教学的开展，使教科书的编写成为当务之急。

本教材已在中山大学新华学院使用6年，效果良好；其他兄弟院校使用后也给予了充分的肯定。我们在总结多年汉英双语教学经验和听取兄弟院校意见的基础上，经过修改和完善后付梓。

本教材为普通高等教育本科法学、知识产权专业学生而编写，也可作为大专和职业培训的教材或教学参考书。作者考虑到教学的需要，力图避免枯燥繁琐的理论演绎和纯粹的操作指南。因此，结合国内新的立法动态，关注社会现实中出现的新问题以及学科的发展趋势，由浅至深，既有中文的基本概念、基本原理、基本制度的阐述，也有英语课文和单词、基本句型，还有课外的英文阅读资料②，以便于拓展学生的视野。为配合教学，按每周3节课(共54课时)的教学时数安排，全书设18章，以便于教学活动之开展。

---

① The Belt and Road，"丝绸之路经济带"和"21世纪海上丝绸之路"之简称。

② 限于教材篇幅的限制，每章的课外阅读资料、试卷样题的参考答案以二维码的方式嵌入书中，读者可以根据需要扫码。

本教材所引用相关专家学者之观点、事例及课外读物，已在注释中列明出处，对相关的著作权人表示谢意！本教材的出版得到了武汉大学出版社的大力支持，胡荣编辑为此付出了辛勤的劳动，特表感谢。

受学识和视角之限制，书中存在疏漏和谬误，敬请各位不吝赐教。

编　者

2017 年 6 月

目　录

第三编　专利权制度

第四编　商标权制度

Contents

PART THREE Patent Legal System

PART FOUR Trademark Legal System

第一编 导　论

PART ONE　Basic Theories of Intellectual Property Law

第一章 知识产权法的基本理论
Chapter 1 Basic Theories of Intellectual Property Law

【引言】民事法律制度(civil law system)是以平等主体之间的人身关系(personal relations)和财产关系(property relations)为调整对象(object)的。知识产权作为无形的财产权(intangible property rights),无论是主体、客体还是其保护,均与传统的有形物权(tangible property rights)有所区别。只有掌握了知识产权法的基本理论问题,才能更好地学习和掌握具体的知识产权制度和根据相关的规定解决实际问题。

【学习目的与要求】在学习具体的知识产权制度之前,必须对相应的知识产权法的基本理论问题有所了解。通过对本章的学习,应当了解知识产权制度的起源与发展,掌握知识产权的主体(subject)、客体(object)、权利内容(content of rights)以及保护方式(protection)。对知识产权法学的相关理论有所了解,理解我国知识产权战略对社会发展的促进作用。

第一节 知识产权及其特点
I The Definition and Features of Intellectual Property

一、有关知识产权的概念(The Definition of Intellectual Property)

知识产权,又称为智力成果权、无形财产权、无体财产权等,是人们对其智力成果所享有法律保护的专有权利之统称。Essentially, intellectual property rights mean civil rights enjoyed by people resulting from creative intellectual achievements.

In the 17th century, intellectual property is first put forward by French scholar Gapzov and later developed by Belgian scholar Picardie. Picardie identified intellectual property as a special kind of legal rights which is different from real rights(物权).

In 1967, the signing of *Convention Establishing the World Intellectual Property Organization* (《建立世界知识产权组织公约》) has gradually accelerated the recognition of intellectual property in many countries and by international organizations over the world.

The American famous scholar Richard Raysman narrates: "Intellectual Property is a term referring to a number of distinct types of creations of the mind for which a set of exclusive rights are recognized—and the corresponding fields of law."①

---

① Richard Raysman. *Intellectual Property Licensing*: *Forms and Analysis* [M]. Law Journal Press, 1998-2008.

Although many of the legal principles governing intellectual property have evolved over centuries, it was not until the 19th century that the term "intellectual property" began to be used, and not until the late 20th century that it became commonplace in the United States. ① *The British Statute of Anne 1709* and *the Statute of Monopolies 1623* are now seen as the origins of copyright and patent law respectively. ②

Law experts have tried to summarize intellectual property rights, and have formed a number of definitions. These definitions can be divided into three types. The first type is the definition of high degree of abstraction. For example, Wu Handong believed that intellectual property rights were exclusive rights enjoyed by persons resulting from creative intellectual achievements. ③The second type is generalized definition. For example, intellectual property rights are the exclusive rights based on creative intellectual achievements and industrial and commercial marks. ④ The third type is defined by samples, listing all the areas where intellectual property rights are protected.

二、知识产权之基本属性与特征(Basic Attributes and Features)

(一)知识产权的基本属性(Basic Attributes of Intellectual Property)

Intellectual property rights are civil rights. Intellectual property law has the nature of civil law.

1. 私权属性(Private Rights)

The private rights nature of intellectual property rights has been confirmed by legislation. In the preamble of *Agreement on Trade-Related Aspects of Intellectual Property Rights* (《知识产权协议》, 简称 TRIPS), there is one provision: "Recognizing the intellectual property rights are private rights"⑤ which sets the tone for the protection of the entire agreement. Private rights are generally understood as civil rights that person (including natural person, legal person and other social organizations) has. Private rights are opposed to public rights.

The main intention of TRIPS emphasizes that intellectual property rights are private rights which emphasizes the equality of subjects of intellectual property rights. The first Intellectual Property Code in the world, French Intellectual Property Code in 1992, provides for protection of literary and artistic property rights and industrial property rights from the perspective of private rights.

2. 人权属性(Human Rights)

---

① Mark A. Lemley. *Property, Intellectual Property and Free Riding* [J]. Texas Law Review, 2005.

② Brad Sherman & Lionel Bently. *The Making of Modern Intellectual Property Law: The British Experience* [M]. 1760-1911. Cambridge University Press, p. 207.

③ 郑成思. 知识产权法教程[M]. 北京: 法律出版社, 1993: 1.

④ 刘春田. 知识产权法教程[M]. 北京: 中国人民大学出版社, 1995: 1.

⑤ Preamble of the Agreement on *Trade-Related Aspects of Intellectual Property Rights*.

Universal Declaration of Human Rights（《世界人权宣言》）is an important treaty on human rights. Human rights are regarded as eternal and inalienable rights beyond the times and nations. According to the theory of natural rights（天赋人权）, intellectual property rights are innate gifts. It is universal and equal to every person.

In 1976, Article 15 of *International Covenant on Economic, Social and Cultural Rights*（《经济、社会和文化权利国际公约》）says: "The States Parties to the present Covenant recognize the rights of everyone:

(1) To take part in cultural life;

(2) To enjoy the benefits of scientific progress and its applications;

(3) To benefit from the protection of the moral and material interests resulting from any scientific, literary or artistic production of which he is the author."①

知识产权具有人权属性，可以从三个方面来理解：第一，知识产权的客体为智力成果，是人们在参与社会文化生活过程中，依靠智力劳动所创造出来的，具有思想性和精神性的智力成果。对知识产权的承认和保护就是对思想自由的认可，是对人的尊严和价值的肯定。第二，知识产权制度必须保证创造者的知识产权得到保护。对智力劳动成果进行保护，有利于提高创造者的积极性，通过激励机制，促进越来越多的智力成果之诞生。第三，对智力成果保护的同时，也要保证这种激励机制能够促进而不是约束社会公众参与文化生活与分享科学进步的利益。因此，从人权属性的角度分析，知识产权制度的关键在于实现保护与限制之间的平衡。

私权与人权在本质上是统一的，理性地把握与处理两者的关系，有利于正确认知知识产权，有助于我们全面考察现代知识产权制度的价值理念和社会功能。②

（二）知识产权的基本特征（Basic Features of Intellectual Property）

As a civil right, intellectual property has the following characteristics in comparison with the real rights:

知识产权作为一种民事权利，其与物权相比较而言，具有下述特征：

1. 行政确认先定性（Administrative Affirmation Bring Ahead）

知识产权的客体具有无形性，而将某一无形客体之知识产权专门归属于某一特定主体行使权利，需要法律作出专门的规定（如著作权自作品创作完成之日起产生，无须履行任何手续），或者通过行政审查而颁发权利证书（如商标权、专利权证书等）。

Although administrative affirmation is not absolute, it has previous effectiveness（先定力）, which means obligee（权利人）has rights until meeting a veto by legal procedure.

Except for the convenience of management or the need for the third person to obtain rights, the formation of real rights usually does not require the administrative agencies to take the approval or certification to confirm the emergence and existence of rights.

2. 专有性（Exclusiveness）

---

① Article 15 of *International Covenant on Economic, Social and Cultural Rights*.

② 吴汉东等．知识产权基本问题研究[M]．北京：中国人民大学出版社，2005：15.

The exclusive right to an intellectual achievement can only be granted once, and only one applicant (including co-ownership) is identified or granted with the exclusive right. The intellectual property rights owned by the obligee(权利人) are unique and the situation of intellectual property rights with different holders does not exist.

而有形的物权，则可以在相同种类的物品上，由不同的主体分别享有不同具体标的之物权，而且互不冲突，如基于同一物品而产生所有权、他物权。

3. 地域性(Territoriality)

Rights are generated based on corresponding laws, while laws depend on the regime. So there will be independent legislation to internal affairs if different countries exist. Therefore, there comes the problem of legal validity scope.

知识产权是依据一国的相关知识产权制度而确定的，当知识产权的拥有者在一国获得法律承认而享有知识产权，并不能理当得到他国知识产权法律制度的自动认可和保护。如果需要在其他的国家获得承认和保护，通常还需要该国家的法律明确规定甚至需要行政性认定。

Regional nature of intellectual property rights and that of tangible property rights are different. It is mainly reflected in applicable principles of international private law, that is, tangible property applies to lex rei sitae(物所在地法), while intellectual property applies to law of the place where right is registered or claimed.

4. 时间性(Timeliness)

Timeliness of intellectual property shows that the duration of the right is limited by law, although the duration of trademark can be renewed, each renewal is still finite. Therefore, intellectual property is timely. That means the obligee shall enjoy the exclusive rights in a legal period. After the legal period, these exclusive rights may be lost or taken from the owner and given to the public. For example, copyright protection has ended for Lu Xun and anyone is free to copy his books *Ah Q Zheng Zhuan* and *Na Han*.

知识应当为人类所共享，但是某些享有知识产权保护的特定知识，因其具有的专有性，就产生了排斥他人使用之功效。如这一功效是无限期的，则社会科技发展和文明进步就会受到影响；而对知识产权的保护时间过短，发明创造或者设计者则难以获得相应的经济回报。

Therefore, the time limit of intellectual property rights is boundary between private rights and social rights.

(三)知识产权体系(Intellectual Property System)

知识产权作为一种权利，而权利通常被理解为一种类型化的自由(typed freedom)，因此权利有其体系性。

According to the object of intellectual property rights, Chinese scholars have made some theoretical classifications of intellectual property rights. Some scholars divided intellectual property rights into copyright and industrial property. Some scholars divided intellectual property rights into copyright, patent and trademark. Some scholars divided intellectual property rights into copyright, patent, trademark and others. However, the theoretical significance of the division should be more inclusive and in accordance with dynamic and open natures of intellectual property rights, which can be divided into rights of intellectual achievements and rights of industrial and commercial designation. ①

There are two typical international conventions providing for the system of intellectual property by complete enumeration(完全列举法):

Convention Establishing the World Intellectual Property Organization (《成立世界知识产权组织公约》), concluded in Stockholm(斯德哥尔摩) on July 14, 1967(Article 2) provides that "Intellectual property shall include the rights relating to:

(1) Literary, artistic and scientific works;

(2) Performances of performing artists, phonograms, and broadcasts;

(3) Inventions in all fields of human endeavor;

(4) Scientific discoveries;

(5) Industrial designs;

(6) Trademarks, service marks, and commercial names and designations;

(7) Protection against unfair competition;

(8) All other rights resulting from intellectual activity in the industrial, scientific, literary or artistic fields". ②

The scope of intellectual property rights provided in the *Agreement on Trade-Related Aspects of Intellectual Property Rights*(《与贸易有关的知识产权协议》, 简称 TRIPS) includes:

"(1) Copyrights and related rights;

(2) Trademarks;

(3) Geographical indications;

(4) Industrial designs;

(5) Patents;

(6) Layout designs of integrated circuits;

(7) Protection of undisclosed information (trade secrets)." ③

Comparing the provisions of two conventions, we can find that, since the purpose of TRIPS is to protect economic rights of trade, so scientific discoveries other designation except trade mark and geographical indications or other rights are not protected.

(四)知识产权与相关权利的关系(Relations Between Intellectual Property Rights and Relevant Rights)

1. 知识产权与无形财产权(intangible property rights)、信息产权(information property rights)

---

① 刘春田. 知识产权法(第三版)[M]. 北京:高等教育出版社,北京大学出版社, 1995: 12-14.

② Article 2 of *the Convention Establishing the World Intellectual Property Organization*.

③ Article 2 of *the Agreement on Trade-Related Aspects of Intellectual Property Rights*.

Judging from the classification, civil rights can be divided into personal rights(人身权) and property rights (财产权). While property rights consists of tangible property rights (有形财产权) and intangible property rights(无形财产权). Intangible property rights include property rights of creative achievements, property rights of profit-making marks(经营性标记财产权) and commercial credit rights (经营性资信权).

Within the perspective of the theory of information property rights(信息产权理论), the products under protection of Intellectual Property Law can be viewed as types of information. Therefore, information property(信息产权), refers to the property rights people enjoy from information collection process.

2. 知识产权与发明权(Right of Invention)、发现权(Right of Discovery)

发明权，是指发明人依法以现有生产技术水平的变革活动的权利以及由此所取得的发明创造性成果取得的权利。它包括发明人对一项不能取得专利或者即便符合授予专利而不愿取得专利的发明所获得的权利。

The right of invention refers to the right of the inventor to make creative achievements in accordance with the existing technology according to the law.

Right of invention is not equal to invention patent. Invention patent is inventor's exclusive right to his invention which is protected by patent law. Some inventions cannot be patented based on the protection restrictions.

Right of discovery refers to the right of the recognition of phenomena, properties or laws of the material universe which hitherto has not been recognized and verified.

发明权和发现权着重于人身权方面，其并非知识产权意义上的“财产权”。因此，将发明权和发现权列入科技(政策)法的范畴似乎更合适些。

3. 知识产权与知识产权的许可使用权(Licensing)

Intellectual property rights are rights of ownership, while licensing of intellectual property rights are rights of use, which uses others' intellectual achievements by acquiring owner's permission or by compulsory licensing.

4. 知识产权与知识产权请求权(Claim for Intellectual Property Right)

知识产权请求权，是指知识产权人或知识产权许可使用人在知识产权受侵害或有受侵害之虞时，得向侵害人主张停止并消除已经存在的妨害或预防妨害发生的请求权。

知识产权是实体性权利(substantive rights)，知识产权请求权是行使实体性权利的程序性权利，二者缺一不可。

第二节 知识产权制度的起源及发展
Ⅱ The Origin and Development of Intellectual Property System

知识产权通常被认为是萌芽于封建社会的特权(privilege)。该特权或由君主个人、封建国家、代表君主的地方官授予。无论是体现“君主对思想的控制”，还是对经济利益的控制或国家以某种形式从事的垄断经营等，都与特定的历史条件有关。专利、商标、著作权制度都有其自身的起源与发展的过程，而其产生又往往伴随着相关的立法进程。

一、专利制度的萌芽与产生(The Germination and Emergence of Patent System)

(一)专利制度的萌芽(The Germination of Patent System)

In 1331, King Edward Ⅲ of England had authorized craftsman John Kempe the right of sewing and dyeing process(缝纫与染织技术).

In 1421, architect Brunelleschi in Florence got three years' exclusive legal protection for inventing a barge with hoisting gear (带吊机的驳船)to transport marbles.

In 1474, Venice was the first city to issue legal document on patent. In 1602, the court of England was the first country which protected patent by Legal Precedent through the case of Darcy v. Allin.

In the 17th century, Queen Elizabeth I authorized invention patent rights for several times. During the period of Jame I, representative of the British bourgeoisie(英国资产阶级代表) tried to have legislation on the patent.

(二)专利制度的产生(The Emergence of Patent System)

After the 16th century, the early British bourgeoisie, in order to pursue wealth and maintain the prosperity of the national economy, encouraged invention. In 1623, the British Parliament(英国国会) passed and promulgated *the Statute of Monopolies*(《垄断法规》), which is the first modern patent law in the world.

At the beginning of the 18th century, in order to break the privilege of ranks and power, the United Kingdom proceeded to improve its patent system further by the rule of autonomy of the will (意思自治)and freedom of contract(合同自由)after the bourgeois revolution.

A patent is a limited property right that the government gives inventors in exchange for their agreement to share details of their inventions with the public.

Patent specification (专利说明书) is the milestone of the establishment of modern patent legal system. By the turn of the 19th century, patent system was carried out in European nations and the United States. So far, more than 170 countries and regions have established their patent system.

二、商标制度的萌芽与产生(The Germination and Emergence of Trademark)

(一)商标制度的萌芽(The Germination of Trademark System)

In English lexicon, the word *brand* originally meant anything hot or burning, such as a firebrand or a burning stick. Cattle brands play an important role in identifying an animal's owner in cattle ranching. The practice of branding is ancient. Some Egyptian tomb paintings at least 4,000 years old depict scenes of roundups and cattle branding, and biblical evidence suggests that Jacob the herdsman branded his stock. ①

Burning an identifying mark into the hide of an animal was, until the invention of the tattoo, the only method of marking that lasted the life of the animal. The practice of branding became particularly widespread in nations with large cattle grazing regions, such as Spain.

(二)商标制度的产生(The Emergence of Trademark System)

In 1803, France first established the legal protection of trade mark. Under *Law on Factory, Manufacturing Field and Workshop* (《关于工厂、制造场和作坊的法律》), counterfeit trademark(假冒商标) was punished as counterfeit legal instrument(私造文书)。

In 1804, France first endowed trade mark the same protection with other property rights *in Codes Napoleon* (《法国民法典》).

In 1857, *Manufacturing Marker and Trademark Law on Use Principle and Non-censorship Principle*(《关于以使用原则和不审查原则为内容的制造标记和商标的法律》) is the first trademark law of French and the world, since then the legal protection of trademark is comprehensively established.

三、著作权制度的萌芽与产生(The Germination and Emergence of Copyright)

(一)著作权制度的萌芽(The Germination of Copyright System)

The history of copyright law starts with early privileges and monopolies granted to printers of books. The first copyright law was issued in England and was classified to Print Law, not copyright law. In 1662, *The Licensing Law* (《许可证法》) which is issued by England specified: 1. Whoever prints shall register with publishing company to get a printing permission; 2. Whoever obtains a permission has right to prohibit others re-print or import relevant books. ②

(二)著作权制度的产生(The Emergence of Copyright System)

The parliament(议会) of United Kingdom passed the first copyright law worldwide—*The Kingdom of Great Britain's Statute of Anne of* 1710 (《安妮女王法令》, *Anne Queen Acts*). *Anne Queen Acts* is the cornerstone of modern copyright theory system.

The Federal Copyright Law (《美国联邦版权法》), which promulgated in 1790, was greatly influenced by *Anne Queen Acts*. Thus America became the second country that possesses copyright law.

In 1834, Spain issued *Royal Law on Printing*(《皇家印刷法》).

In 1791, France promulgated *Performance Rights Law*(《表演权法》). In 1793 a new law was passed giving authors, composers, and artists the exclusive right to sell and distribute their works, and the right was extended to their heirs and assigns for 10 years after the author's death. The National Assembly placed this law firmly on a natural right footing, calling the law the

---

① David Dary. *Cattle Brands*, *Handbook of Texas Online* [M]. Texas State Historical Association, 2011.

② Article 5 of *Licensing Law of* 1662.

"Declaration of the Rights of Genius" and so evoking the famous Declaration of the Rights of Man and of the Citizen.

四、知识产权制度产生的社会条件(Social Conditions of the Emergence of Intellectual Property System)

知识产权制度，仅有先进的科学技术并不能催生之，它还需要有一定的历史条件和环境以及相关制度之匹配。知识产权制度的建立能够促进科技的发展。没有知识产权制度，仅有的一点发明创造成果，也难以使社会得到整体的科技提升。这也就不难理解为什么中国古代就有四大发明，但科技在近代发展得却如此缓慢。因此，社会生产的科学技术化、科学技术成果的商品化、知识财产的法律制度化、知识产权制度的体系化，使知识产权制度得以逐渐的建立和完善。①

知识产权制度产生的社会历史条件可归纳为以下四点：

First, intellectual property appears with the development of new technology. Since the traditional craft is limited to craft workshop, a protection of privilege is enough. But when the developing technology may easily transcend the existing confidential technology, it is necessary to protect the monopoly before entering public domain.

Second, intellectual property develops with the cultural transmission and ideal updating. From the 14th century to the 16th century, Renaissance which highlighted humanism strengthened the protection of private rights and intellectual achievements.

Third, intellectual property is born with political reform. During the 17th century, many ideologists and politicians appeared in bourgeois revolution of Britain, such as Hobbes, Milton and Locke. The principles of sovereignty, equality freedom and private rights which shall not be infringed helped to promote the political reform and the construction of legal system.

Fourth, intellectual property accompany with the revival of the Roman law. The 15th to 16th century, people had a mental reflection of property protection on the Roman law, holding the idea that the intangible assets shall be protected by law. This understanding provided a solid legal foundation to perfect the intellectual property system.

五、知识产权制度的发展(Development of Intellectual Property System)

(一)传统知识产权的范围不断扩大(Expansion of Scope)

As the legal form to protect intellectual achievements, the scope of intellectual property rights expands with the scope of intellectual property constantly. It has grown from copyrights, patents, trademarks to the rights of trade secrets, domain names and so on. Intellectual property rights are not those of a single form, but a combination of a bundle of rights.

(二)知识产权法律体系不断完善(Improvement of Legal System)

著作权、专利权、商标权是传统的知识产权法的三大基本制度。集成电路布图设计

① 吴汉东等．知识产权基本问题研究[M]．北京：中国人民大学出版社，2005：65~68.

(layout-designs of integrated circuits)、计算机软件(computer software)、数据库(data base)、植物新品种(new varieties of plants)、基因(gene)等逐渐由专门的法律加以规范因而出现的相关知识产权立法，无一例外地说明了知识产权制度随着社会的发展而不断得以完善。

(三)知识产权的保护呈现国际化趋势(International Trend)

知识产权的地域性与国际化发展趋势互为存在条件并不断催生对立面。知识产权的国际条约与国内知识产权制度之间不断发生冲突，继而融合。知识产权保护标准的国际化以及协调保护已经成为知识产权的国际话题。

(四)知识产权与人权(Human Rights)、贸易(Trade)等相关联

在贸易国际化的发展态势下，知识产权已经不再是一个国家的内政问题，它不但涉及人权，还涉及贸易，因此也就不难理解在世界贸易组织下所确定了《与贸易有关的知识产权协议》(*Agreement on Trade-Related Aspects of Intellectual Property Rights*，简称 TRIPS)。

(五)知识产权的利益平衡(Balance of Interests)及处置(Management)

Intellectual property is monopolistic, but the development of society needs cultural communication and knowledge dissemination. The protection of intellectual property must be based on the balance of interests.

利益平衡则涉及利益的主体以及利益平衡的处理原则，这不但需要在发达国家与发展中国家、欠发达国家之间取得平衡，还需要在权利人与社会大众之间取得平衡。

第三节 知识产权制度的作用
Ⅲ The Influences of Intellectual Property System

一、鼓励创新(Encouraging Innovation)

Historically, science, technology and inventions certainly can promote the development of the society to some extent. But, if there is no institutional safeguard, even new technology would not create positive effect in long term. Only encouraging the innovation property system can possibly provide appropriate individual stimulation.

In 1624, England carried out *The Statute of Monopolies*. North Douglass (道格拉斯·诺斯) said in his speech: "If there is no guarantee of institutional factors of personal often stimulation and private industry and its income is no guarantee of modern industry, could not have developed." ①It is not difficult to understand the famous remark that "the patent system adds fuel to the fire of genius".

二、保护专有权利(Protecting Proprietary Rights)

Inventions, as intellectual achievements, are not protected by law naturally; it must rely on

① 柳适，张家恕，郝明工等．诺贝尔经济学奖得主讲演集[M]．呼和浩特：内蒙古人民出版社，1998：534.

the construction of legal system. 人是理性的，对财产的“贪欲”和追求，从另一个侧面体现了文明的进程，“营利性”目标成为了对人具有极大支配作用、生机勃勃的力量，① 而“恒产恒心”则反映了人们对财产保护的渴望。

The monopoly rights of intellectual property rights themselves can repel other people's use in a certain period of time, thus guaranteeing the inventor's exclusive right to their intellectual achievements, in order to reclaim their scientific research investment and obtain corresponding profits, and then promote people's creative activities.

三、促进市场交易(Promoting Market Transactions)

作为无形财产权的知识产权，专有权人(patentee)可以通过自己实施来获得经济利益。

Under the doctrines of proprietary sanctions and autonomy of the will, patentee can assign or license his patent rights for benefit. Intangible assets promote the trade circulation of cultural, scientific and technological achievements, accelerating the civilization of material and spirit civilization.

四、维护社会公益(Safeguarding Social Commonweal)

From the aspect of human rights, every single person has the rights to enjoy the benefits of technology. Therefore, intellectual rights are not absolute, but have a certain range of limitations.

在社会利益、他人利益和知识产权人利益之间要实现平衡，仅靠权利人的思想道德制约是难以实现的，必须通过公开透明、可预期的制度加以安排。对知识产权既要保护权利人在一定地域、一定时间内的垄断权，又要打破其永久的垄断性占有，这就需要对知识产权人、社会公众之间有一个利益平衡的考量和安排。

Therefore, the appropriate restrictions on the copyright (such as fair use, legal permission), the trademark rights, and the patent rights become a certainty to safeguard the public interest.

第四节 知识产权的利用、保护与反垄断
Ⅳ The Utilization, Protection and Anti-monopoly of Intellectual Property

一、知识产权的利用(The Utilization of Intellectual Property)

(一)知识产权利用的意义(The Significance of Utilization)

权利的静态支配之法律确认和动态的流转之法律保护，构成了财产权的两大部分并衍生出传统民法的物权法(property law)及合同法(contract law)。从某种意义上说，知识产权的利用是知识产权制度的必然要求。知识产权的利用，具有深刻的社会意义。

1. 实现知识财产的价值

① 刘春田．知识产权法(第三版)[M]．北京：高等教育出版社，北京大学出版社，2007：25.

Intellectual products（知识产品）cannot walk into economic market by themselves. Ownership（所有权）cannot realize its value just by itself, but by possession（占有）, utilization（使用）, seeking profits（收益）and disposition（处分）of the specific products.

充分利用知识产权，将知识产权之标的通过特定的形式传播开来，并得到相应的对价，不但满足了社会对知识产品的需求，也促使了知识产权向社会价值和经济价值的转换。

一个国家的知识产权授权量是衡量一个国家知识产权制度或者科技发达程度的标志，但却不是绝对唯一的标志，知识产权的运用（实施）率，则是深层次地反映知识产权制度对社会发展影响的一个量值标准。

2. 维系创造者、传播者与社会大众利益平衡的关系

The subjects of intellectual property rights are not only the owners of the products, but also the social public who is under lawful and reasonable utilization.

知识产品通过利用，创造者享有所有权，传播者享有传播劳动过程中应有的权利，社会大众享有因知识产品传播而得到的收益，各自从动态的角度来实现利益平衡。知识产品的利用表面上体现出权利人与知识产品之间的关系，而实质上则是反映出了权利人与社会大众之间的利益平衡。

3. 权利保护中排他性权力促使其价值的体现

The values that intellectual products provide lie in serving society（服务社会）, benefiting mankind（造福人类）, and paying corresponding consideration to creators and disseminators. To enjoy intellectual property rights, you must pay certain consideration, which is not only the original investment , but also the expenses in maintaining effectiveness of these rights（such as registration fee of trademark, maintenance fee of patent, etc.）.

作为一种私权向社会公用领域转化的过程中，一定时间的垄断是以相应之对价为交换条件的。因此，在权利保护期限内，权利的排他性要求使用人向知识产权人交付一定的使用费用，来实现所有权的“收益”之权能，而不至于使知识产权成为权利人的“负资产”。权利—利用—效益—再拥有其他新的权利，这样的互动和进入良性循环，才是知识产权制度应有之义。

（二）知识产权利用的主体及方式（The Subjects and Methods of Utilization）

1. 知识产权人的利用（The Utilization of Intellectual Property Owner）

知识产权的权利人（intellectual property owner）对知识产品的利用，是通过实现知识产权的支配权来实现的。

（1）自我实施（Self-enforcement）

自己发表作品，把自己的专利技术运用到自己的产品生产中，将知识产品申请商标注册并在生产、服务中实际使用，等等，都是自我实施知识产权的表现。通过知识产权所有人实施，知识产品在社会中得以传播，社会大众也就获得了带有知识产权相应的商品或服务。

（2）转让（Assignment）

As a private right, intellectual property rights of owner can be partly or wholly assigned to the assignee in a certain period.

由于著作权具有的人身、财产的双重属性，因此著作权的财产权是可以转让的，而著作权的人身权(如署名权等)则不能转让。

(3)授权使用(Authorization)

授权使用又称之为许可使用，国际上又称之为许可证贸易，是指知识产权所有人将其知识产权中的全部或者部分权能许可他人利用的法律行为。

The creative activities evolve to the exclusive activities of professionals gradually. Authorizers of the creative activities may not have corresponding industrial conditions to carry out. Therefore, authorizers obtain intellectual property through creative activities and acquire benefits through transfer or authorization.

(4)设定信托(Trust)

Trust is the property held by trustee for the benefit of the beneficiary. The value of intellectual property lies in its commercialization and not in its mere creation and development per se. Competitive advantage arises out of the way in which corporate organizes and performs activities and the activities are the means by which a firm creates value in its product for its buyers. The value and the value addition for the buyer is the end product for any organization.

专业化创作与职业化管理，凸显了社会分工不断细化的过程。在“凡事皆可信托”的普通法思想影响下，受托人接受委托人交付的知识产权，按照约定之目的进行管理和处分的知识产权信托现象也逐渐为人们所接受。在著作权领域，集体管理就可以理解为一种信托管理方式。

(5)设定质权(Mortgage)

将知识产权设定质权，当债务到期不能履行时，质押权人可要求将知识产权通过法定程序拍卖或者变卖，质押权人对其所得款项有优先的受偿权。知识产权可设定质权，体现了知识产权作为一种财产权应有的性质。

2. 社会大众的利用(The Utilization of Public)

(1)合理使用(Fair Use)

合理使用，是依据法律规定，他人不必征得知识产权人的同意，也无须向其支付报酬而自由使用知识产品的制度性安排。

The legal concept of “Test copyright” was first ratified by *Statute of Anne of* 1710(《安妮女王法令》). As room was not made for the authorized reproduction of copyrighted content within this newly formulated statutory right, the courts created a doctrine of “fair abridgment” in Gyles v. Wilcox, which eventually evolved into the modern concept of “fair use”, that recognized the utility of such actions. The doctrine only existed in the U. S. as common law until it was incorporated into the Copyright Act of 1976, 17 U. S. C. § 107.

Fair use, a limitation and exception to the exclusive right granted by copyright law to the author of a creative work, is a doctrine in United States copyright law that allows limited use of copyrighted material without acquiring permission from the rights holders. Examples of fair use include commentary, criticism, news reporting, research, teaching, library archiving and scholarship. It provides for the legal, non-licensed citation or incorporation of copyrighted material in another author's work under a four-factor balancing test.

尽管在著作权法中有专门的合理使用之规定，在专利法中也有相关的规定，而在商标法中往往没有明文的规定，但是对知识产权的限制，承认社会大众非商业性的合理使用权利，是知识产权制度实现利益平衡的应有之义。

(2)法定许可(Statutory Licensing)

法定许可，是指根据法律的直接规定，以特定方式使用已经公知的知识产品，可不经知识产权人同意但必须支付费用而使用的制度性安排。法定许可，在著作权领域出现。从作品已经向社会公开发表的事实，可以推定著作权人对其作品进入公用领域，允许他人使用，从而促进作品传播的本意。因此，任何人进一步传播作品的使用，是符合著作权人本意的，只是在商业性使用其作品时应当向著作权人付费，而费用标准和具体的支付方式可由双方当事人来意定。

(3)强制许可(Compulsory Licensing)

强制许可，是在特定的条件下，由知识产权主管机关应当事人的请求而强行许可他人使用，使用者向知识产权人支付费用的制度性安排。强制许可具有法定许可的替代功能，① 是在普适性法定许可制度之外的一种特殊性法定程序许可，也是对知识产权最底线的限制。

What happens if a patent owner refuses to license the use of the patented invention by demanding unreasonable terms? The law in many countries provides that where the patented product is not available or is available at exorbitant prices, the government may on grounds of public interest authorize an interested manufacturer to use the patent against payment to the patent holder of an adequate royalty. However, the agreement lays down strict conditions for such licensing to ensure that compulsory licenses are issued only in exceptional situations and on an objective basis. In particular, it provides that compulsory licenses may be granted only when the interested manufacturer has failed in his or her efforts to obtain the authorization on reasonable terms and conditions. Box 49 lists some of the other conditions which must be fulfilled before governments can intervene and license a manufacturer to use patented technology. ②

二、知识产权的保护(The Protection of Intellectual Property)

(一)知识产权的保护范围(The Scope of Protection)

Intellectual property rights are different with traditional real rights(物权) and obligatory rights(债权). The scope of legal protection is varied to different kind of intellectual products.

Copyright law protects works, not its ideological thoughts, but certain form of ideological thoughts. Virtually, technical features and technical scope are specific embodiments of creative thoughts that patent law protects.

---

① 吴汉东等. 知识产权基本问题研究[M]. 北京：中国人民大学出版社，2005：49.

② Article 31 of *Agreement on Trade-Related Aspects of Intellectual Property Rights*.

The exclusive right to registered trademark is not effective when operating beyond the registered conditions.

知识产权保护的不仅是一种专有权，权利人受到保护更多的是以一种禁止权被体现出来，即依法得以禁止他人非法使用知识产品的权利。

(二)知识产权损害赔偿的归责原则(Doctrine of Liability Fixation)

归责原则，是归咎责任的基本准则。

The core point of liability fixation is the causation between wrong action and its liability.

关于知识产权侵权赔偿的归责原则，法学界有不同的认识。有过错归责的“一元归责”学说，也有以过错归责为主、辅以其他归责(无过错、过错推定)原则的“二元归责”学说。①

凡是未经知识产权人同意又没有法定理由而使用享有知识产权的知识产品行为，主观上都是有过错的(明知不可而为之)。知识产权的侵权归责应当采用过错归责原则。理论上，任何的归责均应当基于主观上的过错。根据“谁主张谁举证”的证据规则，就算是无过错归责，也只是法定明确了某些客观情形，不问过错是否存在只要有损害，就要归咎责任；而绝对不是主观上无过错而强行归咎其责任。

尊重知识和尊重他人的知识产权，是社会上每一个人应有的义务；侵犯他人的知识产权在主观上是有过错的，只是在某些特定情形下行为造成的侵害结果并非是行为人的主观追求和放任，在一定程度上可以免除赔偿责任而已。例如，某商场尽到了合理的注意义务，进货后销售，之后发现了该批货物为假冒他人注册商标的，销售者能够提供货物之合法来源并立即停止销售的，可以免除赔偿责任(免除的仅仅是赔偿责任而非全部的侵权责任)。

(三)知识产权的保护方式(The Methods of Protection)

1. 民事保护(Civil Protection)

凡是不符合合理使用、法定许可条件，又没有强制许可的情形下，任何人未经知识产权权利人的许可，不得对知识产品加以利用。换而言之，知识产权人有依法禁止他人非法利用其知识产品的权利；当发生知识产权侵权行为时，知识产权人有权向公权力机关要求获得救济(要求行政查处或者寻求司法救济)。

Intellectual property rights, as private rights, has various relief for resolution when being infringed, including negotiation between the property owner and tort infringers, submitting to arbitration when there is an arbitration clause, or even a civil lawsuit when necessary.

2. 行政查处(Administrative Governance)

Intellectual property infringements not only violate private rights, but also disrupt the normal social order, even encroach on the common interests of the state and the public. Therefore, intellectual property infringements committed thc administrative law, too

知识产权的行政管理机关，可依职权对侵犯知识产权的行为予以查处，可没收侵权工具及设备、销毁侵权复制品，没收非法所得并可处以相应的行政处罚，以打击侵权活动。

---

① 吴汉东等．知识产权基本问题研究[M]．北京：中国人民大学出版社，2005：56.

3. 刑事打击(Criminal Protection)

The article 61 of the *TRIPS* further appeals countries to see that, where there is "willful trademark counterfeiting or copyright piracy on a commercial scale", the infringer is prosecuted under criminal law and imprisoned or fined to an extent sufficient to provide a deterrent. ①

我国的刑法规定了"侵犯知识产权罪",明确了侵犯著作权罪、假冒注册商标罪、假冒专利罪、侵犯商业秘密罪、侵犯商誉权罪等各项罪名,在刑罚上规定了有期徒刑、拘役、管制、罚金等。

三、知识产权的反垄断(Anti-monopoly of Intellectual Property)

知识产权是一种专有性权利(exclusive rights),具有垄断性(monopoly)。《反垄断法》(*Antitrust Law*)所规制的是经济性垄断行为,包括了经营者达成垄断协议;经营者滥用市场支配地位;具有或者可能具有排除、限制竞争效果的经营者集中等。

就著作权、商标权和制止不正当竞争的权利而言,基本上不存在滥用的可能性,只有涉及专利权时,才可能发生滥用的问题。"DVD 专利池"和"华为诉思科"等知识产权案件引起了社会各界的强烈反应和广泛关注。对于专利技术控制所产生的垄断问题,在专利法的强制许可制度中能够加以解决:具备实施条件的单位以合理的条件请求发明或者实用新型专利权人许可实施其专利,而未能在合理长的时间内获得这种许可时,国务院专利行政部门根据该单位的申请,可以给予实施该项发明或者实用新型的强制许可。

第五节 知识产权法学
V The Education of Intellectual Property Law

一、知识产权法学及学科定位(Intellectual Property Law and Its Academic Position)

(一)知识产权法(Intellectual Property Law)

1. 知识产权立法(Legislation)

知识产权法,是调整因知识产品而产生的各种社会关系的法律规范之总称。具体而言,就是调整因知识产权确权、知识产权运用、知识产权保护和知识产权管理所产生的社会关系的法律规范之总称。

The objects of intellectual property are creations of the human mind. Under Intellectual property law, owners are granted certain exclusive rights to a variety of intangible assets, such as musical, literary, and artistic works; discoveries and inventions; and words, phrases, symbols, and designs. Common types of intellectual property include copyrights, trademarks, patents, industrial design rights and trade secrets in some jurisdictions.

Since the 1980s, the state has promulgated and enforced many laws and regulations which

① Article 61 of *the agreement on Trade-Related Aspects of Intellectual Property Rights*.

cover the main content of intellectual property protection, including *Trademark Law of the People's Republic of China*(promulgated in 1982, revised in 1993 , 2001 and 2013), *Patent Law of the People's Republic of China*(promulgated in 1984, revised in 1993 , 2000 and 2008), *Copyright Law of the People's Republic of China* (promulgated in 1990, revised in 2000 and 2010), *Regulations on Computers Software Protection* (promulgated in 2001), *Regulations on the Protection of Layout-designs of Integrated Circuits* (promulgated in 2001), *Regulations on Collective Management of Copyright*(promulgated in 2004), *Regulations on the Protection of New Varieties of Plants* (promulgated in 1997), *Regulations on Customs Protection of Intellectual Property Rights* (promulgated in 1995, revised in 2003 and 2010), *Regulations on the Administration of Special Sign*(promulgated in 2003), etc.

China actively accedes to major conventions and treaties for international intellectual property rights protection. 1980 年 6 月 3 日，中国成为世界知识产权组织成员国。2001 年 12 月 11 日，中国加入世界贸易组织，开始履行《与贸易有关的知识产权协议》(*Agreement on Trade-Related Aspects of Intellectual Property Rights*，简称 TRIPS)项下的义务。多年来，中国还相继加入了《保护工业产权巴黎条约》(*Paris Convention for the Protection of Industrial Property*)、《专利合作条约》(*Patent Cooperation Treaty*，简称 PCT)、《商标国际注册马德里协定》(*Madrid Agreement Concerning the International Registration of Trademarks*)、《国际植物新品种保护公约》(*International Convention for the Protection of New Varieties of Plants*)、《保护文学和艺术作品伯尔尼公约》(*Berne Convention for the Protection of Literary and Artistic Works*)、《世界版权公约》(*Universal Copyright Convention*)等 10 多个国际公约、条约、协定或议定书。

2. 知识产权法的地位(The Status of Intellectual Property Law)

知识产权法的地位，是指知识产权法在整个法律部门体系中所处的位置与作用。知识产权法，是相对于有形财产法而言的。从知识产权的私权性质以及法律调整的范围以及遵从的原则来分析，知识产权法调整的是平等主体之间因创造或使用智力成果而产生的财产关系和人身关系，因此仍然属于民法的范畴。知识产权法在目前不可能脱离民法而成为一个独立的法律部门。

Intellectual property law regulates property relations and personal relations of intellectual achievements between equal subjects, so it belongs to the category of civil law.

为了加强对知识产权的保护，促进科技创新，建设创新型国家，2017 年 3 月 15 日全国人大审议并通过的《中华人民共和国民法总则》(简称《民法总则》)第 123 条规定，民事主体对作品、发明、实用新型、外观设计、商标、地理标志、商业秘密、集成电路布图设计、植物新品种及法律规定的其他客体依法享有知识产权。对比《民法通则》的规定，《民法总则》中规定的商业秘密、集成电路布图设计、植物新品种等均为新增内容。

(二)知识产权法学学科定位(The Discipline Status)

1. 知识产权法学(Intellectual Property Law)

知识产权法学，是指以知识产权法律规范和知识产权社会现象为研究对象的科学。它是以知识产权法律规范和知识产权社会现象作为主要研究对象的一门新兴的法律科学。

2. 知识产权法学的定位(The Discipline Status of Intellectual Property)

知识产权法学，同法学的其他分支学科一样，都是以特定的法律现象作为自己的研究对象，并揭示出这种现象的本质、内容、作用及其产生、发展的规律性。

法学是一个学科体系，传统上我们可以分为宪法学(constitution)、民法学(civil law)、刑法学(criminal law)、行政法学(administrative law)、经济法学(economic law)、诉讼法学(litigation law)等诸多法学的一级学科。知识产权法学属于传统民法学中的主要构成部分之一，与传统的物权法学(real right)、合同法学(contract law)相对应。

二、知识产权法学教育(Education of Intellectual Property Law)

1987年9月，中国人民大学招收全国第一届知识产权第二学士学位学生。自1987年9月以后，又有北京大学、华中科技大学等少数几所学校招收知识产权第二学士学位学生，培养知识产权专门人才。20世纪90年代以后，北京大学率先成立知识产权学院，进行知识产权专门人才的培养。全国至今已有20多所高校成立了知识产权学院。尤其是1998年教育部将知识产权法学作为14门法学核心课之一以后，所有开设法学专业的学校都为本科学生开设了知识产权法学的课程，从而使知识产权法学教育全面展开。我国高等院校进行的知识产权高等教育大致有以下九种模式：将知识产权教育纳入素质教育范畴；为自学考试、成人教育、继续教育、电大学生开设知识产权法课程；为非法学本科生开设选修知识产权法课程；为法学本科生开设知识产权法必修课程；招收知识产权第二学士学位学生；招收知识产权法律方向的硕士；招收知识产权专业法律硕士；招收民法学知识产权法学方向的博士；招收知识产权管理学博士。

近20年，我国培养的知识产权人才包括以下五种模式：知识产权管理型人才；知识产权司法执法型人才；知识产权教研型人才；知识产权服务型人才；知识产权实务型人才。① 归结起来，高校知识产权教育可以分为专业型教育、普及型教育和在职培训教育等三种不同类型的教育形式与教育体系。

为了实现中国由知识产权大国向知识产权强国的转变，充分发挥知识产权制度在中国经济和社会发展中的作用，我们必须大力加强知识产权教育，加强知识产权人才的培养。②

第六节 知识产权战略与社会发展
Ⅵ The Strategy and Social Development of Intellectual Property

一、知识产权战略(The Intellectual Property Strategy)

(一)知识产权战略的提出(The Proposal of Intellectual Property Strategy)

知识产权战略(intellectual property strategy)，是指一个国家或地区运用知识产权制度，

① 曹新明．知识产权高等教育对经济发展与国际经济关系的贡献[DB/OL]．[2016-12-14]．中国知识产权研究网，http：//www.iprcn.com/view_new.asp？idname=1882.

② 陈美章．我国高校知识产权教育和人才培养的思考[J]．知识产权，2006(1)：8.

为充分维护自己的权益，获得与保持竞争优势并遏制竞争对手，谋求最佳经济效益而进行的整体性筹划和采取的一系列策略与手段。

知识产权战略，可以根据不同的层面进行划分，如国家知识产权战略（state intellectual property strategy）、地区知识产权战略（regional intellectual property strategy）、行业知识产权战略（intellectual property strategy of guild）、企业知识产权战略（industrial intellectual property strategy）。

（二）我国的知识产权战略（Intellectual Property Strategy of China）

1.《国家知识产权战略纲要》的制定过程

2005 年 1 月国务院办公厅发文成立了"国家知识产权战略制定工作领导小组"作为制定国家知识产权战略为任务的机构。国家知识产权战略制定工作领导小组由吴仪副总理任组长，国务院副秘书长徐绍史，以及国家知识产权局局长、工商行政管理总局、版权局、发展改革委、科技部、商务部等领导担任副组长，国务院 23 个部门的主要负责人成为该领导小组的成员。

2008 年 6 月 5 日，国务院颁布了《国家知识产权战略纲要》（*Outline of National Intellectual Property Strategy*），决定实施国家知识产权战略。① 这标志着中国的知识产权工作进入了一个新的阶段。

2.《国家知识产权战略纲要》的总体要求

《国家知识产权战略纲要》，分序言（preamble）、指导思想（guiding ideology）和战略目标（strategic objective）、战略重点（strategic focus）、专项任务（special task）、战略措施（strategic measure）共五个部分。明确到 2020 年把我国建设成为知识产权创造（creation）、运用（utilization）、保护（protection）和管理（administration）水平较高的国家，5 年内自主知识产权水平大幅度提高，运用知识产权的效果明显增强，知识产权保护状况明显改善，全社会知识产权意识普遍提高。

3. 指导思想和战略重点（Guiding Ideology and Strategic Focus）

（1）指导思想（Guiding Ideology）

In implementing the national intellectual property strategy, we need to abide by the policy of encouraging creation, effective application, legal protection and scientific administration. We must concentrate our efforts to improve the intellectual property system, actively work to create a favorable legal environment, market environment and cultural environment for the development of intellectual property in order to greatly improve China's capacity to create, utilize, protect and administer intellectual property. This will provide strong support for the effort to make China an innovative country and develop a moderately prosperous society in all respects.

（2）战略重点（Strategic Focus）

---

① 国务院发布《国家知识产权战略纲要》（国发 200818 号），指出到 2020 年把我国建设成为知识产权创造、运用、保护和管理水平较高的国家，5 年内自主知识产权水平大幅度提高，运用知识产权的效果明显增强，知识产权保护状况明显改善，全社会知识产权意识普遍提高。纲要共分序言、指导思想和战略目标、战略重点、专项任务、战略措施五个部分。

①完善知识产权制度，健全知识产权执法和管理体制。Perfect the intellectual property laws and regulations, and strengthen the guiding role of intellectual property rights in the economic, cultural and social policy.

②促进知识产权创造和运用。Use fiscal, financial, investment, government procurement policies and industry, energy, environmental protection policies, to guide and support market subjects to create and apply intellectual property rights, and make enterprises the main body in the creation and application of intellectual property.

③加强知识产权保护。Strengthen the judicial punishment of infringement, reduce the cost of safeguarding rights, and raise the cost of infringing rights.

④防止知识产权滥用。Formulate relevant regulations, define boundaries of reasonable intellectual property, and maintain the market order of fair competition and public legal rights.

⑤培育尊重知识、崇尚创新、诚信守法的知识产权文化。Strengthen the knowledge propagation on intellectual property right and increase the awareness of intellectual property right in the whole society. Carry out the ordinary intellectual property right education extensively.

4. 专项任务(Special Task)

《国家知识产权战略纲要》明确了专利、商标、版权、商业秘密、植物新品种(New Varieties of Plants)、特定领域知识产权、国防知识产权等专项任务，并提出了提升知识产权创造能力、鼓励知识产权转化运用、加快知识产权法制建设、提高知识产权执法水平、加强知识产权行政管理、发展知识产权中介服务、加强知识产权人才队伍建设、推进知识产权文化建设、扩大知识产权对外交流合作等九项战略措施。

5. 战略实施(Strategic Measure)

2008 年 10 月 9 日，国务院批复同意建立国家知识产权战略实施工作部际联席会议(以下简称联席会议)制度，以贯彻落实《国家知识产权战略纲要》。

联席会议由国家知识产权局牵头，知识产权局局长田力普担任召集人。成员由国务院分管副秘书长毕井泉以及中央宣传部、外交部、发展改革委、教育部、科技部、工业和信息化部、公安部、司法部、财政部、人力资源社会保障部、环境保护部、农业部、商务部、文化部、卫生部、国资委、海关总署、质检总局、工商总局、广电总局、版权局、林业局、知识产权局、法制办、中科院、高法院、高检院、解放军总装备部等共 28 个部门和单位的负责同志组成。联席会议办公室设在知识产权局，承担联席会议的日常工作。

联席会议的主要职责是：在国务院领导下，统筹协调国家知识产权战略实施工作。研究制订国家知识产权战略实施计划；指导、督促、检查有关政策措施的落实；协调解决国家知识产权战略实施过程中的重大问题；研究国家知识产权战略实施的重大政策措施，向国务院提出建议；研究协调与国家知识产权战略实施工作有关的其他重要事项。

二、知识产权战略对社会发展的影响(Influences on Social Development)

当今世界，知识产权日益成为国家发展的战略性资源和国际竞争力的核心要素，知识产权战略已成为许多国家提升核心竞争力的重要战略。自 20 世纪 80 年代以来，先后有美、日、法、中、韩、印等十几个国家提出并实施“知识产权立国”战略。

2002年7月3日，日本政府发表了《知识产权战略大纲》，将“知识产权立国”明确为国家战略；同年11月27日，国会通过了政府制定的《知识产权基本法》(共有4章33条，2003年3月1日生效)，为“知识产权立国”提供了法律保障。日本的知识产权战略提出从创造、运用、保护三个战略以及人才基础和实施体制等方面抢占市场竞争制高点。① 同年，日本内阁成立了“知识产权战略本部”，由首相任本部长，并设立了“知识产权推进事务局”，每年发布一次“知识产权推进计划”，对国家主管部门、教学科研单位、各类企业的相关任务与目标都作了规定。② 2005年，日本成立了“知识产权上诉法院”，统一审理知识产权民事和行政上诉案件，以简化程序、优化司法审判资源配置，从而更有效地保护知识产权。③

美国从20世纪80年代开始实行知识产权发展战略：对产业结构进行调整，对相应的知识产权进行改革，制定法律重新界定知识产权的权利归属和利益分配，加强对知识产权的实施和保护。在对外方面，谋求美国知识产权的权利人在全球利益的最大化，推动TRIPS的签署。

我国在2009年的国务院政府工作报告中，知识产权战略与科教兴国战略、人才强国战略并提，知识产权战略已成为我国的三大战略之一。

(一)增强自主创新能力，建设创新型国家(Improving Innovation Capability)

Throughout the science and technology development history of developed countries, we can find that indication of the technological development needs institutional arrangements and strategic plan.

创新型国家总是走在世界其他国家的前列，掌控着最先进的科学技术，在经济领域理所当然地拥有核心的竞争力，并赢取了巨额利润。创新——规模——利润——创新，已经成为了良性循环的一个过程。

(二)完善市场经济体制(Completing Market Economy)

Arrange and implement the intellectual property strategy over the whole nation can strengthen the regulation of economic market construction macroscopically and realize certain expectations of different innovation subjects.

通过知识产权战略，有计划地安排和实施国家整体的知识产权制度，既可以使一个国家或者地区的知识产权在制度构建上纳入规划，也可以使社会不同的创新主体在制度和计划安排下有一定的预期。

(三)增强竞争力(Enhancing Competitiveness)

With the development of globalization and highly technology revolution, the core competitiveness of countries is manifested by cultivation, allocation and command of Intellectual resources and achievements. The technical innovation ability can be greatly improved through

① 李正华．日中の知財立法の比較研究[DB/OL].[2016-05-02]．日本科技振兴会网站，http://www.spc.jst.go.jp/hottopics/0912intellectual property/r0912li zhenghua1.html.

② 康洛奎．日本“知识产权战略推进计划”的启示[J]．电子知识产权，2004(4)：19.

③ 梅术文，曹新明．日本知识产权法院的设置及其启示[J]．电子知识产权，2005(12)：40.

implement of intellectual property strategy. Enterprises as cells of social economic, its innovation ability, talents and property achievement are also the embodiments of core competence.

（四）扩大对外开放，实现互利共赢（Opening Wider to the Outside World and Achieving Mutual Benefits）

Since communications of intellectual property across countries increase, there are more and more trading and investing activities related with intellectual property activities. Intellectual property problems have become more international and have got the common concern of all international communities. 在知识产权制度和知识产权战略的统一安排下，国家在相互发展贸易中才能正确处理贸易冲突和知识流转的相关问题。

【英语词汇】

assignee *n.* 受让人
assignment *n.* 转让
authorization *n.* 授权
beneficiary *n.* 受益人
civil rights 民事权利
copyright *n.* 著作权
commercial names 商号
compulsory licensing 强制许可
doctrine of liability fixation 归责原则
exclusive right 专有权利
exclusiveness *n.* 专有性
fair use 合理使用
geographical indication 地理标记
human right 人权
industrial design 工业品外观设计
industrial property right 工业产权
intangible *adj.* 无形的
intellectual achievement 智力成果
intellectual property 知识产权
layout design of integrated circuits 集成电路布图设计
patent *n.* 专利
private right 私权
phonograms *n.* 录音制品
real right 物权
statutory licensing 法定许可
timeliness *n.* 时间性
territoriality *n.* 地域性
trademark *n.* 商标
trust *n.* 信托
trade secret 商业秘密
unfair competition 不正当竞争
utilization *n.* 使用

【英语句型】

1. Although many of the legal principles governing intellectual property have evolved over centuries, it was not until the 19th century that the term intellectual property began to be used, and not until the late 20th century that it became commonplace in the United States.

"Although..."表示转折，译为"尽管说……但……"。

"It was not until...that"，译为"直到……才……"。

译文：尽管知识产权的很多法律原则已经发展了几个世纪，但直到19世纪，知识产权这个术语才开始被使用，直到20世纪末，知识产权在美国才被看成是司空见惯的事情。

2. Some Egyptian tomb paintings at least 4,000 years old depict scenes of roundups and

cattle branding, and biblical evidence suggests that Jacob the herdsman branded his stock.

"suggests that ..."that 引导的宾语从句，译为"表明了……"。

3. This will provide strong support for the effort to make China an innovative country and develop a moderately prosperous society in all respects.

"provide strong support for..."表示"为……提供了强有力的支撑"。

译文：这为建设创新型国家和全面建设小康社会提供了强有力的支撑。

【阅读资料】

第二编　著作权制度

PART TWO　Copyright Legal System

第二章　著作权制度概述

Chapter 2　Overview of Copyright Legal System

【引言】著作权(copyright)赋予作者(author)有权禁止他人未经许可而复制(copy)其作品，这与房屋所有人有权禁止他人擅自闯入其土地，何其相似。但是，既谓之"知识"，就表示它具有一种不同的特性：著作权并非对诸如一片土地或者一条羊腿之类的有体财产给予保护。著作权所保护的是人的思想成果(intellectual achievements)，这些思想与表达有时可能在书籍篇章中找到，有时又可能存在于一首歌曲或者一部电影之中。这种捉摸不定的"财产"很难确定其界限。一个半世纪以前，约瑟夫·斯托里(Joseph Story)大法官就曾经评论过这一特征："*Compared with other kinds of cases debating in court, copyright is much closer to a so-called legal metaphysics, for its nature, at least so delicate and exquisite, and sometimes almost fleeting.*"①

【学习目的与要求】本章是著作权和著作权制度的基础，是学习知识产权的起点。从保护出版者利益开始，到《安妮女王法令》(*Anne Queen Acts*)的颁发，著作权制度经历了从出版特许权到现代著作权的发展过程。通过本章的学习，需要掌握著作权的概念和特征、著作权法律制度发展和演变的概况，以及我国著作权制度的历史。

第一节　著作权及其特征

Ⅰ　Copyright and Its Features

一、著作权概述(Overview of Copyright)

(一)著作权的概念(The Definition of Copyright)

著作权，亦称版权，是指作者或者其他著作权人在文学、艺术和科学领域对其作品依法所享有的各项专有权利。Copyright is the exclusive right enjoyed by the subjects based on literary, artistic and scientific works. Most copyright laws distinguish between economic and moral rights, which together constitute copyright. Literary, artistic and scientific works are the objects of copyright. Copyright is created based on specific and concrete work. No work, no copyright.

著作权与版权是否为同一概念，在我国《著作权法》立法过程中颇有异议。从历史上看，二者均来自日本，而且当初确有区别。我国《民法通则》认为著作权即版权。我国旧

---

① [美]保罗·戈斯汀．著作权之道：从古登堡到数字点播机[M]．北京：北京大学出版社，2008：6.

时的书刊，也多印有“版权所有，违者必究”字样，这种习惯一直沿袭到今天，表明著作权与版权是通用的。也有学者认为，“使用版权”一词已经过时，不如采用著作权更为准确、科学。实际上，英美法系的“copyright”，传统上译为版权，即制止他人进行复制的权利。大陆法系的“作者权”一词不能译成“copyright”，而应当译成“author's rights”。

使用不同的名词，反映不同法系对该项权利之不同态度。英美法之所以保护一个作品，是出于对复制的不良结果限制之考虑；而大陆法在形式上更倾向于保护作者的权利，认为他有控制和利用其智力成果的道义上之权利。英美法上的“版权”和欧洲大陆法上的“作者权”，既是立法观念的不同，也反映了各自立法的历史传统和当时的经济、社会条件的差异以及保护重点之不同。

In Britain and the U. S., there is a deep-rooted idea in legislation and society: copyright is a kind of property rights fundamentally. Although the nature was changed and the subject was evolved to support authors, the publishers hold the dominant status during the long-term commercial tradition. The copyright of the published book was often turned to the publisher, not the author. The tradition is still found in common law countries today.

The civil law countries, which based on the Roman legal culture and the influence of historical humanism tradition by the bourgeois enlightenment thinkers, make the respect to author the core of rights, even higher than property rights.

在立法之初，如果说“copyright”意在对财产的重视，那么“author's right”则更强调对人权理想追求的关注。今天，在经济进一步全球化之条件下，作为实质上的财产权，“版权”和“作者权”以及“著作权”的称谓留下的更多的是形式上的差别。

The copyright can be divided into a broad sense and narrow sense in the scope. The copyright, in a narrow sense, is the exclusive right of author to his work, including moral rights and property rights. The copyright, in a broad sense includes the copyright in a narrow sense and neighboring rights(邻接权), which are the rights of performers, producers of sound recordings and video recordings, broadcasting organizations and publishers. Neighboring rights protect the rights of communicators, which are adjacent to the author's copyright.

(二)著作权与其他权利的关系(Relations with Other Rights)

1. 著作权和专利权、商标权的区别(Relations between Copyright, Patent and Trademark)

著作权(copyright)和专利权(patent)、商标权(trademark)都是法律赋予人们对智力劳动创造的精神财富所享有的专有权利，同属于知识产权。但三者的区别也是明显的：著作权的行使偏重于社会精神文化财富的传播领域，专利权的行使偏重于科学技术的推广应用领域，商标权的行使则偏重于商品经济的运行领域。其区别具体表现为：

(1)权利保护内容不同

Copyrights protect the expression of ideological content of works, while the ideological content itself is not included. This is the most essential feature of copyright that distinguishes it from other intellectual property rights. On the contrary, patents protect ideas that take the form of useful, novel, and non-obvious inventions—for instance, production methods, devices and mechanical processes.

(2)权利产生途径不同

The birth of patents and trademarks should be regulated under the means of the state administrative license. 著作权的产生一般实行“无手续主义”。

(3)权利独占性程度不同

Copyright cannot reject others enjoying the same rights acquired by independent creative work, while patent rights and trademarks allow others obtain the same exclusive rights by independent creative work.

专利权利、商标权不允许相同构思的表现具有复数的专有权；而相同的思想表达内容则往往能够产生不同主体间的各自著作权。

(4)权利的保护的侧重点不同

Patent focus on property rights(财产权), the personal rights(人身权) involved only confirm who is the inventor or creator. Trade marks do not directly relate to personal rights. Both personal rights and Property rights are important elements of copyright.

2. 著作权与所有权的关系(Relations between Copyright and Ownership)

著作权与所有权虽然都具有绝对性、排他性等共同属性，但它们之间仍存在不同之处。

(1) Copyright is related to the rights of intellectual achievements created by people, including personal rights and property rights. While the ownership of the property only refers to possession, utilization. benefit and dispose of his property (personal property and real property).

(2) As an intangible property right, copyright generally carries out by utilization. While ownership is a tangible property, the owner can directly possess, utilize, benefit and dispose of rights, unless otherwise stipulated by the law.

(3) The ownership is transferred after the property transferred. While the transfer of the original works is not to be considered as the transfer of the copyright. That is to say, copyright owner still enjoys copyright of fine arts.

二、著作权的特征(Features of Copyright)

著作权作为知识产权的重要组成部分，具有知识产权的主要特征。

(一)客体的非物质性(Intangibility of Objects)

知识产权与物权相比最为突出的特征在于其保护的对象不同。

The objects of property rights are concrete matters, mainly tangible assets(有形资产). While objects of intellectual property are abstract matters, usually inventions, designs and trademarks, etc.

Similarly, objects of copyright are intellectual achievements, whose conception and emotions are expressed through paper, books, audio or videotape, computer disk, clay, cavas, etc.

实际上，著作权的对象是一种“信息”，由物质载体所“承载”或“体现”的内核是作品这样的非物质性智力成果(作品)。

（二）地域性（Territoriality）

地域性，是指某一作品的著作权保护受到某一国家地域范围的限制。

Historically, copyright was born to grant the nature of personal privilege or exclusive right authorized by monarch or state, but the awarded copyright was only protected by this state. Legally, copyright of each country won't take effect overseas. Copyright awarded or registered by one country does not necessarily under protect by others. In order to be protected by other countries, the author must make sure his own country and other countries are parties of convention, when his work is protected by the convention, he can enjoy the national treatment（国民待遇）in other parties of the convention.

Authors' rights are internationally protected by *the Berne Convention for the Protection of Literary and Artistic Works* and by other similar treaties. The author is the person whose creativity should be protected while the work has been created, although the exact definition varies from country to country.

According to the article 2 of *Berne Convention for the Protection of Literary and Artistic Works*（《伯尔尼公约》）："The enjoyment and the exercise of these rights shall not be subject to any formality; such enjoyment and such exercise shall be independent of the existence of protection in the country of origin of the work. Consequently, apart from the provisions of this Convention, the extent of protection, as well as the means of redress afforded to the author to protect his rights, shall be governed exclusively by the laws of the country where protection is claimed."

（三）时间性（Timeliness）

时间性，是指法律对著作权财产权规定的保护期之特性。Copyright laws give the property rights of a work temporal protection, and the length of term is different. After a copyright expires, the work goes into the public domain, meaning it becomes available for anyone's use.

In common law counties, copyright was born to have certain duration. In Britain, according to *The Statute of Anne*（《安妮女王法令》），the duration of publishing right（出版权）specified to the author is 14 years since first published. If the author lives as long as this period expires, the term will extend to another 14 years. The purpose of this duration is to reward the investment of publishing.

In civil law countries, take France as an example, the statute in 1793 provided the author a life-long right to authorize the right of performance（表演权），the right of reproduction（复制权）of his literary and article work. The right would be transferred to his heir（继承人），and the duration would last another 10 years after his death. In 1866, the duration would last another 50 years after the death of the author.

从作品本身的角度来看，作品的信息作为一种精神财富，具有永久存续的特点。其本身不会因为使用或时间的推移而消灭。但是，从社会的角度来说，任何作品都不可能凭空产生，总是建立在前人智力活动的基础上。如果权利保护无期限限制，显然不利于社会文化的传承、科学的发展和延续。因此，立法者基于立法政策上的考虑，规定权利人独占控制其信息的期限，期限届满，该信息即进入公有领域，以平衡信息所有人和社会公众的利益，促进社会的发展。

第二节 著作权制度的产生与发展概况
Ⅱ The Origin and Development of Copyright System

著作权的产生和发展与人类传播科技密切相关。从历史的沿革来看，著作权制度经历了从特许出版权到现代著作权的发展过程。

一、著作权制度的产生(The Origin of Copyright System)

Before the invention of the printing machine, a writing could only be physically multiplied by the highly laborious and error prone process of manual copying by scribes(抄写员). Printing allowed for multiple exact copies of a work, leading to a more rapid and widespread circulation of ideas and information. On one hand, publishing industry benefits publishers; on the other hand, illegally pirated copies(盗版) vastly harms businessmen.

Therefore, governments established controls over printers in Britain, requiring them to have official licenses to trade and produce book.

In Britain, the queen Mary I was the first one to award the royal licenses to copyright. The monopolies met the requests of publisher in certain extent, and implemented a system of censorship to prevent the spread of revolutionary ideas.

特许出版权是由君主或地方政府对作品授予的出版专有权，它是一种封建特许权，而非法律意义上的财产权。其利益的主要获取人是出版商，所保护的行为是复制发行。在这种制度下，作者本人从中并无任何受益，他们的利益既未出现在皇家的视野中，也未被追求利润的出版商所重视。因此，特许出版权不过是一种保护出版商利益的出版图书的专有权，并非著作权制度的起源。但是特许权在印刷出版的利益分配方面逐渐朝着有利于作者的方向发展，最终成为孕育现代著作权制度的胚胎。

二、现代著作权制度的发展(The Development of Modern Copyright System)

(一)英美法系著作权制度的诞生(The Origin of Copyright System in Common Law System)

随着资本主义社会的发展，特许权制度引起社会各界的不满和反对。作者团体作为资产阶级的一部分也提出了保护其创作物的利益要求，主张传播作品的行为应当得到法律上的保护。

The Kingdom of Great Britain's Statute of Anne of 1710 was the first act to directly protect the rights of authors The statute was the first to recognize that legal rights flowed from authorship, but it did not provide a coherent understanding of authorship or authors' rights. Given that the statute primarily intended to encourage public learning and to regulate the book trade, any benefits for authors in the statute were incidental.

美国的版权制度源于英国。美国早期版权制度反映了鲜明的实用主义特点。立法者认识到，版权保护能够促进知识和信息交流，而鼓励出版又有利于言论自由。知识的传播同时也有助于确保人民通过更多渠道享受社会和经济发展的利益。

At the Constitutional Convention 1787 both James Madison of Virginia and Charles Pinckney of South Carolina submitted proposals that would allow Congress the power to grant copyright for a limited time. These proposals are the origin of the Copyright Clause in the United States Constitution, namely "to promote the progress of science and useful arts, by securing for limited times to authors and inventors the exclusive rights to their respective writings and discovery". The first federal copyright act, *the Copyright Act of 1790* granted copyright for a term of "fourteen years from the time of recording the title thereof", with a right of renewal for another fourteen years if the author survived to the end of the first term. The act covered not only books, but also maps and charts. With exception of the provision on maps and charts *the Copyright Act of* 1790 is copied almost verbatim from the Statute of Anne.

(二)大陆法系著作权制度的诞生(The Origin of Copyright System in Civil Law System)

大陆法国家保护著作权的法律称为作者权法，该法律制度首创于法国，也曾经历过出版特许权制度。

The concept of "right of the author", which differs from Anglo-American copyright, finds its roots in the practice of printing patents and royal privileges, which first appeared in the 16th century and became common in the 17th century.

18 世纪末法国大革命颁布的法令取消了特许权制度，并代之以自由财产权，其理论基础是"最为神圣不可侵犯的个人财产是作者思想的果实"。

到了 19 世纪中叶，法国法学和哲学都强调"作品体现人格"，作者对其精神创作成果享有人格权利。然而直到 20 世纪早期，作者享有的精神权利才被写入法律。在以后的制度变迁中，法国著作权法又承认了发表权、收回权、发行权和保护作品完整权等作者精神权利。

法国著作权法的产生晚于英国近百年，但它却是著作权制度演变进程中的巨大进步。首先，法国著作权法赋予作者对其作品享有产权。其次，法国著作权法将作者权益的保护范围由图书的复制扩大到了作品的表演。最后，法国著作权理论承认作者的精神权利是著作权的组成部分。

(三)著作权的国际保护(The International Protection of Copyright)

随着世界经济、技术的迅猛发展，人类掌握了越来越多的传播技术。历经图书时代、广播电视时代、互联网时代，传播技术不仅冲破了语言的障碍，而且冲破了地域的限制。著作权保护也随着传播技术的发展而走向世界。

The Berne Convention for the Protection of Literary and Artistic Works, usually known as *the Berne Convention*(《伯尔尼公约》), is an international agreement governing copyright, which was first accepted in Berne, Switzerland in 1886, entering into force in 1887.《伯尔尼公约》已成为当今世界多数国家相互间保护著作权的基础性公约。

After World War Ⅱ, *The Universal Copyright Convention* (UCC,《世界版权公约》), adopted at Geneva in 1952, by the United Nations Educational, Scientific and Cultural Organization(联合国教科文组织) is one of the two principal international conventions protecting copyright. The UCC was developed as an alternative to *the Berne Convention* for those states which disagreed with aspects of the Berne Convention, but still wished to participate in some form of multilateral copyright protection.

三、中国著作权法的概况(Overview of Copyright Law of China)

(一)中国著作权制度的萌芽(The Germination of Copyright System in China)

汉朝蔡伦发明了造纸术，唐朝开始有了雕版印刷技术。宋人毕昇发明活字印刷术后，印书逐渐大规模商业化。我国很早就有了对著作权的保护做法。如公元11世纪即有关于"官府具状，禁止翻刻"的记载，南宋王稱的《东都事略》所附碑记："眉山程舍人宅刊行，已申上司，不许覆板。"①这是迄今为止世界上发现最早的"著作权保留声明"。南宋嘉熙二年(1238年)祝穆刊行的《方舆胜览》，其刻本有"照得雕书，合经使台申明，乞行约束，庶绝翻板之患"。② 这是我国历史上最早记载的出版特许令状。宋代出现的"翻板禁令"比欧洲15、16世纪出现的图书出版垄断权(monopoly of literary works)要早500年左右。如果说版权是随着印刷术的采用而出现的话，那么它应当最早始于我国。毕昇创造活字，实现了印刷技术的革命。印刷方法的进步促进了印书行业的发展。官府曾经根据印书商的请求而颁布过一些保护措施。

宋代出现的以"禁令"保护刻印出版者利益的形式，一直伴随着漫长的封建社会，持续到清末以前。显然，它与欧洲的出版垄断制度有着惊人的相似之处。禁令保护的同样不是作者，而是出版者。但这最终使作者的作品得以完整的保存，便于作者出版权的正确行使，此可看作是我国著作权法制的雏形。

(二)中国著作权制度的发展(The Development of Copyright System in China)

由于种种原因，封建王朝对出版商的特权保护制度并没有演变成现代著作权制度。直至1910年，清政府才颁布了中国历史上第一部著作权法《大清著作权律》(*Copyright Law of Qing Dynasty*)，但该法并没有来得及实施。1915年和1928年北洋政府和国民党政府也曾分别颁布过《著作权法》(*Copyright Law*)。中华人民共和国成立后，中央人民政府虽然陆续颁布过一些有关稿酬和禁止翻版的文件，但并未形成系统的著作权制度。

20世纪70年代末，我国开始了建立著作权制度的进程。当时国家出版局(State Publication Bureau)、文化部(Ministry of Culture)和广播电视部(Department of Broadcasting and Television)分别颁布过《关于书稿稿酬的暂行规定》(*Interim Provisions on Literary Remuneration*)、《图书期刊著作权保护试行条例》(*Proposed Regulations on Copyrights of*

① 李兴才. 中华印刷通史[DB/OL]. [2017-05-02]. 大中华印艺网，http://www.cgan.net/book/books/print/g-history/00722.htm.

② 吴汉东. 关于中国著作权法观念的历史思考[DB/OL]. [2017-05-02]. 中国民商法律网，http://www.xiaoshuo.com/readbook/00152416 12801 1.html.

Periodical and Books)和《录音录像制品管理暂行规定》(*Interim Provisions on Recording Products*)，对著作权给予了一定的保护。1986年颁布实施的《民法通则》(*General Rule of Civil Law*)将著作权等知识产权正式纳入法律保护范围。

1990年9月7日，第七届全国人大常委会通过了新中国第一部《著作权法》，标志着我国初步建立了现代著作权制度，具有重大的历史意义。此后，中国又于1992年加入了《保护文学艺术作品伯尔尼公约》(*The Berne Convention for the Protection of Literary and Artistic Works*)，进一步推动了中国著作权制度与国际的接轨。

中国加入世界贸易组织后，必须承担《与贸易有关的知识产权协议》(*Agreement on Trade-Related Aspects of Intellectual Property Rights*)所规定的义务。为此，我国于2001年修订了《著作权法》，增加了受保护的作品类型和著作权人的专有权利、调整了"法定许可"的范围、增加了对技术措施和权利管理信息的法律保护，从而全面提高了我国著作权的保护水平。2005年和2006年，《著作权集体管理条例》和《信息网络传播权保护条例》的通过又使得著作权集体管理有法可依，并大大加强了网络环境中对著作权的保护力度。

为了适应国际著作权法发展趋势的需要，我国于2010年对《著作权法》进行了第二次修订，将第4条修订为："著作权人行使著作权，不得违反宪法和法律，不得损害公共利益。国家对作品的出版、传播依法进行监督管理。"增加第26条："以著作权出质的，由出质人和质权人向国务院著作权行政管理部门办理出质登记。"2011年，原新闻出版总署启动了《著作权法》第三次修订，国务院法制办就《中华人民共和国著作权法(修订草案送审稿)》已向社会公开征求意见。

【英语词汇】

civil law countries　大陆法系国家
common law countries　普通法系国家
creative work　创作
dismiss　*v.* 驳回
intangibility　*n.* 无形性
literary works　文学作品
national treatment　国民待遇
neighboring right　邻接权
overrule　*v.* 否决
privilege　*n.* 特权
publishing right　出版权
renewal　*n.* 更新，延期
right of performance　表演权
right of reproduction　复制权
right of publication　发行权
tangible carrier　有形物质载体
tangible assets　无形资产

【英语句型】

1. Compared with other kinds of cases debating in court, copyright is much closer to a so-called legal metaphysics, for its nature, at least so delicate and exquisite, and sometimes almost fleeting.

"compared with..."作状语，译为"和……相比较"。

译文：相比其他各类在法庭上争论的案件，著作权更加接近于所谓的法律的形而上学，其特性是，至少看起来可能是如此的微妙与精巧，并且有时几乎是转瞬即逝的。

2. Uses covered under limitations and exceptions to copyright, such as fair use, do not require permission from the copyright owner. All other uses require permission. Copyright owners can license or permanently transfer or assign their exclusive rights to others.

“subject covered…do …”表示“涵盖了……的”。

译文：对著作权限制之内的使用(如合理使用)不需经著作权人许可，但其他的用途的使用则需要许可。著作权人可以许可或永久转让或转让著作权。

3. Historically, copyright was born to grant the nature of personal privilege or exclusive right authorized by monarch or state, but the awarded copyright was only protected by this state.

“…be born to grant…”表示“……是与生俱来的”。

译文：从历史的角度看，著作权最早出现时就具有君主或国家所授予的个人特权或独占权的性质，导致各国都只保护本国授予的、注册的著作权。

【阅读资料】

第三章　著作权的客体与主体

Chapter 3　The Objects and Subjects of Copyright

【引言】著作权(copyright)的对象(object)是作品(works)，但《著作权法》仅为保护作品的表现形式，至于作品的内容(content)、作品的载体(carrier)、作品的素材(materials)等由其他法律调整。本章介绍作品的含义(definition)、作品的构成要件(constitutional elements)和作品的基本分类。作者基于创作行为取得作品的著作权，其他主体可以基于法律规定或者当事人特别约定(special agreement)或者转让(transfer)、赠与(give)等行为取得著作权的部分权能。本章还介绍了一般作品及特殊作品的著作权归属规则。

【学习目的与要求】掌握作品的含义、构成要件，掌握著作权法排除的领域，了解作品的分类。了解著作权主体含义及其分类，重点掌握作者的含义、认定、特殊作品的著作权归属等内容。

第一节　著作权的客体

Ⅰ　The Objects of Copyright

一、作品的概念(The Definition of Works)

作品(works)，是指文学、艺术和科学领域内具有独创性并能以某种有形形式复制的智力成果。

Works means intellectual achievements in the fields of literature, art and science that can be reproduced in a tangible form. In order to deepen our understanding, we can analyze the works in the following three aspects:

1. 作品的实质内容(contents)

As the achievements of the human intelligence, works reflect human thoughts, feelings, ideas, inspirations and cognition, etc. Although the natural view and sound look beautiful and worth appreciation, but they cannot be treated as the works protected by copyright.

2. 作品的表达形式(expression form)

Works are expressions of human thoughts. It relies on certain expression form. The work exists through specific forms, such as word, language, symbol, sound, color, shape, number. Any idea or feeling, if it could not to be expressed in a specific form, cannot be a work.

当作者为了表达“外面的人想进来，里面的人想出去”的思想，他可以采取小说的形式写成《围城》，也可以通过电影的形式拍成《围城》，还可以通过连环画的形式画成《围城》。文字小说形式、电影形式、美术画形式都是作品的表达形式，但其内容却相似。

3. 作品的载体(carrier)

As we know, all human thoughts present via some expression forms. However, expression forms live on certain carriers. 例如，某甲的思想采取文字小说的形式表达为《围城》，该小说如果印刷出版，出版的书籍就是作品《围城》的载体，如果该小说放在网络上供人们欣赏，网络就成为其载体，刻录成 VCD 的光碟，该实物光碟就是其载体。

二、作品的特征(Features of Works)

(一)独创性(Originality)

独创性，是指作品应当具有之独立创作性。Originality of the work means the work must be created independently by the author. A work is original for copyright purposes if it has originated from the author and has not been copied from another work.

Not all creative effort is protected. For protection the output must fall into the category of "works" and must be original. The following aspects can be taken as references to determine the originality of the work:

1. 独立创作(Independent Creation)

The first requirement, it must be independently created by the author. Originality does not require novelty. Originality does not require that a work must be unique or that it be different from preceding works. Suppose that Painter A paints an abstract painting. By coincidence, the painting closely resembles another painting created by Painter B. But Painter A had never seen or heard of the first painting. Painter A's painting would be original because it originated with him.

但是，由于每个人观察世界的角度有所差异，表达手段也会各有特点，独立创作的结果总会不可避免地打上个人烙印，出现一模一样的作品的可能性是很小的。另外，如果相同的作品已经公之于众，每个人都有可能接触到作品，在后创作的人很难证明自己独立创作了与之前一模一样的作品，举证上有困难。但是，不可否认的是，只要能够证明相同或相似的作品并非抄袭的结果，而是来源于巧合，后人的作品就有可能被认定为独立创作。

因此，一般情况下，独立创作出来的作品一般都具有新的表达(new expression)。Compared with the existing expressions, this expression is new (unprecedented). This new expression can be created without precedents as well as innovated on the basis of the existing expressions. In the event that difference can be found between the expression and other expressions, and this difference is not hard to recognize due to extreme subtlety, the expression can be deemed as wholly new.

2. 表达具有一定的创造性(Creative Expression)

Compared with the existing expressions, the expression must have some creativity, that is, it must be produced by exercise of human intellect. There is no hard and fast rule as to how much creativity is enough.

(1) It has the space for creation. For example, if the English version *Besieged City*(《围城》) is only translated into braille, shooting, such "new" expressions lack of creativity, cannot

be copyrighted.

(2) The originality requirement is not particularly stringent(严格的), requiring only some minimal level of creativity.

(3) This expression must be equipped with the minimum of content and length, because the expression only with two or three words cannot be a constitution of creative thought expression at any case.

If B recorded the content of the lecture made by A, the record is not a new work definitively. In another case, if company C made a fixed phone dictionary via a method of collecting phone numbers home by home assisted with a rank according to the alphabet, it is not a new work due to the lack of creative listings. Besides, there is similar case in the games that we play frequently called finding faults. The pictures cannot be considered as new works as each other owes to the negligible differences.

(二)可复制性(Reproducibility)

复制，是作品传播和使用的基本方式。The form of reproduction includes printing, painting, photography, recording and so on.

Works can be aware of and used via and only via certain methods, such as recording the writing by papers, by pictures or by films. The work can be adopted in practical applications when they were recorded. At the same time, the author can benefit from it.

三、不受著作权法保护的对象(Objects without Protection by the Copyright Law)

(一)作者的思想(Thoughts of the Author)

TRIPS provides that: "Copyright protection shall extend to expressions and not to ideas, procedures, and methods of operation or mathematical concepts as such." *Copyright Law of United States* also provides that: " No case does copyright protection for an original work of authorship extend to any idea, procedure, process, system, method of operation, concept, principle, or discovery, regardless of the form in which it is described, explained, illustrated, or embodied(体现) in such work." Copyright does not protect ideas, only their expression.

Human thoughts are free and cannot be monopolized or controlled in democratic society, so it is not legal protected. Besides, the fact that the author has exclusive rights is based on the idea of encouraging the creation of authors.

著作权法是为了鼓励创作，产生更多、更好的作品。如果禁锢人们的思想，将限制创作，这显然与著作权法的立法宗旨相违背。

As thoughts can be delivered in some ways, sometimes it is difficult to distinguish thoughts with expressions.

A写成一部小说《雍正王朝》，B未经过A的同意擅自根据该作品创作出漫画版的《雍正王朝》，是否侵犯A的著作权？著作权法保护表达，但不保护思想。应该如何理解“表达”呢？如果把“表达”理解成为“表达形式”，将他人创作的小说用同义词替换的方法全部改写一遍，以达到具体“表达形式”的不同来规避侵权是十分荒谬的。

Generally speaking, there is a theme for each novel. The author arranges the characters and their traits, main events, the order of appearance, scene, plots, and story structures, etc. The creative idea comes true via composition of words. This process changes the conception to the author.

因此，“表达”不限于“表达形式”。如果抄袭该具体的文字表达则因侵犯了该小说的表达形式而构成侵权；如果使用该小说的主要人物、主要事件、人物性格、场景、情节、结构等具体细节要点，形成一部与原小说等同的小说，各种细节表达都一样，其差别仅仅在于文字的具体组合，也侵犯了前一作品的基本表达。如上文例子，A 写成一部小说《雍正王朝》，B 根据该作品创作出漫画版的《雍正王朝》，虽然二者的具体表达(文字、漫画)不一样，前者用文字表述，后者采图画形式展现，前后作品的人物、情节、顺序、场景、故事结构等具体细节要点均相同，后者就侵犯了前者的作品表达。

对他人作品表达全文照抄，或者通篇采取同义词(如作品的主人翁)替换，对具体细节要点的全部挪用都构成侵权，但仅仅借用他人文章的思想和观念则不构成侵权。以所属领域普通作者和普通读者为标准，以作品的基本细节要点为基础，对两部作品进行全面比较，如果所属领域普通读者和普通作者认为两者完全相同或者是基本相同，基本上可认定为后者侵犯了前者的表达从而可以认定为侵权。

值得注意的是，当某种思想只有一种或有限的几种表达方式之时，该表达方式同样不受著作权法保护，原因是如果保护该表达方式，意味着保护了思想，这显然与著作权法立法宗旨相违背，例如，历法(calendars)、数表(numerical tables)、通用表格和公式(forms of general use and formulas)等，反映对科学规律的认识，或是思想的唯一或最佳表达，属于思想的范畴，不受著作权法保护。

(二)具有实用功能的表达方式(Expressions with Utility Function)

It is not within the protection of copyright law if the presentation form is practical. In general, such as operational approaches, technology programs and processes are out of the protection of copyright law. Only when these two elements are separated from physical or functional aspects, it can fall to the legal protection of copyright law.

例如人形台灯是实用艺术品，其独特的表达“将台灯设计成人形”是为了艺术和美观，而不是照明，因为不设计成人形也可以照明，所以，其照明实用功能与美学艺术成分能够在观念上区分，该种表达受著作权法保护。相反，流线型轿车，设计成流线型是为了最大限度地减少阻力，该表达方式是为了“减少阻力”这一实用功能所必需，其表达与特定实用功能融为一体无法分开，该表达不受著作权法保护。其他如人体力学键盘、倾斜式按摩靠背椅等均因为具体表达不能与实用功能分开，该表达不能受到著作权法保护。

(三)对事实无独创性的汇编(Compilation of Facts without Ingenuity)

The expression to describe the objective facts is not a work. Facts are not copyrightable, but works containing facts may be copyrightable, because they contain other elements created by the author. Where the compilation lacks a certain amount of original authorship, it cannot be copyrighted.

对事实的表达仅具有一种或者有限几种表达方式，该表达方式当然不受著作权法保护，因为事实是客观存在，不是人类创作，如果保护该种表达方式，也就意味着保护该事实，这显然是不恰当的。例如，中央电视台的整点新闻报道，该表达方式与事实本身是重合的，不受著作权法保护。

The news work resulting from the deep investigation, elaborations, comments certainly has a presentation form which is more significant than the event fact. In this case, the presentations full of ingenuity are within the protection of the copyright law.

(四)官方的正式文件(Official Documents)

Copyright law shall not be applicable to laws; regulations; resolutions, decisions and orders of state organs; other documents of legislative, administrative and judicial nature; and their official translations.

Officially issued documents such as laws, rule, work statement and policy decisions, are generally out of the protection of the copyright law. But the published works of officials created originally will be protected by the copyright law.

(五)其他不受保护的对象(Other Objects without Protection)

如体育竞技、公有领域的作品，不受著作权法保护。体育竞技的表达方式不具有独创性；公有领域的作品表达方式虽然具有独创性，但是已经过了保护期限，成为全人类共有财富。

违禁作品的著作权保护问题。2010 年《著作权法》第二次修改以前，第 4 条第 1 款规定："依法禁止出版、传播的作品，不受本法保护。"该规定不符合《伯尔尼公约》和 TRIPS 有关作品应当自动获得保护的规定，为了适应国际著作权保护发展趋势的需要，2010 年 2 月，全国人大常委会决定对《著作权法》进行修改，将第 4 条修改为："著作权人行使著作权，不得违反宪法和法律，不得损害公共利益。国家对作品的出版、传播依法进行监督管理。"这就意味着，依法禁止出版、传播的违禁作品也能受到著作权法的保护，其作者可以通过法律途径起诉未经许可利用其作品的人。

四、作品的分类(The Classification of Works)

按照不同的标准，可以将作品进行若干种类的划分。按照作品创作人不同，将作品分为自然人作品(works of natural person)和单位作品(works of legal person)；按照作者人数不同，将作品分为一人作品(works of one author)与合作作品(works of joint authorship)；按照创作行为性质不同，可以将作品分为原创作品(original works)与演绎作品(derivative works)等。最具实用价值的分类是按照作品表达方不同，将作品分为文字作品(written works)、口述作品(oral works)、音乐戏剧曲艺舞蹈杂技艺术作品(musical, dramatic, qu yi, choreographic and acrobatics works)、美术作品(works of fine art)、摄影作品(photography works)、电影作品(cinematographic works)、图形作品(graphic works)、计算机软件(computer software)、民间艺术作品(folk art works)等。上述的分类最具有实用意义。

(一)文字作品(Written Works)

Written works mean works expressed in written form, such as novels, poems, essays and theses(论文), etc.

There are two key points which should be paid great attention to. For one thing, the work should contain expressions such as Chinese characters(中文), English words(英文), symbols (符号) and numbers, etc. ; for another, written works(文字作品) is not equal to the literature (文学作品). The latter one is included in the former one. As a rule, many written works are written works but not literature, such as computer software which is written in assemble language (汇编语言), original science and engineering papers.

(二)口述作品(Oral Works)

Oral works mean extemporaneous(即兴的) works expressed in oral forms, such as unprepared speeches, lectures and court debate, etc.

There are two core characteristics for oral works, and one of them is the work supposed be improvised. It is different from reading of pre-prepared written works, for example, teachers read lecture, which is not oral works, but only the reappearance of pre-existing works.

The other characteristic is that the oral work should be made orally. If the oral work is fixed in another form such as videos or notes, it will not be oral work any longer.

(三)音乐、戏剧、曲艺、舞蹈、杂技艺术作品(Musical, Dramatic, Qu Yi, Choreographic and Acrobatics Works)

Musical works mean such works as songs and symphonic(交响乐) works, with or without lyrics, which can be sung or performed. A musician who composes music or writes a song is the author of a musical work. A producer who makes a recording of a musician performing musical work is the producer of sound recordings.

Dramatic works mean such works as dramas, operas and local traditional operas for stage performance. A dramatic work would likely fall into another category, such as written work or musical work, for example, music and screenplay in dramatic work.

Qu Yi works(Folk art works) mean such works as "xiang sheng" (cross talk), "kuai shu" (clapper talk), "da gu" (ballad(民谣)) singing with drum accompaniment) and "ping shu" (story telling based on novels), which are mainly performed by recitation(朗诵) or singing, or by both.

Choreographic(舞蹈) works means works in which ideas and feelings are or can be expressed through successive body movements, gestures, facial movements, etc.

Acrobatic works mean works expressed through body movements and skills, such as acrobatics, magic and circus.

All these works are suitable to be performed, so they are called performance works. However, it is necessary to note that all the works stated above mean the content of work not their performances. For example, the song *Colorful Butterfly* means the artistic contents such as lyrics and melody, not the singing performance of Jolin Tsai of this song in the stage.

(四)美术作品(Works of Fine Art)

Works of fine art are two- or three-dimensional(平面或者立体的) works created in lines, colors or other medium which, when being viewed, impart aesthetic(美学的) effect, such as paintings, works of calligraphy(书法), sculptures(雕塑) and works of architecture(建筑).

审美标准并无绝对的统一，只要具有最低限度的创造性便具有审美意义①。美术作品包括平面美术作品(graphic works)、立体雕塑(three-dimensional sculptures)和建筑作品(architecture works)。

An architecture work is the designs of a building—before the building is built, and even if the building is never built. But the definition limits architecture works to the designs of buildings; furniture designed by an architect is not an architecture work.

(五)电影作品和以类似摄制电影的方法创作的作品(Cinematographic Works and Works Created by a Process Analogous to Cinematography)

Cinematographic works and works created by a process analogous to cinematography (cinematographic works for short) mean works which are recorded on some material, consisting of a series of images, with or without accompanying sound and which can be projected with the aid of suitable devices or communicated by other means.

电影作品和以类似摄制电影的方法创作的作品，是指摄制在一定介质上，由一系列有伴音或者无伴音的画面组成，并且借助适当装置放映、播放的作品。

Film is comprehensive special artistic work, which is the work participated and created by many authors and produced by synthesis(合成).

The form of cinematographic work is a movie, not a screenplay(剧本). The work created by a process analogous to cinematography is mainly television or original video. If the video is only recorded without innovation, it cannot be regarded as creative work.

(六)摄影作品(Photography Works)

Photographic works are the kind of artistic works created by recording images on light-sensitive materials with the aid of devices(借助器械在感光材料等介质上记录).

The instrument here is any equipment that has photographic function; the medium here is any device with storage function.

虽然摄像是对客观事物形象的记录，但作者仍然可以通过不同的角度、光线、快门、曝光、场景布置、造型设计、道具摆放、后期处理等使得照片具有独创性从而获得著作权法的保护。

(七)图型作品和模型作品(Graphic Works and Model Works)

Graphic works mean drawings of engineering designs(工程设计图) and drawings of product designs(产品设计图) that are made for construction work or engineering(施工和生产) purposes, and maps, schematic drawings(示意图), etc. that reflect geographical phenomena(反映地形地貌) or illustrate the principles or structures of things(说明事物的原理结构).

Compared with art works, graphic works are mainly used in the field of science and technology due to their practical function, and looks rigorous beauty.

① 唐超华. 知识产权法学[M]. 长沙：湖南大学出版社，2004：46.

Model works mean three-dimensional works made to a certain scale on the basis of the shape and structure of objects, for purposes of display, testing or observation, etc.（为展示、试验或者观测等用途）

（八）计算机软件作品（Computer Software）

计算机软件作品，是指计算机程序（computer programs）及其相关文档。由于计算机软件和传统的文学艺术作品相比有很大的区别，故专开《计算机软件保护条例》保护。该条例规定，计算机程序，是指为了得到某种结果而可以由计算机等具有信息处理能力的装置执行的代码化指令序列，或者可以被自动转换成代码化指令序列的符号化指令序列或者符号化语句序列。同一计算机程序的源程序和目标程序为同一作品。

文档（documents），是指用来描述程序的内容、组成、设计、功能规格、开发情况、测试结果及使用方式的文字资料和图表等，如程序设计说明书、流程图、用户手册等。其实文档本身就是文字作品，并没有什么特殊性。

第二节　著作权的主体
Ⅱ　The Subjects of Copyright

一、著作权主体的概念（The Definition of Copyright Owner）

The copyright owner, also known as the subject of copyright, is the person who enjoys copyright in literary, artistic and scientific works in accordance with the law. The subjects of copyright include natural persons, legal persons and other organizations.

在特定条件下，外国人（foreigners）也能在我国成为著作权主体。根据不同的标准，著作权主体可分为以下几类：

（一）原始主体和继受主体（Original Subjects and Inherit Subjects）

Original subject of copyright is the person who obtains copyright of the work originally by the special legal provisions or contracts. Inherit subject of copyright is the person who obtains the copyright because of the assignment of the copyright, which includes successor（继承人）, legatee（受遗赠人）and assignee（受让人）of the copyright.

著作人身权具有人身依附性不能转让，著作财产权具有财产利益可以转让，所以继受主体只能继受著作财产权。从这个角度讲，继受主体所享有的著作权权能肯定不是完整的著作权之全部。

Inherit subjects have copyright when these two points combined: first, the original right is legal and valid; second, the transmission is legal and valid.

（二）完整的著作权主体和部分著作权主体（Complete Subjects and Incomplete Subjects）

完整的著作权主体，是指对作品享有全部著作人身权和全部著作财产权的主体。部分著作权主体，是指对作品仅享有部分著作财产权或者部分人身权的主体。

Because the moral rights are not transferable, inherit subject can only receive the property rights. In this way, all the inherit subjects are partly subjects for sure. And some original subjects are also partly subjects, for example, works for hire, the copyright belongs to the author, but the employer has priority rights to use it. For special assignment works, the author only has the right of authorship; other copyrights belong to the employer.

既然部分著作权主体只享有著作权的部分权能，该主体在对自己作品权属证明的时候，只要证明自己享有该项权能即可，无须准备多余的资料。相应的，相对方在驳斥部分著作权权能的时候，也应该针对该项权能，而不应该从整体或者从其他权能入手。

(三)国内主体和外国主体(Domestic Subjects and Foreign Subjects)

This is classified by the nationality(国籍) of the copyright owner. Domestic subjects include Chinese citizens, legal person and other organizations. Foreign subjects include foreigners, stateless persons(无国籍人).

由于著作权的地域性，国内主体与外国主体在著作权取得、保护等方面均有较大差异。国内主体，只要创作完成作品，即可取得该作品的著作权，外国主体的作品如果首次在中国出版，按照《著作权法》享有著作权，其著作权自出版之日受到我国法律保护。其在境外的作品，应该根据其所属国或者经常居住国与中国签订的协议或者共同参加的国际条约享有著作权，受我国法律保护。

二、作者(The Author)

Author is the citizen who creates the work. The term "creation" as referred to in the Copyright Law means intellectual activities in which literary, artistic or scientific works are directly created.

另外，《著作权法》还规定，如果由单位主持，代表单位意志创作并由单位承担责任的作品，该单位可以被视为作者。

(一)自然人(Natural Persons)

The author of a work is the citizen who has created the work.

除了法律特别规定或合同特别约定的情形，创作作品的自然人就是作品的著作权人。创作完成，作品产生，著作权随之产生。值得注意的是，此处的创作完成并非指作品的最终完成，即使阶段性的完成，只要能形成一定独创性成果，作者就对该阶段性成果享有著作权。只有实际从事创作的自然人才是作者，没有实际进行创作的人，不是作者。

Any organizational activity, consultation, material support or other auxiliary services(辅助工作) conducted or offered for another person's creation shall not be deemed as creation.

我国实行著作权自动取得制度和著作权鼓励登记制度。

After the registration, author can receive a certificate of registration(登记证书). This certificate is a preliminary proof to his identity which makes the litigation much smoother and more convenient. It is also very important in application and affirmation of high-tech enterprises.

(二)视为作者的法人或者其他组织(The Legal Person and Organization Treated as Authors)

视为作者的法人或者其他组织，又称为单位作者。There are three elements to identify a corporate author: first, the corporation organizes this creative activity; second, the creative activity represents the will of the corporation; third, the corporation is responsible after the work is finished.

三、特殊作品的著作权归属(Attribution of Copyright of Special Works)

(一)职务作品(Work Made for Hire)

1. 职务作品的概念(The Definition of Work Made for Hire)

根据我国《著作权法》的规定，职务作品，是指公民为完成法人或者其他组织工作任务所创作的作品①。

The constitutive requirements of works made for hire involves:

(1) The author and corporation had labor relation or employ relation.

无论是劳动合同关系，还是劳动事实关系，都认为双方存在劳动关系。

(2) The author creates for completing the task of corporation.

该工作任务既可以是本职工作，也可以是单位临时交付的任务。至于该创作是否在工作时间内完成、是否利用了单位物质技术条件、是否受单位的监督等与是否为完成工作任务没有必然联系。

(3) The work is made by the will of the author.

如果该作品是在单位的安排下完成，体现单位某方面意志，该作品就是单位作品而不是职务作品了。例如，十世班禅逝世，西藏自治区政府成立修建灵塔办公室，由该办公室组织相关人员制作十世班禅塑像，该雕塑作品体现的是自治区政府、灵塔办的意志，而非塑造者个人意志，故该雕塑作品是单位作品而不是职务作品。②

2. 职务作品著作权归属(The Attribution of Work Made for Hire)

(1)一般职务作品的著作权归属(The Attribution of General Hire Work)

First, the copyright belongs to the author;

Second, the corporation has priority rights in the scope of business.

(2)特殊职务作品的著作权归属(The Attribution of Special Hire Work)

对某些职务作品，特别是工程设计图(engineering design)、产品设计图(product design)、地图(map)、计算机软件(computer software)等的著作权归属有特别规定。首先，该作品的创作主要是利用了单位的物质技术条件；其次，该作品由单位对外承担责任。满足上述两个要件的职务作品为特殊职务作品，特殊职务作品的著作权，作者仅享有署名权，著作权的其他权能由单位享有。

(二)委托作品(Commissioned Works)

1. 委托作品的概念(The Definition of Commissioned Works)

Commissioned work is a work created by the commissioned party in accordance with the will and requirement of the commissioning party based on the commissioned contract.

---

① 韩松．知识产权法[M]．北京：中国人民大学出版社，2003：79.

② 刘春田．以案说法·知识产权法篇[M]．北京：中国人民大学出版社，2006：42.

例如，新婚夫妇赴影楼请摄影师拍摄的婚纱照、2010年第16届广州亚运会征集的会徽等均是委托作品。

委托作品的创作包含两个要素：委托人的委托要素和受托人的创作要素。

On one hand, the commissioned party and commissioning party have signed a commission contract, creating the working pattern of commission work, which distinguishes the commission work from general work. On the other hand, the commissioned party receives the works commissioned, and completes the creative act in accordance with contractual obligation. The legality and validity of the creative act is the basis for the existence of the commissioned works.

2. 委托作品著作权的归属(The Attribution of Commissioned Works)

(1)当事人对著作权归属有约定的，遵从约定。

(2)无约定，从法定。

如果双方对著作权归属没有约定，应当按照法律规定确定著作权的归属。我国《著作权法》规定，合同未作明确约定的，著作权归属受托人，但委托人可以在约定的范围内免费使用；如果没有约定范围，委托人可以在符合委托创作目的的范围内使用。

3. 委托作品与其他作品的关系(Relations Between Commissioned Works and Other Works)

(1)委托作品与委托作品的关系

If A commissions B to do a painting, then B commissions C to do this painting, who does the copyright belong to?

通说认为，在这种情况下，应该遵循合同相对性原则和保护实际创作者利益原则。

The work is both the commissioned work of A and B. If A and B have not discussed about the attribution, this painting will belongs to B. If A and B made an agreement before, the ownership of this painting follows the contract.

(2)委托作品与职务作品的关系

委托作品的受托方指派自己的员工完成创作，对于创作完成的作品，既是职务作品，又是委托作品，如何确定该著作权的归属?

从实际委托和实际创作过程来看，外部委托关系是内部指派关系的源泉，如果没有外部委托，就不可能产生内部指派。所以，该模式中的外部委托因素优先于内部指派因素。再者，一般情况下的著作权归属约定优先于法定。

(三)合作作品(Works of Joint Authorship)

1. 合作作品的概念(The Definition of Joint Works)

Joint work is a work prepared by two or more authors with the intention that their contributions be merged into inseparable or interdependent parts of a unitary whole. Works of joint authorship constitutes of two elements:

First, consensus of joint work (共同创作的合意). The joint authors have explicit understanding of the behavior and result of joint creation. Each author intend to be a joint author when the work is created.

Second, conduct of joint work(共同创作的行为). The joint authors actually participate in the creative activity. Each author contributes copyrightable expression directly. The person who provides ideas, creative materials, venues, staff organization, fund auxiliary behavior cannot be treated as co-author.

2. 合作作品的著作权归属(The Attribution of Joint Works)

(1)合作作品的著作权归属(The Attribution of Joint Works)

我国《著作权法》规定，两人以上合作创作的作品，著作权由合作作者共同享有。没有参加创作的人，不能成为合作作者。

The creators may not in fact have had a clear understanding of who will own the rights in the work on which they collaborated, the law will divide the ownership equally among the co-authors. As a result, it is a very good idea for the collaborators to work through their agreement, and if they intend to split the proceeds unequally, to say so in a contract binding all the co-authors.

(2)合作作品的利用(The Utilization of Joint Works)

合作作品可以分割使用的，作者对各自创作的部分可以单独享有著作权，但行使著作权时不得侵犯合作作品整体的著作权。

如果合作的作品不可以分割使用的，其著作权由各合作作者共同享有，通过协商一致行使；不能协商一致，又无正当理由的，任何一方不得阻止他方行使除转让以外的其他权利，但是所得收益应当合理分配给所有合作作者。作品的可分割使用，是指该作品在结构上、功能上、价值上都适合分开使用。

作品是否可以分割使用，还须看该作品的性质、长短、使用方式等具体要素。A and B wrote a textbook together. A wrote the former five chapters, B wrote the latter five chapters. In this context, A can use the former five chapters independently, while B can use the latter five chapters as he likes. But if A and B wrote a 4,000-word essay together, this essay cannot be easily separated.

(四)演绎作品(Derivative Works)

1. 演绎作品的概念(The Definition of Derivative Works)

Derivative works, also called deductive works, are the new works created by adaptation(改编), translation, annotation(注释), arrangement or compilation(汇编) of pre-existing work, new work created by recreation of the original work.

Derivative works constitute of two components:

(1) Reserve basic expressions of the original work(保留原作品的基本表达)

后续创作行为所形成的作品保留了原作的基本人物、人物性格、人物关系、事件、情节、场景、对话、动作等基本形式，可以构成演绎作品。相反，如果没有保留原作的基本表达，就不是演绎作品。

(2) Original creation is obliged to original work

必须在原作的基础上加上具有独创性的创作。That is to say, derivative works should have at least the minimum creativity compared with the original one。Otherwise, the work is just a copy of original one.

2. 演绎作品的著作权归属(The Attribution of Derivative Works)

Derivative work is based on the original work, so its ownership of copyright is special. 改编、翻译、注释、整理已有作品而产生的新作品，其著作权由改编、翻译、注释、整理人所享有，但在行使其著作权时不得侵犯原作品的著作权。

According to the Law, there are four components to mention:

(1) Derivative works are new works, the attribution are subject to the author of derivative works.

(2) The copyright of original works are subject to the original owner.

(3) Before creating the derivative works, the creator shall obtain the approval of the owner of original works.

(4) The utilization of derivative works needs double consent of the owner of original works and the author of derivative works.

(五)电影作品和以类似摄制电影方法创作的作品(Cinematographic Works and Works Created by A Process Analogous to Cinematography)

1. 电影作品以及类似摄制电影方法创作的作品的概念(The Definition of Cinematographic Works and Works Created by a Process Analogous to Cinematography)

Cinematographic works and works created by a process analogous to cinematography (cinematographic works for short) mean works which are recorded on some material, consisting of a series of images, with or without accompanying sound and which can be projected with the aid of suitable devices or communicated by other means.

2. 电影作品以及类似摄制电影方法创作的作品的著作权归属(The Attribution of Cinematographic Works and Works Created by a Process Analogous to Cinematography)

电影作品和以类似摄制电影的方法创作的作品是一个特别的作品类型。摄制电影类作品是一个比较复杂的、系统的智力创作过程，要有提供资金和组织拍摄的制片人，要有电影脚本(包括改编和直接创作的剧本和音乐、作词等)，要有导演、摄影、演员、特技设计、美工(包括服装、道具设计)、灯光、布景，等等。摄制电影投资巨大并且编剧、导演、摄影等作者付出了大量的创造性劳动，电影的发行、放映也会带来巨大的商业利益，但也有巨大的商业风险。

In order to ensure investors recover investment in time, most countries agree that the copyright of cinematographic works and works created by a process analogous to cinematography are vested in the film producers.

The copyright in cinematographic works and works created by a process analogous to cinematography shall be enjoyed by the producer of the work, but the scriptwriter(编剧), director, cameraman(摄影师), lyricist, composer, and other authors thereof shall enjoy the right of authorship(署名权) in the work, and have the right to receive remuneration pursuant to(依照) the contract concluded with the producer.

(六)其他作品(Other Works)

1. 美术作品(Works of Fine Art)

Works of fine art are two- or three-dimensional(平面或者立体的) works created in lines, colors or other medium which, when being viewed, impart aesthetic(美学的) effect, such as paintings, works of calligraphy(书法), sculptures(雕塑) and works of architecture(建筑).

The assignment of ownership of the original copy of a work of fine shall not be deemed to include the assignment of the copyright in such work, provided that the right to exhibit(展览权) the original copy of a work of fine art shall be enjoyed by the owner of such original. 美术作品原件的转移，受让人同时也取得了该原件的展览权。

2. 作者身份不明的作品(Works of Unknown Authorship)

Work of unknown authorship means a work by an author whose identity is unknown.

If there does not exist contrary evidence, the citizens, legal persons or any other organizations that signatures in the work will be recognized as the author. If there is no signature in the work, the problem becomes more difficult.

我国《著作权法实施条例》第13条规定，作者身份不明的作品，由作品原件的所有人行使除署名权以外的著作权；作者身份确定后，由作者或者其继承人行使著作权。

【英语词汇】

acrobatics *n.* 杂技
adaptation *n.* 改编
annotation *n.* 注释
assignee *n.* 受让人
choreographic works 舞蹈作品
cinematographic works 电影作品
commissioned works 委托作品
compilation *n.* 汇编
derivative works 演绎作品
folk art works 民间艺术作品
graphic works 图形作品
inherit subject 继受主体
model works 模型作品
oral works 口述作品
originality *n.* 独创性
original subject 原始主体
original works 原创作品
photography works 摄影作品
reproducibility *n.* 可复制性
scriptwriter *n.* 编剧
work *n.* 作品
works of fine art 美术作品
works of joint authorship 合作作品
works made for hire 职务作品
written works 文字作品

【英语句型】

1. Only when these two elements separate from physical or functions can fall to the legal protection of copyright law.

“Only when…”引导的是倒装句，表示“只有当……”。

译文：只有当这两要素能够从物理上或者功能上分离的时候，该具有实用功能的艺术表达才能受到著作权法的保护。

2. On one hand, the commissioned party and commissioning party have signed a commission contract, creating the working pattern of commission work, which distinguishes the commission work to general work. On the other hand, the commissioned party receives the works

commissioned, and completes the creative act in accordance with contractual obligation. The legality and validity of the creative act is the basis for the existence of the commissioned works.

"For one hand..., for the other hand..."表示"一方面……另一方面……"。

译文：对于第一个要素，是委托人与受托人签订委托合同，形成委托创作的工作模式，该模式的有效成型是委托作品区别于一般作品的关键。对于第二个要素，是受托人接收委托并按照委托合同的规定完成作品创作。该创作行为的合法有效是委托作品存在的基础。

3. The assignment of ownership of the original copy of a work of fine shall not be deemed to include the assignment of the copyright in such work, provided that the right to exhibit the original copy of a work of fine art shall be enjoyed by the owner of such original.

"be deemed to... " 表示"被认为……"。

译文：美术作品原件的转让不视为著作权的转让，但是原件的所有人享有美术作品的展览权。

4. As a result, it is a very good idea for the collaborators to work through their agreement, and if they intend to split the proceeds unequally, to say so in a contract binding all the co-authors.

"It is a very good idea..."表示"这对……是个好主意"。

译文：所以，这对合作作者来说是很好的权利制约，一旦他们对所获收益分配不均，那么这个条款能对所有的合作作者产生效力。

【阅读资料】

第四章　著作权的内容
Chapter 4　The Content of Copyright

【引言】著作权的内容包括著作人身权(moral rights)和著作权财产权(property rights)两个部分。著作人身权具体包括发表权(right of publication)、署名权(the right of authorship)、修改权(the right of alteration)和保护作品完整权(the right of integrity)。著作财产权包括复制权(the right of reproduction)、发行权(the right of distribution)、公开传播权(the right of public communication)和演绎权(the right of deduction)，其中公开传播权与演绎权都不是具体的权利，而是权利束，其下又包含若干具体权利。

主体对作品享有的权利为著作权，为了保障著作权人利益的实现，法律赋予该主体17项权能，这些权能的总和即著作权的内容。著作权内容即主体对作品所享有各项专有权利的总和。著作权的权能有两层含义，一层含义是权利人有权以该种方式利用其作品，另一层含义是其他任何人未经许可不得采用与权利人相同的方式使用该作品。著作权是专有权，是对著作权人对作品专有之利用方式，没有法定缘由或未经权利人许可，任何人不得采用与权利人相同的方式使用该作品，否则就是侵权行为。

【学习目的与要求】掌握著作人身权和著作财产权的各项权能，深刻把握每一项权利的含义、特征、范围及权利行使方式，在掌握每一项权能的基础上，深入掌握各项权能之间的相互关系。在深刻把握著作权每一项权能的前提下，较为深刻地理解各种邻接权，掌握邻接权人的权利和各项义务。

第一节　著作人身权
Ⅰ　Moral Rights

一、著作人身权的概念(The Definition of Moral Rights)

Moral rights mean the exclusive rights enjoyed by the author based on his work created by him, the content of which is personal interest without direct economic content.

Copyright can be seen as a type of natural right. Because an author creates a work, he should be able to control what happens to the work. The work is an expression of the author's personality. The author's reputation is tied to the work. Someone that injures the work injures the author.

Moral rights have the nature of civil personal rights, reflecting certain relations between specific subjects and specific interests. This nature is not transferable or inheritable. 但是著作权立法鼓励作品的流转、再流转和再创作，因此有必要对著作权的人身权给予适当之限制。

另外，其人身性质不像普通人身权那样强烈，因而在某些特定之场合下，作者可以放弃、许可他人行使甚至转让。

二、著作人身权的内容(The Content of Moral Rights)

(一)发表权(The Right of Publication)

The right of publication refers to the right to decide whether to make a work available to the public.

The right to publish can be understood from the following three aspects. Firstly, the author is entitled to decide whether to make a work available to the public. Secondly, the author is entitled to decide the time and the means of making a work available to the public. Thirdly, the author is entitled to prohibit unauthorized publication of his work.

公众是指不特定之多数人，室友之间、家人之间、三五个亲朋好友之间并非公众。

The right of publication emphasizes the state of conduct, rather than state of influence, that is, the confirmation of this right is not relevant to the fact that whether the public read it or not.

任何使作品公之于众的方式均受到发表权的控制，传统的如出版发行、公开陈列、现场表演等，现代的方式有广播电视播送、信息网络传输等。

一旦使作品置于为公众能获知的状态，即完成了发表权的行使，其后任何对作品公之于众的行为均不受发表权之控制。发表权一次用尽。法律对发表权还有一些特殊的规定。

(1)当作者转让著作财产权或者许可他人以特定方式使用该作品的时候，推定作者许可他人发表该作品。

(2)发表权的行使可能受到其他民事权利的制约。

(3)发表权在特殊情况下，可以由非著作权人行使。《著作权法实施条例》规定，作者身份不明时，作品原件的合法持有人得发表该作品。该条例第17条规定，作者生前未发表的作品，如果作者未明确表示不发表，在其死后的50年内，其继承人、受遗赠人或者原件所有人(在没有继承人或受遗赠人时)可发表该作品。

(二)署名权(The Right of Authorship)

The right of authorship refers to the right to claim authorship and to have the author's name indicated on his works.

The right of authorship includes the following four aspects. Firstly, the author is entitled to decide whether to sign on his work. No signature does not mean the author has given up his right of authorship. Secondly, the author is entitled to decide to sign real name, pen name or aliases (别名), and the signed sequence when there are two or more authors. Thirdly, the author is entitled to indicate the special relationship between the author and his work, such as screenwriter, director, editor, etc. Fourthly, the author is entitled to prohibit anyone who has not participated in the creation of the work to sign on his work.

至于作者的姓名被他人用在该他人或者第三人作品上的行为，因并不涉及作者本人的作品，因而不属于侵害署名权的行为，作者可以根据姓名权或者竞争法的规定获得救济。例如，张三写武侠小说一本，署名“金庸”，张三并没有侵犯金庸的署名权；如果张三盗版《笑傲江湖》却署名张三或者将之改编为《嘲笑江湖》署名为张三，则侵犯了金庸对《笑傲江湖》的署名权。

In addition, in the judicial practice, if there is no evidence to the contrary(相反证据), the person who signs on this work is the author.

(三)修改权(The Right of Alteration)

The right of alternation refers to the right to alter or authorize others to alter one's work. 根据有关解释，修改是对作品内容作局部的变更以及文字、用语的修正①。

The right of alteration can be understood from the following three aspects.

Firstly, the amendment of the article is the minimum modify under the need of editor. 根据编辑惯例，编辑对文章的错别字、标点符号、断句等的修改，以及为了更好地利用该作品所作的必要修改无须征得作者之同意，亦即编辑基于编辑的需要对文章所做的最低限度之修改不受修改权的控制。②

Secondly, if the basic expression of origin is added with creation to produce a new work, this behavior will fall into the scope of the right of adaptation, not the right of alteration.

Thirdly, if the basic expression of origin is distorted or misrepresented, this behavior will fall into the scope of the right of integrity, not the right of alteration.

此处的修改权仅指非改编、非篡改、非错别字标点改动的一种基本改动权，这种权利范围很狭窄。

(四)保护作品完整权(The Right of Integrity)

The right of integrity refers to the right to protect one's work against distortion(歪曲) and mutilation(篡改). Distortion means changing the real content and expression of the work intentionally. Mutilation means the acts to delete or change the work without permission.

It is important to prove that the author's reputation is damaged in determining whether to infringe the right of integrity or not.

在认定是否侵害保护作品完整权的时候，如果仅仅是一般的改动并没有损害作者的声誉，一般不认为侵害作者的保护作品完整权。例如，某作者针对某重庆拆迁事件发表了评论——《评史上最牛钉子户》，但该报纸编辑仅保留了对拆迁户的评论，而省去了对开发商的评论。一般的人都会认为该种改动是站在开发商的立场上对拆迁户的谴责和抨击，因而这种改动损害了作者声誉，侵害了保护作品完整的权利。

第二节 著作财产权
Ⅱ Property Rights of Copyright

一、著作财产权的概念(The Definition of Property Rights of Copyright)

Property rights mean the rights that copyright owners enjoy to or authorize others to exploit his

① 胡康生．中华人民共和国著作权法释义[M]．北京：法律出版社，2002：43.

② 唐超华．知识产权法学[M]．长沙：湖南大学出版社，2004：55.

works to obtain property interests entitled according to law, that is, the right to receive remuneration.《著作权法》第10条第1款列举了作者对其作品享有的13种专有使用方式。但是，并不是每一种作品的著作权人都享有全部的权利，其权利的具体种类取决于该作品的类型以及有关作品能以什么方式来使用。除了明文列举的12项权利，《著作权法》第10条第1款第17项还规定了“其他权利”，其目的在于使著作权的内容具备一定的灵活性，能够不断适应技术发展带来的挑战。具体的新的权利内容一般需要由法官通过审理案件逐件确立。著作财产权具有财产利益，可以转让和继承，也可以许可他人使用。

二、著作财产权的内容(The Content of Property Rights)

(一)复制权(The Right of Reproduction)

The right of reproduction refers to the right to produce one or more copies of a work by printing, photocopying, lithographing(拓印), making a sound recording or video recording, duplicating a recording(翻录), or duplicating a photographic (翻拍) work or by any other means. Strictly speaking, any utilization of works needs reproduction.

复制是指原作品在有形物质载体上的再现。如果不是在有形物质载体上再现，可能构成对作品的其他利用方式，而非此处所言之复制。

The copyright owner has the right to make copies of the work. Someone else potentially infringes if they copy the work without the author's permission, even if they do not copy the entire work and even if they make a copy that is similar but not identical.

复制是指原作品在有形物质载体上的再现，复制权的核心含义是对原作品之再现。根据再现的方式，可以将复制分为同维度复制和跨维度之复制。

同维度复制(homo-dimension)，包括平面到平面复制(如静电复印、油印、铅印、打印、扫描)和立体到立体的复制。立体到立体的复制，首先要对立体的作品采样，再分解为平面结构图，然后再还原为不同比例的立体形状。

跨维度的复制(multi-dimension)，有平面到立体的复制和立体到平面的复制。需要注意的是，根据建筑图、工程图设计制造相应建筑物和工程物，并不一定受到复制权的控制，因为虽然工程设计图和建筑图均是作品，但是依据该图纸建造的部分建筑物或者工程物可能仅具有实用性并不具有独创性和美感，不能构成作品，此时的复制并不受著作权控制。

In network environment, the reproduction can be:

1. Fix in media by scientific means

In dignity society, the most common copies we know are chips(芯片), disks(磁盘), CD-ROMs(光盘) and floppy disks(软盘) which reproduce through technology.

2. Upload to network servers(网络服务器)

将作品上传至网络服务器是网络环境下最为常见的复制行为。如当下各大高校都架设有FTP (File Transfer Protocol)服务器，学校将大量的影视作品上传到FTP服务器供校园网用户观看欣赏，该上传行为是对影视作品的复制。

3. Download to computer and preserve works

将作品从网络服务器或者他人电脑中下载到本地电脑并保存。

4. Send works to other network node through the network or devices

通过网络向网络中的其他节点或者设备发送作品，如通过手机短信或者电子邮件等形式发送作品的行为也是复制。

(二)发行权(The Right of Distribution)

The right of distribution refers to the right to make available to the public the original or reproductions of a work though sale or other transfer of ownership.

出版发行的主体只能是出版社。发行权与书籍杂志的出版发行不同。出版发行是行业术语，发行权是法律术语。出版发行包括复制和销售两个环节，转移载体的形式只能是销售行为。The right of distribution is different from publishing of books and magazines. The publishing of books and magazines includes two parts：reproduction and sales of works.

The right of distribution contributes to the elements of utilization：

1. Provide works to public(向公众提供作品)

The right of distribution means to provide works to public, that is unspecified persons(不特定多数人), not only his family members or friends. And this right emphasizes the conduct of providing, not the result. 只有向公众提供，才可能会影响到权利人的人身利益和经济利益。

2. Provide works through transferring the ownership of carrier(通过转移作品载体所有权的方式提供作品)

Provide works through transfer the ownership of carrier is the core feature that differs copyright to other intellectual property. Firstly, there must be a carrier and the ownership of carrier can be transferred. Secondly, the behavior of transformation can be transaction(交易) and donation(赠与).

A sold a book to B. Will B have the right to resell this book? The answer is absolutely yes. According to the Property Law, B has the ownership of this book, so he can sell it of course. But there is another question：if B resell it, this action means to provide the book through transferring the ownership of carrier(通过转移作品载体所有权方式向他人提供作品), right under the right of distribution.

在协调物权人利益和知识产权人利益冲突时，各国法律均选择了“适当限制著作权人利益、物权优先原则”，即此时买受人可以自由转售该书籍，该转售行为不受发行权控制，不用向著作权人缴纳“发行费用”。此处所采用的方法称为发行权一次用尽(权利穷竭)原则。发行权一次用尽原则又称为首次销售原则，是指著作权人对某特定复制件，合法有效行使一次发行权后，不可再次享有发行权。

(三)出租权(The Right of Rental)

The right of rental refers to the right to authorize, with payment, others to temporarily use cinematographic works, works created by virtue of an analogous method of film production, and computer software, except any computer software that is not the main subject matter of rental. Compared with other utilizations, the right of rental involves the utilization of carrier; compared with the right of distribution, the right of rental only relates to physical occupy of carrier, but not the change of ownership. What's more, the object of the right of distribution is just cinematographic works, works created by virtue of an analogous method of film production and computer software. For other works, such as books, photos, copyright owners do not have the right of rental.

For instance, when renting an automatic washing machine (or a piece of VCD, a taxi, etc.), the automatic control program is the subsidiary of washing machine, so this action will not be restrained by the right of rental.

与发行权(the right of distribution)一样，出租权同样涉及著作权人与所有权人利益的冲突。买受人合法有效取得该载体的所有权以后，也应该可以自由地占有、使用(出租是使用方式之一)、收益和处分，是否准用发行权一次用尽原则对出租权进行限制，各国都没有规定。

另外，需要注意的是：出租权的构成要件，还须有偿许可他人使用，如果是免费使用似乎不构成此处的出租权。

(四)公开传播权(The Right of Public Dissemination)

公开传播权，是指以不转移作品载体的方式向公众提供作品的权利。对作品财产利益的利用，如果是转移作品载体的方式，可能受发行权和出租权控制，反之就可能是此处的公开传播权。

There are two core features. Firstly, it does not transfer the carriers (不转移作品载体). Secondly, it provides works to the public. Here the public refers to the unspecific majority(不特定多数人).

公开传播权是一权利束，根据具体的利用方式，又可以细分为放映权(the right of showing)、展览权(the right to exhibition)、表演权(the right of performance)、广播权(the right to broadcast)和信息网络传播权(the right of communication of information on networks)。

1. 表演权(The Right of Performance)

The right of performance refers to the right to publicly perform a work and publicly broadcast the performance of a work by various means. Performance includes live performance(现场表演) and mechanical performance(机械表演).

Live performance is acting to reproduces publicly the work by the means of playing music, staging a play, reading a poet, etc. directly. Mechanical performance is to publicly broadcast the performance of the work by means of sound, expression and action through technical equipment. To play a CD in the cafe, supermarket or airport as background music is a typical mechanical performance. Playing background music in the business place can bring profits to the operators, so they have to pay the remuneration to copyright owners, otherwise it will be a copyright infringement.

Copyright owner has the exclusive right to perform his work publicly or has entitled to authorize others to perform his work and receive remuneration. Copyright owner also can prohibit anyone performing his work without permission. But everyone can sing a copyrighted song at home without infringing copyright. That is because copyright owner only can require a commercial performer to obtain permission and pay remuneration,

2. 放映权(The Right of Showing)

The right of showing refers to the right to show to the public a work, of fine art, photography, cinematography and any work created by analogous methods of film production through film projectors(放映机), over-head projectors(幻灯机) or any other technical devices.

例如，央视版的《笑傲江湖》热播，某影厅每天晚上六集连播，学生只用交1元钱就可以观看，该影厅就侵犯了《笑傲江湖》著作权人的放映权。

It is worth noting that the right of showing is different with the right of mechanical performance. The main difference lies in whether the object is suitable to perform. The object of the right of showing is art work, photography work, cinematography work and any work created by analogous methods of film production. The object of the right of mechanical performance is the works which are suitable to perform.

3. 广播权(The Right of Broadcast)

The right of broadcast refers to the right to publicly broadcast or communicate to the public a work by wireless means, to communicate to the public a broadcast work by wire or relay means (有线转播), and to communicate to the public a broadcast work by a loudspeaker or by any other analogous tool used to transmit symbols, sounds or pictures.

(1)无线广播(Wireless Broadcast)

无线广播，是指行为人将作品转化为电磁波，由发射装置将该电磁波通过无线的方式、空中电波方式传送到远端，在远端(客户端)安装接收装置接收并还原该无线电波。Authors of literary and artistic works enjoy the exclusive right to authorizing the broadcasting of their works or the communication thereof to the public by any other means of wireless diffusion of signs, sounds or images. A radio station or television station that broadcasts a published sound recording, does not need a permission from, but shall pay remuneration to the copyright owner, except otherwise agreed by the parties.

(2)以无线或有线方式转播(Wire or Wireless Relay Broadcast)

以无线或有线方式转播，是指通过接收装置接收到他人的无线广播节目，再将该广播节目通过无线电波或有线网络系统对外传播的行为。Authors of literary and artistic works enjoy the exclusive right to authorizing any communication to the public by wire or by rebroadcasting of the broadcast of the work, when this communication is made by an organization other than the original one. 某著作权人授权甲电视台通过无线信号播放电视剧，乙电视台收到甲电视台传送的广播信号后，通过自己的信号发射装置对该广播信号进行实时地传送，或者通过自己经营的有线电缆系统将该广播信号实时传送到用户家中，就属于受广播权控制的转播行为。再如某宾馆通过安装无线信号接收装置，接收无线节目，然后通过在各个房间安设的有线系统，将接收到的无线节目传递到各个房间，该宾馆的行为就是无线转播。

某些地方成立了通过卫星接收器接收其他广播、电视节目的小型转播台，通过架设有线网络，将接收到的节目信号再次传递(转播)到各家庭的行为实际上就落入了有线转播权的控制范围。需要注意的是，转播必须是同步的。如果将信号所载的节目录制下来后，再另行播出是属于重播行为，不是这里的转播。

(3)公开播放接收到的广播(Public Communication of Broadcast the Receipted Program)

公开播放接收到的广播，是指通过接收装置接收到他人的无线广播节目，再将该广播节目通过一定的装置公开播放。Authors of literary and artistic works enjoy the exclusive right to authorizing the public communication by loudspeaker or any other analogous instrument transmitting, by signs, sounds or images, the broadcast of the work.

有线广播和网播并没有落入广播权的保护范围。

4. 展览权(The Right of Exhibition)

The right of exhibition refers to the right to publicly display the original or reproduction of a work of fine art and photography.

According to the definition, only copyright owners of fine article works and photography works have the possibility to enjoy the right of exhibition. Exhibition here includes the display of original works and their copies.

It is worth noting that the transfer of the ownership of such an original work as painting is not regarded as the transfer of copyright in it. However, the right of exhibition of the original of a painting work is still vested in the owner of the original.

5. 信息网络传播权(The Right of Communication of Information on Networks)

The right of communication of information on networks refers to the right to communicate to the public a work, by wire or wireless means in such a way that members of the public may access these works from a place and at a time individually chosen by them.

与其他四种公开传播作品的方式相比，信息网络传播的最大特征是交互式传播，公众可以根据需要随时向服务器下达传送命令，服务器根据用户的指令传送相关信息。

More specifically, communication of information on network shall involve the following characteristics:

(1) Spread by networks.

(2) Disseminate to unspecified majority.

值得注意的是，学校通过校园网向学生提供影视作品，并不因为“在籍学生”而影响对“公众”的认定。Although students is registered which seems to be specific apparently, but the students are changeable through entrance, dropout and graduate. It is a dynamic process. In essential, the students are unspecified majority.

(3) Provide information to public.

Here “provide” means a state of action which give public the possibility to get information, no matter they get it or not actually. 无论是否有人实际进行过下载或浏览，只要作品上传至网络服务器中供网络用户下载或浏览就构成对作品的提供。

(4) Uncertain time and places.

获得作品的时间和地点都必须由公众来选定。

(5) Richness in forms.

任何导致公众在线接触作品内容的行为都构成获得，比如下载、公众在线阅读、欣赏或其他方式的在线使用。

(五)演绎权(The Right of Deduction)

The right of deduction refers to the innovation and utilization of the original works on the basis of preserving the basic expression of the original works. No matter how to process the work, the fundamental idea of the work must be rightly expressed. It means the new work must reserve the basic idea of origin work; if the basic idea or expressions of origin work cannot be recognized, this process has nothing to do with the right of deduction.

与公开传播权(the right of public communication)一样，演绎权也是一权利束，具体包括摄制权(the right of making cinematographic work)、改编权(the right of adaptation)和翻译权(the right of translation)。

1. 摄制权(the Right of Making Cinematographic Work)

The right of making cinematographic work refers to the right to fixate a work on a carrier by way of film production or by virtue of an analogous method of film production.

The result of making cinematography work is to fixate a work on a carrier. The work produced will form a new work which is formed by producing a novel into a movie or TV series. The whole copyright of a cinematography work belongs to the producer(制片人). 例如，将小说版《北京故事》摄制为《蓝宇》，就是行使摄制权的结果。

2. 改编权(the Right of Adaptation)

The right of adaptation refers to the right to change a work to create a new work of originality.

Adaptation is recreation of the original work. It will create a new work with originality by changing the type or form of the original work on the basis of not changing its basic expression. 例如将报告文学改编成为剧本，将长篇小说缩写成为袖珍本，将小说版《围城》改编成漫画版《围城》等。

3. 翻译权(the Right of Translation)

The right of translation refers to the right to translate a work in one language into one in another language. 例如，将英文版的《小王子》翻译成中文版的《小王子》。The resulting work is called as translated work. The copyright of translated work is enjoyed by the translator.

(六)汇编权(the Right of Compilation)

The right of compilation refers to the right to compile works or parts of works into a new work by reason of the selection or arrangement.

In order to form a compilation work, creative intellectual labor of compilation must be reflected in the ideas of compilation and the choice or arrangement of the work. And compiler who compiles others' works shall obtain permission from the author and pay him remuneration.

第三节 邻接权
Ⅲ Neighboring Rights

一、邻接权概述(Overview of Neighboring Rights)

(一)邻接权的概念(The Definition of Neighboring Rights)

邻接权，是指基于作品传播而形成的特定的传播者所享有的与著作权有关之权利。

Creative endeavor is formed when acting, recording, publishing or broadcasting others' works. But this achievement is not as creative as the original work, so this cannot form a new work. However, this creative endeavor needs legal protection.

Under the copyright system, many of the rights covered under neighboring rights are protected as copyrights. For example, under the U. S. copyright law, sound recording producers and performers are regarded as joint authors of sound recordings. Under the French authors' rights systems, such producers' and performers' rights would be protected as neighboring rights. Neighboring rights, while similar in economic character to authors' rights, may be protected at a lower level than authors' rights and are entirely separate and distinct from the higher-level rights granted to authors. ①

Although different countries have different definitions of neighboring rights, the rights of performers, phonogram producers and broadcasting organizations are certainly covered, and are internationally protected by the *Rome Convention for the Protection of Performers, Producers of Phonograms and Broadcasting Organizations*(《保护表演者、音像制品制作者和广播组织罗马公约》，简称《罗马公约》) signed in 1961.

(二)邻接权与著作权的关系(Relations Between Neighboring Rights and Copyrights)

1. 邻接权与著作权联系密切

(1)都与作品相联系(Closely connect with works)

Copyright is the right to protect the creator of a work. Neighboring rights are the rights to protect communicators of a work. Both of them closely connect with works. And copyright is the basis of the neighboring rights. When the neighboring rights owner exercise his rights, he has to respect the copyright owners' right.

(2)权利性质相同(Both rights of the same nature)

著作权与邻接权都具有专有性(exclusiveness)、地域性(territoriality)、时间性(timeliness)。

2. 邻接权与著作权的区别明显

(1)权利主体不同(Different subjects of rights)

---

① Neighboring Rights [DB/OL]. [2017-06-02]. IT Law Wiki, http://itlaw.wikia.com/wiki/Neighboring_rights.

The subject of copyright is the creator of a work and other person who have acquired copyright in accordance with the law. The subjects of neighboring rights are the communicators related to the work, such as performers, producers of sound recordings or video recordings, broadcasting organizations, publishers, and so on.

(2)权利客体不同(Different objects of rights)

著作权的客体是作品；邻接权的客体是对作品的传播行为及该行为的劳动成果，如表演者权的客体是表演活动(performance)，广播组织权的客体是广播信号(broadcast signal)。

(3)权利内容不同(Different contents of rights)

著作权有17项权能，邻接权则只有少数几项权能。

(4)保护期限不同(Different duration of protection)

The rights of authorship, alteration and integrity of an author are not limited in time, and the term of protection for the other rights entitled to the author is the lifetime of the author and fifty years after his death. The term of protection for the other rights entitled to a legal person or other organization is fifty years. The term of protection for the rights of performers, producers of sound recordings or video recordings and broadcasting organizations is fifty years after the communication activity occurred.

二、出版者权(The Rights of the Publisher)

(一)出版者权的概念(The Definition of Rights of the Publisher)

出版者权，是指出版者对其复制、发行的作品复制品依法所享有的专有权利的统称。① 出版是指生产制作作品的复制品，并将其提供给社会公众的行为。出版者是指复制和发行图书、报刊作品的人，一般包括图书、期刊、报纸等出版单位。

Publishing refers to the behavior which distributes reproductions of works to the public. Publisher is the person who copies or distributes books or newspapers, generally including institutions publishing books, periodicals, newspapers. The publisher's rights refer to the rights that publisher enjoys in publishing books, newspapers or other kinds of literary works and these rights shall be associated with publications.

出版是创作作品之著作权人借以传播自己的作品和实现自己的法定权益的重要方式，具体的方式包括对作品的复制和发行。

As mentioned above, copyrights have meaning of two aspects, one is to copy a printing work, and the other is to issue a work. However, the kind of publication won't be legal without authorization, which based on the authorized contracts with its owner.

(二)出版者的义务(The Obligations of the Publisher)

1. 订立图书出版合同(Concluding a Contract for Publication)

A publishing contract is a legal contract between a publisher and a writer or author (or more than one), to publish written material by the writer or author. This may involve a single written

① 张楚. 知识产权法[M]. 北京：高等教育出版社，2004：55.

work, or a series of works. ① The publisher shall conclude a publishing contract with the copyright owner and pay compensation thereto. When involving the exclusive right, a contract in written form would be a better choice.

2. 按约定质量、期限出版(Publishing by Due Quality and Duration)

Since the publishing contract has concluded, it shall be performed legally and entirely in accordance with the contract law and the relevant provisions of the copyright law; otherwise it will cause default, which should be liable for breach. Although our administrative department of copyright has some quality management regulations in reality, many review and proofreading systems are not so rational, which also lead to low publish quality that bring the negative effects to the reputation to authors and their own publishers.

3. 重印和再版(Reprinting and Publishing the Second Edition)

When the book is out of stock, the publisher shall notify the copyright owner and get prepared to reprint or have a second edition. If the publisher refuses to reprint or republish the work after its exhaustion, the copyright owner has the right to terminate the contract.

If a publisher fails to fulfil 2 sets of orders from a copyrights holder within a period of 6 months, it shall be deemed as an "out of stock" situation.

如果经作品著作权人主动请求，出版者拒绝重印或者再版脱销图书，著作权人将有权以出版者违反出版合同义务为由终止合同。

4. 支付报酬(Paying the Remuneration)

A book publisher who publishes a book shall conclude a publishing contract with, and pay remuneration to, the copyright owner.

支付报酬的标准可以由出版者与著作权人协商确定，也可按相关的法定标准执行。出版者应自使用作品之日起，2个月内向作者等著作权人支付使用报酬。

5. 其他义务(Other Obligations)

出版者就出版图书或报刊文章，依据《著作权法》的相关规定，必然建立一种出版合同关系。经报刊出版者与主动投稿者之间可能不需签订书面形式的合同，但法定的合同关系通过投稿、刊登等行为而成立，在出版者与著作权人之间也是一种传播作品的合同关系。② 出版者还应依据各自不同的出版合同关系，承担《著作权法》明确规定的法定义务之外的出版合同约定的义务。

(三)出版者的权利(The Rights of the Publisher)

1. 版式设计权(Format Design Rights)

版式设计是指出版图书、刊登文章所使用的排版格式和版面布局造型，诸如图书、报纸、杂志刊载文章所使用的开本、字体、篇章结构，以及版心、抬头、字号、行距、边距、页眉、花边、插图等使用方式的设计与装饰安排。其保护期至使用该版式设计的图书

① Publishing Contract [DB/OL]. [2017-06-05]. Wikipedia, http://en.wikipedia.org/wiki/Publishing_contract.

② 张楚. 知识产权法[M]. 北京：高等教育出版社，2004：56.

期刊首次出版后第10年的12月31日。

Format design refers to the original achievements issue from publishers' editing through reproduction progress. These intelligent achievements belong to the publishers as exclusive rights. Format design rights are typical neighboring rights which belong to the communicators.

2. 专有出版权(Exclusive Publishing Rights)

Exclusive publishing rights means that the publisher has right to publish, within the contract term and within the territories stipulated in the contract, a work in its original language and in the form of original edition, revised version.

Facing numerous types of publishers, only the book publisher can negotiate an agreement with the copyright owner for the exclusive right, according to the Chinese copyright law. This exclusive right actually comes from the authorization of the copyright owner, usually the author. The exclusive right of the book publisher means that only one publisher has the right to publish, any others including the copyright owner shall not publish in the same way. If the publisher violates the contract for publication, he will probably lose it.

专有出版权还受到出版物文字或版本的限制，除专有出版合同另有约定外，出版者只能就著作权人交付的作品所使用的文字及合同约定的出版物版本享有出版权。

For instance, an author had set up exclusive publishing contract of with one Chinese press on issuing his work in Chinese version. Although the publisher had got the exclusive right on the basis of the contract, the author certainly can publish his work in English version, and entitle to find other press for cooperation in China, the former publisher with the exclusive right of Chinese version have no right to interfere in any way.

3. 作品文字修改权(Rights of Modification)

对作品文字性的修改是指出版者对准备复制发行的作品所作的语句通顺、文字润色、标点符号使用的修正等不改动作品内容的文字变动和处理。

图书出版者对文字作品的修改、删节需经过作者的许可；报社、期刊社对作品文字内容的修改，应该经过作者的许可，而对于作品只作文字性的修改、删节则无须经过作者的许可同意。

The reason is that the newspaper relatively has more readers, in addition, its publishing cycle is short, and the layout is fixed. In order to avoid unnecessary manpower loss and resource loss, the newspaper and journal clubs are entitled with legal rights to modify or abridge the written language. But if the author's manuscript is truncated(删节) overmuch to damage his original intention, the publisher must get authorization from the author. Without the authorization, it will for certain cause a dispute over copyright infringement.

4. 报刊出版者的作品转载权、摘编权(Rights of Reprinting and Excerpting of Newspaper and Magazine Publisher)

After a work is published, other newspapers or magazines may reprint it or print it as an abstract or as reference materials, except where the copyright owner has declared that reprinting or excerpting is not allowed, however, compensation shall be paid to the copyright owner according to regulation.

If the copyright owners, usually the authors, don't want to be reproduced by other newspaper publishers, they need submit a statement to the former publisher in advance together with their manuscripts. Thus, the former publisher should put the author's attached statement along with his manuscript, forbidding any kind of reprint or excerpt. Otherwise, the other newspaper publishers can exercise their rights on reprint and excerpt legally.

5. 重印、再版作品权(Rights of Reprinting and Publishing the Second Edition)

When the book is out of stock, the publisher shall notify the copyright owner and get prepared to reprint or have a second edition. If the publisher refuses to reprint or republish the work after its exhaustion, the copyright owner has the right to terminate the contract.

三、表演者权(The Rights of Performers)

(一)表演者权的概念(The Definition of Rights of Performers)

Performers shall be natural persons, legal persons or other organizations, who reproduce publicly the work by means of playing music, staging a play, reading a poem, etc. directly or by means of sound, expression and action through technical equipment.

The rights of performers means the exclusive rights of performance enjoyed by performers. There are two points to mention: firstly, the object of performance must be a work. If not, the performance has nothing with the rights of performers, such as fashion shows or football competitions. Secondly, no matter the object is under the duration of legal protection or not, the rights of performers are not affected. Although the poetry is no longer under legal protection, the performer still has the rights of performers.

(二)表演者的义务(The Obligations of Performers)

表演者在使用他人作品时，应履行相应的义务：

1. 征得著作权人同意并支付报酬的义务

In using a work of another for performance, the performer shall acquire the license of the copyright owner and pay remuneration thereto. Because the copyright owner has the performer rights, any performance that making profits is under the regulation of performance rights. In organizing a performance, the organizer shall acquire the license of the copyright owner and pay remuneration thereto.

2. 征得原著作权人和演绎权人双重同意并支付报酬的义务

Because derivative works keep basic expressions of original work, the performance of derivative works are both utilization of derivative works and original works. In this way, performance of a work derived from adaptation, translation, annotation or arrangement of the preexistent work shall be in possession of the license of both the copyright owner of original works and the copyright owner of derivative works.

3. 举办者的获权义务

组织他人表演(如举办音乐会等)的，组织者应当征得著作权人同意并支付报酬。

(三)表演者的权利(The Rights of Performers)

1. 表演者人身权(Personal Rights of Performers)

表演者人身权，是指表演者对其表演活动享有的与其人身利益相关的权利。表演活动与表演者个人对艺术的独特理解和表达紧密相连，在某种程度上可以认为表演也是表演者人格的延伸。Performers have rights to show their identities and protect the image inherent in his performance from distortion.

根据利用表演活动的方式不同，表明表演者身份的方式也各异。剧院可采用报幕的方式表明表演者身份，电视台可通过字幕方式表明表演者身份。

In addition, if the identity cannot be exposed to public according to commercial customs, this action will not be treated as infringement. Take the ringtones of mobile phones as an example. The ringtones need performance of singers, but the singers may not be known to public, and this act which does not show singers' identity is completely legal.

2. 现场直播权(The Right to Live Broadcast)

Live broadcast is an act that a radio and television station transmits the live performance to the public by wireless means. 现场直播权，是指许可他人通过广播或电视系统等通信手段把现场表演直接传送给用户的权利。现场直播权控制的是将表演传播到现场以外其他场所的行为，该传播行为还必须是与现场表演同步直播。In addition, if it is not simultaneously live broadcast, but broadcasting the records of live concert, this will not be regulate by this right.

3. 首次固定权(The Right of Fixation for the First Time)

The right of fixation for the first time is the right to license others to make sound or visual recordings and to get remuneration. 该权利控制的是将表演活动无载体到有载体的复制，将无载体的表演活动通过录制行为首次固定在有形载体上。

4. 复制发行权(The Right of Reproduction and Distribution)

The right of reproduction and distribution is the right to license others to reproduce or distribute sound or visual recording products on which their performance is fixed and to get remuneration. 复制发行权控制的是对已经固定在有形载体上的表演活动再加以复制，形成新的有形载体。

5. 信息网络传播权(The Right of Dissemination Through Information Networks)

The right of dissemination through information networks is the right to license others to make information network dissemination of their performance to the public and to get remuneration.

It is worth noting that the five kinds of right mentioned above are forbidden rights, not permission rights. In other words, performers have rights to prohibit live broadcasting, recording, taping, reproduction of distribution and network transmission which have not been authorized yet.

In using a work of another for performance, the performer shall acquire the license of the copyright owner and pay remuneration thereto.

四、录音录像制作者权(The Rights of Producers of Sound Recordings and Video Recordings)

(一)录音录像制作者概念(The Definition of Producers of Sound Recordings and Video Recordings)

Producer of sound recording means a person who first produces a sound recording. Producer of video recording means a person who first produces a video recording. Sound recordings include recordings of performances or other sounds. Video recording mean any recording of continuous, related images or pictures with or without accompanying sound other than a cinematographic work or a work created by a process analogous to cinematography.

(二)录音录像制作者的义务(The Obligations of Producers of Sound Recordings and Video Recordings)

1. 取得著作权人的许可并支付报酬(Obtain permission from, and pay remuneration to, the copyright owner)

2. 征得改编、翻译、注释、整理作品的著作权人的许可的同意并支付报酬(Obtain permission from, and pay remuneration to, the owner of the copyright in the work created by adaptation, translation, annotation or arrangement)

录音录像制作者对他人表演活动进行录制的，应当征得表演者的同意并支付报酬。

3. 使用他人已经合法录制为录音制品的应当支付报酬(Pay remuneration to the copyright owner for exploiting a music work another person has duly made into a sound recording to produce sound recordings)

录音制作者使用他人已经合法录制为录音制品的音乐作品制作录音制品的，可以不用征得著作权人同意，但是应该支付报酬，著作权人声明不许使用的不得使用。此规定的执法目的是防止对音乐的垄断。另外，该录音制作者还应征得表演者同意和原录音制作者同意并支付报酬。例如，甲创作音乐作品《花蝴蝶》，由乙演唱，丙对表演录制形成录音制品的母带，丁现在利用该录音制品制作录音制品，不用征得甲的同意，但是应该向甲支付报酬，并且应该征得乙、丙的同意并支付报酬。

(三)录音录像制作者的权利(The Rights of Producers of Sound Recordings and Video Recordings)

Producers of sound recording or video recordings have paid creative activities in the process to communicate the work, in the way of using scientific a technical means to record a work in the form of sounds and pictures in the carriers. So producers of sound recordings and video recordings shall be entitled the corresponding rights.

1. 复制权(The Right of Reproduction)

复制权，是指将录音录像制品翻录成一份或者多份的权利。行使该复制权，可以将录音录像制品中所包含的声音和画面固定在另一个载体上。

2. 发行权(The Right of Distribution)

发行权，是指以出售或者赠予方式向公众提供录音、录像制品的权利。

3. 出租权(The Right of Rental)

出租权，是指有偿许可他人临时使用录制品的权利。

4. 信息网络传播权(The Right of Dissemination Through Information Networks)

信息网络传播权，是指以有线或者无线方式向公众提供作品、表演或者录音录像制品，使公众可以在其个人选定的时间和地点获得作品、表演或者录音录像制品的权利。

5. 许可电视台播放权(The Right to Permit Television Broadcasting)

许可电视台播放权，是指录像制作者许可电视台播放其录像制品的权利。录像制作者享有许可电视台播放的权利，但录音制作者并无此项权利。

The same with performance rights, the rights of video recording producer are forbidden rights, not permission rights.

五、广播组织者权(The Rights of Broadcasting Organizations)

(一)广播组织者概念(The Definition of Broadcasting Organizations)

Broadcasting organizations are those who transmit works, facts or recordings by radio waves. In China's Copyright Law, broadcasting organizations refer to radio stations or television stations that transmit signals of sounds and/or pictures by wireless or wire means for purpose of being accepted by the public. The rights of broadcasting organizations are the exclusive rights enjoyed by broadcasting organizations in their program signals. Therefore, the object of the rights of broadcasting organization is the program signals transmitted by broadcasting organizations. It is important to note that the radio stations of enterprises, schools and towns which is established for propagating policy are not include in broadcasting here.

(二)广播组织者的义务(The Obligations of Broadcasting Organizations)

(1) In broadcasting an unpublished work created by another person, the radio or television station shall obtain permission from the copyright owner and pay remuneration thereto(播放未发表作品应征得同意并支付报酬).

(2) In broadcasting a published work created by another person, the radio or television station does not need a permission from, but shall pay remuneration to, the copyright owner (播放已经发表的作品可以不经著作权人的许可，但应支付报酬).

The reasons are as follows: firstly, the broadcasting of radio and television are highly time-limited. In order to maintain a normal operation, the stations do not have to ask for permission; secondly, the station must award the owner to guarantee the persistence of creative activities.

(3) In broadcasting a cinematography work, a work created by virtue of an analogous method of film production or a video graphic work produced by another person, the television station shall obtain permission from, and pay remuneration to, the producer of cinematographic or video graphic work(播放录像制品和电影作品均应征得同意并支付报酬).

(4) In broadcasting a published sound recording product, the radio or television station does not need a permission from, but shall pay remuneration to, the copyright owner, unless otherwise (除非) agreed by the parties concerned(播放已经出版的录音制品，可不经著作权人许可，

但应当支付报酬，当事人另有约定的除外）.

（三）广播组织者权的内容（The Content of Rights of Broadcasting Organizations）

1. 转播权（the Right of Relay）

The radio or television station shall have the right to prohibit relaying（转播）its broadcast radio or television program without permission. Relay means that programs of a broadcasting organization are broadcasted by another broadcasting organization at the same time. 有些地方电视台未经许可将央视的春晚节目录制存储，在以后的节目中播放。因为非同步播放，所以这些电视台并没有侵犯央视的转播权。

2. 对广播信号的录制和复制（Records and Copies of Broadcasting Single）

A radio or television station shall have the right to prohibit fixing its radio or television program on a sound or video recording carrier and to reproduce the sound or video recording carrier（将其播放的广播、电视录制在音像载体上以及复制音像载体）录制，是指将广播信号录制在有形物质载体上，形成载有该广播信号的复制件。复制则是对该复制件的再次复制。

International rules to protect television broadcasts from piracy have not been updated since the 1961 Rome treaty, drafted at a time when cable was in its infancy（有线电视处于起步阶段）and the Internet not even invented. Now that perfect digital copies of television programmers can be made and transmitted with a few mouse clicks, signal theft has become a big commercial headache for broadcasting organizations around the world. ① Therefore, new institutions shall be explored to better safeguard the rights of broadcasting organizations.

【英语词汇】

derivative *adj.* /*n.* 衍生的/衍生物
disseminate *v.* 传播，宣传
distribution *n.* 分配，散发，供销
donation *n.* 赠与
distortion *n.* 歪曲，曲解
impromptu *adj.* 即兴的，临时的
misrepresent *v.* 歪曲，扭曲
moral rights 人身权
publisher *n.* 出版者
propagate *v.* 传播，宣传
property right 财产权
remuneration *n.* 报酬
the right of adaptation 改编权
the right of alteration 修改权
the right of authorship 署名权
the right of broadcast 广播权
the right of communication of information on networks 信息网络传播权
the right of compilation 汇编权
the right of exhibition 展览权
the right of integrity 保护作品完整权
the right of making cinematographic work 摄制权
the right of publication 发表权
the right of public dissemination 公开传播权
the right of rental 出租权
the right of showing 放映权

---

① WIPO. Protection of Broadcasting Organizations—Background Brief. [DB/OL]. [2017-05-25]. http：//www. wipo. int/pressroom/en/briefs/broadcasting. html.

the right of translation 翻译权
transaction *n.* 交易
unspecified persons 不特定的多数人
subsidiary *n./adj.* 附属物/附属的

【英语句型】

1. Firstly, the author is entitled to decide whether to make a work available to the public.

“be entitled to…”意思是“有权……”。

译文：首先，作者有权决定是否发表作品。

2. It is worth noting that the right of show is different with mechanical broadcasting. The main difference lies in whether the object is suitable to perform. The object of the right of show is art work, photography work and film production. The object of mechanical performance is music works which is suitable to perform.

“It is worth noting that…”意思是“值得注意的是……”。

译文：值得注意的是机械表演权和放映权有所不同，其最主要的不同在于播放的对象不同，机械表演播放的是音乐作品等“适合于表演”的作品的表演，而放映权播放的是美术作品、摄影作品和电影作品。

3. Creative endeavor is formed when acting, recording, publishing or broadcasting others' works. But this achievement is not as creative as the original work, so this cannot form a new work. However, this creative endeavor needs legal protection.

“ not as… as…”意思是“不像，不如……”。

译文：对他人的作品进行表演、录制、出版、播放等行为会形成一定的劳动成果，该成果与原作相比，不具有创造性，不能形成新的作品，但是对上述劳动成果也应该予以保护。

4. In this way, performance of a work derived from adaptation, translation, annotation or arrangement of the preexistent work shall be in possession of the license of both the copyright owner of original works and the copyright owner of derivative works.

“… be in possession of…”意思是“占有，拥有，获得”。

译文：这样，使用改编、翻译、注释、整理已有作品而产生的作品进行演出，应当取得演绎作品和原作品著作权人的许可。

【阅读资料】

第五章　著作权的限制与利用

Chapter 5　The Limitations and Utilization of Copyright

【引言】为了鼓励人们的创作积极性，我国著作权法规定了著作权人享有 13 项财产权利。但是，著作权法的立法目的并非仅仅为了保护著作权人的个体权益(individual rights and interests)，通过对个体权益的保护来促进社会科学文化艺术的发展，为社会提供更加丰富的文化艺术产品，满足广大公众的精神文化需求才是其最终的目标。因此，著作权法需要在著作权人的个体权益与公共利益(public interests)之间寻找平衡，著作权限制度(restriction system of copyright)正是这种利益平衡的产物。著作权限制是为了公共利益，但并不是否定个体利益，著作权人必须对其作品加以利用，通过转让(assignment)、许可(licensing)等方式来获取报酬，以最终实现其著作权。

【学习目的与要求】通过对本章的学习，首先要理解著作权限制制度的概念，认识其产生的根源，熟悉著作权保护期的起止时间，理解并掌握合理使用的判断标准以及合理使用和法定许可的构成条件。其次要明白著作权利用是著作权人实现著作财产权的途径，了解著作权利用的主要方式，熟知著作权许可合同的主要内容，掌握著作权转让应该注意的问题。

第一节　著作权的限制

Ⅰ　The Limitations of Copyright

一、著作权限制概述(Overview of the Limitations of Copyright)

The limitation of copyright refers to situations in which the exclusive rights of copyright owners do not apply or are limited for public interest reasons. These limitations keep a balance between the rights granted to the owners of copyrighted works and the social benefit that arises from their use by others.

广义的著作权限制，是指凡是对著作权权利各要素起到约束作用的规范均属著作权限制的范畴，其不仅包括时间限制(time limits)、地域限制(geographical limits)和权能限制(power limits)，还包括对著作权的主体、客体、权利内容的约束。狭义的著作权限制仅是指对著作权权利行使的约束，与著作权的主体、客体、权利内容无关。

Copyrights refer to a series of proprietary rights empowered by laws to creators. The proprietary rights are given to ensure creators' monopoly economic interests through reasonable access, encouraging more participators join in writing.

保障创作者的个人利益并不是著作权法的最终目的，“保护创作者正当权益，鼓励创作的目的在于广泛传播优秀作品，促进知识的积累和交流，丰富人们的精神文化生活，提高全民族的科学文化素质以推动经济的发展和人类社会的进步”①。“版权立法的最终目的是为了促进学术与公共福利文化的增长，授予作者在有限时间内的独占权是达到该目的的一种手段。”②著作权法的立法宗旨所决定的公共利益与创作者利益的目的与手段的关系表明，著作权法保护创作者的权利并不是绝对的，著作权的行使必须具有促进公共利益的效果，著作权限制制度正是实现这一效果的工具。

Despite most countries have made regulations on copyright limitations, however, they have significant differences in name and provision. In European countries, various provisions of copyright limitations are called “exception and limitation of rights clause”(权利的例外和限制条款). In United States Copyright Act, it is named after “fair use”(合理使用) and “legal license”(法定许可); in Britain, Canada and other countries, it is “fair trade”(公平交易). What's more, relevant international conventions and treaties (TRIPS, WPPT, WCT, etc.) adopt expressions as “restriction or exception” (限制或者例外).

根据著作权限制的定义并结合我国《著作权法》的规定，我国著作权限制的外延包括两类：第一类是著作权保护期制度，第二类是著作权行使限制制度，包括合理使用和法定许可。此外，《伯尔尼公约》(*Berne Convention for the Protection of Literary and Artistic Works*)和《世界版权公约》(*Universal Copyright Convention*)中还规定了强制许可制度，因我国已加入该两个公约，故强制许可(compulsory licensing)也应成为我国著作权限制制度的组成部分。但由于公约规定的强制许可范围十分有限，我国《著作权法》对此并未作出相应的规定。

二、著作权的保护期(The Term of Protection for Copyright)

The term of protection for copyright is the time limit for copyright to be protected by the law. If the period expires, the rights of publication and property rights of the work are not subject to legal protection. The work enters into the public domain, and anyone can exploit it freely without permission from and without payment of remuneration to the author.

值得指出的是，有关国际公约或条约中关于著作权保护期的规定均为最低国际标准，并不禁止各国国内法对著作权规定更长的保护期，故世界各国国内法所规定的著作权保护期长短不一。③

---

① 宋木文. 关于《中华人民共和国著作权法(草案)》的说明[DB/OL]. [2016-12-08]. 西湖法律图书馆网，http: //www. law-lib. com/fzdt/newshtml/20/20050722192552htm.

② Register's Report on the General Revision of the U. S. Copyright Law [DB/OL]. [2017-06-15]. Wikisource, http: //en. wikisource. org/wiki/Register's Report on the General Revision of the U. S. Copyright Law.

③ 保护期较短的有：波兰、伊拉克、马来西亚、坦桑尼亚、赞比亚、苏丹、利比亚、古巴等国 25 年；保护期较长的有：巴西 60 年，德国、奥地利等国 70 年，西班牙、巴拿马、哥伦比亚等国 80 年。

(一)著作人身权的保护期(The Term of Protection for Moral Rights)

Due to the different perception and legislative tradition, the expiration of moral rights is varied with different countries. Generally, there are two kinds:

One is in most civil law countries. Works are inseparable with authors' moral rights. Expiration of moral rights is perpetual and should be permanently enjoyed by authors.

The other is most common law countries and few European countries. Duration of moral rights is not perpetual and expires after a set amount of time, maybe a certain duration after the death of author or contemporary when property rights terminate.

我国《著作权法》采取折中办法。The term of protection of author's rights of authorship, alteration and integrity are timeless, they can be permanently protected. The right of publication is limited by the period. And the term of protection for the right of publication is the lifetime of the author and fifty years after his death.

(二)著作财产权的保护期(The Term of Protection for Property Rights)

对著作财产权的保护期进行限制，是为了促进作品的有效、合理之利用，保证作品从私有领域向公有领域的转移，从而丰富社会的文化生活。基于上述目的和原则，我国《著作权法》根据权利主体、客体和发表行为的不同而对著作财产权的保护期分别作出了不同的规定：

1. 自然人的作品(Works of Natural Person)

自然人作品的著作财产权的保护期为作者终生及其死亡后 50 年，截止于作者死亡后的第 50 年的 12 月 31 日。如果是合作作品，则截止于最后死亡的作者死亡后第 50 年的 12 月 31 日。

As to the expiration of people's property rights, all the countries have the same expression, such as "author's all life and several years after his death", but the duration after his death is different in different countries.

我国的《著作权法》之所以规定为 50 年而不是较短或更长，一是考虑我国著作权保护的发展水平和社会对作品需求方面的要求，二是考虑对外开放和国际文化、科技交流的需要以及国际上通行的做法。①

2. 法人或其他组织的作品(Works of Legal Person and Other Organizations)

著作财产权由法人或其他组织享有的作品，包括法人作品和职务作品，其著作财产权的保护期为 50 年，截止于作品首次发表后第 50 年的 12 月 31 日，但作品自创作完成后 50 年未发表的，不再受著作权法保护。

3. 电影作品和摄影作品(Cinematographic and Photography Works)

此两类作品的著作财产权保护期为 50 年，截止于作品首次发表后第 50 年的 12 月 31 日，但作品自创作完成后 50 年未发表的，不再受著作权法保护。

4. 作者身份不明的作品(Works of Unidentified Authors)

根据《著作权法实施条例》的规定，作者身份不明的作品，其著作财产权的保护期为

① 郑友德. 知识产权法(第二版)[M]. 北京：高等教育出版社，2009：78.

50 年，截止于作品首次发表后第 50 年的 12 月 31 日。值得注意的是保护期限的转换，即作者身份一旦确定后，则转而适用《著作权法》第 21 条，即作者终生加死后 50 年。

三、合理使用(Fair Use)

Fair use means that in some cases, a work may be used without the permission from, and remuneration to, the copyright owner. Examples of fair use include commentary, criticism, news reporting, research, teaching, library archiving and scholarship. 合理使用的价值目标在于通过对著作权的适当限制，来平衡作品创作者、传播者以及使用者之间的利益，以促进社会的科学文化发展。

The term "fair use" originated in the United States. According to the United States Code, notwithstanding the provisions of sections 106 and 106A, the fair use of a copyrighted work, including such use by reproduction in copies or phonorecords or by any other means specified by that section, for purposes such as criticism, comment, news reporting, teaching, scholarship, or research, is not an infringement of copyright. In determining whether the use made of a work in any particular case is a fair use the factors to be considered shall include:

(1) The purpose and character of the use, including whether such use is of a commercial nature or is for nonprofit educational purposes;

(2) The nature of the copyrighted work;

(3) The amount and substantiality of the portion used in relation to the copyrighted work as a whole; and

(4) The effect of the use upon the potential market for or value of the copyrighted work. (U. S. Code, § 107)

The fact that a work is unpublished shall not itself bar a finding of fair use if such finding is made upon consideration of all the above factors. ①

在实践中，合理使用常常被使用人作为侵权抗辩的理由加以运用。但合理使用必须具备一定的条件。根据《伯尔尼公约》(*Berne Convention*)、《与贸易有关的知识产权协议》(*TRIPS*)和《世界知识产权组织版权条约》(*Universal Copyright Convention*)的规定，各国规定著作权的合理使用，只能在特殊情况下作出、与作品的正常利用不相冲突、不会损害权利人的合法利益，这就是学界通称的“三步检验标准”。我国《著作权法》中虽然没有直接规定这个标准，但我国已加入上述三个国际条约，有遵守“三步检验标准”之义务，故在《著作权法实施条例》中作出了相应的补充规定，实践中应以“三步检验标准”作为判断是否为合理使用的最终标准。

在我国，使用人除了应遵守“三步检验标准”外，还须承担以下两项义务：一是合理使用的作品必须是已经发表的作品，未发表的作品不属于合理使用的范围；二是合理使用不得损害作者的人身权，即必须注明作品的名称、作者姓名，并不得歪曲、篡改作品的内

① 17 USC § 107 - Limitations on exclusive rights: Fair Use [DB/OL]. [2017-06-16]. Cornell University Law School, http://www.law.cornell.edu/uscode/17/107.html.

容。

In the following cases, a work may be exploited without the permission from, and without payment of remuneration to, the copyright owner, provided that the name of the author and the title of the work are mentioned and the other rights enjoyed by the copyright owner by virtue of this Law are not infringed upon:

(一)为个人目的使用(Use for Personal Purpose)

为个人目的使用，是指为个人学习、研究或者欣赏，使用他人已经发表的作品。

许多国家的著作权法都把某种情况下的个人使用列入合理使用的范围。我国《著作权法》也作了类似的规定，并强调这种使用必须是为了纯粹的个人目的。如个人为了自我娱乐而歌唱、演奏他人的音乐作品等，这里的目的是指直接目的，至于学习、研究或欣赏的间接目的，是否具有营业性，在所不问。①

需要指出的是，不能认为只要是为个人学习、研究或者欣赏而进行的使用都是合理使用，“三步检验标准”仍然是最终的判断标准。For example, someone downloads songs, movies from Internet or reproduces phonograph records for personal appreciation. It is treated as an infringement in most countries on the ground that this action damages the legitimate interests of the right holder unreasonably.

(二)在作品中适当引用(Appropriate Quotation)

在作品中适当引用，是指为介绍、评论某一作品或者说明某一问题，在作品中适当引用他人已经发表的作品，包括通过信息网络提供他人作品中适当引用已经发表的作品。

在这里，引用的目的是为了介绍、评论或者说明，而且引用的程度要“适当”。“适当”意味着引用作品在自己创作的作品中处于从属地位，不能以引用为主导，更不能以引用代替自己的创作，作品中的主要部分或实质部分应为自己创作。从量上看，引用一般应只是他人作品的片断，只有在极其特殊的情况下才会发生全文引用。这种“转换性使用”(transformative use)②同样构成合理使用。

Copying the entire work is less likely to quality for fair use than using only a portion. But fair use may also protect the use of entire work. This is especially true if work is thinly protected, where copying the entire work still copies only a little protected expression. As discussed above, many aspects of copyrighted work are not protected by copyright, such as ideas, facts, functional aspects, no original elements, and so on. Someone may copy such elements from a copyrighted work without infringing.

While the particular portion copied is important. There was no fair use in copying less than one percent of a book, where the copier chose the “heart” of the book. Whether the portion

① 李扬. 知识产权法总论[M]. 北京：中国人民大学出版社，2008：87.

② 转换性使用是指对原作的使用并非为了再现原作本身的艺术价值，而是通过该种使用使其在表达形式、意义或传达的信息等方面与原作相比，具有了新的功能或价值. 该术语最早由皮埃尔(Pierre N. Leval)在1990年《哈佛法学评论》上发表的《论合理使用标准》(*Toward a Fair Use Standard*)一文中提出的，由美国最高法院在坎贝尔诉阿卡夫洛斯音乐公司一案中所采纳。

chosen is itself highly protected, creative expression is also relevant. ①

特别值得说明的是，引用通常不会发生改动被引用作品的情形，但在某些特殊情况下(比如滑稽模仿(parody)或讽刺作品)，对他人的作品进行改动并引用也可以构成适当引用。

(三)在时事新闻报道中使用(Utilization in News Report)

在时事新闻报道中使用，是指为报道时事新闻，在报纸、期刊、广播电台、电视台等媒体中，以及在通过网络向公众提供的作品中不可避免地再现或者引用已发表的作品。Copying from informational works like news report encourages the free spread of ideas which benefits the public.

在新闻报道中使用他人已经发表的作品，必须是附带性的。

When reporting the news of our bid for the Olympic Games, some scenes of Yimou Zhang's propaganda video leap to the eyes. In this case, it is collateral use(附带使用). However, a song was fully recorded and broadcast to public when reporting the music concert. This is not a reasonable use, because it is beyond the necessary or supplementary range of reasonable use(必要或附带性的范围).

(四)对时事性文章的使用(Utilization of Newsletter)

对时事性文章的使用，是指报纸、期刊、广播电台、电视台等媒体刊登或播放其他报纸、期刊、广播电台、电视台等媒体已发表的关于政治、经济、宗教问题的时事性文章，以及向公众通过网络提供已经在网络上发表的上述时事性文章，但作者声明不许刊登、播放的除外。

Newsletter is created to propagate the national guidelines, policy, political and economic situations, promoting democratic construction and political civilization. All countries allow newspapers and broadcasting organizations to publish the released newsletters on the condition that the author made no reservation.

《信息网络传播权保护条例》规定的合理使用中，并没有规定作者可以声明保留。这就意味着，只要关于政治、经济、宗教问题的时事性文章已经在网络上发表，他人就可以通过信息网络再传播，作者不享有禁止权。

(五)对公众集会上讲话的使用(Utilization of Speeches Delivered at a Public Gathering)

对公众集会上讲话的使用，是指报纸、期刊、广播电台、电视台等媒体刊登或播放或者通过网络传播他人在公众集会上发表的讲话。

"公众集会"(public gathering)，是指群众性的政治集会、庆祝活动或者纪念性的集会，学术讨论会不在此列，因为它是某一特定范围内的人的会议。② A government official made a public speech on current political and economic situation in public conference. Although

① Stephen M. Mc John. Interllectual Propery[M]. Fifth edition. New York: Wolters Kluver, 2014: 254-255.

② 柳松．谈谈我国著作权法中的合理使用[J]．中国专利与商标，1991(4).

this report fit the components of work, it has a more important function to deliver information on public policy. In this case, the report can be published and broadcast as long as the authors made no reservation.

需要注意的是，根据多数国家的著作权法，媒体刊登或播放他人在公众集会上的讲话，其内容必须是有关时事性，涉及政治、经济、文化等重大社会问题的讲话，与时事无关的内容，如学术演讲、诗歌朗诵、科学报告等都被排除在外。因此，应该对我国《著作权法》的此项规定做限制性解释。

(六)课堂教学和科研中的使用(Utilization for Teaching and Scientific Research)

课堂教学和科研中的使用，是指为学校课堂教学或者科学研究，翻译或者少量复制已经发表的作品，供教学或者科研人员使用以及通过网络向少数教学、科研人员提供少量已经发表的作品，但不得出版发行。这里有几个问题需要注意：

1. 学校的范围

The scope of school includes full-time school(全日制学校), spare time school(业余学校), primary school(小学), middle school(中学), university(大学), public school(公立学校) and private school(私立学校).

2. 课堂应为泛指进行教学活动的场所，并不局限于学校内部的教室

It refers to all teaching places, no matter inside school or outside school. Nevertheless, when comes to temporary or special training institutions which earn expense through training, it is not a teaching place even during classroom instruction.

3. 使用的形式

限于翻译和少量复制。

For the purpose of teaching, music schools teach the music works, songs made by others. For the purpose of teaching, film schools recompose others' plays or films to new works and take them to the stage or screen. All these should be treated as utilization for teaching.

此类合理使用中最为复杂的问题在于何为少量复制？少量复制是指复制的部分在被复制的整部作品中只占少量，还是指复制的部分在新作品中只占少量？还是两者同时满足？一般而言，复制应以满足教学和科研人员的需要为标准，并以“三步检验标准”来进行判定，看该单位的复制是否不合理地损害了著作权人的利益。

(七)国家机关执行公务中的使用(Utilization in Official Execution)

国家机关执行公务中的使用，是指国家机关为执行公务在合理范围内使用已经发表的作品，包括在合理范围内通过网络向公众提供已经发表的作品。

国家机关包括立法、行政、司法和军事机关；使用的目的是为了执行公务。如果虽为国家机关使用，但并非为了执行公务则不属于合理使用的范围。至于国家机关为执行公务而使用是否在合理范围内，则同样需要符合“三步检验标准”。In case of trial, the court can reproduce works for evidence or reference material. But if the court reproduces another's works for publishing a case book, it is not belong to fair use.

(八)图书馆等为收藏作品而复制或者通过网络为特定对象提供数字作品中的使用(Production by Libraries for Collection and Supply of Digital Works to Specific Objects

through Network）

图书馆等为收藏作品而复制或者通过网络为特定对象提供数字作品中的使用包括两种情形：

1. 复制作品（Works of Reproduction）

复制作品，是指图书馆、档案馆、纪念馆、博物馆、美术馆等为了陈列或保存版本的需要，复制（包括以数字化形式复制）本馆收藏的作品。这里需要注意的是，复制作品的目的是为了陈列或保存，而不是借阅或出租；被复制的作品必须是本馆收藏的作品，而不能复制他人包括他馆收藏的作品。以数字化形式复制时，被复制的作品应当是已经损毁或者濒临损毁、丢失或者失窃，或者其存储格式已经过时，并且在市场上无法购买或者只能以明显高于标定的价格购买的作品。

If the library book was lost, and the same book is available on the market, the library cannot copy, but only buy one book on the market. The early films collected by library are saved in video tapes, but most video tapes have already outdated and damaged, so as long as the films are available in the market, library cannot copy the films, but only purchase the films.

2. 网络传播作品（Works Disseminated Through Networks）

网络传播作品，是指图书馆、档案馆、纪念馆、博物馆、美术馆等通过信息网络向本馆馆舍内服务对象提供本馆收藏的合法出版的数字作品和依法为陈列或者保存版本的需要而以数字化形式复制的作品。

There are some limitations to this kind of fair use：

First, the collections of the library are (i) open to the public, or (ii) Libraries only give service to those people stay indoors. They cannot provide service to those people outside libraries, no matter through network or dedicated circuit.

Second, the right of reproduction duplicated solely for the purpose of replacement of a copy that is damaged, deteriorating, lost, or stolen, the library has, after a reasonable effort, determined that digital works of library provided to public must be first fixed in digital form for display or preservation. This means the library cannot provide his digital works to public through internet at random.

Third, digital works must be read online, under the protection of encryption, identity authentication technology measures. The service object cannot download the digital works. ①

（九）免费表演中的使用（Utilization in Free-of-charge Live Performances）

Free-of-charge live performance of a published work means that the performance neither collects any fees from the members of the public nor pays remuneration to the performers.

著作权法上的表演分为现场表演（live performance）和机械表演（mechanical performance）两种方式。法律虽然没有直接表明构成合理使用的“免费表演”是指现场表演还是机械表演，但从“未向表演者支付报酬”的表述来推断，这里的表演应指现场表演。

The “free” here constitute with two conditions. First, the performance is free. Performers

① Fair Use [DB/OL]. [2017-05-13]. Wikipedia, http://en.wikipedia.org/wiki/Fair_use.

and organizations are not paid. Second, the show is free open to the general public. In other words, organizers can neither pay performers, nor charge the public.

(十)室外公共场所艺术品的复制(Copy of Artistic Work Located or on Display in Outdoor Public Places)

室外公共场所艺术品的复制，是指对设置或者陈列在室外公共场所的艺术作品通过临摹、绘画、摄影、录像等方式进行复制。

之所以将室外公共场所艺术品的复制规定为合理使用，一方面是因为这些艺术品本身就具有公益性质；另一方面，如果要求复制这些室外艺术品的人都去征得著作权人的同意和支付报酬，实际上也无法做到。因此，《伯尔尼公约》和世界上大多数国家都肯定了这种情形下的使用为合理使用。

"Public place" here refers to a social place that is generally open and accessible to people. Roads (including the pavement), public squares, parks and beaches are typically considered public place. In addition, it also includes places where sight can be reached, such as the appearance of an aircraft, the exterior of a building, etc.

艺术品主要指雕塑作品、绘画作品、摄影作品等。使用的方式是复制。①

(十一)制作成少数民族语言文字版本的使用(Utilization of Minority Nationality Language Version)

制作成少数民族语言文字版本，是指将中国公民、法人或者其他组织已经发表的以汉语言文字创作的作品翻译成少数民族语言文字作品在国内出版发行以及通过网络向中国境内少数民族提供。

这样规定的目的是为了增加少数民族获得信息和受教育的机会，促进少数民族的社会经济发展和教育、文化以及科学技术的进步。

However, there are some strictly legal limitations:

First, it is limit to the Chinese works(汉语作品) of Chinese citizens and organizations.

Second, it only refers to translation of language, no matter the translation is done for remuneration or not. For example, it is not a fair use, even if the author recomposes a Chinese novel into a drama and provides its ethnic linguistic version to ethnic majorities for free.

Third, it is only used in mainland. Hong Kong, Taiwan and Macao are not included.

(十二)制作成盲文版本的使用(Utilization of Braille Edition)

制作成盲文版本的使用，是指将已经发表的作品改成盲文出版，以及不以营利为目的而通过网络以盲人能够感知的独特方式向盲人提供已经发表的文字作品。

法律之所以这样规定，完全是出于对盲人的关怀与扶持，增进盲人的福利。The work here has no limitation, regardless of the nationality of copyright holder, regardless of what

① 对绘画、摄影作品进行临摹、绘画、摄影、录像，是典型的以无接触方式实施的"平面到平面"的复制行为，而对雕塑作品进行临摹、绘画、摄影、录像，则是以无接触方式实施的"立体到平面"的复制行为。

language it uses. All works can rewrite into braille for publication, no matter profitable or not. But if the works are sensible to blinds through the network, the works must be not profitable to obtain fair use.

Under the current Copyright Law, it uses a "closed list" in limitations to copyrights, similar to the system used by many Commonwealth countries (such as Canada and the UK)(如加拿大和英国等英联邦国家), often referred to as "fair dealing." Under this system, use of a copyright without the right holder's permission is limited to certain circumstances enumerated in law.

Revised draft (June 2014) of the Article 42 of the Chinese Copyright Law includes an additional acceptable case for fair use of copyrighted material: "(13) Other Circumstances"(其他情形). This open-ended category will change the Chinese system on limitations and exceptions to copyright from a closed list to an "open list" (such as Section 107 of the United States Copyright Act), giving a much broader scope to allowable uses of copyrighted material.

四、法定许可(Statutory Licensing)

Statutory licensing means the exploitation of a published work in accordance with the law, may not obtain permission from, but pay remuneration to the copyright owner, and shall respect the other rights enjoyed by the copyright owner under the law.

In essence, under a statutory licensing, an individual or company seeking to use another's copyright can do so without seeking the copyright holder's consent, and pays the copyright holder a set fee for the license. This is an exception to the general rule under intellectual property laws.

The similarities between statutory licensing and fair use lies in two points: first, both don't need the consent of the copyright holder; second, both use the published works. The difference between statutory licensing and fair use lies in the fact that users under statutory licensing have to pay the copyright holder, while the users of fair use don't have to pay.

In a number of countries, copyright law provides for statutory licensing of copyrighted works for specific uses, but the scope is different in accordance with their national conditions and legislative purposes. Generally speaking, the scope of statutory licensing of copyright in common law countries is not as broad as that in civil law countries.

There are five main conditions of statutory licensing in China's Copyright Law.

(一)报刊转载的法定许可(Reprinting in Newspapers)

Except where the copyright owner has declared that reprinting or excerpting is not permitted (除著作权人声明保留外), other newspaper or periodical publishers may, after the publication of the work by a newspaper or periodical, reprint(转载) the work or print an abstract of it or print it as reference material(作为文摘、资料刊登), but such other publishers shall pay remuneration to the copyright owner as prescribed in regulations(按规定支付报酬).

转载，是指原封不动或不涉及实质内容的略有改动后刊登；作为文摘、资料刊登，是指对原文主要内容进行摘录、缩写后刊登。该种法定许可主要是对文字作品“复制权”的限制，旨在通过为报刊转载作品提供便利，使优秀的作品能够迅速传播，满足公众的文化需求。

It is worth noting, such statutory licensing of reprinting or excerpting applies to the work published in a newspaper or periodical, and can only be reprinted or excerpted in other newspapers or periodicals. Otherwise, it is beyond the scope of statutory licensing, in addition, reprinting or excerpting can not infringe authors' moral rights. The author's name and the work's title shall be indicated.

(二)制作录音作品的法定许可(Producing Sound Recordings)

A producer of sound recordings who exploits a musical work another person has duly made into a sound recording to produce sound recordings, may not obtain permission from, but shall pay remuneration to the copyright owner as prescribed by regulations, such work shall not be exploited where the copyright owner has declared that such exploitation is not permitted.

需要注意的是，制作录音制品的法定许可只适用于已经被合法录制为录音制品的音乐作品。如果音乐作品还未合法录制为录音制品，如仅仅在网上进行传播，就不能未经著作人许可而制作录音制品。

制作录音制品法定许可的出现是为了防止唱片公司对音乐的垄断。① Meanwhile, considering many recording products often stored in one contain medium, it is against with the dissemination if let every phonograph producer obtain the consent of all copyright holders.

There are four points to illustrate:

First, the objects are only restrained to music works.

Second, producers can use others' music works under the statutory licensing. But producers cannot simply reproduce music works; they must hire bands and singers to react the music works.

Third, the music works here are works with legal permission. Without permission, the works published in newspaper or transmitted in internet are not allowed to use.

Fourth, the work cannot be used if the copyright holder has a reservation.

(三)播放作品和录音制品的法定许可(Broadcasting Works and Sound Recordings)

A radio station or television station that broadcasts a published work created by another person, or a published sound recording, does not need permission from, but shall pay remuneration to the copyright owner. Such work and sound recording shall not be broadcasted where the copyright owner has declared that such broadcast is not permitted.

The "work" here is not including films, music works in sound recordings or video products. 因为,《著作权法》第 44 条对播放录音制品、第 46 条对播放电影作品和录像制品做了特

---

① See Melvile B. Nimmer & David Nimmer. *Nimmer on Copyright* [M]. Matthew Bender & Company, 1978: 4.

殊的规定,① 根据特别法优于普通法的原则，对电影作品包括以类似摄制电影的方法创作的作品的播放，应该直接适用法律的特别规定，而不适用此种法定许可。

（四）编写出版教科书以及制作和提供课件的法定许可（Composition and Publication of Textbooks）

编写出版教科书的法定许可，是指在编写出版特定的教科书时，可以不经著作权人许可而在教科书中直接使用他人已经发表的特定作品。The main purpose of this statutory licensing is to promote the implementation of the nine-year compulsory education and national education program without prejudice to the author's right to publish and other economic interests.

此种法定许可的适用范围较广，不仅限制著作权人的汇编权、复制权和发行权，还限制出版者的专有出版权，广播电台、电视台对其所播出节目的复制权，以及表演者、录制录像制品对其表演和制品的复制权、发行权。②

First, the "textbook" here refers to the official books used in classroom instruction. 一般是指课本，但应不限于课本，有些与课本配套的教师用书和辅助图册也应包括其中。也有学者认为"教科书"不应当包含教学参考书、辅导丛书等。

Second, not all textbooks are suitable to have statutory licensing. Only the textbooks of the nine-year compulsory education and those for the implementation of the national education program are "textbooks" under statutory licensing.

Third, there are strict limitations on the objects and quantity of works. 文字作品、音乐作品仅限于"片断"、"短小"篇幅，美术作品、摄影作品则限于"单幅"。

《信息网络传播权保护条例》将这一法定许可向网络进行了延伸，规定为实施九年制义务教育和国家教育规划，可以使用已经发表的作品片断来制作课件，并通过远程教育网络向学生提供。通过网络提供课件并非可以任意传播，提供者应当采取技术措施，以防止其服务对象以外的人获得作品。

（五）扶助贫困的准法定许可（Quasi Statutory Licensing of Assisting Impoverished）

扶助贫困的准法定许可，是指在遵循一定程序和著作权人无异议的前提下，网络提供者可以通过信息网络向农村地区的公众免费提供他人已经发表的与扶助贫困有关的特定作品。

《信息网络传播权保护条例》规定，为扶助贫困，通过信息网络向农村地区的公众免费提供中国公民、法人或者其他组织已经发表的种植养殖、防病治病、防灾减灾等与扶助贫困有关的作品和适应基本文化需求的作品，网络服务提供者应当在提供前公告拟提供的作品及其作者、拟支付报酬的标准。自公告之日起 30 日内，著作权人不同意提供的，网络服务提供者不得提供其作品；自公告之日起满 30 日，著作权人没有异议的，网络服务

① 《著作权法》第 46 条规定："电视台播放他人的电影作品和以类似摄制电影的方法创作的作品、录像制品，应当取得制片者或者录像制作者许可，并支付报酬；播放他人的录像制品，还应当取得著作权人许可，并支付报酬。"

② 郑友德．知识产权法(第二版)[M]．北京：高等教育出版社，2009：89.

提供者可以提供其作品，并按照公告的标准向著作权人支付报酬。网络服务提供者提供著作权人的作品后，著作权人不同意提供的，网络服务提供者应当立即删除著作权人的作品，并按照公告的标准向著作权人支付提供作品期间的报酬。It is notable that the user must not gain economic interests directly or indirectly in doing public welfare.

普通法定许可虽然允许著作权人声明保留，但如果著作权人在发表时没有声明保留，符合法定许可条件的使用人则可以直接使用，著作权人无权再阻止。而在为扶助贫困而实施的法定许可中，符合条件的使用人首先应当公告，著作权人不仅可以在公告期内阻止其使用，而且在公告期满后，仍然可以提出异议，阻止其使用。这就使得此种法定许可并不能像其他普通的法定许可那样具有强制效力，故称为准法定许可。

第二节 著作权的利用
Ⅱ The Utilization of Copyright

一、著作权利用概述(Overview of Copyright Utilization)

著作权的利用，大体分为著作权人自己使用、许可他人使用(licensing)和著作权的转让(transfer)、质押(pledge)三种方式。Among them, the first utilization represents in a small proportion without much reward; although pledge is able to obtain secured financing, but this way itself cannot produce reward, not under the regulation of copyright strictly. Therefore, the main methods of copyright utilization are copyright licensing and transfer.

二、著作权许可使用(Licensing of Copyright)

(一)著作权许可使用的概念(The Definition of Licensing)

Copyright licensing is the act that the owner of a copyright authorizes others to exploit his work and receives remuneration. This is the basic way of copyright holder to use his work. Because the essence of a copyright is the exclusive right to make copies, in order to commercially exploit the product, a copyright owner needs to pass some rights to publisher or distributor.

A license may be ether exclusive or nonexclusive and can be restricted by territory, time, media, purpose, or buy virtually any factor desired by the parties.

著作权许可既可以是著作权的整体许可，也可以是一项或几项权利的部分许可，实践中绝大多数都是一项或几项权利的部分许可，少有整体许可的方式。

(二)著作权许可使用的方式(Measures to Implement)

我国著作权许可分为专有许可(exclusive licensing)和非专有许可(non-exclusive licensing)。专有许可是指除非另有约定，著作权人授权被许可人以一定的方式使用作品后，其他任何人包括著作权人自己也不得再以同样的方式使用该作品，又称独占许可。非专有许可是指著作权人授权被许可人以一定的方式使用作品后，自己还可以同样的方式使用该作品，也可以授权其他人以同样的方式使用该作品，也称一般许可。

First, no matter exclusive licensing or non-exclusive licensing, the licensee(被许可人) are not bound to have the right to distribute licensing. That is to say, without consent of the copyright holder, licensee cannot allow other person to use the work again.

Second, copyright licensing is usually permission to several copyrights. Licensee can't exercise those rights that are not clearly stipulated.

Third, the copyright holder files the lawsuit when infringement incurs. The licensee can just file on behalf of the copyright owner, following standard international practices.

Fourth, pay attention to the specialty of derivative works. After copyright holder A licenses B to deduce his works, C cannot produce derivative work on grounds of B's derivative work and B's licensing, without A's permission.

(三)著作权许可使用合同(Copyright Licensing Contracts)

1. 著作权许可使用合同的概念(The Definition of Copyright Licensing Contracts)

Copyright licensing contracts can clarify the rights and obligations between the copyright owner and the licensee.

Copyright licensing agreement plays a vital role in stipulating the rights and obligations of both parties, especially the property rights. Because of the importance of copyright licensing contracts and "natural" authors are always in the weaker situation, as a result, many countries formulate copyright contract law, or stipulate details in the copyright law.

2. 著作权许可使用合同的形式(Forms of Copyright Licensing Contracts)

A licensing contract shall be concluded between a copyright holder and a user for exclusive use of the copyright holder's works by the user, with the exception of works published in newspapers or periodicals.

现实中，各个报社、期刊社往往都公开了自己的约稿办法、作品刊登条件或计酬标准等类似于格式合同的文件，作者投稿即视为接受，这实际上也等于以积极的投稿行为接受了该约稿办法的约束。

As to the non-exclusive licensing contract, there is no provision in the copyright law. Based on the principle and the spirit of contract law, licensing contract shall be construed as either written form or oral form. However, in order to avoid further disputes, it is better to have a written licensing contract, no matter exclusive copyright licensing or non-exclusive copyright agreement.

3. 著作权许可使用合同的内容(The Contents of Copyright Licensing Contracts)

In order to regulate acts to conclude the contract of both parties, clarify the rights and obligations of both parties, avoid and reduce contract disputes, China's "*Copyright Law*" specifies the main provisions of copyright licensing contracts, including:

(1) The category of the licensed right(许可使用的权利种类)

合同首先必须明确被许可人使用作品的方式，是一项、多项或全部的著作财产权。

(2) Exclusive or non-exclusive nature of licensed right(许可使用的权利是专有许可或者

非专有许可）

因为两者的禁止权范围不同，被许可人的诉讼地位不同，报酬标准也相去甚远。An exclusive license must be in writing. If contracts stipulated unclearly, the court only can identify the contract as the non-exclusive licensing.

Exclusive license is a contact in which a copyright owner authorizes licensee (another person or entity) to exclusively exercise one or more of the rights that belong to the copyright owner under the copyright, under the exclusive license; the licensee has the right to file an infringement action in court to stop all infringing activities.

(3) The geographic area, term of the license（许可使用的地域范围、期间）

许可使用的地域范围通常表现为被许可人在哪些地域可以出版（publish）、发行（issue）、表演（perform）、播放（broadcast）等；期间则是指许可使用的起止时间（beginning to ending）。

(4) The standard of remuneration and the method of payment of the license（付酬标准和办法）

The standard of remuneration for exploitation of a work may agree by both parties or may be paid according to the standard established by the copyright administration department. 由于作者的相对弱势地位，以及著作权市场的非常不确定性，许多国家都对作者的报酬权给予强制保护。

(5) Liability for breach of contract（违约责任）

当事人应当在合同中约定一方违反合同时，另一方可以采取的补救措施、赔偿方法等。

(6) Other necessary particulars deemed by both the parties（双方认为需要约定的其他条款）

合同双方可以根据不同的使用方式和双方的实际情况，对双方认为需要明晰的问题进行约定。如：担保条款（guarantee clause）、保密条款（secrecy and confidentiality clause）、合同解除条件（terminated conditions）、争议解决条款（dispute resolution terms）等，只要双方达成一致，都可以成为合同的内容。

三、著作权转让（Assignment of Copyright）

（一）著作权转让概述（Overview of Assignment of Copyright）

Assignment of copyright means that copyright owner transfers all or a portion of his own copyright to another person.

Usually, total assignment involves the permanent transfer of the entire copyright. Partial assignment is the copyright owner assigns one or more of the copyrights to another person. For example, an author might assign the right to reproduce and distribute a novel to a publisher while reserving the right to create derivative work from that novel.

著作权的转让是对著作权本身的处分，也是著作权脱离作者归属他人所有。Once

transferred, it means a permanent loss to the original copyrights. The assignee would become the new copyright holder. He is not only entitled with rights to use, but also to give licensing or retransfer to others.

由于世界各国的政治、经济、文化环境和传统不同，各民族法律观念差异，从而形成不同的著作权转让观念和立法规定。①

(二)著作权转让的实务问题(Practical Issues of Assignment of Copyright)

1. 著作权转让的范围(The Scope of Assignment)

根据我国《著作权法》的规定，著作权转让仅限于著作财产权，著作人身权不得转让。而著作财产权既可以全部转让，也可以部分转让。

2. 著作权转让的形式(The Form of Assignment)

Copyright assignment shall be completed through the contract, and shall be in writing. 但是，即使未通过书面形式签订，著作权转让合同也有可能因为履行而成立。

3. 著作权转让合同的内容(The Content of Contracts of Assignment)

The assignment contract shall contain the following key particulars: work's title, category and geographic area of the assigned work, assignment price, date and method of price payment, liability for breach of contract, and other necessary particulars deemed by both the parties.

The other party ought not to exercise the right which is not expressly(明确地) agreed to transfer. This means rights not expressly transferred in contract still belong to the copyright holder, without the exercise of assignee.

4. 著作权转让合同的备案(Filing for Contracts of Assignment)

Assignment contracts may be filed(备案) with copyright administration departments. 但备案不是合同生效的要件，法律也没有规定备案具有何种效力。从理论上讲，备案应该具有对抗效力。如果著作权人就同一权利进行多重转让的情况下，如果多个受让人均主张权利，则备案应该成为对抗要件。同时，也可以借鉴美国版权法的规定，当先后进行的几项著作权转移发生冲突时，以备案的移转优先。②

5. 著作权转让与作品载体的关系(Relations between Assignment and Carrier)

The transfer of copyright does not mean that the ownership of the carriers of the original work will be transferred accordingly. 如果受让人行使著作权需要使用作品原件，著作权人应当提供给其使用，但使用完毕应返还给著作权人。作品原件物权的转让也不意味着作品的著作权随之转让。但值得提醒的是，美术作品的原件转移，则该作品的展览权随之转移，这是一个例外。

【英语词汇】

assignment *n.* 转让　　appropriate quotation 适当引用

① 来小鹏．版权交易制度研究[M]．北京：中国政法大学出版社，2009：146.

② 李永明主编．知识产权法[M]．杭州：浙江大学出版社，2000：162.

collateral use 附带使用
excerpt *v./n.* 摘录、节选
file *v./n.* 备案
license *v./n.* 许可，特许
non-exclusive license 非专有许可
pledge *n.* 质押
public interests 公共利益
reprint 转载
transformative use 转换性使用
dispute resolution term 争议解决条款
exclusive license 专有许可
geographical limits 地域限制
licensee *n.* 被许可人
permanently *adv.* 长久地
public gathering 公众集会
quasi statutory license 准法定许可
restriction or exception 限制和例外

【英语句型】

1. Though copyright law provides the author with several critical and powerful rights over their work, those rights are not unlimited.

"provide… with…"表示"给某人某物"。

译文：虽然著作权法赋予作者对作品享有决定性的权利，但是权利并不是无限的。

2. In the public domain, the work is considered to be a part of our cultural heritage and is not subject to any copyright limitations.

"… is considered to be…"表示"……被认为是……"。

译文：公共领域的作品被认为是文化遗产的一部分，不受著作权法限制。

3. Due to the different perception and legislative tradition, the expiration of moral rights is varied with different countries.

"due to…"的意思是"正是由于……"。

译文：正是因为各国的看法和立法传统的不同，著作人身权的期限有所不同。

4. As to the expiration of people's property rights, all the countries have the same expression.

"as to…"的意思是"至于……"。

译文：至于著作财产权的期限，所有国家的表述都相同。

5. In case of trial, the court can reproduce works for evidence or reference material.

"in case of …"表达的意思是"如果/一旦……"。

译文：如果在诉讼中，法院可以复制作品作为证据和资料。

6. The work here has no limitation, regardless of the nationality of copyright holder, regardless of what language it uses.

"regardless of …"的意思是"不管……"。

译文：这里的作品对著作权人的国籍和作品使用的语言都没有限制。

7. The main purpose of this statutory licensing is to promote the implementation of the nine-year compulsory education and national education program without prejudice to the author's right to publish and other economic interests.

“without prejudice to”表示“没有对……造成不利”。

译文：此种法定许可主要目的在于不损害作者发表权和其经济利益的前提下，促进九年义务教育和国家教育规划的实施。

【阅读资料】

第六章　著作权的管理与保护
Chapter 6　The Administration and Protection of Copyright

【引言】著作权是一种民事权利(civil rights)，但是在很多情况下，作者无法直接行使权利，也无法了解自己作品被使用的情况，特别是在信息时代，作品的数字化(digitization)和网络化(networked)，使个人实施和管理著作权权利越来越不现实，著作权集体管理(collective administration)则越来越有必要了。保护著作权，是著作权法的核心问题，而在信息网络高速发展的今天，形形色色的著作权纠纷(copyright disputes)给传统的著作权保护制度提出了诸多新的课题。

【学习目的与要求】了解著作权行政管理的概念(definition)、特征(characteristic)、职能(function)，理解著作权集体管理概念、必要性(necessity)，掌握著作权集体管理组织概念与职能、著作权侵权的认定标准(recognition criteria)、侵权所导致的责任(responsibility)以及相应的执法措施(enforcement)。理解《著作权法》第46条和第47条的规定，重点掌握并能综合应用著作权侵权行为的相关理论及其法律规定。

第一节　著作权的管理
Ⅰ　The Administration of Copyright

一、著作权的行政管理(Administrative Management of Copyright)

(一)著作权行政管理的概念与特征(The Definition and Features of Administrative Management of Copyright)

著作权行政管理，是指国家著作权行政管理机关，通过行政行为，代表国家对著作权工作进行管理的行为。

著作权的行政管理是著作权管理不可缺少的一部分，著作权行政管理的特征主要有：第一，著作权行政管理的性质是行政行为(administrative act)；第二，以著作权管理为内容。

(二)著作权行政管理机构的职能(The Functions of Administrative Agencies)

根据《著作权法》的规定，国家设立中央和地方著作权行政机关。其中国务院著作权行政管理部门主管全国的著作权管理工作；各省、自治区、直辖市人民政府的著作权行政管理部门主管本行政区域的著作权管理工作。

1. 国务院著作权行政管理部门的职能

在我国，国务院著作权行政管理部门是指国家版权局(National Copyright Administration

of China)。国家版权局的著作权行政管理职能主要包括以下内容：贯彻实施著作权法律、法规，制定与著作权行政管理有关的办法；查处在全国有重大影响的著作权侵权案件；指导地方著作权行政管理部门的工作；批准设立著作权集体管理机构(copyright collective management organizations)、涉外代理机构(foreign related agencies)，并监督、指导其工作；管理国家享有著作权的作品的使用；负责著作权涉外管理工作；承担国务院交办的其他著作权管理工作。

2. 地方著作权行政管理部门的职能

地方著作权行政管理机关是指各省、自治区、直辖市版权局。地方版权局的职能主要包括：主管本行政区域的著作权管理工作(management)；查处著作权违法行为(infringement)；监督、指导本地区的著作权贸易活动(trading)；拟订地方性著作权法规、管理措施并组织实施和监督检查，等等。

二、著作权的集体管理(Collective Administration of Copyright)

(一)著作权集体管理的概念与必要性(The Definition and Necessity of Collective Administration of Copyright)

1. 著作权集体管理的概念

Collective management of copyright shall mean a collective management organization, upon authorization of a right owner, collectively exercises the copyrights and related rights of the rights owners and conducts the related activities in its own name.

2. 著作权集体管理的必要性

To the copyright owner, the development of science and technology is a double-edged sword. On one hand, high-technology plays a vital effect on expanding the scope, strengthening integrity of copyright and holding new methods to control works. But on the other hand, unexpected advantages are acquired by more unearned participators(不劳而获的参与者) through new technology of information dissemination.

The owner of copyright has the right to allow or to prohibit the use of his of his works. A writer can negotiate a contract with a publisher for the publication and distribution of his book. A composer or a musician can agree to have his music or performance recorded on CD. These examples mean the owners of copyrights can exercise their rights in person. But an author is not capable of monitoring all uses of his works. And he cannot contact every single radio or television station to negotiate licenses and remuneration for the use of his works. It is not practical for a radio station or a television station to seek specific permission from every author for the use of every copyrighted work. Therefore collective management organizations are like a bridge that connects the copyright owners and the users.

(二)著作权集体管理组织(Collective Management Organizations of Copyright)

1. 著作权集体管理组织的概念(The Definition of Collective Management Organizations of Copyright)

著作权集体管理组织，是指为权利人的利益依法设立，根据权利人授权、对权利人的著作权或者与著作权有关的权利进行集体管理的社会团体。

国家版权局于1992年批准设立了我国第一个著作权集体管理组织，中国音乐著作权协会。其会员主要是词、曲作者和部分音像制作者和创作团体。主要管理音乐作品的表演权(包括现场表演和播放背景音乐)、广播权和录制发行权(包括制作广播电视节目、背景音乐制作、音像制品制作、网络下载等)。

In 1847, the works of living authors could not be performed in a public theater without the author's assent based on a 1793 French law. Songwriter Ernest Bourget along with composers Victor Parizot and Paul Henrion refused to pay for food or drink consumed at the fashionable Ambassadeurs cafe on the Avenue des Champ-Elysees in Paris. They argued that the cafe benefitted by playing their scores every day, without payment and without acknowledgement. They had to pay for their seats and meals but neither the cafe proprietor nor fellow customers intended to pay for their creativity. The proprietor agreed that the music was important, but declined to pay the creators.

The court ruled that justice meant the composers (and their publisher) should share in the benefits from that amenity. It ordered payment (the trio supposedly received exemplary damages), but left the copyright owners to identify the use of their works and secure payment from thousands of cafes, theaters and other venues.

As a result, Society of French Writers was established in France as a copyright collecting society for creators and publishers. ①

2. 著作权集体管理组织的构成条件(The Recognition Criteria of Collective Management Organizations of Copyright)

除相关法律法规规定设立的著作权集体管理组织外，任何组织和个人不得从事著作权集体管理活动。根据2005年3月1日起施行，于2011年和2013年两次修订的《著作权集体管理条例》的规定，设立著作权集体管理组织，应当具备下列条件：①发起设立著作权集体管理组织的权利人不少于50人；②不与已经依法登记的著作权集体管理组织的业务范围交叉、重合；③能在全国范围代表相关权利人的利益；④有著作权集体管理组织的章程草案、使用费收取标准草案和向权利人转付使用费的办法草案。

3. 著作权集体管理组织的职责范围(The Scope of Administrative Duty of Collective Management Organizations of Copyright)

表演权、放映权、广播权、出租权、信息网络传播权、复制权等权利人自己难以有效行使的权利，可以由著作权集体管理组织进行集体管理。Collecting societies in Australia, New Zealand, the UK and other locales have five main functions:

(1) License works in which they hold the copyright or for which they act as agent on behalf of their members for specific uses;

(2) Monitor use of those rights;

---

① Copyright Infringement [DB/OL]. [2017-06-12]. Wikipedia, http://en.wikipedia.org/wiki/Copyright_infringement.

(3) Collect revenue relating to use of the rights;

(4) Distribute revenues as royalties to members;

(5) Enter into reciprocal arrangements with foreign collecting societies to collect and distribute local royalties to foreign rights holders and to receive and distribute royalties earned overseas to local rights holders.

第二节　著作权的保护
Ⅱ　The Protection of Copyright

一、著作权侵权行为概述(Overview of Copyright Infringements)

(一)著作权侵权行为的概念(The Definition of Copyright Infringements)

Copyright infringement is the unauthorized or prohibited use of works under copyright, infringing the copyright holder's exclusive rights. ① 著作权侵权行为，是指未经著作权人同意，又无法律上的根据，擅自对著作权作品进行使用以及其他非法手段行使著作权的行为。②

《著作权法》第 46 条规定了承担民事责任的侵权行为，第 47 条规定了承担民事责任或因同时损害公共利益，除民事责任外，还需要承担行政或刑事责任的侵权行为。

(二)著作权侵权行为的内容(The Contents of Copyright Infringements)

1. 承担民事责任的侵权行为(Infringements Bearing Civil Liability)

有下列侵权行为的，应当根据具体情况，承担停止侵害、消除影响、赔礼道歉、赔偿损失等民事责任：

(1) Publishing a work without the permission of the copyright owner

Once the work is finished, the author himself obtains copyright immediately. The author has right to decide whether publish or not. If he decided to share it with the public, he can also decide the time, place and form of publication. It is an infringement if you publish the author's work without his permission. Such act violates the right of publication enjoyed by the copyright owner.

(2) Publishing a work of joint authorship as a work created solely by oneself(当做自己单独创作的作品), without the permission of the other co-authors

Joint authors have equal undivided interests in the copyright. Without the permission from co-author, the author published the work of joint authorship in name of himself is obviously an infringement of the right of publication and authorship of the co-author.

(3) Having one's name indicated on a work created by others, in order to seek personal fame and interest , where one has not participate in the creation of the work

---

① Copyright Infringement [DB/OL]. [2017-05-20]. Wikipedia, http://cn.wikipedia.org/wiki/Copyright_infringement.

② 吴汉东. 知识产权法(第五版)[M]. 北京：中国政法大学出版社，2009：113.

The right of authorship is the exclusive right of author. The author is the only person who is entitled to sign his real name, pen name and pseudonym(化名、笔名). The others who didn't contribute to this work cannot pursue personal benefits from it. Such act violates the right of authorship enjoyed by the copyright owner.

应当注意的是，此种侵权行为是在他人作品上署名，并未删去作者名。如果是删去作者名，就是剽窃(plagiarize)他人作品。

(4) Distorting or mutilating (歪曲、篡改) a work created by another

此种行为会导致作品原意发生改变，作者要表达的思想发生了曲解，损坏了作品的价值，对作者的名誉造成了不利的影响，是对作者的修改权和保护作品完整权的侵犯。

For the court to impose liability for distortion, tamper with(篡改) other's works, at least one the following element must be proven:

One is to revise the original work by misinterpret original intention or distort the context(语境) under the authorization of the author. The other is to revise original intention or distort the context without the author's permission.

(5) Plagiarizing(剽窃) a work of another person

Contrary to popular belief, the word plagiarism is not synonymous with copyright infringement. Not every incident of plagiarism is copyright infringement, especially when public domain works are involved. But the plagiarism in copyright law is a kind of infringement.

Plagiarism is using works of others without obtaining a proper permission, or citing inappropriately; while copyright infringement is using creative works of others without authorization or compensation.

Plagiarism means that one person copies a whole work of another person and publishes it in his name, or plagiarizes the core of a work of another person and takes it as the content of his article.

应当注意的是，从著作权的相关原理来看，法律保护的是思想的表达而不是思想本身，所以剽窃，也只是对表达的剽窃，而不包括对思想的剽窃。

(6) Exploiting by exhibition, film production or any analogous method of film production or by adaption, translation, annotation, or by other means, without the permission of the copyright owner, unless otherwise provided in this Law

The author is entitled to have the right of exhibition, the right of production, the right of translation, the right of adaptation, the right of making cinematography work, etc.. The author can exercise the copyright by licensing or receive remuneration through above rights.

除了使用已经超过著作权法保护期限的作品或者其使用行为属于规定的合理使用或法定许可的范围外，上述行为侵犯了作者对其作品的展览、摄制、改编、翻译和注释等使用权和获得报酬的权利，而美术作品的原件所有人展览该作品的原件则不在此列。

(7) Exploiting a work created by another person without paying remuneration as prescribed by regulations

The user should pay the copyright owner appropriate remuneration. If not, this will be the infringement of owner's property rights. The copyright owner can exercise their copyright by licensing or receiving remuneration through performances, exhibitions, issuance, film and shoot in the similar method in adaptation, translation, assembly, annotation of copyright owners' works. This is the embodiment of property rights.

除著作权法规定的可以不付报酬的以外，都应当依照合同约定或者法律的相关规定给付报酬。

(8) Rending a work, sound recording or video recording, without the permission of the copyright owner of a cinematographic work, a work created by virtue of an analogous method of film production, computer software, sound recording or video recording or the owner of a copyright-related right unless otherwise provided in this law

According to the copyright law, the copyright owner are paid to license the temporarily use in film or similar production, and computer soft wares (except those computer software are produced for rental). Without the copyright owners' permission, it will be an infringement of the right of rental. Rental are different with borrowing. Rental contains requirement of consideration. The tortfeasor(侵权人) shall compensate for the loss of copyright owner.

(9) Exploiting the typographic arrangement of a book or periodical without the permission of the publisher

由于出版者对其版式设计享有专有使用权。对于改动较小的复制以及变化比例尺的复制，也可能会构成侵权。

(10) Broadcasting a live performance or communicating the live performance to the public, or recording his performance without the permission of the performer

Live broadcast or transmit openly or record the performance without the permission of the performers, constitute an infringement.

表演者享有许可他人从现场直播和公开传送其现场表演，并获得报酬的而权利；有许可他人录音录像，并获得报酬的权利。任何人未经许可，实施上述行为，即构成侵权。

(11) Committing any other act of infringement of copyright and of other rights and interests relating to copyright

The copyright infringements are more complex in social life and more difficult to list in the legal provisions. But the actions violate copyrights and neighboring rights shall stop the infringement(停止侵害), eliminate the impact(消除影响), offer the apology(赔礼道歉), compensate for the damage(赔偿损失), compel restitution(责令赔偿) and other civil liabilities.

只要是属于侵犯著作权及邻接权的其他行为，即可责令侵权人承担停止侵害、消除影响、赔礼道歉、赔偿损失等民事责任。此项规定为兜底性条款作为完善法律规定的补充。

2. 承担综合法律责任的侵权行为(Infringements Bearing Multiple Liabilities)

《著作权法》第 47 条分八项列举了一些侵权行为，并规定有此类侵权行为的，应当根据不同的情况，分三种情况来承担责任：一是有相应侵权行为的但没有损害公共利益(public interests)的，应当承担民事责任(civil liability)；二是相应之侵权行为，损害了公共利益，除承担民事责任外，还要承担行政责任(administrative responsibility)；三是有相应之侵权行为构成犯罪的，依法追究刑事责任(criminal liability)，还可能承担民事责任。

(1) Without the license of the copyright owner, to reproduce, distribute, perform, show, broadcast, compile or disseminate to the public through information networks his work, unless this Law provided otherwise

无论行为人是否以营利为目的，只要未经著作权人许可，以上述方式向公众传播其作品，就要视其侵权行为的情节，适用《著作权法》第47条规定的法律责任。加大了保护著作权人对作品使用权的力度。但是法律另有规定的除外，如合理使用。

(2) To publish a book in which the exclusive right of publication shall vest in another

According to the copyright law, publishers enjoy the exclusive right of publishing in accordance with the contract. The permitted press can only issue by itself during the exclusive duration, and has no right to permit others' publishing.

擅自出版他人享有专有出版权的图书，即侵犯了图书出版者的专有出版权。著作权人在出版合同约定的专有出版权期限和约定的地区内，不能再行使出版权。只在合同期满或者出版社严重违反合同义务时，出版权才重新回归著作权人。

(3) Without the license of the performer, to reproduce or distribute a sound or visual recording product on which his performance was fixed or to disseminate his performance to the public through information networks, unless this Law provided otherwise

表演者享有许可他人复制、发行录有其表演的录音录像制品；许可他人通过信息网络向公众传播其表演，并获得报酬的权利。侵权行为人未经表演者许可，擅自复制、发行录有其表演的录音录像制品，或者通过信息网络向公众传播其表演，侵犯了表演者的财产权利。表演者有权要求停止侵权行为(stop infringement acts)，赔偿损失(compensate damages)。著作权行政管理部门应当根据行为人侵权情节的轻重对侵权行为人给予行政处罚。但是，行为人未经表演者许可，以上述方式合理使用的，不属于侵权行为。

(4) Without the license of the producer, to reproduce, distribute or disseminate a sound or visual recording product to the public through information networks, unless this Law provided otherwise

Reproduce, publish or transmission through network to public without the permission of producers of audio and visual recordings lead to an infringement, except as otherwise stipulated by the copyright law.

录音录像制作者对其制作的录音录像制品享有许可他人复制、发行、出租、通过信息网络向公众传播并获得报酬的权利。对于未经录音录像制作者许可，复制、发行或者通过信息网络向公众传播其录音录像制品的侵权行为，权利人有权要求行为人停止侵害、赔偿损失。著作权行政管理部门应当根据行为人侵权情节的轻重对行为人给予行政处罚。但行为人合理使用的除外。

(5) Without the license, to broadcast or reproduce a radio or television program, unless this Law provided otherwise

Broadcast or reproduce the radio, television without permission of broadcasting stations or television stations lead to an copyright infringement, except as otherwise stipulated by the copyright law.

广播电台、电视台有权禁止未经其许可，将其播放的广播、电视转播或者录制在音像载体上以及复制音像载体。除法律另有规定外，转播或复制广播电台、电视台播放的广播、电视，应当取得广播电台、电视台的许可，并支付报酬，否则，构成对广播组织权的侵犯，广播电台、电视台有权要求侵权行为人停止侵权行为，赔偿损失。著作权行政管理部门应视其情节轻重给予行政处罚。

(6) Without the license of the copyright owner or copyright-related right owner, intentionally to escape or infringe(故意避开或者破坏) the technical measures(技术措施) adopted by the right owner for protecting the copyright or copyright-related rights in his work or sound or visual recording product, unless laws and administrative regulations provided otherwise

Deliberately avoid or damage the technical measures for owners' protection of copyrights or neighboring rights in works, without the license of the owner of copyrights or neighboring rights, leads to an infringement, except as otherwise stipulated by the law or administrative regulations.

技术措施(technical measure)，是指用于防止、限制未经权利人许可浏览、欣赏作品、表演、录音录像制品的或者通过信息网络向公众提供作品、表演、录音录像制品的有效技术、装置或者部件。权利人对其作品、录音录像制品采取保护性的技术措施，是为了防止他人不经许可，擅自使用作品和音像制品，侵犯相关的权利。但是，近年来出现了针对这种技术措施而产生的破坏或者故意规避的反向技术，极大地损害了著作权人和相关的权利人的利益，也将给文化市场秩序造成极大的混乱。侵权行为人应当承担民事责任，著作权行政管理部门对侵权行为人给予行政处罚。但法律、行政法规为保护文化市场秩序另有规定的除外。

(7) Without the license of the copyright owner or copyright-related right owner, intentionally to cancel or alter electric data for management of his work or sound or visual recording product, unless laws and administrative regulations provided otherwise

Intentionally delete or alter electric data for the management of works, audio and visual recording, without the license of the owner of copyrights or neighboring rights, lead to the copyright infringement, except as otherwise stipulated by the law or administrative regulations.

权利管理电子信息(electric data for the management)，是指说明作品及其作者、表演及其表演者、录音录像制品及其制作者的信息，作品、表演、录音录像制品权利人的信息和使用条件的信息以及表示上述信息的数字或者代码。在互联网上，以数字化形式出现的权利管理信息很容易被他人伪造、篡改和消除，给权利人权利的实现带来很大的损害和风险。这类侵权行为不仅会侵害著作权人或与著作权人有关的权利人的合法权益，而且会给著作权的管理和作品的使用带来混乱，扰乱国家的文化市场秩序。

(8) To produce or sell a work on which the author's name is forged

制作、出售假冒他人署名的作品其表现形式主要有三种：第一种是把自己的作品署他人的姓名，假冒他人的作品出售；第二种是将第三人的作品署他人的姓名，假冒他人的作品出售；第三种是临摹名家的作品(主要是美术作品)，署上名家的名。这种侵权行为不仅侵犯被假冒者的权利，严重损害被假冒者的声誉，而且还欺骗社会公众，扰乱文化市场的秩序。侵权行为人不仅应当承担民事责任，还应当受到应有的行政处罚。

上述八项侵犯著作权的行为，符合我国《刑法》的有关规定，构成犯罪的，应当依法追究刑事责任。

二、法律责任和执法措施(Legal Liability and Executive Measures)

(一)著作权侵权行为的民事责任(Civil Liability of Copyright Infringements)

侵犯著作权和与著作权有关的权益是一种侵权行为，对权利人的人身权和财产权造成了损害，侵权行为人对其造成的损害后果应当承担法律责任。

针对本条规定的侵权行为，承担民事法律责任的方式有：

1. 停止侵害(Cessation of Infringement)

侵权行为人正在实施侵害他人著作权或邻接权的行为，受害人可以依法请求其停止侵害行为，这实际上是权利人为了防止损害后果的扩大，要求侵权人不实施某种侵害行为。

Performers who have right to require the tortfeasor stop the copyright infringement immediately, when tortfeasor televised the live concert or transmitted the live show openly, without the permission of performers.

2. 消除影响、赔礼道歉(Elimination of Impact and Offering Apologies)

消除影响(eliminate impact)和赔礼道歉(offer an apology)是《民法通则》就侵权民事责任的承担所规定的两种非财产性的方式。消除影响主要针对的是侵权行为给权利人造成不良影响；赔礼道歉主要针对的是权利人所享有的精神权利受到侵害。

As a general rule, the scope of eliminating the impact and apology should be in accordance with the scope of influence caused by the infringement act, except those solved in special methods both parties agreed. Reprint which did not indicate original authors and original publications shall be liable for such civil responsibilities like eliminating the impact or offering an apology.

3. 赔偿损失(Compensation for Loss)

侵权行为人造成著作权以及与著作权有关的权益的损失时，应当以其财产赔偿权利人的经济损失(economic losses)。

Money damages in copyright infringement actions are commonly awarded under three legal theories, actual damages(实际损失), profits(获益), and statuary damages(法定损失、法定赔偿).

Actual damages also called compensatory damages, consists of the amount of any demonstrable loss the owner suffered as a result of the infringing activity. This loss may be from loss sales, lost licensing revenue, or any other provable financial loss directly attributable to the infringement.

Profits consist of any money made by the infringer as a result of the infringement. These damages are only awarded if they exceed(超过) the amount of profits lost by the copyright owner as a result of the infringement.

In many copyright cases, both actual damages and profits are difficult to prove. For that reason, the copyright law provides for statutory damages—that is, damages set by law. ①

《著作权法》第 48 条规定，侵犯著作权或者与著作权有关的权利的，侵权人应当按照权利人的实际损失给予赔偿；实际损失难以计算的，可以按照侵权人的违法所得给予赔偿。赔偿数额还应当包括权利人为制止侵权行为所支付的合理开支。权利人的实际损失或者侵权人的违法所得不能确定的，由人民法院根据侵权行为的情节，判决给予 50 万元以下的赔偿。

人民法院在确定赔偿数额时，应当考虑作品类型(type)、合理使用费(royalty of fair use)、侵权行为性质(nature of infringement)、后果(consequence)等情节(circumstance)综合确定。②

制止侵权行为所支付的合理开支，包括权利人或者委托代理人对侵权行为进行调查、取证的合理费用。人民法院根据当事人的诉讼请求和具体案情，可以将符合国家有关部门规定的律师费用计算在赔偿范围内。③

(二)著作权侵权行为的行政责任(Administrative Responsibility of Copyright Infringements)

The copyright administrative authority has right to investigate and prosecute the infringement acts that have profound influence around the nation. The tort acts listed in Article 47 of the Copyright Law, concurrently with damages to the public interests, the copyright administrative authority of local people government has right to investigate and prosecute the infringement acts.

对于《著作权法》第 47 条规定的行为，损害社会公共利益的，著作权行政管理部门可以责令停止侵权行为，没收违法所得，没收、销毁侵权复制品，并处罚款；情节严重的，著作权行政管理部门还可以没收主要用于制作侵权复制品的材料、工具、设备等。对于前述的罚款，《著作权法实施条例》第 36 条又进一步规定："有著作权法第 48 条所列侵权行为，同时损害社会公共利益，非法经营额 5 万元以上的，著作权行政管理部门可处非法经营额 1 倍以上 5 倍以下的罚款；没有非法经营额或者非法经营额 5 万元以下的，著作权行政管理部门根据情节轻重，可处 25 万元以下的罚款。"

(三)著作权侵权行为的刑事责任(Criminal Liability of Copyright Infringements)

《著作权法》第 47 条列举了 8 项侵权行为，对其中情节严重，构成犯罪的依法追究刑事责任。为此，刑法规定了侵犯著作权罪、销售侵犯著作权作品复制品罪。

1. 侵犯著作权罪

侵犯著作权罪(copyright crime)，是指以营利(seek profits)为目的，侵犯他人著作权，违法所得数额较大或者有其他严重情节(serious circumstance)的行为。

2. 销售侵犯著作权作品复制品罪

销售侵犯著作权作品复制品罪，是指以营利为目的，销售明知是刑法第 217 条规定的侵犯著作权罪中所列的侵权复制品，违法所得数额巨大的行为。具体而言，违法所得数额

① Attorney Richard Stim. Patent, Copyright & Trademark[M]. Berkeley: Bang Printing, 2014: 290-291.

② 《最高人民法院关于审理著作权民事纠纷案件适用法律若干问题的解释》第 25 条第 2 款。

③ 《最高人民法院关于审理著作权民事纠纷案件适用法律若干问题的解释》第 26 条。

在10万元以上的，属于“违法所得数额巨大”。单位犯以上两罪的，对单位判处罚金，并对其直接负责的主管人员(chief executive staff)和其他直接责任人员(directly responsible staff)，依照相应规定处罚。

(四)执法措施(Executive Measures)

1. 诉前禁止令和财产保全(Interim Preservation before Initiating Legal Proceedings)

著作权人或者与著作权有关的权利人有证据证明他人正在实施或者即将实施侵犯其权利的行为，如不及时制止将会使其合法权益受到难以弥补的损害的，可以在起诉前向人民法院申请采取责令停止有关行为的禁止令(injunction)和财产保全(property preservation)的措施。这是2001年《著作权法》修改时为保护著作权增加的重要措施。

In judicial practice, holders' losses often expand due to delayed legal measures to copyright infringement. In the trial, the evidences such as infringing products, tort tools, equipment and belongings have been moved or destroyed. As a result, it is more difficult to verify the facts of copyright infringements.

一旦权利人在起诉前已经有证据证明他人正在实施或者即将实施侵犯其权利的行为，权利人即可在起诉之前申请责令停止这种行为或进行财产保全，及早停止侵权行为，减少财产损失，有效保护著作权。

According to the copyright law and civil procedure, all the following conditions must be proven simultaneously before applying for junctions and property preservation:

Have enough evidence to prove the tortfeasor is doing or will do such infringement; in urgency, if don't take steps, the copyright or benefits related to copyright will encounter losses difficult to redeeming; the person who apply legal measures is due to copyright holder or obligee related to copyright; the applicant should provide guarantees.

2. 诉前证据保全(Perpetuation of Evidence before Initiating Leal Proceeding)

证据保全(perpetuation of evidence)是指在证据有可能灭失或以后难以取得的情况下，人民法院根据诉讼参加人的请求或依职权采取措施，对证据加以固定和保全的制度。此措施是2001年《著作权法》增加的规定。

根据《著作权法》的规定，为制止侵权行为，在证据可能灭失(might be destroyed)或者以后难以取得(difficult to obtain)的情况下，著作权人或者与著作权有关的权利人可以在起诉前向人民法院申请保全证据(preserve evidence)。人民法院接受申请后，必须在48小时内作出裁定(adjudication)；裁定采取保全措施的，应当立即开始执行。人民法院可以责令(order)申请人提供担保(provide guarantee)，申请人不提供担保的，驳回(reject)申请。申请人在人民法院采取保全措施(security measures)后15日内不起诉的，人民法院应当解除保全措施。

(五)复制品侵权的举证责任(Burden of Proof in Copyright Infringements)

基于对著作权人和邻接权人的正当权益的保护，复制品侵权采取了举证责任倒置的原则(inverted burden of proof)。《著作权法》规定，复制品的出版者(publisher)、制作者(producer)不能证明其出版、制作有合法授权的，复制品的发行者或者电影作品(cinematographic works)或者以类似摄制电影的方法创作的作品(works created by virtue of the analogous method of film production ）、计算机软件(computer software)、录音录像制品(audio and visual recording)的复制品的出租者(renter)不能证明其发行、出租的复制品有合法来源(legal resource)的，应当承担法律责任(legal liability)。如果这些主体不能证明行为的合法性，可能就会承担败诉的风险。

【英语词汇】

administrative responsibility　行政责任
administrative management　行政管理
burden of proof　举证责任
civil liability　民事责任
criminal liability　刑事责任
cessation of infringement　停止侵害
collective administration　集体管理
compensate for the damage　赔偿损失
detention　*n.*　拘役
injunction　*n.*　禁止令
eliminate the impact　消除影响
fine　*v./n.*　罚款/罚金
interim preservation　临时保护
monitor　*n.* *v.*　监控
offer an apology　赔礼道歉
order　*n.*　责令
perpetuation of evidence　证据保全
plagiarize　*v.*　剽窃
plagiarism　*n.*　剽窃
provide guarantee　提供担保
reject　*v.*　驳回
statuary damages　法定赔偿
term imprisonment　有期徒刑

【英语句型】

1. But on the other hand, unexpected advantages were acquired by more unearned participators through new technology of information dissemination, partitioning others' delicious cakes.

"be acquired by…"意思是"通过……得到"。

译文：但是另一方面，信息传播手段的多样化给一些人带来更多的可乘之机，作者的利益蛋糕被更多的不劳而获者瓜分。

2. Songwriter Ernest Bourget along with composers Victor Parizot and Paul Henrion refused to pay for food or drink consumed at the fashionable Ambassadeurs cafe on the Avenue des Champ-Elysees in Paris.

"…along with…"意思是"和……一起……"。

译文：作词家欧尼斯特·布尔歇和作曲家维克托·帕里佐，保罗·亨利翁都拒绝向巴黎爱丽舍田园大街的一家咖啡馆的食物和饮品付账。

3. In much of the world that administration is performed by a network of not-for-profit copyright collecting societies (sometimes known as authors' societies or reproduction rights organizations, RROs).

"be performed by…"意思是"由……执行"。

译文：世界上很多国家的著作权行政管理都是由非营利性的著作权集体管理组织(有时被称为著作者协会或者版权组织)来执行的。

4. These examples mean the owners of copyrights can exercise their rights in person.

"...in person"意思是"亲自"。

译文：上述例子表明著作权人能够自行实施著作权。

【阅读资料】

第三编　专利权制度

PART THREE　Patent Legal System

第七章　专利权制度概述
Chapter 7　Overview of Patent Law System

【引言】专利法律制度(patent law system)是一种利用法律、行政和经济手段保护发明创造专利权(patent of invention and innovation)，鼓励人们进行发明创造活动，促进科学技术进步与创新，推动发明创造推广应用和经济发展的知识产权保护制度。专利战略(patent strategy)在我国知识产权战略中占有十分重要的地位。建立和完善专利制度，有利于鼓励发明人进行科技创新，有利于提高我国专利创造、运用、管理和保护的能力，从而增强我国的自主创新能力(capacity for independent innovation)。

【学习目的与要求】专利权法律制度概述是专利权法律制度学习的基础。学习本章内容，应当掌握专利(patent)的概念(definition)，以及专利权(patent rights)的概念和特征(features)；了解专利制度(patent system)产生和发展的历史；了解我国专利法制定和修改的情况。

第一节　专利权及其特征
Ⅰ　Patent Right and Its Features

一、专利概述(Overview of Patent Right)

The word patent originates from the Latin "patere", which means "to lay open" (i. e., to make available for public inspection), and more directly as a shortened version of the term letters patent, which originally denoted an open for public reading royal decree granting exclusive rights to a person.① In the 13th century, the king of England began to reward the people who specialized in technical innovation and brought benefit to the society through issuing special permissions. In 1331, King Edward Ⅲ of England had authorized craftsman John Kempe the right of sewing and dyeing(缝纫和印染) process.

英王颁发这些诏书时，并不封口，这种"敞开"的证书只在底部盖有封印，不像普通证书那样密封，目的是为了让所有人都能知道该文书的内容。专利的本意源于此，即"垄断"(monopoly)和"公开"(open)。

现代社会中所谓的专利，主要有以下三种情况：

其一，指取得专利权的发明创造本身，即专利权的客体(object of patent)。从技术发

① Patent [DB/OL]. [2017-05-28]. Wikipedia, http://en.wikipedia.org/wiki/Patent.

明角度来看，专利是具有独占权的公开技术。我国《专利法》规定了三种专利：发明专利(patent of invention)、实用新型专利(patent of utility model)和外观设计专利(design patent)。发明(invention)，是指对产品(product)、方法(method)或者其改进所提出的新的技术方案(technical proposal)。实用新型(utility model)，是指对产品的形状(shape)、构造(structure)或者其结合所提出的适于实用(practical)的新的技术方案。外观设计(design)，是指对产品的形状、图案(image)或者其结合以及色彩(color)与形状、图案的结合所作出的富有美感(aesthetic)并适于工业应用(industrial appliance)的新设计。

其二，指记载发明创造内容的专利证书或者专利文献，即具体的物质文件(material documents)，如说明书(specification)、权利要求书(claims)等。如《专利法》规定，"发明专利申请(patent application for invention and innovation)经实质审查(substantial examination)没有发现驳回理由(rejected reasons)的，由国务院专利行政部门(the patent administrative department of the State Council)作出授予发明专利权的决定，发给发明专利证书(invent patent certificate)，同时予以登记和公告"。

其三，指专利权，即专利权人对其发明创造依法享有的排他性独占权，如某公司"对某种技术享有专利"中的"专利"就是指专利权。

二、专利权的概念(The Definition of Patent Right)

The term patent usually refers to an exclusive right granted to anyone who invents any new, useful, and non-obvious process, machine, article of manufacture, or composition of matter, or any new and useful improvement thereof, and claims that right in a formal patent application.

Patents are frequently referred to as "monopolies", but a patent does not give the right to the inventor or the owner of a patented invention to make, use or sell anything. The effects(作用) of the grant of a patent are that the patented invention may not be exploited(使用) in the country by persons other than the owner of the patent unless the owner agrees to such exploitation. Thus, while the owner is not given a statutory right(法定权利) to practice his invention, he is given a statutory right to prevent others from commercially exploiting his invention, which is frequently referred to(经常被提及) as a right to exclude others from making, using or selling the invention.

The right to take action against any person exploiting the patented invention in the country without his agreement constitutes the patent owner's most important right, since it permits him to derive the material benefits to which he is entitled as a reward for his intellectual effort and work, and compensation for the expenses which his research and experimentation(实验) leading to the invention have entailed. ①

A patent is the right granted by the State to an inventor to exclude others from commercially exploiting the invention for a limited period, in return for the disclosure of the invention, so that patent holder may gain the benefit of the invention.

---

① WIPO Intellectual Property Handbook: Policy, Law and Use(2nd Edition) [M]. New York: World Intellectual Property Organization, 2004: 17.

三、专利权的特征(Features of Patent Right)

作为知识产权的重要组成部分，专利权具有以下特征：

(一)无形性(Intangibility)

专利保护的客体，是一种无形财产，本身看不见、摸不着，难以实际控制，却可以通过有形的物质载体具体表现出来。一经公开，就可以被许多人同时所使用。因此，专利权的无形性为权利人带来巨大的经济效益，因为权利人可以“一女两嫁”、“货许三家”。

Compared with the tangible property rights, the intangible patent rights are easier to be infringed. The characteristics of invisibility determine the special forms in patent infringement acts. Because patents may be transferred or licensed to more than two subjects, and the utilization may not cause any wastage or losses to patents themselves in certain conditions, patent infringement acts are not obvious in most situations.

(二)独占性(Exclusiveness)

Exclusiveness means the patent rights are exclusive rights belong to patentee and often represented from these two aspects:

On one hand, everyone cannot implement patents for the commercial purpose without the permission from patentee or special legal provisions.

On the other hand, only one patent can be granted for the same invention. However, where the same applicant applies for a utility model patent and an invention patent with regard to the same invention on the same day, if the utility model patent acquired earlier is not terminated yet and the applicant declares his waiver of the same, the invention patent may be granted.

(三)公开性(Openness)

The basic functions of the patent system are to encourage the development of technology by making patent applications public documents which are disclosed information about new inventions to everyone. The disclosure requires the specifications to contain a complete description of the new invention, revealing how it works and how to reproduce it.

在现代专利法律制度中，“以技术本身的公开，换取法律的保护”成为普遍遵循的重要原则。技术公开是指专利申请人必须以说明书(written description)等专利申请文件(patent application document)的形式公开其申请专利的发明创造的内容。专利主管机关也应当向社会公开通报申请专利的发明创造。技术公开是发明人向社会换取专利权的条件，也是专利权人对社会应尽的义务。一方面使公众了解该专利的内容，监督专利权的授予；另一方面为公众提供利用该专利的机会。The written description shall contain a clear and comprehensive description of the invention or utility model so that a technician in the field of the relevant technology can carry it out; when necessary, pictures shall be attached to it.

(四)时间性(Timeliness)

The protection conferred by the patent is limited in time. After the legal expiration, the patent rights are missing, and the technology enters into public domain, becoming the common wealth of the whole society, free to every individual or unit. The term of protection for the patent right for invention shall normally be calculated between 10 and 20 years from the date of application. For the period of patent for utility models and industrial designs, most countries set 5 to 10 years. In China, the duration of the invention patent right shall be 20 years and that of the utility model patent right and of the design patent right shall be ten years respectively, all commencing from the date of application(从申请日起算).

(五)地域性(Territoriality)

专利权的地域性是指根据一国法律取得的专利权，原则上只在该国范围内发生法律效力，在其他国家或者地区不发生法律效力。权利人希望就同一专利在其他国家享有专利权，必须按照其他国家的法律另行提出专利申请。

为了克服专利权地域性给国际交往带来的弊端，各个国家之间缔结了专利权双边协定或者国际公约，一定程度上扩大了专利权的地域范围。

Under the World Trade Organization's (WTO) *Agreement on Trade-Related Aspects of Intellectual Property Rights*(《与贸易有关的知识产权协议》, TRIPS), patents should be available in WTO member states for any inventions, in all fields of technology, and the term of protection available should be the minimum twenty years. Different types of patents may have varying patent terms. By far, *Paris Convention for the Protection of Industrial Property*(《保护工业产权巴黎公约》) is one of the most widespread and the most basic international conventions protecting industrial property. It covers fundamental principles like, invention patent(发明专利), utility model(实用新型), industrial design(工业品外观设计) and unfair competition prohibition(制止不正当竞争), national treatment principle(国民待遇原则), the priority principle(优先权原则) and independence principle(独立性原则).

(六)法定性(Legalism)

专利权必须由国家专利主管部门授予方可获得。各国专利法关于授予专利的条件规定虽有不同，但都规定了一项专利申请必须经过专利主管部门审查批准，颁发专利证书，才能受到法律保护。

On the contrary, if there is no application or approval, the invention cannot be protected by law even it is an independent creation. This feature makes patent rights different from copyrights. The copyrights are automatic acquisition based on the facts that authors create the complete works. The acquisition of copyrights has no business with legal procedures.

第二节 专利制度的产生与发展概况
Ⅱ The Origin and Development of Patent System

一、专利制度的产生(The Origin of Patent System)

(一)国外专利制度的起源(The Origin of Patent System Overseas)

专利制度是科学技术和商品经济发展到一定阶段的产物，以科技和经济的发展水平相适应为前提。专利制度的产生可以追溯到中世纪甚至更远的时代。当时欧洲各国还处在封建社会的末期，但手工业作坊已出现，封建王室为了发展经济，便赐予商人或能工巧匠在一定期间内独家经营或者独家生产某种新产品的特权。

The Florentine architect Filippo Brunelleschi received a three-year patent for a barge with hoisting gear, that carried marble along the Arno River in 1421. In 1449, King Henry VI granted the first patent with a license of 20 years to John of Utynam for introducing the making of colored glass to England. ①

Patents in the modern sense originated in 1474, when the Republic of Venice enacted a decree that new and inventive devices, once put into practice, had to be communicated to the Republic to obtain the right to prevent others from using them. ②

England followed with the Statute of Monopolies in 1623 under King James I, which declared that patents could only be granted for "projects of new invention."

因此，真正具有现代意义的专利法是 17 世纪以来随着资本主义经济的不断发展和资本主义生产方式的牢固确立而逐步形成的。1623 年英国颁布了《垄断法规》，该法确立的基本原则和某些具体规定被许多国家制定专利法时采用和借鉴。《垄断法规》是英国资产阶级革命最重大的成就之一，也是世界上第一部正式而完整的专利法，标志着现代专利制度的开端。

进入 18 世纪以后，欧美各国相继颁布了专利法。美国于 1790 年颁布了专利法。1793 年对该法进行了修正，采用审查制原则，成为专利制度现代化的标志。法国在资产阶级大革命胜利后，于 1791 年颁布了专利法，并在序言中明确规定无视他人对技术发明的专利权就等于无视人权，从而确立了专利权作为一种人权的法律地位。到了 19 世纪，许多国家纷纷建立自己的专利制度，如西班牙于 1820 年、德国于 1877 年、日本于 1885 年相继建立专利制度。尤其是 1877 年德国专利法规定了强制审查原则，是最早实行专利审查的国家。截至 2006 年，全世界建立专利制度的国家和地区已达 184 个。许多对人类文明产生重大影响的发明被授予专利权，如 1752 年弗拉克林发明的避雷针，1867 年诺贝尔发明的炸药(安全雷管引爆装置)，1893 年狄塞尔发明的内燃机等。

In France, patents were granted by the monarchy and by other institutions like the "Maison du Roi". The Academy examined novelty. Examinations were generally done in secret with no requirement to publish a description of the invention. Actual use of the invention was deemed adequate disclosure to the public. The modern French patent system was created during the Revolution in 1791. Patents were granted without examination since inventor's right was considered as a natural one.

In the United States, during the so-called colonial period and Articles of Confederation years (1778—1789), several states adopted patent systems of their own. The first Congress adopted a Patent Act, in 1790, and the first patent was issued under this Act on July 31, 1790. ③

---

① Patent [DB/OL]. [2017-05-22]. Wikipedia, http://en.wikipedia.org/wiki/Patent.

② Patent [DB/OL]. [2017-05-22]. Wikipedia, http://en.wikipedia.org/wiki/Patent.

③ Patent [DB/OL]. [2017-06-18]. Wikipedia, http://en.wikipedia.org/wiki/Patent.

(二)我国专利制度的起源(The Origin of Patent System in China)

我国历史上有过许多发明创造，但专利制度的建立比其他国家晚了200多年。西汉时对盐、铁、茶叶、丝绸等实行官办或者商卖的垄断经营制度，是独占经营制度的体现，并非是技术的专利制度之萌芽。

直到19世纪中叶之后，西方的专利制度思想才传入我国。1859年太平天国在《施政新篇》中规定对新机器的发明给予奖励。1882年光绪皇帝授予郑观应等人创立的上海机器纺布局机器织布工艺10年的专利，这是我国历史上的第一个专利。1898年清政府颁布《振兴工艺给奖章程》，是我国近代史上第一个有关专利的法规。

辛亥革命后，我国才正式建立了专利制度。1912年中华民国工商部颁布《奖励工艺品暂行章程》，规定有关发明或者改良的制造品经工商部考验合格将予以奖励。1923年农商部公布《奖励工艺品暂行章程》，将保护对象扩大到制造方法的发明或改进，专利期限为3年或者5年。

1932年国民党政府颁布《奖励工业技术暂行条例》。该条例于1939年修正时增加“新型”和“新式样”两种专利，使其初步具备了专利法的雏形。1944年5月29日国民党政府公布我国历史上第一部正式的“专利法”。这部“专利法”几经修改，在台湾地区沿用至今。

二、专利制度的发展(The Development of Patent System)

(一)国外专利制度的发展(The Development of Patent System Overseas)

专利制度从出现到为各个国家所接受仅仅经历了短短数百年的时间。其间专利制度的发展并非一帆风顺，甚至一度出现倒退的现象。19世纪中叶第一次工业革命完成后，出现了一场关于专利制度的大论战。反对专利立法的主张盛行起来，他们认为：

第一，专利导致垄断。

Patent leads to monopoly. In the laissez-faire capitalism period(自由资本主义时期), free and fair are concepts firmly entrenched thorough public. Under the slogan of “free trade”, most people believe that law support monopoly must be immoral law, while patent law is law about monopoly. Hence patent law leads to monopoly conflict with the political principle of free market.

第二，专利制度作用有限。

Britain once thought that the costly process of patent examination, lengthy process of authorized review is high cost of patent protection. In 1851, it is fully demonstrated that innovation activities will be more active without the protection of patent system in series of hearings sponsored by parliament(一系列议会的听证会上).

第三，废除专利制度将对消费者有利。

When European economists in mainstream economic journal(主流经济期刊) think patent fee will eventually passed on to consumers, and the monopoly profits which patentees obtained also come from exploitation to consumers. Because of large-scale resistance, some countries vote against patent law. In 1869, Holland announced the abolition of patent law which carried out more than one and a half century. Until 1910, Holland resumed its patent system for the sake of joining the Paris convention.

但是，经过工业革命的洗礼和战胜自由贸易理论的挑战后，曾经废除专利制度的国家开始重新建立专利制度。尤其是第二次世界大战之后，随着国际经济与科技的高度发展，专利制度以前所未有的速度在世界上普及开来。经济的全球化趋势迫切要求专利制度趋于国际一体化。因而，一系列多边专利保护的国际或地区性条约相继出现。

1883年，以法国为首的十几个国家在巴黎签订《保护工业产权巴黎公约》(*Paris Convention for the Protection of Industrial Property*)。《巴黎公约》开创了专利法国际协调的先河。截至2009年10月已有173个成员国，是目前世界上最重要的知识产权公约。巴黎公约的基本目的是保证一成员国的工业产权在所有其他成员国都得到保护。但由于各成员国间的利益矛盾和立法差别，该公约没能制定统一的工业产权法，而是以各成员国内立法为基础进行保护，因此它没有排除专利权效力的地域性。

Paris convention provides the basic principles each member must abide by, in respect of each member's domestic legislation at the same time. Each member must guarantee their domestic legislation is consistent with the provisions of the convention, such as the national treatment principle(国民待遇原则), the priority principle(优先权原则), independence principle(独立性原则), compulsory licensing principle(强制许可原则), etc.

1970年关于专利申请国际合作的《专利合作条约》(*Patent Cooperation Treaty*)规定，这可以说是专利制度国际化的第一步。

If an invention aims at the world market, its patent application ranks among several countries. To grant the patent right over several countries, the applicant may choose to apply in a single channel and retrieve and examine by a single agency. Of course, whether patent application is approved will depends on the domestic legislation.

1971年《巴黎公约》成员国在法国斯特拉斯堡签订《国际专利分类斯特拉斯堡协定》。该协定根据1954年发明专利国际分类欧洲公约创建的发明专利国际分类法制定，是有关建立专利国际分类的专门协定之一。该协定的分类法不但对巴黎公约全体缔约国十分重要，而且对发展中国家同样重要。

This agreement is managed by the world intellectual property organization, and open to the all parties of Paris convention. This agreement stipulates that all parties should mark appropriate international patent symbols upon patent documents. Every country, no matter members or not, must use contracting methods according to this agreement. International patent classification system revises every five years.

《欧洲专利公约》(*The European Patent Convention*)于1973年被制定。根据本公约，申请人依照统一的程序和实体标准提出申请，就可以获得欧洲专利。该专利在经专利权人指定的所有缔约国成员中得到保护，并享有和缔约国专利相等的优惠和权利。新修订的欧洲专利公约于2007年12月13日正式生效，公约简化了欧洲专利保护的途径和程序，便利了专利申请人和专利权人，同时保留欧洲专利局高质量的审查标准。此外，由于欧洲专利公约是欧洲专利组织及其执行机构EPO的法律基础，公约各缔约国专利法及EPO的审查程序也将因欧洲专利公约的修订而发生改变。欧洲专利制度朝着更加灵活和更加友好的组织结构迈出了重要的一步。截至2008年1月1日，该公约的成员国达到34个，成为国际专利保护领域中一项重要的国际公约。

全球经济的一体化对于专利法律制度提出了新的要求。1994 年,《与贸易有关的知识产权协议》(*Agreement on Trade-Related Aspects of Intellectual Property Rights*)获得通过。

The significance of the TRIPS Agreement is three-fold:

(1) It is the first single, truly international agreement that establishes minimum standards of protection for several forms of intellectual property rights (IPR);

(2) It is the first international intellectual property agreement that mandates detailed civil, criminal, and border enforcement provisions; and

(3) It is the first international intellectual property agreement that is subject to binding, enforceable dispute settlement.

(二)我国专利制度的发展(The Development of Domestic Patent System)

新中国成立后,1950 年政务院颁布《保障发明权与专利权暂行条例》。该条例采用了前苏联的发明证书(invention certificate)和专利证书(patent certificate)的双轨制。1954 年又批准颁布了《有关生产的发明、技术改进及合理化建议的奖励暂行条例》。1963 年上述条例被废止,国务院颁布了新的《发明奖励条例》,由发明奖励制度取代了发明保护制度。

The patent system of China has been established with the adoption of the reform-open policy in China. The Standing Committee of the National People's Congress approved the Chinese Patent Law on March 12, 1984. This law took effect on April 1, 1985. 该法采取单一的专利保护制度,并分别规定职务发明(service invention)和非职务发明(non-service invention)的权利归属,规定了三种专利,即发明、实用新型和外观设计。对发明专利申请采取早期公开、延迟审查制,即自申请日起 18 个月公开,然后再进入实质程序;实用新型和外观设计专利申请,采用登记制,只进行形式审查。考虑我国存在全民所有制和集体所有制等公有制形式,该法对这些单位所产生的重大职务发明创造,规定有关主管部门可以根据国家计划指定其他单位实施。而对于一些具备实施条件的单位以合理条件请求专利权人许可实施其专利未能获得许可的情况,国家专利局根据该单位的请求,可以颁发强制实施许可证。赋予专利管理机关以准司法的行政职能是专利法的重要特点之一。

To handle the infringing acts, the Patent Law provided that the patentee and interested party could request the administrative authority for patent affairs or file a lawsuit directly. This law had adopted from the basic principles of the Paris convention and the hundreds of years' experience on patent system overseas. It is a modern patent law in consistent with China's national conditions and international characteristics.

The Patent Law has been revised triple in the past, firstly on September 4, 1992 to further promote the economic reform. The revision entered into force on January 1, 1993.

The main points of the first revision:

(1) enlarging the scope of patentable subject matter to cover pharmaceuticals and materials obtained by chemical process;

(2) prolonging the term of patent protection, for invention to 20 years, for utility model or industrial design to 10 years;

(3) adding the regulation of import right, conferring the patentee with the right to prohibit others from importing patented products without his permission;

(4) extending the legal effect for patented process to the products obtained directly by the patented process;

(5) replacing the pre-granting opposition procedure by the post-granting revocation procedure;

(6) adding the regulation of national priorities;

(7) resetting the scope of the patent application modification; 将原来修改范围仅限于说明书扩大到说明书(specification)和权利要求书(claims);

(8) expanding the scope of patent protection in technical fields;

(9) advancing the time granted for patent, 即去掉审定公告程序(determine and notification process), 在实质审查(substantive examination)后没有发现驳回理由的, 即作出授予发明专利权的决定, 发给发明专利证书(inventive patent certification), 并予以登记(registration)和公告(announcement)。

In addition, the amendment also increased penalties for counterfeit products or methods.

In order to meet the needs of establishing market economic system, and aligning the patent system with the provisions of TRIPS prior China's accession to the WTO, China revised the Patent Law secondly on Aug. 25, 2000. The revision entered into force on July 1, 2001.

The main points of the second Revision:

(1) stating explicitly the purpose of patent legislation to promote scientific and technological progress and innovation;

(2) allowing scientific and technological personnel and companies to agree on the ownership of invention and creation through contracts;

(3) stating explicitly the service inventors should be given "remuneration" instead of "reward";

(4) canceling the revocation procedure (撤销程序) to eliminate its conflicts with the procedure of invalidation(无效程序) putting the decisions made by the reexamination board(专利复审委员会) on utility model and industrial design application;

(5) adding search report(专利检索报告) for utility model patent as reference for court trial of infringement cases;

(6) empowering administrative authority to order infringers immediately stop infringement;

(7) adding provision on methods for calculation of damages to punish counterfeit patent;

(8) clearing the legal basis for submitting international patent applications (Patent Cooperation Treaty).

The latest amendment of Chinese Patent Law (hereinafter referred to as Patent Law (2008)) was adopted on 27 December 2008 and entered into force from 1 October 2009. The latest amendment changes or eliminates many provisions in the 2000 revision. Unlike the first two revisions, which were focused mainly on fulfilling China's international commitments, the third revision responds to China's internal demands to increase innovation capacity and strengthen patent protection. To achieve these goals, the legislation encompasses the following changes:

(1) clarifying the ownership of patent rights: exploitation of the co-owner's right;

(2) enhancing the quality and stability of patent right: from relative novelty standard to absolute novelty standard(绝对新颖性标准);

(3) strengthening the protection of genetic resources: no patent shall be granted for any invention or creation that is completed depending on genetic resources of which the access or use violates provisions of State laws and administrative regulations;

(4) improving the design patent system: requirement of "brief description"(简要说明); adjustment on the protection scope of the patent right for design exclusion of the plane presswork of logo design (平面印刷标记的设计); increase criteria for granting design patent; allow filing a single application for similar designs;

(5) strengthening the protection of patent right: raise threshold for punishment; the calculation method for the amount of compensations for infringement; preservation of evidence (证据保全) before litigation administrative enforcement against patent infringement prohibition of offering for sale of patented designs;

(6) safeguarding the legitimate rights and interests of the public: provisions on compulsory license; allow "parallel import"(平行进口); add "bolar exception"; add "defense of prior art"(现有技术抗辩);

(7) building up service orientated government: canceling the designation of foreign-related patent agencies.

Ever since the enactment and implementation of the *Patent Law*, it has played a significant role in encouraging the inventions and creations, protecting the achievements made in them, promoting the scientific advancement and technological innovation, and boosting the overall economic and social development of China.

与此同时，我国于 1980 年 6 月 3 日参加世界知识产权组织，1985 年 3 月 19 日加入《保护工业产权巴黎公约》(*Paris Convention for the Protection of Industrial Property*)。1994 年 1 月 1 日我国正式成为《专利合作条约》(*Patent Cooperation Treaty*)的成员国，获得与美、日、欧等工业发达国家和地区同等的地位。1996 年 6 月 17 日，我国政府向世界知识产权组织递交加入书，1997 年 6 月 19 日成为《国际专利分类斯特拉斯堡协定》(*Strasbourg Agreement Concerning the International Patent Classification*)成员国，2001 年 12 月 11 日我国加入《与贸易有关的知识产权协议》(*Related Aspects of Intellectual Property Rights*)，该协议是综合性的知识产权保护协议。所有这些标志着我国的专利工作进入到崭新的发展阶段。

After the Third Amendments to the Chinese Patent Law, *Tort Liability Law* (2009)(侵权责任法), the New *Civil Procedure Law* (2012)(《民事诉讼法》), and Judicial Interpretation of Civil Procedure Law (2015)(《民事诉讼法司法解释》) have been promulgated consecutively, and China is preparing to join *The Hague Agreements concerning the International Deposit of Industrial Designs*(《工业品外观设计国际保存海牙协定》). For the purpose to enhance patent enforcement and adapt to these treaties, laws and regulations, the State Intellectual Property Office (国家知识产权局，简称 SIPO), on April 1, 2015, published *Draft of the Fourth Amendments to the Chinese Patent Law* (*for public comments*)(《中华人民共和国专利法修改草案(征求意见稿)》), which contains revisions to 18 articles, addition of 11 articles, deletion of 1 article, and addition of one Chapter "Patent Enforcement and Application". This draft of the fourth revision focuses on improving the existing patent protection mechanism of China in five aspects as related to protection of legal rights of patent owners, exploitation and application of patent rights, roles of patent administration departments, patent examination system, and patent agency.

【英语词汇】

absolute innovation standard 绝对新颖标准
announcement *n.* 公告
authorization *n.* 授权
claims *n.* 权利要求书
design patent 外观设计专利
duration of patent 专利权的保护期限
genetic resources 遗传资源
independence principle 独立性原则
industrial designs 工业品外观设计
intangibility *n.* 无形性
national treatment principle 国民待遇原则
non-service invention 非职务发明
openness *n.* 公开性
parallel import 平行进口
patent application document 专利申请文件
patentee *n.* 专利人
patent of invention 发明专利
patent of utility model 实用新型专利
preliminary examination 初步审查
preservation of evidence 证据保全
registration *n.* 登记
remuneration *n.* 报酬
revocation procedure 撤销程序
reward *v./n.* 奖励
service invention 职务发明
specification *n.* 说明书
substantial examination 实质审查
statutory right 法定权利
the priority principle 优先权原则
the procedure of invalidation 无效程序
the reexamination board 专利复审委员会

【英语句型】

1. The effects(作用) of the grant of a patent are that the patented invention may not be exploited in the country by persons other than the owner of the patent unless the owner agrees to such exploitation.

"... other than..." (用于否定陈述后)是指"除了……以外"。

译文：专利授权的作用在于，对已经获得专利的发明，除专利权人以外任何人不得在该国使用，除非这种使用已经得到专利权人的统一。

2. The right to take action against(提起诉讼) any person exploiting the patented invention in the country without his agreement constitutes the patent owner's most important right.

"take action against" 指 "对……起诉"。

译文：这种对为经专利权人同意而在该国使用其专利发明的人提出诉讼的权利，成为专利权人最重要的一项权利。

3. Of course, whether patent application is approved will depend on the domestic legislation.

“whether…depend on…”是指“是否……取决于……”。

译文：当然，专利申请能否获得批准，还要由各国依据本国的《专利法》决定。

4. Every country, no matter members or not, must use contracting methods according to this agreement.

“no matter …or not…”的意思是“不论是否……”。

译文：任何国家，不论是否协定的缔约国，均可使用该分类法。

5. This law had adopted from the basic principles of the Paris convention and the hundreds of years’ experience on patent system overseas.

“…had adopted from…”是过去完成时，意思是“采用了……”。

译文：本法是在国外几百年来的专利经验和《巴黎公约》基本原则的基础上制定的。

【阅读资料】

第八章　专利权的主体与客体
Chapter 8　The Subjects and Objects of Patent Right

【引言】专利权法律关系(legal relations)的主体(subject)，是指专利权利义务(rights and obligations)的主体，在权利主体一方表现为专利权人(patentee)。而在专利权产生的前后，发明人(inventor)和申请人(applicant)往往也有重要的作用。专利权的客体(object)，也成为专利权的对象，在我国专利法中，包括发明(invention)、实用新型(utility model)和外观设计(appearance design)。专利权的内容主要是指，专利权人的权利和义务，在权利方面，主要表现为专利权人享有独占实施权(exclusive right to exploit)、转让权(assignment right)、许可权(right of licensing)和标记权(right of mark)；在义务方面主要表现为专利权人应当缴纳专利费用(patent fees)以及不得滥用专利权。同时，专利权也受到一定的限制，比如强制许可的限制和不视为侵犯专利权的立法规定的限制。

【学习目的与要求】通过本章的学习，要求能够区别发明人、申请人与专利权人的不同。掌握职务发明创造、合作发明创造以及委托发明创造的申请权和专利权的归属。准确理解发明、实用新型和外观设计的含义特征和要求。熟悉专利权人的权利和义务。掌握专利权的几种受限制情形。

第一节　专利权的主体
Ⅰ　The Subjects of Patent Right

在专利权法律关系中，专利权的主体即专利权人(patentee)。但是，在专利权产生之前的发明创造过程中、专利权申请(utility patent application)过程中也会涉及不同主体的法律地位。对此本节予以一并讨论。

一、发明人(Inventor)

The inventor is the person who has completed the invention-creations(发明创造) which include inventions, utility models and (industrial) designs. 我国《专利法》把发明和实用新型的完成者称为发明人(inventor)，把外观设计的完成者成为设计人(designer)。故此，这里发明人既包括发明(invention)和实用新型(utility model)的完成者，也包括外观设计(design)的完成者。

Implementing Regulations of the Patent Law(《专利法实施细则》) in rule 13 provides "inventor" or "creator" referred to in the Patent Law means any person who makes creative contributions to the substantive features of an invention-creation. Any person who, during the course of accomplishing the invention-creation, is responsible only for organizational work(组织工作), or who offers facilities(设施) for making use of material and technical means, or who takes part in other auxiliary(辅助的) functions, shall not be considered as inventor or creator. According to this provision, inventor must fulfill two conditions: direct participation(直接参与) and creative contribution(创造性贡献).

如果两个或两个以上的人对同一发明创造的实质性特点共同作出了创造性贡献，其被称为共同发明人(co-inventor)。

二、申请人(Applicant)

Patent applicant means a citizen, legal person or other organization that has the right to apply for a patent in accordance with the provisions of the law or the contract. Patent applicants shall submit patent applications to the state in accordance with the law, and may obtain the patent right after the examination and thus become the patent holder.

Where a foreigner, foreign enterprise or other foreign organization without a regular residence or business site in China applies for a patent in China, the application shall be handled in accordance with the agreements concluded by the country he or it belongs to and China or the international treaties to which both the countries have acceded(加入) or in accordance with this Law on the principle of reciprocity(互惠原则).

If a foreigner, foreign enterprise, or other foreign organization without a regular residence or business site in China intends to apply for a patent or handle other patent-related matters in China, he or it shall entrust(委托) a legally established patent agency(依法设立的专利代理机构) with the application and such matters.

一般地，完成发明创造的人有权就其发明创造申请专利。但是，在发明人之外的其他人通过合同、继承等情形下，存在发明创造完成人和申请人不一致的情形。

Moreover, patent applicants are different according to the different kinds of innovation-creations.

1. Applicant of service invention-creation (职务发明创造的申请人)

An invention-creation that is accomplished in the course of performing the duties of an employee, or mainly by using the material and technical conditions of an employer shall be deemed a service invention-creation. For a service invention-creation, the employer has the right to apply for a patent. After such application is granted, the employer shall be the patentee.

2. Applicant of non-service invention or creation (非职务发明创造申请人)

For a non-service invention-creation, the inventor or designer has the right to apply for a patent. After such application is granted, the said inventor or designer shall be the patentee.

3. Applicant of cooperate invention (合作发明创造申请人)

With regard to an invention-creation accomplished by two or more units or individuals in collaboration(协作), the right to apply for a patent shall be vested in(被授予) the units or individuals that have accomplished the invention-creation in collaboration unless it is otherwise agreed upon. After the application is granted, the applying unit(s) or individual(s) shall be deemed the patentee(s).

4. Applicant of commissioned invention (委托发明创造申请人)

根据《专利法》的规定，一个单位或者个人接受其他单位或者个人委托所完成的发明创造，除另有协议的以外，申请专利的权利属于完成的单位或者个人。With regard to an invention-creation accomplished by an unit or individual under the entrustment(委托) of another unit or individual, the right to apply for a patent shall be vested in the unit or individual that has done so under entrustment, unless it is otherwise agreed upon.

三、专利权人(Patentee)

The patentee is different from the patent applicant. The applicant is not definitely the patentee. On one hand, the applicant is not patentee on the account of his failure in innovation and creation patent application. On the other hand, the patent rights can be acquired by ordinary assignment and inheritance.

除以上两种情况外，在一般情况下专利权人就是专利申请人。

第二节　专利权的客体
Ⅱ　The Objects of Patent Right

专利权的客体(the object of patent)，又称为专利权的对象或可获专利的客体，是指我国专利法规定的可以获得专利的主题。Patent Law in article 2 provides that for the purposes of this Law, invention-creations mean inventions (发明), utility models (实用新型) and (industrial) designs(外观设计). Therefore, the objects of patent rights include invention, utility model and industrial designs.

一、发明(Invention)

(一)发明的概念(The Definition of Invention)

Inventions mean new technical solutions(技术方案) proposed for a product, a process or the improvement thereof(其). The technical solution here refers to the use of natural law to solve technical problems in production, scientific research and experiment.

Inventions often extend the boundaries of human knowledge or experience. An invention that is novel and not obvious to others skilled in the same field may be able to obtain the legal protection of a patent.

First of all, inventions must take advantage of the laws of nature(自然规律)，没有利用自然规律的不能称为发明，如体育比赛规则；违背自然规律的不能称为发明，如所谓的永动机；自然规律本身也不是发明，科学发现(scientific discovery)与技术发明(technological invention)不同，前者是对自然规律或自然现象的揭示，只是人类对自然界的认识，并非是人类的创造，后者则是技术方案。

Second, inventions should be innovative. 创新是指相对于已有技术(existing technologies)而言，发明有一定的改进或提高(improve or enhance)。

Third, the invention should be a specific technical scheme(具体的技术方案). 如果只是一种思想，并没有形成具体的技术方案，则不属于发明。①

(二)发明的分类(The Classification of Invention)

我国《专利法》将发明规定为产品发明(product invention)和方法发明(method invention)两种。

产品发明(product innovation)是指人们通过智力劳动(intellectual work)研究开发出来的关于新产品、新材料、新物质等的技术方案。产品发明是用物品来表现其技术方案的，诸如车辆、航空器、家电产品等发明均属于产品发明。专利法上的产品，可以是一个独立、完整的产品，也可以是一个设备或仪器中的零部件。

方法发明(process invention)是指人们通过智力劳动研究开发出来的关于操作方法、制作方法以及工艺流程等的技术方案。方法可以是由一系列步骤构成的一个完整过程，也可以是一个步骤。

产品发明和方法发明的分类意义在于：

1. 专利权人在享有权利的范围(the scope of patent rights)上因产品发明和方法发明的不同而有一定的差异

After the patent right is granted for an invention, unless otherwise provided for in this Law, no unit or individual may exploit the patent without permission of the patentee, i. e. , it or he may not, for production or business purposes(生产经营为目的), manufacture, use, offer to sell(许诺销售), sell, or import the patented products, use the patented method, or use, offer to sell, sell or import the products that are developed directly through the use of the patented method.

2. 专利侵权诉讼(patent infringement litigation)中，当事人因产品发明和方法发明的不同而存在举证责任(burden of proof)的差异

产品发明专利权被侵权后，诉讼中的举证责任在专利权人(patentee)一方；方法发明专利权被侵权后，诉讼中的举证责任在侵权行为人(tort-feasor)一方。

If a dispute over patent infringement involves an invention patent for the method of manufacturing a new product, the unit or individual manufacturing the same product shall provide evidence to show that the manufacturing method of their own product is different from the patented method.

二、实用新型(Utility Model)

Utility model in the *Patent Law* means any new technical solution relating to the shape, the structure(构造), or their combination, of a product, which is fit for practical use. Terms such as

① 刘春田 . 知识产权法(第二版)[M]. 北京：高等教育出版社，北京大学出版社，2003：152 ~ 155.

“petty patent”, “innovation patent”, “minor patent”, and “small patent” may also be considered to fall within the definition of “utility model”.

作为一种实用的技术方案，应当符合两个基本的条件：

(1) Patent for utility model can be granted only for products.

The products shall be objects manufactured by industrial methods, having definite shape and structure, and occupying a certain space. 如果不是产品或者虽是产品，但没有一定的形状和构造，则不能取得实用新型。

(2) Patent for utility model must be practical applicability(实用性).

The subject matter of a patent application for utility model must one which can be made or used in an industry or can produce effective results. In other words, if the application relates to a product, the product shall be able to be made industrially and solve a technical problem. 比如粉笔以前多是圆的，后来人们为了防止粉笔滚落到地面摔碎，于是制造出了六角粉笔。

实用新型和外观发明具有一些相似之处，所以也有人把实用新型称为“小发明”。但是，两者之间还是具有较大的差别，具体体现在以下几个方面：

1. 两者的保护范围(the scope of protection)不同

根据我国《专利法》及《专利法实施细则》中对两者的定义我们可以看出，发明专利既保护产品发明，又保护方法发明；而实用新型则只针对产品进行保护，并且限定在具有一定的形状、构造或者形状和构造结合的产品。如对于某种胡椒粉的成分进行改进而形成的技术方案，由于不具备一定的形状和构造，故不能申请实用新型专利。

2. 两者在专利实质性要件(substantive elements)的创造性上要求(the requirement of creativity)不同

《专利法》规定，创造性是指与现有技术相比，该发明具有突出的实质性特点和显著的进步，该实用新型具有实质性特点和进步。据此规定，实用新型专利的创造性要求比发明专利的创造性低，只要具有实质性特点和进步即可。

3. 两者的保护期限(the term of protection)不同

The duration of patent right for inventions shall be twenty years, and the duration of patent right for utility models and patent right for designs shall be ten years, counted from the date of filing.

可见，实用新型专利权的保护期限要比发明专利短。究其原因，大概是我国专利法对授予发明专利和实用新型专利的实质性条件要求不同，研发时间和投入的经费也不同，相应地要回收投资所需要的时间也应当有所区别。因此，基于创造性水平的高低，自然对实用新型专利权的保护时间也相对于发明专利要短。

4. 两者的审查程序(review process)不同

我国《专利法》对发明专利权的授予采取实质审查制度(substantive examination system)，而对实用新型则属于形式审查(preliminary examination)，故实用新型专利权的审查程序要简单一些。

Where it is found after examination as to substance that there is no cause for rejection of the application for a patent for invention, the Patent Office shall make a decision to grant the patent right for invention, issue the certificate of patent for invention, and register and announce it.

Where it is found after preliminary examination that there is no cause for rejection of the application for a patent for utility model or design, the Patent Office shall make a decision to grant the patent right for utility model or the patent right for design, issue the relevant patent certificate, and register and announce it.

据此，实用新型专利权授予是不进行严格的“三性”——新颖性(novelty)、创造性(creativity)、实用性(practicability)审查的。

三、外观设计(Industrial Design)

Designs mean, with respect to a product, new designs of the shape, pattern, or the combination thereof, or the combination of the color with shape and pattern, which are rich in an aesthetic appeal and are fit for industrial application.《保护工业产权巴黎公约》明确将外观设计纳入其保护范围。

Firstly, the carrier of a design must be a product. Agricultural products, livestock products or natural products, which cannot be produced repeatedly, shall not be the cattier of the design.

Secondly, products that include designs must be suitable for industrial applications. That means the designs can be used in industry and may be manufactured in batches(成批的). 否则不能申请外观设计专利。这里所说的能够在工业上应用，不代表外观设计一定具有实用性(practical)，外观设计解决的是产品的美感问题，不解决实用性的技术问题。

Thirdly, the combinations are rich in an aesthetic appeal. When judging whether the subject matter is patentable, the visual sensation(视觉感受) of the appearance of the product shall be taken into consideration, but not the function or technical effect of the product(产品的功能特性或技术效果).

即在审美主体身上所引起的愉悦感受和欣赏、评价等心理活动与心理过程。美感具有情感性，人们在审美活动中，总是伴随着好恶爱憎，充满了情感色彩，表现得比较主观。所以这里的美感应该做相对宽松的解释，即只要和目前已经存在的设计(existing design)相比，具有差异性(difference)，能够为人们所接受，并且也不违背公序良俗原则(the principle of public order and good morals)，应该可以认定该外观设计具有美感。

四、不授予专利权的对象(Unpatentable Objects)

根据国际条约，如《与贸易有关的知识产权协议》第27条第2款，以及我国《专利法》及《专利法实施细则》的规定，不应授予专利权的对象可以归结为以下四类：

(一)违反法律、社会公德或妨害社会公共利益的发明创造(Invention Contrary to the Laws or Social Morality, or Detrimental to Public Interest)

1. Invention Contrary to the Laws(违反法律规定的发明创造)

Where an invention-reation is contrary to the laws, it cannot be granted for a patent right.

For example, gambling facilities, devices or instruments, drug-taking appliances are all invention-creations contravening(违反) the laws and no patent rights shall be granted for them.

The laws refer to the laws formulated and promulgated by National People's Congress or its Standing Committee following the legislative procedure. They do not include administrative regulations made by the State Council or its departments or local governments.

另外，对于违反法律、行政法规的规定获取或者利用遗传资源(genetic resources)，并依赖该遗传资源完成的发明创造，也不能被授予专利权。如果发明创造的物品仅其在其使用中有可能被法律所禁止的，该项发明创造技术符合条件的亦可取得专利权。例如，各种武器的生产、销售及使用虽然受到国家法律的限制，但这些武器作为物品本身及其制造的方法仍可依法授予专利权。

2. Invention-Creations Contrary to Social Morality or Detrimental to Public Interest (违反社会公德或者妨害公共利益的发明创造)

Social morality refers to ethical or moral norms and rules(伦理道德观念和行为准则) generally recognized as justifiable(正当的) and accepted by the public. Its connotation is based on certain cultural background, continuously changes with time and social progress, and varies from region to region.

Where an invention-creation is contrary to social morality, it shall not be granted a patent right. Inventions-creations such as a design with drawings or photographs of violence, murder or obscenity(淫秽), or a method of mating a human-being with an animal, a process for cloning human beings or a cloned human being, are contrary to social morality and thus shall not be granted patent rights.

公共利益(public interest)，是指全体社会成员对公共秩序(public order)、公共安全(public safety)、公共社会环境(public social environment)等各方面的基本的共同需要而形成的利益。

Where an invention-creation is detrimental to public interest, it shall not be granted a patent right. "Detrimental(有害的) to public interest" means that the exploitation or use of an invention-creation may cause detriment to the public or the society or may disrupt(破坏) the normal order(正常秩序) of the State and the society.

Where an invention-creation employs the means of disabling or injuring a person or damaging property, such as an anti-theft device or process by causing blindness to the thief, it shall not be granted a patent right.

Where the exploitation or use an invention-creation may serious pollute the environment, seriously waste energy or resources, disrupt(破坏) ecological balance, or impair(损害) the health of the public, the invention-creation shall not be granted a patent right.

(二)科学发现(Scientific Discovery)

Scientific discovery refers to the revelations (揭示) of substances, phenomena, transformation processes and their features and laws, which objectively exist in the nature. 科学发现属于人们对客观世界中的物质、现象等的认识，而这些物质、现象等在人们认识它们之前就已经存在，只是随着人们认识水平的提高而逐渐进入了人们的认识世界里面而已。由于科学发现并不是一项具体的技术方案，所以其不被授予专利权。发明则是属于人们对客观世界的改造行为，是人们通过其智力创造活动，使某一产品或方法从无到有的产生。亦即在人们发明某种产品或方法之前，其是并不存在的。

(三)智力活动的规则和方法(Rules and Methods for Mental Activities)

Mental activities(智力活动) refer to human's thinking movements. They originate from human's thinking, and produce abstract results through inference, analysis and judgment, or, via human's thinking movement, produce results by indirectly acting on the nature.

Rules and methods for mental activities are rules and methods governing people's thinking, expression, judgment, and memorization. Because they do not use technical means or apply the laws of nature, nor do they solve any technical problem or produce any technical effect, they do not constitute technical solutions. Therefore, rules and methods instructing people on how to perform this kind of activities cannot be granted patent rights.

For example, methods of deduction, inference, or operations; rules and methods of editing calendar; operating instructions of an instrument or an apparatus; or computer languages, computing rules, all of there shall not be granted a patent right.

(四)疾病的诊断和治疗方法(Methods for Diagnosis or for Treatment of Diseases)

Methods for diagnosis or for treatment of diseases refer to the processes of identifying, determining, or eliminating the cause or focus (消除病因或病灶) of diseases which are practiced directly on living human or animal bodies.

For humanity(人道主义) and ethical(社会理论) reasons, it is acknowledged that a doctor shall be given the freedom to choose any means in the course of diagnosis or treatment of diseases. Moreover, this kind of methods are not susceptible of (不适用于) industrial application because they are practiced directly on living human or animal bodies. Therefore, methods for diagnosis or for treatment of diseases shall not be granted patent rights.

However, instruments or apparatus(仪器) for implementing these methods of diagnosis or treatment, or substances or materials for use in such methods are subject matters for which patent right may be granted.

除以上所述四种不授予专利权情形之外，在我国，动物和植物品种(animal and plant varieties)也是不授予专利权的，但是培育动植物品种的方法(method of plant and animal species' cultivation)则可以授予专利权。此外，原子核变换方法以及用该方法获得的物质(methods of nuclear transformation and the substances obtained therefrom)关系到国家的重大利益，不宜为人垄断，不宜公开，因此也不授予专利权。

第三节 专利权的内容以及限制
Ⅲ The Contents and Limitations of Patent Right

一、专利权的内容(The Contents of Patent Rights)

(一)专利权人的权利(The Rights of the Patentee)

According to China's Patent Law, after the grant of the patent right for an invention or utility model, except where otherwise provided for in this Law, no entity or individual may, without the authorization of the patentee, exploit the patent, that is, make, use, offer to sell, sell or import the patented product, or use the patented process, and use, offer to sell, sell or import the product directly obtained by the patented process, for production or business purposes.

After the grant of the patent right for a design, no entity or individual may, without the authorization of the patentee, exploit the patent, that is, make, sell or import the product incorporating its or his patented design, for production or business purposes.

A patent grants only the right to exclude others, not an affirmative right to make, use or sell an invention. The patent owner may be prevented from making, using, or selling a product embodying the patented invention because another patent's claim cover the same product, or because government regulations restrain its marketing.

根据上述之规定，专利权人的权利(the rights of the patentee)可归纳为以下几个方面：

1. 独占实施权(Rights of Exclusive Implementation)

独占实施权，是指专利权人对其专利产品或者专利方法依法享有的进行制造、使用、许诺销售、销售、进口的专有权利。①

The patent confers on its proprietor the right to prevent third parties (第三人) from manufacturing, using, offering for sale, selling or importing for such purposes, without his consent(许可), a product that is the object of the patent or the process. Under U. S. Law, a patentee also has the right to exclude others from making, using, or selling a protected invention. The patentee may choose to obtain sole benefit of the patent by withholding the practice of the invention from others or may license one or more parties to practice the invention.

(1)制造权(Manufacturing Rights)

制造权是指专利权人(patentee)享有独占地制造专利产品，禁止他人未经其许可制造相同或相似于专利产品的权利。制造专利产品，对发明和实用新型专利而言，指作出或者形成具有权利要求所记载的全部技术特征的产品；对外观设计专利权而言，是指作出或者形成采用外观设计专利的图片或者照片所表示的设计方案的产品。② 在未经许可的情况下，只要他人生产制造的产品与专利产品相同，不论使用什么设备装置或方法，也不管制

① 吴汉东．知识产权法学(第三版)[M]．北京：北京大学出版社，2005：203.

② 尹新天．中国专利法详解[M]．北京：知识产权出版社，2011：130.

造数量多少，只要结果相同，即构成侵权(infringement)。

(2)使用权(Using Rights)

使用权，是指专利权人享有的使用专利产品或专利方法及依照专利方法直接获得的产品的专有权(exclusive rights)。非经专利权人的许可，任何人不得使用其专利产品或使用其专利方法。使用者可以直接利用专利产品，如用专利电风扇乘凉，利用专利产品作为手段来自制造其他按产品，还可以采用专利产品作为零件来生产其他产品。

After a design patent right is granted, no unit or individual may exploit the patent without permission of the patentee, i. e. , it or he may not, for production or business purposes, manufacture, offer to sell, sell or import the design patent products.

由此可见，与发明和实用新型专利权相比，外观设计专利权人不具有禁止他人未经许可使用外观设计专利的产品的权利。

(3)许诺销售权(Offering for Sale Rights)

许诺销售权，是专利权人有明确表示愿意出售具有权利要求书所述技术特征的专利产品以及禁止他人未经专利权人许可许诺销售专利产品的权利。许诺销售行为可以表现为面向特定和不特定的对象(specific and non-specific objects)，以口头或书面等形式(oral or written form)，以及以产品展示、展览、陈列及各种广告明确表示愿意销售专利产品的愿望的行为。该权利在于禁止他人进行销售前的推销或促销。

(4)销售权(Marketing Rights)

销售权，是指专利权人享有的独自销售专利产品或依照专利方法直接获得的产品的权利。销售与通常意义的货物买卖一样，是将其产品的所有权按市场价格从一个单位或者个人转移到另一个单位或个人。

(5)进口权(Importing Rights)

进口权，是除法律另有规定外，专利权人享有自己进口或禁止他人未经许可为制造、许诺销售、销售、使用等生产经营目的进口其专利产品或进口依照其专利方法直接获得的产品的权利。

2. 转让权(Rights of Assignment)

转让权，是指专利权人享有的将自己的专利所有权依法转让给他人的权利。转让专利权的，当事人应当订立书面合同(written contract)，并向国务院专利行政部门(the patent administration department)登记(registration)，由国务院专利行政部门予以公告(announce)。专利权的转让自登记之日起生效。

If a Chinese unit or individual intends to transfer the right to apply for a patent(专利申请权) or patent rights to a foreigner, foreign enterprise or other foreign organization, it or he shall perform the procedures in accordance with the provisions of relevant laws and administrative regulations.

For the transfer of the right to apply for a patent or of patent rights, the parties concerned shall conclude a written contract and file for registration at the patent administration department under the State Council, and the latter shall make an announcement thereof. The transfer of the right to apply for a patent or of patent rights shall become effective as of the registration date.

3. 许可权(Rights of License)

许可权，是指专利权人享有的许可(license)他人实施其专利的权利。

一般来说，专利权人自己实施其发明创造，受到资金、市场或人员等限制，经常不能满足市场的需求，当专利权人为个人时更是如此，为了能够推动发明创造的实施应用，促进经济社会的发展，让民众能够更好地享受科技进步带来的利益，许可其他单位或者个人实施该专利，是实施应用被授予专利权的发明创造的主要方式。

Any unit or individual that intends to exploit the patent of another unit or individual shall conclude a contract with the patentee for permitted exploitation and pay the royalties. The permittee shall not have the right to allow any unit or individual not specified in the contract to exploit the said patent.

根据专利实施许可内容的不同，专利实施许可分为独占许可(monopolistic license)、排他许可(exclusive license)、普通许可(ordinary license)、交叉许可(cross-license)与分许可(sub-license)。

独占许可，是指在一定地域内，被许可方(licensee)在合同有效期间(effective period of the contract)对被许可使用的专利技术(patented technology)拥有独占的权利(monopolistic rights)，许可方(licensor)自己不能在该地域内使用其专利技术，也不得把该技术再许可第三方(the third party)使用。但专利的所有权(ownership)仍属于许可方。

排他许可，是指在一定地域内，被许可方在合同有效期间对被许可使用的专利技术享有排他的使用权(exclusive rights)，许可方不得把该专利技术再许可第三方使用，但许可方自己有权在该地域内使用该项技术。

普通许可(ordinary license)是指许可方允许被许可方在指定的地域内使用其专利技术，同时，许可方自己有权在该地域内使用该技术，也可以许可第三方使用。

交叉许可，是指两个专利权人互相许可对方实施自己的专利。两个专利的价值大体相等，一般可以彼此免交专利许可费用。但若二者的技术效果或者经济效益差距较大，也可以约定由一方给予另一方以适当的补偿。

分许可(sub-license)，是指许可方允许被许可方在指定的地域内使用其专利技术以及允许被许可方在一定条件下再许可第三方使用该技术。被许可方分许可权利的取得，应当有原许可合同的明确规定(clear provisions)或者双方的明确约定为条件。

4. 标记权(Rights of Marking)

标记权，是指专利权人在其专利产品或者该产品的包装上标明(indicate)专利标记、专利类型和专利号(patent marks, patents type and patent number)的权利。

5. 出质权(Rights of Pledging)

出质权，实质是专利权人独占权的体现，是指专利权人作为出质人(pledger)，将其拥有的专利权中的财产权(property rights)进行出质(pledge)，以担保其债务的履行(guarantee the fulfillment of its obligations)，在出质人不履行或不能履行债务的情形下，质权人享有对其专利权中的财产优先受偿(priority for repayment)的权利。我国《物权法》、《担保法》、《专利法实施细则》都对专利权人所享有的出质权进行了规定。

In the case of the pledge of registered patent rights, copyrights or other property rights in the intellectual property, the parties concerned shall conclude a written contract, and the right of pledge shall be established when the relevant competent authority has registered the pledge.

After the property rights in the intellectual property have been pledged, the pledger shall not transfer the pledge or permit anyone else to use it, unless it is otherwise agreed to between the pledger and the pledgee after negotiations. The pledger shall use the money incurred from transferring the pledged intellectual property or permitting anyone else to use it to fulfill the obligee's rights in advance, or submit the aforesaid(上述的) money to a competent authority(主管部门) for keeping.

(二)专利权人的义务(The Obligations of the Patentee)

专利权人在享有上述各项权利的同时，必须承担相应的义务。

1. 缴纳专利费用的义务(The Obligation to Pay Royalties)

The patent applicant shall pay all kinds of application fees when applying for the patent. And the patentee shall pay annual fees(年费) commencing from the year when the patent right is granted. If failure to pay the annual fee as required, the patent right shall be terminated before the expiration of the duration.

The main purpose of setting the obligation to pay annual fee is, to promote the patentee to give up the patent which is have no more actual commercial value as soon as possible, and adjust the interest relationship between the patentee and the society through the economic levers.

2. 不得滥用专利权(Do Not Abuse the Patent Rights)

专利权人应促进专利技术早日为社会所用，为人类作贡献。在具备实施条件的单位以合理的条件请求专利权人许可实施时，专利权人应该在合理长的时间内给予许可。

The entity or individual requesting, in accordance with the provisions of this Law, a compulsory license for exploitation shall furnish proof that it or he has not been able to conclude with the patentee a license contract for exploitation on reasonable terms and conditions.

如果新专利技术的实施依赖于前一发明创造，则前一发明创造的专利权人更应该给予后一发明创造专利权人实施其发明的许可。拒绝许可可能构成专利权的滥用或限制竞争行为(restriction of competition)，导致专利被强制许可(compulsory licensing)。

二、专利权的限制(The Limitations of Patent Rights)

《与贸易有关的知识产权协议》第30条规定了专利独占权(exclusive rights to the patent)的例外。其认为，成员方可对专利授予的独占权规定有限的例外，条件是该例外规定没有无理地与专利的正常利用相冲突，也未损害专利所有者的合法利益，同时考虑到第三者的合法利益。

专利权的限制，是指依专利法的规定，允许他人(the third parties)在某些特殊情况下可以不经专利权人许可而实施其专利，且其实施行为并不构成侵权(infringement)的一种法律制度。

(一)不视为侵犯专利权的行为(The Defense of Patent Infringements)

根据《专利法》的规定，以下情形不视为侵犯专利权：

1. 专利权用尽(Exhaustion of Patent)

当专利权人自己制造、进口或者经专利权人许可而制造、进口的专利产品或者依照专利方法直接获得的产品售出后，即认为其专利权已经“用尽”，他人对该产品再次进行分销、转卖或零售(distribution, resale or retail)，都无须征得专利权人的许可。这一原则又称为“专利权穷竭原则”(the doctrine of patent exhaustion)，也被称为“首次销售原则”(the doctrine of first sale)。当然，专利权用尽原则只适用于合法投入市场的专利产品。

After a patented product or a product directly obtained by using the patented method is sold by the patentee or sold by any unit or individual with the permission of the patentee, any other person using, offering to sell, selling or importing that product, shall not to be deem to be patent right infringement.

2. 在先实施(Earlier Implementation)

The circumstance of having made identical product or having used the identical process or having made necessary preparations for making such a product or using such a process prior to the date of application, and continuing making such product or using such a process only within the original scope, shall not be deemed an infringement upon a patent right.

先用权可以转让，但不能脱离原来的生产实体单独转让(individual assignment)。先用权是对专利权的又一种限制，这种限制可以消除实际生活中存在的已经投入人力、物力完成的发明创造的单位或者个人，因没有先申请专利而带来的不能再实施自己的智力成果的不“公平”结果。但是，需要说明的是，先用权人不视为侵犯专利权的行为，只限于在原有的范围内继续制造和使用。超过原有的范围内制造和使用的，则属于侵犯专利权的行为。

3. 临时过境(Temporary Transit)

《专利法》规定，临时通过中国领陆、领水、领空的外国运输工具，依照其所属国同中国签订的协议或者共同参加的国际条约，或者依照互惠原则，为运输工具自身需要而在其装置和设备中使用有关专利的，不视为侵犯专利权。对专利权的这一限制，是为了保证国际交通的国际惯例(international practice)，在《保护工业产权巴黎公约》中对此作了明确规定。

In respect to any foreign means of transportation that temporarily passes through the territory, territorial waters, or territorial airspace (领空) of China, the relevant patent is used in the devices and installations for its own needs, in accordance with the agreement concluded between the country it belong to and China, or in accordance with any international treaty to which both countries have acceded, or on the principle of mutual benefit. This circumstance shall not be deemed an infringement according to the *Patent Law*.

According to the Article 5 of *Paris Convention for the Protection of Industrial Property*(《保护工业产权的巴黎公约》):

In any country of the Union the following shall not be considered as infringements of the rights of a patentee:

(i) the use on board vessels of other countries of the Union of devices forming the subject of his patent in the body of the vessel, in the machinery, tackle, gear and other accessories, when such vessels temporarily or accidentally enter the waters of the said country, provided that such devices are used there exclusively for the needs of the vessel;

(ii) the use of devices forming the subject of the patent in the construction or operation of aircraft or land vehicles of other countries of the Union, or of accessories of such aircraft or land vehicles, when those aircraft or land vehicles temporarily or accidentally enter the said country. ①

4. 科研和实验目的而使用(Using for the Scientific Research)

The circumstance that using relevant patents solely for the purposes of scientific research and experiment shall not be deemed an infringement upon a patent right.

The experimental use exception applies only if there is genuine experimentation directed to the features of invention that are the subject of the patent claim. It does not apply to market testing to determine customer preferences. Testing to obtain government approval to market a product is not necessarily experimental in a patent law sense.

5. 行政审批需要(Administrative Examination and Approval's Demand)

此规定是2008年《专利法》修改时新增加的条款。

Any person produces, uses, or imports patented drugs or patented medical apparatus and instruments, for the purpose of providing information required for administrative examination and approval, or produces or any other person imports patented drugs or patented medical apparatus and instruments especially for that person shall not be deemed an infringement upon a patent right.

此外，我国《专利法》规定了现有技术抗辩(existing technology defense)或现有设计抗辩，即在专利侵权纠纷中，被控侵权人有证据证明其实施的技术或者设计属于现有技术或者现有设计的，不构成侵犯专利权。

值得注意的是，《专利法》规定，为生产经营目的使用、许诺销售或者销售不知道是未经专利权人许可而制造并售出的专利侵权产品，能证明该产品合法来源的，不承担赔偿责任。也就是说，即使能证明该产品来源合法，仍然构成侵权，只是不承担赔偿责任，不属于以上所列举的不视为侵犯专利权的情形。

(二)强制许可(Compulsory License)

强制许可，也称非自愿许可(non-voluntary license)，是指国务院专利行政部门(the patent administration department)根据具体情况，不经专利权人同意，通过行政程序(administrative procedures)授权他人实施发明或者实用新型专利的一种法律制度。

强制许可分为以下几种类型：

1. 合理条件的强制许可(Compulsory License on Reasonable Conditions)

When it has been three years since the date the patent right is granted and four years since the date the patent application is submitted, the patentee, without legitimate reasons, fails to have

① Article 5 of *Paris Convention for the Protection of Industrial Property*.

the patent exploited or fully exploited. In this situation, the patent administrative department of the State Council may, upon the application of an eligible entity or individual, grant it or him a compulsory license to exploit the patent for an invention or utility model.

申请强制许可的主体可以是单位，也可以是个人；申请强制许可的时间(the term of compulsory license's application)应当是在专利权被授予之日起满3年(after the lapse of 3 full years from the date when a patent is granted)，且自提出专利申请之日起满4年之后(after the lapse of 4 full years from the date when a patent application is filed)；申请强制许可的对象(the object of compulsory license's application)是发明专利(invention patent)或者实用新型专利(utility model patent)，不包括外观设计(industrial design)。

The entity or individual requesting a compulsory license for exploitation shall prove that it or he has not been able to conclude with the patentee a license contract for exploitation on reasonable terms within a reasonable timeframe.

2. 防止垄断的强制许可(Compulsory Licenses to Prevent Monopoly)

专利权人行使专利权的行为被依法认定为垄断行为，为消除或者减少该行为对竞争产生的不利影响的，国务院专利行政部门根据具备实施条件的单位或者个人的申请，可以给予实施发明专利或者实用新型专利的强制许可。这一条款规定的强制许可主要是为了防止垄断，维护竞争。

If the patentee's exercise of the patent right is in accordance with law, confirmed as monopoly and its negative impact on competition needs to be eliminated or reduced, the patent administrative department of the State Council may, upon the application of an eligible entity or individual, grant it or him a compulsory license to exploit the patent for an invention or utility model.

3. 国家强制许可(National Compulsory Licensing)

所谓国家强制许可(national compulsory licensing)，是指为了国家安全(national security)、公共利益(public interest)、公共健康(public health)等目的而实施的强制许可。

Where a national emergency or any extraordinary state of affairs occurs, or public interests so require, the patent administration department under the State Council may grant a compulsory license for exploitation of an invention patent or utility model patent.

For the benefit of public health, the patent administration department under the State Council may grant a compulsory license for manufacture of the drug, for which a patent right has been obtained, and for its export to the countries or regions that conform to the provisions of the relevant international treaties to which the People's Republic of China has acceded.

4. 交叉强制许可(Cross-compulsory Licensing)

If an invention or utility model, for which the patent right has been obtained, represents a major technological advancement of remarkable economic significance, compared with an earlier invention or utility model for which the patent right has already been obtained, and exploitation of the former relies on exploitation of the latter, the patent administration department under the State Council may, upon application made by the latter, grant it a compulsory license to exploit the earlier invention or utility model. 这种强制许可情形，被称为交叉强制许可(cross-compulsory licensing)。

针对以上四种强制许可类型，我国专利法作出了相应的一些限定事项。强制许可涉及的发明创造为半导体技术(semiconductor technology)的，其实施限于公共利益(public interest)的目的和《专利法》第48条第(2)项规定的防止垄断(prevent monopoly)之情形。此外，第50条还有基于公共健康的原因而给予强制许可的规定，强制许可的实施应当主要为了供应国内市场(domestic market)。

Where the patent administrative department of the State Council decides to grant a compulsory license for exploitation, it shall notify the patentee in time, and register it and make an announcement.

A decision on granting a compulsory license for exploitation shall, on the basis of the reasons for compulsory license, specify the scope and time of exploitation. When the reasons for compulsory license have been eliminated and will no longer occur, the patent administrative department of the State Council shall, upon request of the patentee, make a decision after examination on terminating the compulsory license.

The entity or individual that is granted a compulsory license for exploitation shall pay to the patentee a reasonable royalty or deal with the royalty issue under the relevant international treaties to which the People's Republic of China has acceded. If a royalty is to be paid, the amount of the royalty shall be decided by both parties upon negotiation. If the parties fail to reach an agreement, the issue shall be settled by the patent administrative department of the State Council.

【英语词汇】

accede *v.* 答应；同意；加入
applicant *n.* 申请人
auxiliary *adj.* 辅助的
co-inventor *n.* 共同发明人
contravene *v.* 违反
detrimental *adj.* 有害的；不利的
disrupt *v.* 破坏
entrustment *n.* 委托
exclusive right to exploit 独占实施权
exhaustion of patent 专利权用尽
expiration *n.* 期满，终止
genetic resource 遗传资源
impair *v.* 损害
invention-creations *n.* 发明创造
inventor *n.* 发明人
licensee *n.* 被许可方
licensor *n.* 许可方
method invention 方法发明
patent fee 专利费用
product invention 产品发明
preliminary examination 形式审查
public interest 公共利益
social morality 社会公德
sub-license *n.* 分许可
superstition *n.* 迷信
temporary transit 临时过境
the doctrine of patent exhaustion 专利权穷竭原则
the principle of reciprocity 互惠原则

【英语句型】

1. Where a foreigner, foreign enterprise or other foreign organization without a regular residence or business site in China applies for a patent in China, the application shall be handled in accordance with the agreements concluded by the country he or it belongs to and China or the international treaties to which both the countries have acceded or in accordance with this Law on the principle of reciprocity.

"where"译成"如果……"、"如……"、"倘……"等"显性"条件结构，但在这里不译成通常表示条件的词语，只是通过描述具体情况来表达此意。

译文：在中国没有经常居所或者营业执照的外国人、外国企业或者外国其他组织在中国申请专利的，依照其所属国同中国签订的协议或者共同参加的国际条约，或者依照互惠原则，根据本法办理。

2. With regard to an invention-creation accomplished by two or more units or individuals in collaboration, the right to apply for a patent shall be vested in(被授予) the units or individuals that have accomplished the invention-creation in collaboration , unless it is otherwise agreed upon.

"...be vested in ..."是指"……被授予(被批准)……"。

译文：两个以上单位或者个人合作完成的发明创造，除另有协议的以外，申请专利的权利属于共同完成的单位或者个人；申请被批准后，申请的单位或者个人为专利权人。

3. Inventions mean new technical solutions proposed for a product, a process or the improvement thereof.

"...thereof"是指"其……"置于所修饰词后，紧邻修饰词。

译文：发明，是指对产品、方法或者其改进所提出的新的技术方案。

4. Designs mean, with respect to a product, new designs of the shape, pattern, or the combination thereof, or the combination of the color with shape and pattern, which are rich in an aesthetic appeal and are fit for industrial application.

"with respect to..." 是指" 关于，至于……"。

译文：外观设计，是指对产品的形状、图案或者其结合以及色彩与形状、图案的结合所作出的富有美观并适于工业应用的新设计。

【阅读资料】

第九章　专利授权的实质性条件与程序

Chapter 9　Substantial Conditions and Procedures of Patent Authorization

【引言】取得专利权需要什么样的条件(conditions)和手续(procedures)，以及申请专利(application of patent)时需要提交哪些专利文件(patent documents)，国家专利局(the National Patent Office)的审查员(examiner)如何来审查所申请的专利文件，并且在审查过程中申请人需要配合哪些工作内容。各国专利局都对这些内容有全面的规定，虽略有区别，但实质精神却基本一致。

【学习目的与要求】专利的申请(application)与授权(authorization)是比较复杂也是比较有难度的内容，不仅需要深刻理解专利授权的实质性条件，以及三种专利的授权条件的区别，同时还需要了解在申请与授权中的各种流程、手续及相关文书。

第一节　专利授权的实质性条件

Ⅰ　Substantial Conditions of Patent Authorization

一项发明创造要取得专利权，必须满足形式性条件(formal conditions)和实质性条件(substantial conditions)。

所谓形式性条件，是指专利局对专利申请进行审查及授予专利权所必要的文件格式和应履行的必需手续。In other words, the applicant needs to submit application document with certain format and content in application.

实质性条件是指申请专利的发明创造自身具备的属性要求，即指确定申请专利保护的发明创造有无专利性(patentability)，这是确定专利申请能否授予专利权的关键。

Inventions and utility models for which patent rights are to be granted shall be ones which are novel(新颖的), creative(有创造性的) and of practical use(实用性).

A design for which the patent right is granted is not an existing design, and no application is filed by any unit or individual for any identical design with the patent administration department under the State Council before the date of application for patent right and no identical design is recorded in the patent documentations announced after the date of application.

一、发明或实用新型专利的实质性条件(Substantial Conditions)

(一)新颖性(Novelty)

Novelty means that the invention or utility model concerned is not prior art(现有技术，

existing technology); no patent application is filed by any unit or individual for any identical invention or utility model with the patent administration department under the State Council before the date of application(申请日) for patent right, and no identical invention or utility model is recorded in the patent application documents or the patent documentations which are published or announced after the date of application.

If technologies are already exposed to the public, no matter how hard he worked or how heavy the investment was, the inventor or designer have no justification to grant the patent rights.

1. 现有技术(Prior Art)

Prior art refers to the technologies known to the public both domestically and abroad before the date of application.

The prior art includes any technology which has been disclosed in publications in China or abroad, or has been publicly used or made known to the public by any other means in China or abroad, before the date of filing (or the priority date where priority is claimed).

所谓"为公众所知"(known to the public),是指技术的实质内容处于能够被公众获得的状态,这种状态是指公众想要了解即能得知,想要获取即能得到,并不要求公众必须已经得知、或者必须已经获得,也不要求公众中每一个人必须都已经得知。所谓"公众"(the public),是指非特定的社会公众,而不是指特定的某部分人。所以为公众所知的准确含义是指记载有该技术方案的技术信息的载体已经存在于社会公众中。

(1)现有技术的公开方式(Means of Disclosure of Prior Art)

"技术信息有三种载体,第一种是载有技术信息的机器设备、物质产品;第二是载有技术信息的纸张、胶片、磁带、磁盘、光盘、软盘、硬盘、闪存等技术资料载体,也就是专利法中常说的出版物;第三种是掌握技术的人。"①因此,技术公开的方式有三种:

①出版物公开(Disclosure by Publications)

出版物公开是指通过出版物在国内外公开披露技术信息。

Publications in the context of the Patent Law mean the independently existing disseminating carriers(传播载体) of technical or designing contents, which shall indicate or have other evidence to prove the date of public issue or publication.

公开披露技术信息,是指技术内容向不负有保密义务的不特定相关公众公开。

The determination of whether a document is a publication shall not be affected by the place or language of issue, the manner of acquisition, or its age. The amount of distribution(发行量), whether it has been read, or whether the applicant is aware of it is of no relevance either.

The printing date(出版日) of a publication is regarded as the date of disclosure(公开日), except where the date of disclosure can be evidenced otherwise.

②使用公开(Disclosure by Use)

Disclosure by use means that by use the technical solution is disclosed or placed in the state of being available to the public.

---

① 张晓都. 专利实质条件[M]. 北京:法律出版社,2002:73.

Means of disclosure by use include making, using, selling, importing exchanging, presenting(馈赠), demonstrating(展示), exhibiting(展出) and the like that can make the technical content available to the public.

So long as by the above means the relevant technical content is placed in such a state that the public can know it if they wish, disclosure by use can be established, and it is of no relevance whether the public had actually known it. However, if at an exhibition or demonstration of a product no explanation of the technical contents thereof is provided so that the structure and function or composition of the product is not known to a person skilled in the art, the exhibition or demonstration does not constitute a disclosure by use. ①

③其他方式的公开(Disclosure by Other Means)

以其他方式公开指以出版物和使用以外的方式公开。它主要是口头方式公开(oral disclosure),主要是"掌握技术的人"(person skilled in the art)口头的公开方式,如口头报告、讨论会发言、讲课、广播、电视播放以及科研鉴定、科研总结等。其他还包括对外开放的展台、展厅、橱窗内放置的可供公众阅读的包括技术内容的宣传资料或者技术材料。

现有技术,无论以何种方式公开,其地域标准均是全世界范围内。也就是说,一项技术只要在申请日以前不论世界各地何处的出版物上刊载过、公开使用过或者以其他方式公开过,就不具备新颖性。

(2)现有技术公开的时间标准(Temporal Demarcation of Disclosure of Prior Art)

现在技术公开的时间是判断一项发明创造新颖性的重要标准,目前世界上主要存在两种标准:一种是以完成发明创造的时间作为判断新颖性的时间标准,即专利权授予最先完成发明创造的申请人(inventor)。这就是所谓的"先发明制"(first-to-invent principle),即只要发明创造在发明完成之前未被公开,就确认该发明创造具有新颖性,而不论该发明在申请专利时是否公开。

但发明创造完成的时间有时候非常难确认,尤其是在发生纠纷时,真正的第一个发明人要提出强有力的证据来证明其真正的完成时间有时是非常困难的。因此大多数国家都不采用先发明制。以先发明制作为专利独特制度的美国,在专利法国际协调和融合趋势下,面临着前所未有的挑战。经过各方利益的博弈和妥协,美国于2011年9月16日通过了发明法案AIA,于2013年3月16日生效,标志着美国由先发明制转为了先申请制。

大多数国家采用的以申请日(filing date)为判断标准的"先申请制"(first-to-file principle),即两个以上的申请人就同样的发明创造申请专利的,专利权授予最先申请人。A first-to-file rule is followed in most countries. Under the rule, regardless of which the first inventor was, the person or legal entity who files a patent application first is the one who is granted the patent. 依照该标准,凡是发明创造的实质内容在申请日以前未被公众所知,就认为其具有新颖性。广义上讲,申请日以前公开的技术都属于现有技术,但申请日当天公开的技术不属于现有技术。

① State Intellectual Property Office of The People's Republic of China. Guidelines for Patent Examination 2010[M]. Beijing: Intellectual Property Publishing House, 2010: 173.

China's *Patent Law* provides, if two or more applicants apply for a patent for the same invention separately, the patent right shall be granted to the first applicant. From this we can see that the *Patent Law* of China adopts the standard of "first-to-file principle".

(3)现有技术公开的地域标准(District Range of Disclosure)

判断一项发明创造是否具备新颖性，除了考虑在什么时间内，以什么方式公开以外，还要考虑在什么地域范围内公开，这就是判断发明创造的空间范围，也称为地域标准。通常世界上有三种地域标准：

①绝对新颖性标准(Standard of Absolute Novelty)

绝对新颖性标准又称"世界新颖性标准"(international application)。一项提出专利申请的发明创造在全世界范围与已知技术进行比较，没有以任何方式在全世界范围内公开过，才能视为具备新颖性。法国、联邦德国、英国等欧洲国家专利法均采用这种新颖性标准。

②相对新颖性标准(Standard of Relative Novelty)

相对新颖性标准又称"本国新颖性标准"或"国内新颖性标准"(national application)。一项提出专利申请的发明创造在本国范围内没有以任何方式公开过，才能视为具备新颖性。如许多发展中国家，为保护本国有关发明创造，多采取相对新颖性标准。

③混合新颖性标准(Standard of Mixed Novelty)

所谓混和新颖性标准兼顾了绝对新颖性标准和相对新颖性标准，具体指对于出版物公开而言，采用绝对新颖性标准；对于使用公开和以其他方式公开，则采用相对新颖性标准。日本和美国均采用混和新颖性标准。

中国《专利法》在2009年10月1日之前申请的专利采用混合新颖性标准，需要注意的是，对于使用公开或以其他方式公开所采用的境内新颖性标准，将香港、澳门和台湾归入境外，即在港、澳、台采用使用公开或以其他方式公开不会影响中国专利申请的新颖性。

根据中华人民共和国第十一届全国人民代表大会常务委员会第六次会议于2008年12月27日通过的、并于2009年10月1日起施行的第三次修改的《专利法》(2009年第三次修改版，以下所提专利法均为该专利法)，将原《专利法》规定的混和新颖性修改为了绝对新颖性，即将对现有技术的各种公开方式的判断标准的地域范围均扩展到全世界范围。

2. 抵触申请(Conflicting Application)

Conflicting application refers to the applications relating to the identical invention or utility model which have been filed by any entity or individual prior to the filing date of the application being examined with the Patent Office and published or announced on or after said filing date.

如果在申请日之前已有同样的发明或实用新型(包括进入中国国家阶段的国际专利申请)提出过申请并记载在申请日以后公布的专利文献中，这种情况被称为抵触申请(conflicting application)。

如果在提出专利申请A之前已有相同发明的专利申请B向国家专利局提出了，但在申请A提出之时申请B并未公开，申请人在提出申请时进行新颖性检索时不能够检索得到；但申请A提出后或者当日，申请B若为发明专利申请则经过了18个月进行了专利申请文件的公布，或者实用新型专利申请进行了授权公告。因此，申请B称为申请A的前一申请，而申请A称之为申请B的后一申请；申请B为申请A的抵触申请，申请A不具有新颖性。抵触申请不属于现有技术。

但如果前一申请没有公开而中止申请，则不属于抵触申请，后一申请的新颖性不被破坏，抵触申请只能发生同一国家的专利申请之间，不同国家间的申请不存在抵触。

因此，一件“在先申请”(prior application)要构成抵触申请，应当满足如下两个条件：一是申请在先，公布在后；二是在中国的专利申请。第三次修改《专利法》时，将抵触申请的申请主体由“他人”(other person)修改为了“任何单位或者个人”(entity or individual)，扩大了抵触申请的范围，即同一申请人的申请之间也可能存在抵触申请问题。

3. 不视为丧失新颖性的公开(Disclosure without Losing Its Novelty)

通常情况下，一项发明创造在申请日前公开则丧失了新颖性而不具有专利性，但为了鼓励技术交流，各国专利法大多有不丧失新颖性公开的例外，给予了新颖性宽限期(grace period)的规定。根据这种规定，申请专利的发明虽然已经公开，但只要申请人在宽限期内提出了专利申请，则视为不丧失新颖性。

Article 24 of Patent Law in China provides: within six months before the date of application, an invention for which an application is filed for a patent does not lose its novelty under any of the following circumstances:

(1) It is exhibited for the first time at an international exhibition sponsored or recognized by the Chinese Government;

(2) It is published for the first time at a specified academic or technological conference; and

(3) Its contents are divulged by others without the consent of the applicant.

就上述(1)、(2)两种情况，即使在我国，也仅仅对首次展出、首次发表的公开加以保护，宽限期内的再次公开以及他人独立作出同样发明后进行的专利申请，都会导致发明创造新颖性的丧失。

4. 新颖性的判断原则(Principles of Novelty Examination)

新颖性判断，是指审查是否存在与申请专利的发明或实用新型存在相同的技术方案的现有技术和抵触申请。审查新颖性时，应当根据以下原则进行判断：

(1)同样的发明或者实用新型(Identical inventions or utility models)

根据《专利审查指南(2010年版)》规定，被审查的发明或者使用新型专利申请与现有技术或者申请日前有任何单位或者个人向专利局提出申请并在申请日后(含申请日)公布或公告的发明或实用新型的相关内容相比，如果其技术领域、所解决的技术问题、技术方案和预期效果实质上相同，则认为两者为同样的发明或者实用新型。

Therefore, in comparing the application being examined with prior art or conflicting application, the following factors should be taken into consideration: the technical fields, the technical problems to be solved, the technical solutions, and the expected effects.

相同的技术方案包括两个含义：第一，两个技术方案相同；第二，两个技术方案等同。

相同，是指技术内容完全相同，或者仅仅是简单的文字变换。如专利申请“一种治疗贫血的药物，包括人参和文无”；而对比文件公开“一种治疗贫血的药物，包括人参和当归”。但实际上“文无”就是“当归”，因此这是完全相同的技术方案。

等同，是指技术内容并不完全相同，但其区别之处仅仅在于所属技术领域的惯用手段的直接置换，或者说是等同物的替换。如对比文件公开了采用螺钉固定的装置，而要求保护的发明或者实用新型仅将该装置的螺钉固定方式改换为螺栓固定方式，该两个技术方案实质上相同，也即等同。

(2)单独对比(Separate comparison)

所谓单独对比是指所申请的发明或实用新型中的技术方案与对比文件中的每一项技术方案分别单独进行对比，即一对一的对比。

When determining novelty, the examiner shall compare each claim of the application separately with the relevant technical contents disclosed in each item of the prior art or each previously filed (在先申请) and later published or announced(公布或公告在后) invention or utility model, rather than with a combination of the contents disclosed in several items of the prior art or several previously filed and later published or announced applications or with a combination of several technical solutions disclosed in one reference document.

(二)创造性(Creativity)

1. 创造性的定义(Definition of Creativity)

Creativity also called inventive step , means that, compared with the prior arts, the invention possesses prominent substantive features (突出的实质性特点) and indicates remarkable advancements, and the utility model possesses substantive features(实质性特点) and indicates advancements(进步).

因此，创造性是一项发明创造获得专利的必备条件，英美国家通常称之为“非显而易见性”(non-obviousness)。

“Non-obviousness” is the term used in US patent law to describe one of the requirements that an invention must meet to qualify for patentability. One of the main requirements of patentability is that the invention being patented is not obvious, meaning that a “person having ordinary skill in the art(所属技术领域的普通技术人员)” would not know how to solve the problem at which the invention is directed by using exactly the same mechanism.

Person with ordinary skill in the art is a hypothetical(假设的) person whose educational or occupational credentials(职业资格) would make him or her competent(有能力的) in the field of the invention.

突出的实质性特点(prominent substantive features)，是指发明与现有技术相比具有明显的本质区别，对于发明所属技术领域的普通技术人员来说是非显而易见的。If the person skilled in the art can obtain the invention just by logical analysis, inference, or limited experimentation on the basis of the prior art, the invention is obvious and therefore has no prominent substantive feature.

显著的进步(notable progress)，是指从发明的技术效果上看，与现有技术相比具有长足的进步和能够产生有益的技术效果。For instance, the invention has overcome the defects and deficiencies(缺点和不足) in the existing technology, or has provided a different technical solution to solve a certain technical problem, or represents a certain new trend of technical development.

发明专利必须具有“突出的实质性特点”和“显著的进步”，而实用新型仅需要具有“实质性特点”和“进步”(progress)即可，而不需要长足的进步。可见我国《专利法》对发明专利的创造性具有比实用新型专利更高的要求。

2. 创造性的判断标准(Criterion for Inventiveness)

Whether or not an invention involves an inventive step shall be evaluated on the basis of the knowledge and capability of the person skilled in the art. 因此，我们通常称这个人为“所属技术领域的普通技术人员”(person skilled in the art)，是为了统一审查标准而虚拟的人。

The person skilled in the art is supposed to be aware of all the common technical knowledge and have access to the entire technical field to which the invention pertains(属，与……相关), and have capacity to apply all the routine experimental means(常规的实验方法) before that date. However, he is not presumed to have creativity. This fictional person mainly serves as a reference for determining, or at least evaluating, whether an invention is non-obvious or not (in US patent law), or does involve an inventive step or not (in European patent laws). If it would have been obvious for this fictional person to come up with the invention while starting from the prior art, then the particular invention is considered not patentable.

需要注意的是，抵触申请不属于现有技术，而创造性是与现有技术相比，发明有突出的实质性特点和显著的进步，实用新型有实质性特点和进步，因此在评价发明和实用新型创造性时，不需要考虑抵触申请。

这也是新颖性判断和创造性判断中的一个区别，即判断新颖性的参照基准为现有技术和抵触申请，而判断创造性的参照基准仅为现有技术。与新颖性单独对比的审查原则不同，审查创造性时，将一份或者多份对比文件中的不同的技术内容组合在一起进行判断，通常按照以下三个步骤(通常称为“三步法”)进行：

(1)确定最接近的现有技术(Determining the closest prior art)

最接近的现有技术，是指现有技术中与要求保护的发明最密切相关的一个技术方案，它是判断发明是否有突出的实质性特点的基础。

The closest prior art may, for example, be an existing technology in the same technical field as the claimed invention, and its technical problem to be solved, technical effects, or intended use are the closest to the claimed invention, and/or has disclosed the greatest number of technical features of the claimed invention; or be an existing technology which, despite being in a different technical field from the claimed invention, is capable of performing the function of the invention and has disclosed the greatest number of technical features of the invention.

(2)确定发明的区别特征和其实际解决的技术问题(Determining the distinguishing features of the invention and the technical problem actually solved by the invention)

For this purpose, the examiner shall first determine the distinguishing features of the claimed invention as compared with the closest prior art and then determine the technical problem that is actually solved by the invention on the basis of the technical effect of the distinguishing features. 发明实际解决的技术问题，是指为获得更好的技术效果而需对最接近的现有技术进行的技

术任务。

(3)判断要求保护的发明对本领域的技术人员来说是否显而易见(Determining whether or not the claimed invention is obvious to a person skilled in the art)

In the course of judgment, what is to be determined is whether or not there exists such a technical motivation(技术启示) in the prior art so as to apply said distinguishing features(上述区别特征运用到) to the closest prior art in solving the existing technical problem (that is, the technical problem actually solved by the invention), where such motivation would prompt a person skilled in the art, when confronted with the technical problem, to improve the closest prior art and thus reach the claimed invention. If there exists such a technical motivation in the prior art, the invention is obvious and thus fails to have prominent substantive features.

如所述区别特征为公知常识，例如本领域中解决该技术问题的惯用手段，或者教科书或者工具书中披露的解决技术问题的手段，则因为缺乏创造性而不能授予专利。

(三)实用性(Practical Applicability)

1. 实用性的含义(Definition of Practical Applicability)

Practical applicability means that the said invention or utility model can be used for production or be utilized, and may produce positive results.

If the application relates to a product (subject matter for invention or utility model), the product shall be able to be made industrially and solve a technical problem; if it relates to a process (subject matter for invention only), the process shall be able to be used industrially and solve a technical problem.

2. 实用性的判断标准 (Criterion of Practical Applicability)

判断发明或实用新型的实用性时要以申请文件所公开的整体技术内容为基准，包括权利要求书(claims)、说明书(description)和附图(drawings)中的内容。判断实用性要从以下两个方面判断：

(1)可实施性(Practical Utility)

可实施性的第一层含义是指发明创造应当能够在产业上制造或使用(can be made or used in an industry)。

There must be a technical solution that can be made or used industrially. Those only raise problems or conceive are of no practical applicability.

如科学原理的发现不具有实用性，但以这种原理为依据的具体技术实施方案及手段可以申请专利。其次，技术方案必须符合自然法则(comply with the laws of nature)，不能违背自然规律。An invention or utility model application that violates the laws of nature cannot be implemented, such as perpetual motion machines, definitely do not possess practical applicability. 例如，“永动机”发明因违背了能量守恒定律，不能获得专利保护。

可实施性的另一层含义则是要求一项发明创造可以重复实施，具有再现性(reproducibility)，即所属技术领域的技术人员可以根据公开的技术内容，能够重复实施(implemented repeatedly)专利申请中为解决技术问题所采用的技术方案。有些方案尽管翔实、具体，但不可能在产业上重复实施，比如利用独一无二的自然条件的创造性设计，比如武汉长江大桥就不具有再现性。

(2)有益性(Beneficial Utility)

一项申请专利的发明创造必须能够产生积极效果(effective results)，这些效果应当是积极的和有益的(positive and advantageous)，比如同现有技术相比，可以表现为提高产品质量、提高生产效率、降低资源或能耗、改善工作和生产环境、减少环境污染、降低生产成本等。明显无益、脱离社会需要的发明或者实用新型(an invention or utility model that is obviously of no utility or deviates from the needs of society)专利申请的技术方案不具备实用性。

二、外观设计专利的实质性条件(Substantial Conditions)

我国原《专利法》(2000年第二次修改版)第23条规定："授予专利权的外观设计，应当同申请日以前在国内外出版物上公开发表过或者国内公开使用过的外观设计不相同和不相近似，并不得与他人在先取得的合法权利相冲突。"

The substantial conditions set in this article may be unclear and cause misunderstanding. For instance, there is no provision on conflicting application, as well as on known by other means; "must not be identical with and similar to any design" can be interpreted as a requirement of novelty or of both novelty and inventiveness, or "identical" and "similar" should be read separately; and whether the date of "prior right" is determined by the date of filing or the date of grant.

为了解决这些问题，现行《专利法》对原第23条进行了比较大的修改，一是修改了授权条件的表述方式，将易混淆的表述明确化；二是提高了外观设计专利的授权标准；三是引入了抵触申请。将外观设计专利的实质性条件明确规定新颖性、独创性和不与他人在先取得的合法权利相冲突。

(一)新颖性(Novelty)

A design for which the patent right is granted is not an existing design, and no application is filed by any unit or individual for any identical design with the patent administration department under the State Council before the date of application for patent right and no identical design is recorded in the patent documentations announced after the date of application.

The term "existing design" refers to a design known to the general public both at home and abroad prior to the date of application.

因此，外观设计专利的新颖性与发明或实用新型的新颖性一致，也属于绝对新颖性标准。

(二)独创性(Originality)

Designs for which the patent right is to be granted shall be ones which are distinctly different from the existing designs or the combinations of the features of existing designs.

这一规定包括两层含义：一是授予专利权的外观设计与每一项现有设计单独相比，不仅在整体上与视觉效果上实质不相同，而且还具有明显区别；排除了与现有设计不相同但与现有设计的区别对产品的整体视觉效果不具有显著影响的外观设计；二是允许将两项或者两项以上现有设计的特征组合起来判断所申请的外观设计是否具有明显区别，排除了将惯常(usual)设计特征、知名产品(well-known product)的设计特征组合而成的设计，也排除了对多项现有设计的特征进行简单组合而成的设计。①

It should be noted that, the subject of inventive step of design patent refers to general consumers, which is different from "person skilled in the art" of novelty of invention or utility model.

(三)不得与他人在先取得的合法权利相冲突(To consist with Prior Right)

授予专利权的外观设计不得与他人在申请日以前已经取得的合法权利相冲突。新《专利法》将原专利法中他人"在先"(prior)取得的合法权利明确为"申请日以前"(prior to the date of application)，这里应该还包括外观设计专利申请有优先权日(priority date)的，是指在优先权日以前。

第二节 专利申请的原则
Ⅱ Principles of Patent Application

与著作权的取得不同，专利权不能自动获得，必须依专利法的规定向国务院专利行政部门提出专利申请，经审查合格后才能被授予专利权。根据中国专利法的规定，专利的申请一般要遵循四个原则：形式法定、先申请原则、单一性原则和优先权原则。

一、形式法定(Legal Form)

形式法定原则之前称为书面原则(principle of written examination)，即专利申请必须以书面形式提交国务院专利行政部门，不能以口头说明或者提交实物的方式代替书面形式。不仅申请必须以书面形式办理，整个审批过程中的所有手续也必须以书面形式办理。

随着计算机和网络技术的发展与普及，美国于2003年3月率先实现了电子文件形式专利申请，并于2007年开始受理PCT电子申请，于2009年7月21日实现专利申请审批全电子化，以电子发文取代传统的纸质邮件通知。WIPO自2004年2月开始受理PCT电子申请以来，澳大利亚、丹麦、芬兰、法国、德国、英国、日本、荷兰、菲律宾、波兰、韩国、罗马尼亚、斯洛文尼亚、西班牙、美国的国家局以及欧洲专利局均可受理通过PCT-SAFE系统提交PCT电子申请。2004年3月12日，国家知识产权局"中国电子专利申请系统"正式开通，中国成为继日本、美国、韩国之后提供网上申请专利服务的国家之一。

因此，目前申请专利可采取书面形式，也可以采取电子文件形式。Any formalities prescribed by the Patent Law and these Implementing Regulations shall be complied with in a written form or in any other form prescribed by the Patent Administration Department under the State Council. 但电子申请也需要采用专用的系统，而诸如传真、电报、电子邮件等方式不

① 国家知识产权局条法司.《专利法》第三次修改导读[M]. 北京：知识产权出版社，2009：54~55.

被接受。

二、先申请原则(First-to-file Principle)

目前国际上有先发明制(first-to-invent)和先申请制(first-to-file)两种标准，中国专利法采用了先申请制。If two or more applicants apply for a patent for the same invention separately, the patent right shall be granted to the first applicant.

相同的发明创造在同一天申请专利，包含不同申请人和同一申请人在同一天就同样的发明创造提交专利申请的两种情况，其处理方式不同。对于前一种情况，申请人应当在收到国务院专利行政部门通知后自行协商确定申请人，可以协商为共同申请人也可以协商为一方为申请人；协商不成的，都不授予专利权让其成为社会公有技术。对于后一种情况，国务院专利行政部门只能授予其中一件专利申请专利权，另一件专利申请，若申请人自己不主动撤回，则予以驳回。

三、单一性原则(Principle of Unity)

Unity means that a patent application for invention or utility model shall be limited to one invention or utility model. Two or more inventions or utility models belonging to a single general inventive concept may be filed as one application. That is, where there are several inventions or utility models in one application, the application is acceptable only if all the inventions or utility models are so linked as to form a single general inventive concept. This is the requirement of unity of a patent application.

An application for a patent for design shall be limited to one design. Two or more similar designs for the same product or two or more designs which are incorporated in products belonging to the same class(统一类别) and sold or used in sets (成套出售或使用) may be filed as one application (combination application for short)(合案申请).

The requirement of unity for patent applications consists in the following two reasons:

The first reason is economic reason, in order to prevent an applicant from obtaining patent protection for several diverse inventions or utility models by paying for one patent;

And the second reason is technical reason, in order to facilitate the classification, search and examination of a patent application.

四、优先权原则 (Principle of Priority Right)

The priority right which originates from the *Paris Convention for the Protection of Industrial Property*(《保护工业的巴黎公约》), means that, on the basis of a regular application for an industrial property right filed by a given applicant in one of the member countries, the same applicant (or its or his successor in title) may, within a specified period of time (six or twelve months) , apply for protection in all the other member countries. These later applications will then be regarded as if they had been filed on the same day as the earliest application. 发明和实用新型的优先权期限为 12 个月，外观设计的优先权期限为 6 个月。

Therefore, when a priority is validly claimed, the date of filing of the first application, called the "priority date", is considered to be the "effective date of filing" for the examination of novelty and inventive step or non-obviousness for the subsequent application claiming the priority of the first application. In other words, the prior art which is taken into account for examining the novelty and inventive step or non-obviousness of the invention claimed in the subsequent application would not be everything made available to the public before the filing date (of the subsequent application) but everything made available to the public before the priority date, i. e. the date of filing of the first application.

根据我国《专利法》的规定，申请人就相同主题的发明或者实用新型在外国第一次提出专利申请之日起12个月内，或者就相同主题的外观设计在外国第一次提出专利申请之日起6个月内，又在中国提出申请的，依照该国同中国签订的协议或者共同参加的国际条约，或者依照相互承认优先权的原则，可以享有优先权。这称之为外国优先权(foreign priority right)。外国优先权适用于发明、实用新型和外观设计三种专利。

我国《专利法》还规定，申请人自发明或者实用新型在中国第一次提出专利申请之日起12个月内，又向国务院专利行政部门就相同主题提出专利申请的，可以享有优先权。这通常称之为本国优先权或国内优先权(national priority right)。国内优先权不适用于外观设计专利申请，并且只适用于两次申请均在国内的申请人。

申请人依照规定享有优先权的，应当在申请专利时提出书面声明(written declaration)，并且自申请日起3个月内提交第一次提出专利申请文件的副本(a copy of the patent application document which was first filed)，否则视为未要求优先权(the claim to the right to priority shall be deemed as having not been made)。

第三节 专利申请手续及相关文书
Ⅲ Formalities and Documents of Patent Application

专利申请人向国务院专利行政部门提出专利申请以及在专利审批程序中办理的各种与专利申请有关的手续统称为专利申请手续。

一、办理申请手续的途径及方式(Forms of Patent Application)

申请人可以委托专利代理机构办理专利申请，也可以自己直接向国务院专利行政管理机关办理专利申请。委托专利代理机构办理的，需提交专利代理委托书，并在请求书中填写专利代理机构及专利代理人的相关信息。

考虑到一些专利申请可能涉及我国国家安全，《专利法》规定："任何单位或者个人将在中国完成的发明或者实用新型向外国申请专利的，应当事先报经国务院专利行政部门进行保密审查。保密审查的程序、期限等按照国务院的规定执行。"

办理专利申请手续可以直接面交，也可以邮寄方式递交，以及可以通过电子网络的方式申请。

二、办理相关手续的地点(Location of Patent Application)

办理专利申请手续的地点可以是国家知识产权局专利局受理处，也可以是国家知识产权局的派出机构——地方专利代办处，目前全国共有北京、广州、深圳、成都等33个代办处。如果是申请国防专利还可以到国防专利分局办理。

地方专利代办处的职能主要包括中国内地申请人面交或者寄交的发明、实用新型、外观设计专利申请文件，以及港、澳、台地区的个人委托内地专利代理机构代理的发明、实用新型、外观设计专利申请文件。以下几类手续不能在代办处办理：(1)PCT国际申请的申请文件；(2)境外申请人及港、澳、台地区法人专利申请文件；(3)分案申请文件；(4)有优先权声明的专利；(5)专利申请被受理后提交的中间文件等。

三、专利申请应提交的文件(Documents for Patent Application)

When a person intends to apply for an invention or utility model patent, he shall submit the relevant documents, such as a written request(请求书), a written description(说明书) and its abstract(摘要), and a written claim(权利要求书). When a person intends to apply for a design patent, he shall submit a written request, drawings(图片) or pictures of the design, a brief description(简要说明) of the design, and other relevant documents.

It is obvious that the filing of an application for a patent for invention or utility model is different from that of an application for a design patent.

(一)发明或实用新型专利所需提交的文件(Documents for patents of invention or utility model)

In accordance with the provisions of the patent law, applications for inventions or utility models are required to submit at least a request, a description, an abstract and a claim.

1. 请求书(Request)

请求书是申请人向国务院专利行政部门表述请求授予专利权愿望的书面文件。申请人在请求书中要写明发明或实用新型的名称、发明人的姓名、申请人的姓名或名称、地址，委托代理的，应写明代理人及代理机构的情况；要求优先权的，应当写明与优先权相关的信息。

The title of the invention in the request should be identical with the one in the description. The inventor should be an individual who has made creative contributions to the substantive features of an invention. The applicant can be an individual or an entity. For a service invention, the right to apply for a patent belongs to the entity for which the inventor serves. While for a non-service invention, the right to apply for a patent belongs to the inventor himself.

2. 说明书及附图(Description with Drawings)

A description is an important legal document in which the applicant discloses his invention or utility model. The main functions include the following three aspects:

(1)The description contains a clear(清楚的) and comprehensive(完整的) description of the invention or utility model so that a technician in the field of the relevant technology can carry it out。所谓“清楚”是指主题明确、表述清楚，即应当写明发明或者实用新型所要解决的技术问题以及解决其技术问题采用的技术方案，并对照现有技术写明发明或者实用新型的有益效果。“完整”是指说明书应当包括有关理解、实现发明或者实用新型所需的全部技术内容。“能够实现”是指所属技术领域的技术人员按照说明书记载的内容，就能够实现该发明或者实用新型的技术方案，解决其技术问题，并且产生预期的技术效果。

(2) The description provides detailed information for the State Intellectual Property Office to review patent applications and decide whether to grant patent rights.

(3) The description is the basis of the claim. After the patent has been authorized, especially in the case of a patent infringement dispute, the description and their drawings can be used to interpret the claims so as to correctly determine the scope of protection of the patent right for inventions and utility models.

The instruction shall contain the following parts: the title of the invention, technical field, background art, contents of invention, description of figures (if necessary), and specific mode for implementing the invention. Each part shall bear the headings respectively.

The technical field(技术领域) of an invention or utility model shall be the specific technical field to which the claimed technical solution of the invention or utility model pertains or is directly applied, rather than a general or adjacent technical field or the invention or utility model per se. 技术领域不能写得太上位，即技术领域的范围不能太宽泛，也不能是技术方案本身。

The part of background art(背景技术) shall indicate the background art which can be regarded as useful for the understanding, searching, and examination of the invention or utility model, and when possible, cite the documents reflecting such art. 在背景技术中可以引证与专利申请最接近的现有技术文件，引证的文件可以是专利文件，也可以是非专利文件。此外，在说明书背景技术部分中，还要客观地指出背景技术中存在的、由本专利申请的技术方案能够解决的问题和缺点。

The part of contents of the invention(发明内容) shall disclose the technical problem the invention or utility model aims to settle and the technical solution adopted to resolve the problem; and stating, with reference to the prior art, the advantageous effects of the invention or utility model. 技术方案是专利申请的核心，是清楚、完整地描述发明或者实用新型解决其技术问题所采取的技术方案的技术特征。有益效果是指发明或实用新型的技术方案解决现有技术的技术问题所产生的技术效果，有益效果是确定发明是否具有“显著的进步”，实用新型是否具有“进步”的重要依据。

Where the description has appended drawings(附图), it shall state the title of each figure (图形) in the drawings and briefly describe the contents as illustrated.

The part of mode of carrying out (具体实施方式) the invention or utility model shall describe in detail the optimally(最优的) selected mode contemplated by the applicant for carrying out the invention or utility model; where appropriate, this shall be done in terms of examples, and with reference to the drawings, if any.

The drawings(附图) are a component part of the description. The function of drawings is to supplement the explanation in the text of the description with figures to enable a person to intuitively(直观的) and visually understand each technical feature and the whole technical solution of the invention or utility model. For patent applications in the field of mechanics or electricity, the function of drawings is particularly outstanding. Therefore, the drawings shall clearly reflect the contents of the invention or utility model.

Description of utility models must contain drawings, while there is no provision on that of invention.

3. 摘要(Abstract)

说明书摘要是对整个发明创造的简短概述，它仅是一种供有关人员迅速获知发明或实用新型内容的情报检索性文件，不具有法律效力，不能作为以后修改说明书和权利要求书的根据，也不能用来解释专利权的保护范围。

The abstract shall indicate the title and the technical field of the invention or utility model, the gist and principal use and the improvement as compared with the prior art. The abstract shall contain a figure accompanying the abstract which is submitted by the applicant and selected from the drawings of the description and can show the technical solution. The abstract shall not be written as a commercial advertisement.

4. 权利要求书(Claims)

权利要求书是申请文件中最重要也是最基本的文件，是申请人请求给予专利保护范围的书面表达，是确定专利权的依据，并划定了专利的保护范围。

按照性质划分，权利要求有两种基本类型，即物的权利要求和活动的权利要求，也称为产品权利要求和方法权利要求。产品权利要求保护的是人类技术生产的物，包括物品、物质、材料、工具、装置、设备等权利要求；由于计算机软件和网络的发展，产品权利要求还包括虚拟装置的权利要求。方法权利要求保护有时间过程要素的活动，包括有制造方法、使用方法、通信方法、处理方法以及将产品用于特定用途的方法等权利要求，在软件或者数控专利中，主要是涉及各种处理流程。

The claims shall state the technical features of the invention or utility model. The claims shall have an independent claim(独立权利要求), and may also contain dependent claims(从属权利要求).

The independent claim shall outline(概述) the technical solution of an invention or utility model and state the essential technical features necessary for the solution of its technical problem.

The dependent claim shall, by additional technical features, further define (进一步限定) the claim which it refers to.

一件专利申请的权利要求中，应当至少有一项独立权利要求。当有两项或者两项以上独立权利要求时，写在最前面的独立权利要求被称为第一独立权利要求，其他独立权利要求称为并列独立权利要求。

独立权利要求由两部分构成——前序部分和特征部分。前序部分应当写明发明或者实用新型的名称，以及发明或者实用新型的技术特征与一份最接近的现有技术共有的必要技术特征；特征部分的开头应当采用“其特征是……”，或者类似的用语，接着写明发明或者使用新型区别于最接近现有技术的技术特征。从属权利要求也应当由两部分构成——引用部分和特征部分。引用部分应当写明被引用的权利要求的编号及其主题名称；特征部分应当写明该从权利要求所要求保护的技术方案在被引用权利要求基础上附加的技术特征。需要注意的是，从属权利要求的主题名称应当与被引用的权利要求的主题名称一致。

If there are several claims, they shall be numbered consecutively in Arabic numerals. The scientific and technical terminology should be identical with those in the description. The claims shall contain no drawings or forms.

通常一项权利要求用一个自然段表述。开放式权利要求宜采用“包含”、“包括”等表达方式，如有数值范围的，数值范围尽量以数学方式表达。

Requirements that the claims shall satisfy: support in the description(以说明书为依据); clarity (清楚)and conciseness(简要).

The claims shall be supported by the description and define the extent of the patent protection in a clear and concise manner.

权利要求书中的每一项权利要求所要求保护的技术方案应当是所属技术领域的技术人员能够从说明书充分公开的内容中得到或概括得出的技术方案，并且不得超出说明书公开的范围。如某专利申请的说明书提到生产某产品的温度范围为0℃～1000℃，权利要求书将其限定为更小范围20℃～50℃，则该权利要求得到了说明书支持。又如另一专利申请的说明书中仅提及发明采用钢材料作为电镀材料，权利要求书将其概括为采用金属材料作为电镀材料，则因说明书中只提到了钢，没有提到其他电镀材料，所以权利要求书得不到说明书支持。

权利要求书应当“清楚”(clear)。首先，权利要求的主题名称应当清楚，要与权利要求的技术内容相适应，并要清楚地表明是产品权利要求还是方法权利要求，不能写成“一种……产品及其制造方法”。其次，权利要求所确定的保护范围也应当清楚，不得使用含义不确定的用语，如“厚”、“薄”、“强”、“弱”、“高温”、“高压”、“很宽范围”等类似用语。最后，构成权利要求书的所有权利要求作为一个整体也应当清楚，这是指权利要求之间的引用关系应当清楚。

权利要求书应当“简要”(concise)，权利要求的数目应当合理，表述应当简要，除记载技术特征外，不得对原因或者理由作不必要的描述，也不得使用商业性宣传用语。为避免权利要求之间相同内容的不必要重复，在可能的情况下，权利要求应尽量采取引用在前权利要求的方式撰写。

(二)外观设计专利所需提交的文件(Documents for a Patent of Design)

When a person intends to apply for a design patent, he shall submit a written request, drawings or pictures of the design, a brief description(简要说明) of the design, and other relevant documents.

1. 请求书(Request)

首先应填写使用外观设计的产品名称。使用外观设计的产品名称对图片或者照片中表示的外观设计所应用的产品种类具有说明作用。The name of the product incorporating the design(使用外观设计的产品名称) shall be in accordance with the design as shown in the drawings or photographs and indicate the design for which protection is sought accurately and concisely. The name of the product shall generally be in conformity with the name listed in the subclass(小分类) of the International Classification for Industrial Design(国际外观设计分类表). It shall generally contain no more than 20 Chinese characters.

The following names shall generally be avoided: the name of a person , a place, a nation, an entity, a trademark, a code, a model or a historical age; improper generic or abstract names; names describing the internal structure, technical effect; and names with specification, size, scale or numerical unit of the product.

申请人还应当写明产品所属类别，即该产品在国际外观设计分类表中的类别。申请人不明确该产品所属类别的，应当写明产品所属领域、用途、使用方法或使用场所。

申请外观设计专利的请求书中的其他栏目的要求同发明和实用新型专利的请求书相同。

2. 图片或照片(Pictures or Photos)

The extent of protection of the patent right for design shall be determined by the design of the product as shown in the drawings or photographs. The brief explanation may be used to interpret the design of the product as shown in the drawings or photographs. The relevant drawings or photographs submitted by applicant shall clearly indicate the design of the product for which patent protection is sought.

对于立体产品的外观设计，如果产品设计要点(essential features)涉及六个面的，应当提交六面正投影图(orthographic projection views)；若仅设计一个或者几个面的，应当至少提交所涉及面的正投影图和立体图，并应当在简要说明中写明省略视图的原因。

对于平面产品的外观设计，设计要点涉及一个面的，可以仅提交该面的正投影视图；如果涉及两个面的，应该提交两个面的正投影视图。

图片可以使用包括计算机在内的制图工具绘制，但不得使用铅笔、蜡笔、圆珠笔绘制，也不得使用蓝图、草图、油印件。请求保护的外观设计包含色彩的专利申请，申请人应当提交着色的图片或者照片一式两份。

3. 简要说明(Brief Explanation)

简要说明是对产品图片或者照片的说明或限定，用来对外观设计产品的设计要点、省略视图以及请求保护色彩等情况进行扼要的描述。The brief explanation shall include the following contents: the title(名称) of the product incorporating the design; the use(用途) of the product incorporating the design; the essential features(设计要点) of the design; drawing or photograph is designated to best show the essential features of the design.

The brief explanation shall contain no language of commercial advertisement and not be used to show the function of the product.

除此而外，根据《专利法实施细则》的规定，国务院专利行政部门认为必要时，可以要求外观设计专利申请人提交使用外观设计的产品样品或者模型。

四、专利申请文件的提交、修改及撤回（Submittal, Modification and Withdrawal of Patent Application Documents）

（一）专利申请文件的提交（Submittal）

申请人准备好专利申请文件后，即可向国务院专利行政部门或地方专利代办处递交。可以直接面交、邮寄递交，或者电子申请。

如果发明创造涉及国家安全或者重大利益的，则需要依照《专利法》第 4 条和《专利法实施细则》第 9 条中有关保密的规定进行。

如果申请专利的发明涉及新的生物材料，该生物材料公众不能得到，并且对该生物材料的说明不足以使所属领域的技术人员实施其发明的，申请人还必须按《专利法实施细则》第 24 条的规定办理特定的手续，包括在申请日前要将生物材料提交国务院专利行政部门认可的保藏单位保藏，申请文件中提供有关该生物材料特征的材料，在请求书和说明书中写明该生物材料的分类命名、保藏单位、保藏日期、保藏编号等。

（二）专利申请文件的主动修改（Proactive Amendment）

申请文件的修改分为主动修改和根据专利局审查员的要求进行被动修改（amendment made by examiner）两种。

为使专利申请文件清晰、完整地表明专利申请的发明内容，根据《专利法》和《专利法实施细则》的规定，申请人提交申请文件后，可以对专利申请文件进行主动修改。为了保持申请秩序的稳定，法律对修改的范围和时间作了限制，其中，对发明和实用新型专利申请文件的修改不得超出原说明书和权利要求书记载的范围，对外观设计专利申请文件的修改不得超出原图片或者照片表示的范围。对于发明专利申请，提出修改应该在提出实质审查请求或者在收到中国专利局发出的实质审查通知书之日起 3 个月内；对于实用新型或外观设计提出修改外观设计专利申请文件，应在申请日起 2 个月内。

With regard to the proactive amendment, the examiner shall first examine the date of amendment which should be within two months from the filing date. To the amendment made within two months, the examiner shall examine whether the amendment goes beyond the scope described in the initial description and claims. With regard to the amendment made two months later, if the amended documents remove the defects existing in the initial application documents, and have the prospect of being granted the patent right, the amended documents may be accepted.

（三）专利申请的撤回（Withdrawal）

专利申请的撤回分为申请人主动撤回（proactive withdrawal）和因申请人不作为被动的视为撤回（withdrawal for nonfeasance of applicant）两种方式。

主动撤回，根据《专利法》的规定，提交申请后，在被授予专利权前，申请人还可以随时撤回专利申请。主动撤回申请的声明应向国务院专利行政部门提出，并在其收到时生效。

申请人若不作为，如自申请日起 3 年内，发明专利申请人不正当理由不请求实质审查的，或者申请人后没有缴纳申请费的，该申请即被视为撤回。

若申请在公开前撤回，视为该申请自始不存在，不影响其在后申请的新颖性；但如果是在公开后撤回的，则该发明创始将丧失新颖性。

第四节 专利审查程序
Ⅳ Patent Examination

关于专利审查制度，目前世界上主要有三种不同的制度。

一是登记制(registration)，是指只对专利申请进行形式审查(formal examination)，即只审查专利申请文件是否完备、文书格式是否符合规定，形式审查合格后便直接授予专利证书。并不对申请的内容作新颖性、创造性和实用性审查。

二是完全审查制(full examination)，指国家专利主管机关除对专利申请进行形式审查外，还需对每一件专利申请进行新颖性、创造性和实用性等进行专利性实质审查(substantial examination)，仅对符合实质审查要求的专利申请授予专利权。并且在进行形式审查后，无须申请人提实质审查请求即直接进行实质审查。目前，美国、加拿大、瑞典等国家实行这种审查制度。

三是早期公开、延迟审查制(early disclosure and deferred examination)，是指专利申请交到国家主管部门后，国家主管部门应首先对其进行形式审查，符合形式审查要求的，国家主管部门将在自申请日(application date)起(有优先权的自优先权日起)18个月期满时在专利公报上公布；国家专利主管部门在完成形式审查后并不立即进行实质审查，而是只对在一定期限内提出实质审查请求的专利申请才进行实质审查。早期公开延迟审查制的优点是：加速了专利信息的交流；给申请人充分时间来考虑是否提出实质审查请求和什么时候提出实审请求，申请人中有一部分将根据实际情况放弃实质审查请求的，从申请人来讲避免了被驳回的情形，节约了审查费用，从专利局来讲减轻了审批的工作量。

我国的发明专利实行这种早期公开、延迟审查制，对实用新型和外观设计专利的审查采取登记制，即只进行形式审查。

一、受理申请(Acceptance of Application)

国务院专利行政管理机关收到发明专利申请的请求书、说明书(有附图的应包括附图)和权利要求书等申请文件后，应当发出受理通知书，明确申请日，给予申请号。对于缺少文件或者有其他违反法律要求的，国家专利局不予受理或要求在指定期限内补交或补正。

二、初步审查(Preliminary Examination)

初步审查也称为“形式审查”或“格式审查”(formal examination)，是国务院专利行政部门对申请人所提交的专利申请进行是否符合形式条件的审查。

The purpose of the preliminary examination lies in preparing for substantial examination in later steps. The authority will check the applicant according to the provisions of the patent law and the implementing regulations. Typically, the review to utility models and designs aim at whether they meet the condition of granting patent rights.

根据《专利法》的规定，发明专利申请初步审查的主要内容包括：(1)审查申请人提交的申请文件是否完整，文件格式是否正确，撰写是否符合《专利法》及《专利法实施细则》的规定；(2)申请文件的明显实质性缺陷审查，申请主题是否属于违反国家法律、社会公德或者妨害公共利益的发明创造，以及《专利法》第25条规定的不授权专利权的对象；(3)申请人的身份是否合法，申请人是外国人的，是否有依法委托中国专利代理机构；(4)是否有享有优先权的及相关文件的审查；(5)申请人是否缴纳了申请费等。

实用新型和外观设计初步审查的内容除了包括与发明专利初步审查相同的内容外，还包括：(1)实用新型专利申请的主题是否符合《专利法实施细则》规定的实用新型的定义；(2)申请是否符合单一性规定；(3)是否会违反重复授权原则；(4)申请的修改或分案申请是否超出原说明书和权利要求书记载的范围。由此可见，对实用新型和外观设计的初步审查既有格式审查，也包含了部分必要的实质审查。

三、早期公开(Earlier Disclosure)

Upon receipt of an invention patent application, if the patent administration department under the State Council, after preliminary examination, confirms that the application meets the requirements of this Law, it shall publish the application within 18 full months(满18个月) from the date of application. And it may do so at an earlier date upon request of the applicant.

四、实质审查(Substantive Examination)

Within three years from the date an invention patent application is filed, the patent administration department under the State Council may, upon request made by the applicant at any time, carry out substantive examination of the application. If the applicant, without legitimate reasons, fails to request substantive examination at the expiration of the time limit, such application shall be deemed to have been withdrawn(撤回).

国务院专利行政部门(administrative department of the State Council)根据申请人实质审查的请求，对发明专利申请进行实质审查，实质审查的主要内容包括：第一，对发明主题的新颖性、创造性、实用性进行审查。不符合三性要求的，书面通知申请人或代理人，在指定的期限内陈述意见(pronounce)，进行修改。第二，单一性审查。对于不符合单一性要求，应通知申请人或代理人作分案处理。第三，对说明书和权利要求书的审查，说明书应当清楚完整地说明发明的主要技术特征(main technical features)，充分公开使同领域的技术人员能够实施，同时，还要对权利要求给予支持。

五、授权公告(Announcement of Grant of Patent Right)

If no reason for rejection is discerned after an invention patent application is substantively examined, or no reason for rejection is discerned after preliminary examination of a utility model or design patent application, the patent administration department under the State Council shall make a decision on granting of the invention patent right, issue a corresponding patent certificate (发给相应的专利证书), and meanwhile register and announce the same. The patent right shall become effective as of the date of announcement(公告之日).

国务院专利行政部门发出授予专利权通知书的同时，应当发出办理登记手续的通知书，申请人应当在收到该通知之日起2个月内办理登记手续、缴纳专利登记费、授权当年(办理登记手续通知书中指明的年度)的年费(annual fee)、公告印刷费(printing expenses)，同时还应当缴纳专利证书印花税(stamp duty of patent certificate)。发明专利申请还应当一并缴纳除授权当年之外的各年度的申请维持费(maintenance fee)。

【英语词汇】

absolute novelty 绝对新颖性
brief description 简要说明
claims *n.* 权利要求书
comprehensive *adv.* 完整的
conciseness *n.* 简要
conflicting application 抵触申请
creativity *n.* 创造性
dependent claims 从属权利要求
description *n.* 说明书
drawing *n.* 附图
early disclosure and deferred examination 早期公开、延迟审查制
essential features 设计要点
first-to-file principle 先申请原则
first-to-invent principle 先发明原则
grace period 宽限期
independent claim 独立权利要求
non-obviousness *n.* 非显而易见性
novelty *n.* 新颖性
practical applicability 实用性
person skilled in the art 所属技术领域的普通技术人员
preliminary examination 初步审查
principle of unity 单一性原则
prior art 现有技术
priority right 优先权
relative novelty 相对新颖性
request *n.* 请求书
submit *v.* 提交
substantive examination 实质审查
technical motivation 技术启示
the date of application 申请日
withdraw *v.* 撤回，撤销

【英语句型】

1. The determination of whether a document is a publication shall not be affected by the place or language of issue, the manner of acquisition, or its age.

"be affected by..."表示"受……影响"。

译文：出版物不受地理位置、语言或者获得方式的限制，也不受年代的限制。

2. That is, where there are several inventions or utility models in one application, the application is acceptable only if all the inventions or utility models are so linked as to form a single

general inventive concept.

"so…as to"表示"那么地……以至于……"。

译文：也就是说，如果一件申请包括几项发明或者实用新型，则只有在所有这几项发明或实用新型之间有一个总的发明构思之相互关联的情况下才被允许。

3. The title of the invention in the request should be identical with the one in the description.

"be identical with"表示"与……相同"。

译文：请求书中的发明名称和说明书中的发明名称应当一致。

4. If technologies are exposed to the public, no matter how hard he worked or how heavy the investment was, the inventor or designer have no justification to grant the patent rights.

"no matter how… "表示"不论如何……"。

译文：如果一项技术公众已经可以得到，无论发明人、设计人在该项发明创造上投入了多大的智力，都没有授予专利权的正当理由。

5. The disclosure made by any other person without the consent of the applicant includes the disclosure of the contents of an invention-creation by another person for his failure to comply with the explicit or implicit confidentiality agreement, and disclosure caused after another person gets to know the contents of an invention-creation from the inventor or applicant by means of coercion, fraud or espionage.

"without the consent of…"意思是"未经……同意……"。

译文：他人未经申请人同意而泄露其内容的公开，包括他人未遵守明示的或者默示的保密约定而将发明创造的内容公开，也包括他人用威胁、欺诈或者间谍活动等手段从发明人或者经发明人告诉而得知发明创造内容的任何其他人那里得知发明创造的内容而后公开。

6. The person skilled in the art is supposed to be aware of all the common technical knowledge and have access to the entire technical field to which the invention pertains, and have capacity to apply all the routine experimental means before that date. Otherwise, he is not presumed to have creativity.

"be supposed to be…"意思是"应该……"。

译文：掌握技术的人应该与申请专利的发明创造属于相同的技术领域，具有该技术领域的通常的技术知识和能力，知晓申请日或者优先权日之前发明所属技术领域所有的普通技术知识，能够进行常规设计和实验，能够在现有技术的基础上作简单的逻辑推理和组合，但不具有创新能力。

7. If the application relates to a product (subject matter for invention or utility model), the product shall be able to be made industrially and solve a technical problem; if it relates to a process (subject matter for invention only), the process shall be able to be used industrially and solve a technical problem.

"relate to…"的意思是"涉及……"。

译文：如果申请的是以一种产品(包括发明和实用新型)，那么该产品必须在产业中能够制造，并且能够解决技术问题；如果申请的是一种方法(仅限发明)，那么这种方法必须在产业中能够使用，并且能够解决技术问题。

【阅读资料】

第十章　专利的复审、无效及终止
Chapter 10　Patent Reexamination, Invalidation and Expiration

【引言】在专利申请人（patent applicant）递交了申请文件之后，发明（invention）专利经过初步审查（preliminary examination）与实质审查（substantive examination），实用新型（utility model）、外观设计（industrial design）专利经过专利主管部门的初步审查（preliminary examination），会产生授予（grant）专利或驳回（reject）请求的结果。针对被驳回的专利申请，申请人不服（dissatisfied）时有何救济措施（remedies），针对不符合专利要件却被授予专利的情况，有何补救措施（remedial measures），以及专利产生之后在何种情况下终止，这些都具有重要的意义。

【学习目的与要求】掌握专利复审的条件及程序；理解专利无效的事由、程序及后果；熟悉专利终止的情形。在学习的过程中学生需密切关注专利无效的相关案例，并能结合《专利法》及《专利法实施细则》进行相应的分析。

第一节　专利复审
Ⅰ　Patent Reexamination

一、复审的原因及条件（Causes and Conditions of Reexamination）

If a patent applicant is dissatisfied with the decision made by the Patent Administration Department under the State Council on rejecting of the application, he may, within three months from the date of receipt of the notification, file a request with the patent review board for review. After review（复审）, the Patent Review Board（专利复审委员会）shall make a decision and notify the patent applicant of the same.

Reexamination is used to provide a reevaluation of an issued patent based on prior art not considered by the examiner in the initial patent issuance. It is particularly useful for patent holders when an alleged infringer（侵权人）raises prior art as a reason for invalidity as a defense in an infringement or declaratory judgment action.

The patent holder in such a situation has two choices: to slug the matter out before the court, or to request reexamination by the PTO（美国专利商标局）and request a stay of the court proceedings. ①

(一)复审的原因(Causes)

Cases of request for reexamination include those made out of dissatisfaction with the decisions of rejection（驳回决定）in preliminary examination stage and in substantive examination stage.

设立复审程序主要基于以下几方面原因(The reasons of setting the reexamination process)：②

(1)保障当事人的申诉权利(To protect the appeal rights of involved parties)。

(2)确保审查结论的合法性与合理性(To ensure the legitimacy and rationality of the examination conclusions)。

(3)给予当事人补救的途径(To support the remedy to involved parties)。复审程序中设有前置审查程序(interlocutory examination)，从而为申请人提供一种可能通过修改文件(modify the file)或陈述理由(state of reasons)而及时撤销驳回决定(revocation the decision of rejection)的快捷的补救途径。

(4)节省司法资源(To save judicial resources)。

(二)申请复审应满足的条件(Conditions)

1. 专利申请被驳回(Patent application rejected)

The applicant who is not satisfied with the decision of rejection by the Patent Office may file a request for reexamination with the Patent Reexamination Board. A request for reexamination shall not be accepted if it is not directed to a decision of rejection by the Patent Office.

2. 请求人应当是被驳回专利申请的专利申请人(The applicant should be the one who was rejected in reexamination)

只有被驳回的专利申请的申请人才能够请求复审，其他个人或组织不得提出请求。Only the applicant of a rejected application may file a request for reexamination with the Patent Reexamination Board, others shall not request. Where the person filing a request for reexaminanon is not the applicant of the rejected application, the request shall not be accepted. Where a rejected application has two or more applicants and the petitioner（请求人）for reexamination does not include all the applicants, the Patent Reexamination Board shall notify the petitioner to make rectification within a specified time limit. If the defect is not rectified within the time limit, the request for reexamination shall be deemed not to have been made.

3. 向专利复审委员会提出请求(The request should be made to Patent Reexamination Board)

The Patent Reexamination Board shall consist of technical and legal experts designated by the

① Robert J. Yarbrough. Patent Reexamination [DB/OL]. [2017-05-23]. http://www.yarbroughlaw.com/publications/ pubs%20patent3%20Patent%20Reexamination. htm.

② 国家知识产权专利局. 发明专利审查基础教程[M]. 北京：知识产权出版社，2004：305.

administrative department for patent under the State Council.

专利复审委员会对专利的复审、无效宣告进行受理、审理和决定。

4. 应当在法定的期限内提出(The request should be submitted within the statutory time limit)

The applicant may file a request for reexamination with the Patent Reexamination Board within three months from the date of receipt of the decision of rejection by the Patent Office. The request for reexamination shall not be accepted if the time of filing the request does not meet this requirement.

5. 提交符合要求的复审请求书(Reexamination application should comply with the prescribed form)

If the applicant requests the Patent Reexamination Board to make a re-examination in accordance with the Patent Law, he shall file a written request and state the reasons, when necessary, affix relevant supporting documents. Request for reexamination shall comply with the prescribed format.

6. 按照规定交纳相应的复审费用(Appropriate reexamination fees should be paid)

专利申请人提出复审请求时，应当依法缴纳相应的费用，当时未缴纳的，应在一定期限内补交。

二、复审的程序(Reexamination Process)

(一)形式审查(Formal Examination)

专利复审委员会在收到复审请求书(the request for reexamination)之后，首先要进行形式审查(form of review)，判断该请求是否满足申请复审的条件，从而决定是否受理。形式审查主要是审查复审请求的客体、复审请求人的资格、复审请求的期限、文件形式等是否符合复审要求。复审申请人的复审请求不符合《专利法》第19条第1款或者第41条第1款规定的，专利复审委员会不予受理，书面通知复审请求人并说明理由。

(二)前置审查(Interlocutory Examination)

The Patent Reexamination Board shall transfer the written request for reexamination to the original examination department(原审查部门) which made the decision of rejection for interlocutory examination.

The previous examination department shall provide its opinion on interlocutory examination, and make a Note of Interlocutory Examination Opinion.

There are three types of interlocutory examination opinion:

The first one is that the request for reexamination is allowable, and the decision of rejection is agreed to be revoked(撤销).

The second one is that the amended text of the application submitted by the petitioner has overcome the previous defects, and the decision of rejection is agreed to be revoked on the basis of the amendments.

The third one is that the observations and the amendments submitted by the petitioner are not sufficient to revoke the decision of rejection, and the decision of rejection is maintained(坚持驳回决定).

针对第一种、第二种前置审查意见，专利复审委员会应当直接据此作出复审决定，不需要再进行合议审查。而针对第三种前置审查意见，专利复审委员会需要进行合议审查，然后再作出复审决定。

(三)专利复审委员会合议审查(Collegiate Examination of the Patent Reexamination Board)

经过前置审查程序(interlocutory examination)，原审查部门作出坚持原驳回申请决定的意见时，专利复审委员会需要对该复审请求进行审查。专利复审委员会的审查采取合议的方式。

If the patent reexamination board considers after reexamination that the request is not legal, it shall require the person requesting reexamination to state his opinions within a specified time limit. If no response has been made at the expiry of the time limit, the request shall be deemed to have been withdrawn.

In the reexamination procedure, the panel(合议组) normally examines only the grounds(理由) and evidence on which the decision of rejection is based.

(四)复审决定(The Decision of Reexamination)

经过复审程序，复审委员会应当对该复审请求作出复审决定。复审决定主要包括以下几种：

第一，依照原审查机关的意见直接撤销原决定(to rescind the original decision directly)。

If the original examination department agrees to revoke its former decision upon the request of the applicant requesting reexamination, the Patent Reexamination Board shall make a reexamination decision accordingly and notify the applicant. 复审决定只能由专利复审委员会以其自己的名义作出，而不得以原审查机关的名义作出。

第二，经合议审查维持原驳回决定(to uphold the original rejection decision)。

If after the opinions have been stated or the rectifications have been made, the Patent Reexamination Board still considers the request illegal, it shall make a reexamination decision sustaining the original decision of rejection.

第三，经合议审查撤销原驳回决定(to rescind the original rejection decision)。专利申请人提出专利申请复审请求，经原审查机关的前置审查，作出坚持驳回决定的意见。专利复审委员会进行合议审查后，认为原驳回决定不符合《专利法》或《专利法实施细则》有关规定的，或者认为经过修改的专利申请文件消除了原驳回决定指出的缺陷的，应当撤销原驳回决定。专利复审委员会作出撤销原驳回决定的，该专利申请由原审查部门继续进行专利审查程序。复审请求人对于复审决定不服的，可在接到复审决定通知之日起3个月内以专利复审委员会为被告，提起行政诉讼。

第二节　专利权的无效宣告
Ⅱ　Patent Invalidation

一、专利权无效宣告的事由及条件(Reasons and Conditions for Patent Invalidation)

专利权的无效宣告(invalidation)，是指专利被授予后，认为该专利权的授予不符合法律的有关规定的单位或个人，依法向专利委员会提出宣告该专利无效的申请，该申请经过复审委员会审查作出决定的制度。

(一)申请专利权无效宣告的理由(Reasons)

If, as of the announcement of the granting of the patent by the patent administrative department of the State Council, any entity or individual considers that the granting of patent does not conform to the relevant provisions of this Law, it or he may request the Board of Patent Appeals and Interferences to invalidate the patent right.

可见，专利权被授予以后，并不是绝对稳定(absolutely stable)的。因为，在专利审查过程中可能会有疏漏(omission)，使不满足专利条件的申请获得授权，尤其是对于实用新型、外观设计，在我国只进行形式审查(formalistic examination)就更容易出现这种现象。为了及时更正这种错误，就需要社会监督(social supervision)的介入，从而产生了专利权的无效宣告制度。

专利权的无效宣告制度，虽是为了引入社会监督，纠正错误授权(error authorization)，但为了保护合法的专利权人以及防止他人恶意申请无效宣告，申请专利权的无效宣告需要具有法定理由(statutory grounds)。根据《专利法实施细则》的规定，被授予专利的发明创造不符合《专利法》第 2 条，第 20 条第 1 款，第 22 条，第 23 条，第 26 条第 3 款、第 4 款，第 27 条第 2 款，第 33 条或者《专利法实施细则》第 20 条第 2 款、第 43 条第 1 款的规定，或者属于《专利法》第 5 条、第 25 条的规定，或者依照《专利法》第 9 条规定不能取得专利权的，可以申请宣告专利权无效。对以上法条进行整理，这些理由主要包括以下几种：

(1)不属于《专利法》所规定的发明创造(The unqualified inventions under the patent law)；

(2)违反法律、社会公德或者妨害公共利益的发明创造，或者违反法律、行政法规的规定获取或者利用遗传资源，并依赖该遗传资源完成的发明创造(Invention that contravenes any law or social moral or is detrimental to public interests or invention based on genetic resources which arc get through illegal sources)；

(3)违反了先申请原则的(Inventions violating the principle of advance application)；

(4)违反法律规定，向境外申请专利的(To apply for a patent abroad against the law)；

(5)不符合专利“三性”标准的(Do not meet with the novelty, inventiveness and practical applicability standards)；

(6)说明书为能够对发明或者实用新型作出清楚、完整的说明，未达到使所属技术领域的技术人员能够实现的标准，权利要求书未能以说明书为依据，清楚、简要地限定要求专利保护的范围(The description cannot clearly and completely describe the invention or utility model so as to enable a person skilled in the relevant field to carry it out; the claims cannot clearly and concisely state the requested patent protection scope in accordance with the specifications);

(7)对发明和实用新型专利申请文件的修改超出原说明书和权利要求书记载的范围，对外观设计专利申请文件的修改超出原图片或者照片表示的范围(The modifications to the application for a patent for invention or utility model beyond the scope of the disclosure contained in the initial description and claims, and the modifications to the patent application for design beyond the scope of the disclosure as shown in the initial drawings or photographs);

(8)不符合单一性原则的(Contrary to the principle of unity)。

(二)申请专利权无效宣告应满足的条件(Conditions of Patent Invalidation)

1. 请求权人(Claimant)

任何组织和个人都可以申请宣告专利无效。自然人(natural person)为请求人的需要具备完全民事行为能力(full civil capacity)。以授予专利权的外观设计与他人在申请日以前已经取的合法权利相冲突为理由请求宣告外观设计专利权无效，但请求人不能证明是在先权利人或者利害关系人的，专利复审委员会不予受理。专利权人对自己的专利权请求宣告无效，且申请宣告该专利全部无效、所提交的证据不是公开出版物的，专利复审委员会不予受理。当专利权由多个专利权人共有，而部分专利权人对该专利提出无效请求时，专利复审委员也会不予受理。

2. 提出请求的时间(Time Requirement)

在专利被授权公告之日起，才能提出专利权宣告无效申请。自专利申请公开之日起至公告授予专利权之日止任何人认为该申请不符合法律规定的都可以提出意见，并说明理由，从而阻止该发明被授予专利。该项异议制度是与专利权的无效宣告制度不同的。只有在专利权产生之后才谈得上专利权的无效问题。对于被授权的专利，即使该专利已经终止，也可以被请求宣告其无效。

3. 提交符合规定的请求书(The Request Should Comply with the Prescribed Form)

Anyone requesting invalidation or part invalidation of a patent right shall submit a written request and necessary evidence in duplicate(一式两份). The request for invalidation shall state in detail the grounds for filing the request, making reference to all the evidence as submitted, and indicate the piece of evidence on which each ground is based.

专利权无效宣告请求书不符合规定格式的，无效宣告请求人应当在专利复审委员会指定的期限内补正；期满未补正的，该无效宣告请求视为未提出。

4. 请求的理由及证据(Reasons and Evidences of the Request)

无效宣告请求书应当结合提交的所有证据，具体说明无效宣告请求的理由，并指明每项理由所依据的证据。无效宣告的理由(reason for invalidation)是指发明创造不符合《专利法》第2条，第20条第1款，第22条，第23条，第26条第3款、第4款，第27条第2

款，第 33 条或者《专利法实施细则》第 20 条第 2 款、第 43 条第 1 款的规定，或者属于《专利法》第 5 条、第 25 条的规定，或者依照《专利法》第 9 条规定不能取得专利权的情形。

以授予专利权的外观设计与他人在先取得的合法权利相冲突为理由请求宣告外观设计专利权无效，但是未提交生效的能够证明权利冲突的处理决定或者判决的，专利复审委员会不予受理。

5. 缴纳费用(Fees)

Where the petitioner fails to pay in full the fee for request for invalidation within one month from the submitting date of the request, the request for invalidation shall be deemed not to have been made.

二、专利权无效宣告的审查原则(Examination Principles for Patent Invalidation)

专利复审委员会在受理了专利权的无效宣告申请之后，要对该申请进行审查，其审查要坚持以下原则：

(一)一事不再审原则(Principle of *Res Judicata*)

After an examination decision on a request for invalidation of a patent has been made, any new request for invalidation of the same patent based on the same causes and evidence shall not be accepted or examined.

如果再次提出无效宣告的理由或证据等因时限等原因未被在先的无效宣告审查决定所考虑，则该请求不属于上述不予受理和审理的情形。

(二)当事人处置原则(Principle of Disposal by the Party Concerned)

The petitioner may renounce part or all of the scope, causes and evidence he has raised for the request for invalidation. For the scope, causes or evidence renounced by the petitioner, usually the Patent Reexamination Board will not investigate or examine them anymore.

In the invalidation procedure (无效宣告程序), the party concerned is entitled to compromise(和解) with the opposite party at his own wish. 对于请求人与专利权人均向专利复审委员会表示有和解愿望的，合议组应当给予双方当事人一定的期间进行和解，并暂缓作出审查决定。

In the invalidation procedure, if, in response to the request for invalidation, the patentee narrowed the extent of protection of the patent right on his own initiative (主动) and the corresponding(相应的) amended text was accepted by the Patent Reexamination Board, then it shall be deemed that the patentee admitted a larger extent of protection did not conform to the relevant provisions of the Patent Law and its Implementing Regulations and acknowledged(同意) the request for invalidation concerning the claim(该权利要求), and thus the burden of proof(举证责任) on the petitioner for invalidation of said claim is exempted.

(三)保密原则(Confidentiality Principle)

Before an examination decision is made, any member of the panel (合议组) without authorization shall neither explicitly nor implicitly (明示或者暗示) reveal to any side of the parties the opinion on the case of himself, of any other panel member, or of the Director(主任委员) or Deputy Director(副主任委员) of the Board responsible for the approval of the case.

In order to ensure impartiality(公正执法) and confidentiality, any member of the panel in principle(原则上) shall not individually meet with any side of the parties.

(四)可补正原则(Corrected Principle)

可补正原则体现在两方面：一方面，无效宣告请求人在提出请求后，可补充证据及理由(supplementary evidence and reasons)。在专利复审委员会受理无效宣告请求后，请求人可以在提出无效宣告请求之日起1个月内增加理由或者补充证据。另一方面，在无效宣告请求的审查过程中，专利权人可以修改其权利要求书(amend its claims)以补正其不足。在无效宣告请求的审查过程中，发明或者实用新型专利的专利权人可以修改其权利要求书，但是不得扩大原专利的保护范围。在修改时注意，发明或者实用新型专利的专利权人不得修改专利说明书和附图，外观设计专利的专利权人不得修改图片、照片和简要说明。

三、专利权无效宣告的审查程序(Examination Process of Invalidation)

(一)初步形式审查(Initial Form Examination)

After the Patent Reexamination Board receives a request for invalidation, it shall perform initial formal examination on it. 专利复审委员会，收到专利权无效宣告的申请后，首先要进行初步审查以决定是否受理。初步审查主要是看请求的文件是否符合法定的格式、理由是否符合法律规定以及是否违反了一事不再审原则。

(二)通知专利权人(Notifying the Patent Holder)

专利复审委员会应当将专利权无效宣告请求书和有关文件的副本送交专利权人，要求其在指定的期限内陈述意见。专利权人和无效宣告请求人应当在指定期限内答复专利复审委员会发出的转送文件通知书或者无效宣告请求审查通知书；期满未答复的，不影响专利复审委员会审理。

(三)实质审查(Substantive Examination)

专利复审委员会根据当事人的请求或者案情需要，可以决定对无效宣告请求进行口头审理(oral hearing)。专利复审委员会决定对无效宣告请求进行口头审理的，应当向当事人发出口头审理通知书，告知举行口头审理的日期和地点。当事人应当在通知书指定的期限内作出答复。无效宣告请求人对专利复审委员会发出的口头审理通知书在指定的期限内未作答复，并且不参加口头审理的，视为撤回；专利权人不参加口头审理的，可以缺席审理。

(四)审查决定(The Decision of Examination)

There are three types of examination decisions for a request for invalidation, which are: declaring a patent right invalid in whole; declaring a patent right invalid in part; and maintaining the validity of a patent right.

The Patent Reexamination Board shall timely examine the request for invalidating a patent, decide and notify the petitioner and the patentee. The decision shall be registered and announced by the patent administrative department of the State Council.

对专利复审委员会宣告专利权无效或者维持专利权的决定不服的，可以自收到通知之日起3个月内向人民法院起诉。人民法院受理后应当通知无效宣告请求程序的对方当事人作为第三人参加诉讼。

四、宣告无效的法律效力(The Legal Effectiveness of Invalidation)

Where a patent right is declared invalid in part, the part of the patent right so invalidated(专利权无效部分) shall be deemed non-existent from the date of filing, and the part of the patent right that are maintained valid (including the amended claims) shall be deemed existent from the date of filing at the same time.

第三节　专利权的终止
Ⅲ　Patent Expiration

一、专利权终止的概念(Definition of Patent Expiration)

专利权的终止，是指由于某种法律事实(legal facts)的发生而导致专利权消灭(eliminate)的情形。

专利权的终止有广义与狭义之分。广义(broad sense)上的专利权的终止包括一切使专利权消灭的情形，既包括专利的期限届满(the expiration of the patent)也包括专利的无效宣告(invalidation of the patent)，既包括专利权的绝对消灭(absolute elimination)，又包括专利权因转让(transfer)而使原专利权人相对丧失(relative loss)专利权的情形。狭义(narrow sense)的专利权的终止是指，原有效的专利权因为特定法律事实(specific legal facts)的出现而权利消灭的情形，其不包括专利权自始无效的无效宣告情形，也不包括专利权因转让而使原专利权人丧失专利权的情形。本书所讲的专利的终止，专指在狭义上的专利的终止。

专利权的终止与专利权的无效宣告制度虽然都是原本被授予的专利权消灭，但却有很大的不同：第一，前提(premise)不同。专利权的终止针对的是满足专利法要求的合法有效的专利，而专利的无效宣告针对的是不满足专利法的要求却错误授予的情形。第二，原因(reason)不同。专利权的消灭主要是因为期限届满、专利权人弃权等原因，而专利权的无效宣告主要是因为原专利不符合法律的规定要件。第三，后果(result)不同。专利权的消灭没有溯及力，而专利权的无效宣告却使专利权自始无效，具有溯及力。第四，程序(procedure)不同。

二、专利权终止的事由(Reasons of Patent Expiration)

(一)专利权期限届满自然终止(Natural Termination)

知识产权与有形财产权(tangible property)的主要区别之一就是其具有时间性(timeliness)，一旦超过了法律规定的有效期限，这一权利就消灭。知识财富应该是社会的共同财富，其除了为权利人带来利益外，也应当为整个社会的进步作出贡献。为了提高智力劳动者的创造性、积极性，应给予其一定时间内的专有权利，同时为了促进社会的进步，在期限届满后该知识产品即转变成整个社会的公共财富，任何人都可以使用。

The duration of the invention patent right shall be 20 years and that of the utility model patent right and of the design patent right shall be ten years respectively, all commencing from the date of application. 需要注意的是，专利权的产生时间是从其授权公告之日起，而专利期限的起算点是其申请日而不是授权公告之日。

在专利的有效期限内，专利权人死亡，该专利可由专利权人的继承人继承(inheritance)。在无人继承该权利时，该专利权是否终止，不同的国家有不同的规定。日本专利法中规定，在规定的期间内，无人主张继承权时，专利权自行消失。① 我国《专利法》对此问题没有明确的规定，这在司法实践中存在着法律适用的空白，我国应明确这方面的规定。

(二)专利权因欠缴年费而终止(Default of Payment)

《专利法》规定，专利权人自被授予专利的当年开始应当缴纳年费。

A patentee shall pay an annual fee since the year when the patent is granted. If an annual fee is not paid under relevant provisions, the patent shall be terminated before the expiration of its duration.

专利权人自被授予专利权自后，若要使其专利权中持续存在，就需要依照法律规定按时足额地缴纳专利年费。

专利权人未按时缴纳年费(不包括授予专利权当年的年费)或者缴纳的数额不足的，可以在年费期满之日起6个月内补缴，并缴纳滞纳金(late fees)。在该期限内按照规定补缴了年费及滞纳金的专利权依然存续。补缴时间超过规定时间不足1个月的不需要缴纳滞纳金，超过1个月的滞纳金按照一定的比例缴纳。

专利年费滞纳期(delaying payment)满仍未缴纳或者缴足专利年费或者滞纳金的，自滞纳期满之日起2个月后审查员应当发出专利权终止通知书(franchise termination notice)。因未及时缴纳年费，专利权终止的，其权利从上一专利年度届满之日起终止。

(三)专利权因权利人放弃而终止(Termination for Renunciation)

专利权作为一种私权，权利人可以按照自己的意志对其进行处分。维持专利的有效，虽然可以在一定期间能享有对该知识产品的专有使用权，排斥他人未经许可使用该专利，但同时其每年要缴纳专利年费。所以，当维持专利权不能给权利人带来大的利益时，权利人可能会选择放弃专利权(renunciation)。当然，放弃专利权的理由还有很多，只要是权利人的真实意思表示(true intention)都是允许的。

但放弃专利权是一个要式行为，按照《专利法》第44条的规定，专利权人需要以书面声明(written declaration)的方式放弃其专利。放弃专利权的声明一旦作出，专利权人无正当理由不得撤销(revocation)。

当专利权属于多个专利权人共有时，放弃专利权的声明应当经全体专利权人的同意。如果只有部分专利权人声明放弃专利权，则该专利权并不会产生终止的后果，只导致声明

① 日本专利法[M]. 杜颖，易继明，译. 北京：法律出版社，2001：35.

放弃权利者丧失其专利权，该专利权由未声明放弃权利的专利权人继续享有。

【英语词汇】

accused infringer 被控侵权的人
collegiate examination 合议审查
dissented from 对……持有异议
interlocutory examination 前置审查
patent expiration 专利权终止
petitioner *n.* 请求人
revoke *v.* 撤销
termination *n.* 终止
confidentiality principle 保密原则
dismiss *v.* 驳回
grant *v.* 授予
patentability *n.* 专利性
patent reexamination 专利复审
rejection *n.* 驳回
revocation *n.* 撤回
unpatentable *adj.* 不可取得专利的

【英语句型】

1. The description cannot clearly and completely describe the invention or utility model so as to enable a person skilled in the relevant field of technology to carry it out; the claims cannot clearly and concisely state the requested patent protection scope in accordance with the specifications.

"in accordance with..."表示"与……一致"。

译文：说明书为能够对发明或者实用新型作出清楚、完整的说明，未达到使所属技术领域的技术人员能够实现的标准，权利要求书未能以说明书为依据，清楚、简要地限定要求专利保护的范围。

2. If an annual fee is not paid under relevant provisions, the patent shall be terminated before the expiration of its duration.

"the expiration of..."意思是"……的终结"。

译文：专利权人没有按规定缴纳年费的，专利权终止。

【阅读资料】

第十一章　专利管理与专利权的保护
Chapter 11　Patent Management and Protection of Patent Right

【引言】现实中有很多的专利纠纷(patent disputes)都涉及专利权的保护问题，而专利权保护的关键在于解决专利侵权(patent infringement)的认定问题，故此我们必须要明确专利权的保护范围，以及专利侵权行为的构成要件(constitutive requirements)、种类。同时要完善对专利权利用的过程中发生纠纷后的保护措施。

【学习目的与要求】了解我国专利权的行政管理(public administration)，明确如何界定专利的权利范围和认定专利侵权行为，掌握专利纠纷的解决方法。

第一节　专利管理
Ⅰ　Patent Management

一、专利管理机关(Administrative Authority for Patent Affairs)

专利管理，是指以行政手段(administrative means)和法律手段(legal means)管理有关专利事务的活动。

专利管理是现代专利制度(patent system)的产物。纵观世界各国专利制度的产生和发展，凡是建立了专利制度的国家都相应地建立了较完整的专利管理体制。

Patent management is becoming increasingly important as the complexities involved in managing patents increase due to technological advancement.

我国的专利管理体系是随着我国专利制度的发展而逐步建立和健全起来的。专利管理的内容包括：宣传普及专利知识；推动发明创造活动；培训专利业务干部；对基层专利业务进行指导；调处专利纠纷等。其目的是推动专利制度更好地为经济发展和科技进步服务。

现在，我国专利管理机构主要可以分为国家专利行政部门(national patent administrative department)和地方各级人民政府管理专利工作的部门(patent administrative department of local people's governments)。国家专利行政部门，在1998年机构改革之前为中国专利局，现更名为国家知识产权局(State Intellectual Property Office)。地方管理专利工作的部门主要指由省、自治区、直辖市人民政府以及专利管理工作量大又有实际处理能力的设区的市人民政府设立的管理专利工作的部门。目前，一般由省级政府所设的知识产权局负责其辖区内的专利管理工作。

二、专利管理机关的职责(Administrative Authority for Patent Affairs and Its Obligations)

(一)国务院专利行政部门及其职能(The Patent Administrative Department of the State Council and Its Functions)

国务院专利行政部门(the patent administrative department of the State Council)，是在国务院领导下的负责专利管理的最高机构，负责管理全国的专利工作，统一受理和审查专利申请，依法授予专利权。

The patent administrative department of the State Council has the authoritative right to accept and examine applications for patents, and grant patents in accordance with the law.

在我国负责专利管理的最高机构为国家知识产权局(State Intellectual Property Office)。我国《专利法》规定的其对专利权的管理上的职能具体主要体现在以下方面：

(1)根据《专利法》的规定，转让(assign)专利申请权或者专利权的，须向国务院专利行政部门登记(register)，由国务院专利行政部门予以公告(announce)。专利申请权或者专利权的转让自登记之日起生效。

(2)根据《专利法》的规定，任何单位或者个人将在中国完成的发明或者实用新型向外国申请专利的，应当事先报经国务院专利行政部门进行保密审查(confidentiality review)。保密审查的程序、期限等按照国务院的规定执行。

(二)地方管理专利工作部门及其职能(The Patent Administrative Department of Local Place and Its Functions)

地方管理专利工作的部门是指省、自治区、直辖市人民政府管理专利工作的部门(the patent administrative department of the people's government of each province, autonomous region, or municipality directly under the Central Government)。实践中，由地方知识产权局负责本行政区域内的专利管理工作，具体履行以下工作职能：

1. 执法职能 (Enforcement Function)

专利管理机关的执法职能主要体现为调解和处理各种专利纠纷，监督各项专利法律、法规的执行，对违法侵权行为进行处罚等方面。Such as mediating disputes over the ownership of patent right, disputes over patent infringement, and disputes over patent contracts.

2. 管理职能 (Management Function)

专利管理机关的管理职能主要指专利管理机关开展企业专利工作、进行专利宣传、培训专利业务干部和专利法制建设等方面所做的工作。专利管理机关具有以下管理职能：宣传专利法，普及专利知识，组织培训专利工作人员；起草、制定本地区、本部门的专利工作，并进行业务指导，管理本地区、本部门技术进出口中有关专利工作；领导本地区、本部门的专利服务机构、专利技术实施机构、专利文献和咨询服务机构；组织制定本地区、本部门专利工作的发展规划；逐步建立和完善本地区、本部门的专利工作体系；协助有关部门监督和检查本地区、本部门贯彻执行《专利法》及其《专利法实施细则》的情况。

三、单位的自我管理(Self-Management of an Entity)

为了明确企业技术的研究开发、申请专利保护、管理专利技术的职责，规范专利技术的使用，保护企业无形资产，单位应加强其专利权的管理，促进企业的可持续发展，鼓励员工积极进行发明创造。单位应设立专利管理部门，负责日常专利事务，提出技术方案保密、技术方案法律保护的方式及具体的措施设想，监督市场相同技术方案产品的状态以及侵权信息的收集。如企业的知识产权部或者法务部，教学科研机构的科技处等。

Patent management of an entity includes: (1) development of patent technology(专利技术开发); (2) application(申请), preservation(维持) and abandonment(放弃) of a patent, and examination of a service invention(职务发明) and non-service invention(非职务发明); (3) evaluation and assessment of a patent; (4) assignment(转让), licensing trade(许可贸易), application of the patent right, investment in the form of the patent right at certain value(专利作价投资), and pledge(质押) of patent right; (5) behavioral norms for personnel involved in the development of patent technology; (6) protection of the patent right, such as surveillance of patent infringement(专利侵权监视), action of a patent, and boarder protection of the patent right(专利权边境保护); (7) and other business in patent management of an entity.

第二节 专利权的保护
Ⅱ The Protection of Patent Right

一、专利权的保护范围(Scope of Patent Right Protection)

(一)专利权的保护范围及认定原则(Scope of Protection and Principles of Patent Rights)

1. 专利权的保护范围(Scope of Patent Right Protection)

专利权的保护范围，是指专利权法律效力所涉及的发明创造的范围。对于发明和实用新型，专利权的保护范围由权利要求书确定。一般来说，如果他人实施的技术方案再现了一项权利要求中记载的全部技术特征，就落入了该权利要求的保护范围。如果他人实施权利的技术方案除了包含权利要求中记载的全部技术特征以外，还包括一个或者多个权利要求中没有的技术特征，也同样是落入了该权利要求的保护范围。反之，如果让人实施的技术方案没有包括一项权利要求记载的某一技术特征，一般就会被认为没有落入该项权利要求的保护范围。

2. 专利权保护范围的认定原则(Principles in Determining Scope of Protection of Patent Rights)

考察各国专利法的实施，在对权利要求书的解释方面主要有三种原则：第一种是以德国为代表的“中心限定”原则，第二种是以英美为代表的“周边限定”原则，第三种是对上述两种原则的折中原则。

(1)中心限定原则 (Central Claiming Principle)

中心限定原则，是指权利要求书是专利保护范围的依据，但在解释权利要求书时，应当以权利要求书表达的实质内容为中心，全面考虑发明创造的目的、性质以及说明书和附图，将中心一定范围内的技术也包含在保护范围之内的权利保护原则。According to the central claiming system, the claims identify the "center" of the patented invention. The exact scope of the protection depends on the actual nature of the inventor's contribution to the art in the concerned technology. 中心限定原则的采用，不必拘泥于权利要求书的文字记载。这种解释原则给专利权人提供了充分的保护，但对第三人而言，专利权的保护范围处在难以明确的状态，实际并不利于公平竞争。

(2)周边限定原则(Peripheral Claiming Principle)

周边限定原则，是指要求严格依照权利要求书的字面记载进行解释，对专利权的保护范围不能超出权利要求书文字记载的范围的权利保护原则。According to the peripheral claiming system, claims identify the exact periphery of the conferred protection. In this system, the burden of drafting good claims is much higher on the patent applicant (or on his counsel). The applicant receives the protection he or she requested and almost nothing more, provided that the invention is new and non-obvious. This theoretically makes it easier for third parties to examine whether infringement may exist. 说明书(description)和附图(drawings)不能成为确定专利权保护范围的依据，只有在权利要求书不明确的情况下，才能用来对保护范围作限制性解释(restrictive explanation)。这种解释，对第三人是有利的，稍稍进行修改，就可能逃出专利保护的范围，依照此种解释，对权利要求书的撰写提出了很高的要求，但实际上在申请专利时就找到一个保护范围较为恰当的概念来表达是比较困难的。

(3)折中原则(Principle of Mediocrity)

折中原则，即以权利要求书的内容为准，但不拘泥于权利要求书的文字或措辞，而是结合说明书和附图划定专利权的保护范围。当权利要求书中表示的技术特征有疑义时，可以引用说明书和附图进行解释。欧洲专利公约及其成员国采用折中原则，我国《专利法》也采用这一原则。

3. 专利侵权行为的判断(Elements of Patent Infringement)

发明和实用新型专利的保护范围以权利要求书中记载的必要技术特征所确定的范围为准。侵权指的是一种产品或者方法具有他人专利产品或者方法权利要求书中全部技术特征。只要被控侵权的技术方案包含了专利权利要求书中的全部技术特征，即使增加了新的技术特征，仍属于侵权。

在判定侵权与否时，需将侵权物与权利要求书所描述的技术方案加以比较，具体可通过以下步骤进行特征分析：第一，分析被指控侵权的方案的技术特征，其特征是否包含专利方案独立权利要求中的全部技术特征。这是因为在所有权利要求中，独立权利要求的范围是最大的，所以只要没有纳入独立权利要求的范围，就不会纳入其他引用该独立权利要求的从属权利要求的范围。第二，比较前述所有与独立权利要求相同的技术特征是否都与专利独立权利要求所述方案具有相同的功能或形式、所有特征间的相互关系是否亦相同。第三，判断所有特征按这种关系的组合所产生的效果是否相同。即使是两个由若干相同技术特征构成的发明，由于这些特征组合的方式不同，完全可能构成不同的发明。如果上述问题的答案均为肯定，则构成侵权。在分析比较和概括技术特征的过程中，应当运用前述对权利要求的解释原则。

(二)我国对专利权的保护范围(Scope of Patent Right Protection in China)

1. 发明和实用新型专利的保护范围(Scope for Invention or Utility Models)

Article 59 of China's Patent Law provides that: for the patent right of an invention or a utility model, the scope of protection shall be confined to what is claimed, and the written description and the pictures attached may be used to explain what is claimed.

在确定专利权的保护范围时应当以权利要求书中明确记载的必要技术特征所确定的范围为准，也包括与该必要技术特征相等同的特征所确定的范围。等同特征(equivalent features)是指与所记载的技术特征以基本相同的手段，实现基本相同的功能，达到基本相同的效果，并且本领域的普通技术人员(person skilled in the art)无须经过创造性劳动就能够认识到的特征。

一项技术特征如在权利要求中叙述不清的，可以通过说明书和附图加以理解，必要时，可以依说明书和附图公开的内容去修改。但如果在权利要求中没有记载的，则不能受到法律保护，说明书本身不能确定保护范围。

2. 外观设计专利权的保护范围(Scope of Patent Right Protection for Design)

Article 59 of China's Patent Law provides that: for the design patent right, the scope of protection shall be confined to the design of the product as shown in the drawings or pictures, and the brief description may be used to explain the said design as shown in the drawings or pictures.

The scope of protection depends on two factors: (1) the patented design as shown in the drawings or photographs; (2) that incorporated in the product specified in the grant of patent.

二、专利侵权行为(Patent Infringements)

(一)专利侵权行为的界定和构成要件(Definition and Constitutive Requirements of Patent Infringements)

Patent infringement occurs when someone enforces others' patent for profit during the patent protection period without the patent owner's permission or statutory reasons for exemption. If a court finds that infringement occurred, every patent infringer can be ordered by a court to stop all infringing activity. Any of the infringers who profited from the infringement may also be found liable for money damages.

The definition of patent infringement may vary by jurisdiction, but it typically includes using or selling the patented invention. In many countries, a use is required to be commercial (or to have a commercial purpose) to constitute patent infringement.

专利侵权行为的构成必须符合以下要件:

1. 侵害的对象是有效的专利(A Valid Patent Is Being Infringed)

专利侵权必须以存在有效的专利为前提，即被侵害的专利必须是在《专利法》规定的保护期限内。If it was not practicing the patented invention, the patent is invalid or abandoned, or the patent has expired, the act does not infringe the patent.

If an appropriate royalty is not paid for using an invention during the period from the publication of the invention patent application to the grant of the patent right, patentee may take legal action to request the payment.

2. 有实际的侵害行为(The Act of Infringement Is Actual)

即行为人在客观上实施了侵害他人专利的行为。包括直接侵权行为(direct infringement)和间接侵权行为(indirect infringement)。

3. 以生产经营为目的(The Purpose Is for Production and Business Operation)

The essence of patent rights lies in the monopoly of the market. The patent right is not infringed if it causes no harm to the patentee's interests.

4. 违反法律的规定(The Act Violates the Law)

违反法律的规定，即行为人实施了专利的行为未经专利权人的许可，又无法律依据。对于直接侵权行为，根据我国现有的法律规定不要求行为人主观上有过错，只要客观上实施的行为没有法律依据(no legal basis)即成立侵权；但对于间接侵权行为，则要求行为人主观上必须有过错(be faulty subjectively)。

(二)专利侵权行为的种类(Types of Patent Infringement)

依照侵权行为是否由行为人本身的行为所造成，将专利侵权行为划分为直接侵权行为(direct infringement)和间接侵权行为(indirect infringement)。

1. 直接侵权行为(Direct Infringement)

直接侵权行为是指直接由行为人实施的侵犯他人专利权的行为。只要侵权人实施了受专利权控制的行为，不论主观状态如何，均认为是侵权。其表现形式包括：

(1)制造、使用、许诺销售、销售、进口发明或实用新型专利产品，或者使用发明专利方法以及使用、许诺销售、销售、进口依照该专利方法直接获得的产品。

(2)制造、许诺销售、销售、进口外观设计专利产品。

(3)假冒专利的行为，是指在与他人专利产品类似的产品或者产品的包装上，加上专利权人的专利标记或者专利号，使他人相信该产品是专利权人的专利产品的行为。这种行为不仅直接侵害了专利权人的权利，而且严重损害了消费者的利益，扰乱了市场秩序，带有较大的社会危害性。

2. 间接侵权行为(Indirect Infringement)

间接侵权行为，是指行为人本身的行为并不直接构成对专利权的侵害，但实施了诱导、怂恿、教唆、帮助他人侵害专利权的行为。

If an act of actively inducing, abetting, instigating or helping another to infringe a patent shall itself be treated as an act of infringement.

To prove inducement to infringe, the patent owner must demonstrate some positive act of inducement by the person being sued. That may include instructing, directing, or advising the third-party as to how to carry out an infringement.

间接侵权促使和导致了直接侵权行为的发生，行为人主观上有过错，对专利权人造成了损害，与直接侵权构成共同侵权(joint tort)。

三、对专利权的保护方式(Types of Protection)

(一)民事保护(Civil Protection)

1. 管辖(Jurisdiction)

《最高人民法院关于审理专利纠纷案件适用法律问题的若干规定》规定，专利纠纷第一审案件(case of the first instance)，由省、自治区、直辖市人民政府所在地的中级人民法院和最高人民法院指定的中级人民法院管辖。2014 年 11 月 3 日起施行的《最高人民法院关于北京、上海、广州知识产权法院案件管辖的规定》规定，北京市、上海市各中级人民法院和广州市中级人民法院不再受理知识产权民事和行政案件；广东省其他中级人民法院不再受理本规定第 1 条第(1)项和第(3)项规定的案件。也就是说在北京、上海和广东专利侵权案件一审由知识产权法院管辖。

因侵犯专利权的行为提起的诉讼，由侵权行为地(the place if the tort is committed)或者被告住所地(the place if the defendant lives)人民法院管辖。

2. 诉讼时效(Statute of Limitation)

我国《专利法》规定，侵犯专利权的诉讼时效为 2 年，自专利权人或者利害关系人得知或者应当得知侵权行为之日起计算。权利人超过 2 年起诉的，如果侵权行为在起诉时仍在继续，在该项专利权有效期内，人民法院应当判决被告停止侵权行为，侵权损害赔偿数额应当自权利人向人民法院起诉之日起向前推算 2 年计算。需要注意的是，2017 年 3 月 15 日颁布的《中华人民共和国民法总则》第 188 条规定，将诉讼时效期间由 2 年延长为 3 年，并将诉讼期间的起算点调整为“自权利人知道或者应当知道权利受到损害以及义务人之日起计算”。《民法总则》实施以后，《专利法》中的诉讼时效期间应如何适用?

我国《立法法》第 92 条规定：“同一机关制定的法律、行政法规、地方性法规、自治条例和单行条例、规章，特别规定与一般规定不一致的，适用特别规定；新的规定与旧的规定不一致的，适用新的规定。”知识产权属于私权，专利权属于民事权利，因此《民法总则》颁布与实施后，根据新法优于旧法的基本原则，专利实际上也应使用 3 年的诉讼时效。延长诉讼时效，以适应社会生活中新情况的不断出现，交易方式与类型不断创新，权利义务关系更趋复杂的现实与司法实践，有利于建设诚信社会。

3. 专利侵权的民事责任(Civil Liability of Patent Infringements)

民事责任的方式主要有停止侵害(cessation of infringement)、消除影响(elimination of ill effects)、赔礼道歉(extending a formal apology)和赔偿损失(compensation for a loss)。

(1)停止侵害(Cessation of Infringement)

停止侵害，是指专利侵权行为人应当根据管理专利工作的部门的处理决定或者人民法院的生效判决，立即停止正在实施的专利侵权行为。

If a patentee or interested party has evidence to prove that someone is committing or is going to commit an infringement upon the patent right, no matter whether one is faulty subjectively, or its or his lawful rights and interests are damaged, he may, apply to the court for taking such measures as ordering the stop of the relevant act. The act of infringement shall not continue for any reason.

(2)赔偿损失(Compensation for a Loss)

Regarding an act of patent infringement, whether the tortfeasor should compensate for the loss of the patentee, and in accordance with what standard of compensation, there are two theories at present: one is punitive damages(惩罚性赔偿论), the other is compensatory damages(补偿性赔偿论).

根据我国《专利法》的相关规定，专利侵权的损害赔偿，应当贯彻公平原则，让专利权人因侵权行为而受到的实际损失能够得到合理的赔偿。专利权人的损失赔偿数额可按照以下标准进行:

The amount of compensation for patent right infringement shall be determined according to the patentee's actual losses(实际损失)caused by the infringement. If it is hard to determine the actual losses, the amount of compensation may be determined according to the benefits acquired by the infringer through the infringement. If it is hard to determine the losses of the patentee or the benefits acquired by the infringer, the amount of compensation may be determined according to the reasonably multiplied amount of the royalties of that patent(专利许可费的倍数). The amount of compensation shall include the reasonable expenses paid by the patentee for putting an end to the infringement.

If the losses of the patentee, benefits of the infringer, or royalties of the patent are all hard to determine, the people's court may, on the basis of the factors such as the type of patent right, nature of the infringement, and seriousness of the case, determine the amount of compensation within the range from 10,000 Yuan to 1,000,000 Yuan.

(3)消除影响、赔礼道歉(Elimination of Ill Effects, Formal Apology)

If patent rights are infringed, patentee shall have the right to demand that the infringement be stopped, its ill effects be eliminated and the damages be compensated for. 在侵权行为人实施侵权行为给专利产品在市场上的商业信誉造成损害，影响其专利产品的销售、使用时，侵权行为人就应当承担消除影响、赔礼道歉的法律责任。

4. 诉前临时措施 (Interim Measures Before an Action)

为了更好地保护专利权人的权利，我国《专利法》规定了起诉前可对侵权行为采取的措施：诉前行为保全、诉前财产保全和诉前证据保全。

That is, if a patentee or interested party has evidence to prove that someone is committing or is going to commit an infringement upon the patent right, and his lawful rights and interests will be damaged and are difficult to be remedied if the said infringement is not stopped in time, he may, prior to initiating a lawsuit, apply to the court for taking such measures as ordering the stop of the relevant act.

To stop a patent infringement, the patentee or any interested party may apply to the court for preserving the evidence prior to filing the lawsuit when such evidence is likely to be destroyed and hard to be obtained again.

5. 举证责任 (Burden of Proof)

If any dispute over patent infringement involves a patent for invention for the manufacturing process of a new product, the entity or individual manufacturing the identical product shall prove the difference of its own process used in the manufacture of its product from the patented process.

专利侵权纠纷涉及实用新型专利或者外观设计专利的，人民法院或者管理专利工作的部门可以要求专利权人或者利害关系人出具由国务院专利行政部门对相关实用新型或者外观设计进行检索、分析和评价后作出的专利权评价报告，作为审理、处理专利侵权纠纷的证据。

(二)行政保护(Administrative Protection)

If a dispute arises as a result of exploitation of a patent without permission of the patentee, that is, the patent right of the patentee is infringed, the dispute shall be settled through consultation(调解) between the parties. If the parties are not willing to consult or if consultation fails, the patentee or interested party may take legal action before a people's court, and may also request the administration department for patent-related work to handle the dispute.

经管理专利工作的部门调解，当事人双方达成调解协议的，应当制作调解书(mediation agreement)。调解书经当事人签名盖章，调解人员签名，并加盖管理专利工作的部门公章。如调解不成，管理专利工作的部门应当及时作出处理决定。处理决定书应由调解人员签名，并加盖管理专利工作的部门公章。当事人不服管理专利工作的部门的处理决定的，可以在收到通知之日起 3 个月内向人民法院起诉。当事人在规定期限内未起诉的，管理专利工作的部门的处理决定即发生法律效力。一方不按照处理决定履行的，另一方可请求人民法院强制执行。

(三)刑事保护(Criminal Protection)

对于假冒专利的行为，侵权人除要承担停止侵害、赔偿损失等民事责任及行政责任外，情节严重，构成犯罪的，则依法追究侵权人的刑事责任。我国《刑法》规定，假冒他人专利，情节严重的，处 3 年以下有期徒刑或者拘役，并处或者单处罚金。

四、其他专利纠纷及其解决(Other Patent Disputes and Solutions)

(一)专利权属纠纷(Disputes over the Ownership of a Patent)

专利权属纠纷包括专利申请权纠纷和专利权归属纠纷

1. 专利申请权纠纷(Disputes over the Right to Apply for a Patent)

专利申请权纠纷，是指一件发明创造完成后，当事人之间在确认谁有权申请专利而发生的争议。Including disputes over the right to apply for a patent for a non-service invention(非职务发明), for a service invention(职务发明), for an entrusted invention(委托发明), and for a joint invention(合作发明).

2. 专利权归属纠纷(Disputes over the Ownership of a Patent Right)

专利权归属纠纷，是指在专利授权后，当事人之间在确认谁是真正权利人而发生的争议。Such as disputes over joint patentees(共同专利权人), over demarcation of a non-service invention and a service invention, over an entrusted research(委托研究).

3. 纠纷解决的方法(Dispute Resolutions)

非职务发明(non-service invention)与职务发明(service invention)的申请权、专利权归

属的纠纷。According to the Patent Law, for an employment invention-creation, the employer has the right to apply for a patent. After such application is granted, the employer shall be the patentee; for a non-employment invention-creation, the inventor or designer has the right to apply for a patent. After such application is granted, the said inventor or designer shall be the patentee; for an invention-creation that is accomplished by using the material and technical conditions of an employer, if the employer has concluded a contract with the inventor or designer providing the ownership of the right to apply for the patent or the ownership of the patent right, such provision shall prevail.

对于委托发明与合作发明的申请权、专利权归属的纠纷。According to the *Patent Law*, with regard to an invention-creation accomplished by two or more units or individuals in collaboration, or an invention-creation accomplished by an unit or individual under the entrustment of another unit or individual, the right to apply for a patent shall be vested in the units or individuals that have accomplished the invention-creation in collaboration or in the unit or individual that has done so under entrustment, unless it is otherwise agreed upon. After the application is granted, the applying unit(s) or individual(s) shall be deemed the patentee(s).

(二)专利合同纠纷(Disputes over Patent Contracts)

专利合同纠纷主要是指在专利申请权、专利权转让合同，专利技术许可实施合同，专利技术中介服务合同中各方当事人就权利义务的履行，合同条款的解释等发生的争议。As a whole, negotiation is the most convenient way in settling disputes over patent contracts. If the parties are not willing to negotiate or fail to reach an agreement, the patentee or any interested party may either bring a lawsuit, or request the arbitration agency for arbitration.

需要指出的是，这两种程序是相互排斥的，只能择其一。选择了仲裁程序，即意味着排除了司法管辖，仲裁机构的裁定具有终局效力(final)。但若要选择仲裁程序，当事人之间必须达成仲裁协议，即当事人各方同意将其合同纠纷交予某仲裁委员会仲裁。仲裁协议可以在合同订立时一并达成，也可以在纠纷发生时再行约定。如果当事人双方在合同订立时及纠纷发生后都没有达成仲裁协议，则纠纷的解决只有向法院起诉了。

(三)专利行政纠纷(Administrative Patent Disputes)

专利行政纠纷是指当事人对专利行政机关所作出的决定不服而引起的争议。其中专利行政机关包括国家专利局、专利复审委员会及专利管理机构。

依照我国《专利法》的规定，有关专利的行政纠纷有许多种类，在专利审查的各个环节都有可能产生纠纷。

For instance, the patent applicant is dissatisfied with the decision of the patent administrative department of the State Council on rejecting the application; a patentee is dissatisfied with the decision of the patent administrative department of the State Council on granting a compulsory license for exploitation, and the ruling on the royalties payable for compulsorily licensed exploitation; any party is dissatisfied with the review decision of the Patent Reexamination Board (专利复审委员会); any party is dissatisfied with the decision of the Patent Reexamination Board on declaring a patent invalid or maintaining a patent, etc.

主要专利行政纠纷的解决程序如下:

第一，因不服驳回专利申请(dissatisfied with the decision on rejecting the application)而产生的行政纠纷。If a patent applicant is dissatisfied with the decision made by the Patent Administration Department under the State Council on rejecting of the application, he may, within three months from the date of receipt of the notification, file a request with the patent review board for review. After review, the Patent Review Board shall make a decision and notify the patent applicant of the same.

第二，因宣告专利权无效(declaring a patent invalid)而产生的纠纷。A person that is dissatisfied with the patent review board's decision on declaring a patent right invalid or its decision on affirming the patent right may take legal action before a people's court, within three months from the date of receipt of the notification. The people's court shall notify the opposite party in the invalidation procedure to participate in the litigation as a third party.

第三，因强制许可决定(the decision on granting a compulsory license for exploitation)或强制许可费用裁定(the ruling on the royalties payable for compulsorily licensed exploitation)而产生的行政纠纷。If a patentee is dissatisfied with the decision made by the patent administration department under the State Council, on granting of the compulsory license for exploitation, or if the patentee, or the unit or individual that has obtained the compulsory license for exploitation is dissatisfied with the ruling made by the patent administration department under the State Council regarding the royalties for the compulsorily licensed exploitation, it or he may take legal action before the people's court within three months from the date of receipt of the notification of the ruling.

(四)发明专利临时保护使用费的纠纷(Disputes over Access Fee of Temporary Protection Patent of Invention)

由于我国专利法对发明专利采取“早期公开、延迟审查”(early disclosure and deferred examination)的审查制度，必然导致发明专利申请在公开之后、授权之前期间技术的权属处于或然状态。

On the one hand, the applicant may request a substantive examination after the disclosure of technology, the key stage of patent examination. On the other hand, others may implement the technology without compensation after the disclosure of technology.

After the application for an invention patent is published, the applicant may require the unit or individual that exploits the said patent to pay an appropriate amount of royalties(适当的使用费). 但此时由于申请人尚不享有对技术的绝对支配权，当其要求技术实施人支付相应的使用费时，实施人可以拒绝支付，由此必然导致了纠纷的产生。

这种纠纷的产生，是完全由于审查制度的设计造成的，故解决此种纠纷，必须等到专利申请程序结束，除非当事人之间自愿达成协议(agreement based on voluntariness of both parties)。如果专利申请未能通过专利审查，即专利申请被驳回(rejected)，申请人则没有任何理由再向实施人索取技术使用费。如果专利申请被批准授予了专利权，根据法律的规定，专利权人可以对该技术享有专有权。此时，专利权人可以就公开之后、授权之前期间实施其技术的使用费纠纷，请求管理专利工作的部门调解，或者直接向人民法院起诉。

【英语词汇】

abandonment *n.* 放弃
constitutive requirement 构成要件
equivalent feature 等同特征出
joint tort 共同侵权
mediation agreement 调解书
patent dispute 专利纠纷
passing off a Patent 假冒专利行为
temporary protection 临时保护
statute of limitations 诉讼时效
burden of proof 举证责任
direct infringement 直接侵权行为
indirect infringement 间接侵权行为
jurisdiction *n.* 管辖
Non-service invention 非职务发明
patent number 专利号
peripheral claiming principle 周边限定原则
preserve *v.* 维持
service invention 职务发明

【英语句型】

1. No administrative authorities for patent affairs but the patent administrative department of the State Council have the right to accept and examine applications for patents, and grant patents in accordance with the law.

"no...but..."引导的是倒装句，意思是"只有……才……"。

译文：除国务院专利行政部门有权受理、审查专利申请和依法授予专利权外，其他任何专利管理机关均无权受理、审查专利申请和授予专利权。

2. If a patentee or interested party has evidence to prove that someone else is committing or is going to commit an infringement upon the patent right, and its (his) lawful rights and interests will be damaged and are difficult to be remedied if the said infringement is not stopped in time, he may, prior to initiating a lawsuit, apply to the court for taking such measures as ordering the stop of the relevant act.

"is doing or is going to do..."是现在时和一般将来时态并用，意思是"正在或者即将……"。

译文：专利权人或者利害关系人有证据证明他人正在实施或者即将实施侵犯专利权的行为，如不及时制止将会使其合法权益受到难以弥补的损害的，可以在起诉前向人民法院申请采取责令停止有关行为的措施。

3. If any dispute over patent infringement involves a patent for invention for the manufacturing process of a new product, the entity or individual manufacturing the identical product shall provide proof on the difference of its own process used in the manufacture of its product from the patented process.

"dispute over..."的意思是"对于……的纠纷"。

译文：专利侵权纠纷涉及新产品制造方法的发明专利的，制造同样产品的单位或者个人应当提供其产品制造方法不同于专利方法的证明。

4. If the parties are not willing to negotiate or fail to reach an agreement through

negotiations, the patentee or any interested party may either bring a lawsuit with the court, or request the arbitration agency for arbitration.

"be willing to..."的意思是"愿意……"。

译文：如果经协商无法解决，当事人在法律程序方面可以有两种选择：一是请求合同各方当事人认可的仲裁机构仲裁，二是向法院起诉。

【阅读资料】

第四编　商标权制度

PART FOUR　Trademark Legal System

第十二章　商标权制度概述

Chapter 12　Overview of Trademark Legal System

【引言】随着市场经济(market economy)的发展，越来越多的商标(trademark)映入我们的眼帘。商标法律制度(trademark law)作为市场经济制度不断完善的产物，同样也在不断地成长。一个商标所代表的不仅仅是产品的本身，同时也代表着生产者或销售者在消费者心目中的形象。因此，商标制度的发展，对商标注册(trademark registration)、商标使用(trademark use)、商标管理(trademark management)、商标权的法律保护(legal protection of trademark rights)等均具有重要的意义。

【学习目的与要求】商标的问题不仅涉及商业的宣传广告，而且涉及商业竞争行为和法律保护的基本原理和制度，要真正地把握好这一章的内容，应了解商标的概念、特征，商标的分类和商标制度的产生与发展。还要关注社会现实中出现的与商标有关的纠纷，了解相关的立法和司法解释。

第一节　商标的特征及商标的作用

Ⅰ　The Features and Functions of Trademark

一、商标(Trademark)

(一)商标的概念(Concept of Trademark)

A trademark is a symbol used by a person or an entity in commerce to indicate the source of the goods or services and to distinguish them from others. The symbol can be a word, a phrase, a design, an image, or even a sound. Some well-known trademarks are Lenovo for computers, GREE for air conditioner, NIKE for shoes, and COCA-COLA for beverages. Well-known service marks include EBAY for online auction(拍卖) and trading services, the Walmart for retail and wholesale services, and CCTV for television broadcasting. But beyond such well-known marks, trademarks are practically everywhere in modern society.

(二)商标的出现(The Emergence of Trade Mark)

有学者认为，商标的出现可追溯到自人类有交易(trading)生活开始，① 还有学者认为

---

① 陈明汝．商标法原理[M]．北京：中国人民大学出版社，2003：4.

物品上使用标记(mark)的历史与人类和宗教(religion)的历史一样悠久。① 而关于商标在中国的起源，也存在多种不同的说法。不过，在中国的商标历史上，被公认的，最早具有现代商标特性的商标来自北宋时期。当时，济南有家姓刘的针铺店，以白兔为商标，颇负盛名。这个商标是用铜版印刷的，近似方形，印版上方标明店铺字号“济南刘家功夫针铺”，正中有店铺标记——白兔捣药图，并注明“认门前白兔儿为记”，下方是广告语：“收买上等钢条，造功夫细针。不误宅院使用，转卖兴贩，别有加饶，请记白。”②

The origin of trademarks can be traced back to the beginning of the circulation of goods. The history of marks is nearly as old as the histories of mankind and religion. Scientists have come across excavated(挖掘) artifacts(古器物) from places such as ancient Egypt with various symbols carved thereon for religious and superstitious(迷信的) reasons. "Potters marks" appeared in relics(遗迹) left from the Greek and Roman periods and were used to identify the maker (potter) of a particular vessel.

Over time, different methods of identification and distinction developed. Loved ones and pets were given names. "Proprietary marks(专有标记)" (in the form of a name or symbol) were affixed to goods to enable one person to distinguish their own possessions from those of others. Craftsmen(技工) applied their names, unique drawings, or simple inscriptions to identify goods they created.

Around the 10th century, a mark called a "merchants mark"(商人标记), appeared, and symbols among traders and merchants increased significantly. These marks, which can be considered one kind of "proprietary mark", essentially were used to prove ownership rights(所有权) of goods whose owners were missing due to shipwrecks(沉船), pirates(海盗), and other disasters. Even now, in every part of the world, horses, sheep, and other animals are still branded with a mark identifying the owner.

尽管以上个案可以说明中国早期商标的出现，但商标(trademark)这一名词乃至现代商标制度是一舶来之物(exotic things)，是清朝政府在与西方列强的战争失败后，被西方人强加给中国人的，尽管这在后来被证明是进入现代化商业及工业化(modern commercial and industrial)的必需品(necessity)。“Trademark”这个词最早见于1902年的《中英续议通商行船条约》(*The Sino-British Treaty of Mackay*)，当时被翻译为“贸易牌号”，后来在《中英续议通商行船条约》中被改译为“商标”，而该词被沿用至今。③

(三)商标与其他标志的关系(The Relation between Trademark and Other Marks)

1. 商标与广告宣传(Trademarks and Advertising)

从商品营销(marketing)的角度来看，商标(trademark)和广告(advertise)都是营销的一

---

① [日]小野昌延，江口俊夫．商标知识[M]．魏启学，译．北京：中国财政经济出版社，1981：16.

② 刘春田．知识产权法(第三版)[M]．北京：高等教育出版社，北京大学出版社，2007：251.

③ 孟庆法．六十年：中国商标制度经历戏剧变迁[DB/OL]．[2017-05-20]．网上看报，http://newspaper.mofcom.gov.cn/aarticle/guojsb/200909/20090906509467.html.

种方式，都是以促销商品为目的。但是，从法律的角度上看，商标和广告存在着不同之处。

(1)法律的要求不同(The Differences of Legal Requirements)

商标的功能是区别他人产品或者服务，必须具备“显著性”(distinctiveness)，而且商标是相对固定不变的，一旦经过注册即受法律的保护，他人不得冒用；而广告宣传是用来宣传企业或者产品的信息传播手段，可根据宣传的对象灵活地采取不同的形式，还可以在一定的程度上采用夸张的手法。

(2)法律保护的对象不同(Different Objects of Legal Protection)

商标权所保护的是特定标志与相关商品间的关系，任何破坏这种联系的行为都属于侵权行为(infringement)；而一些具有独创性的广告是作为作品受到著作权的保护，这种保护是针对广告本身的，与其所宣传的商品没有直接关系。①

2. 商标与商品名称(Trademark and Trade Name)

商品名称(trade name)，是指为了区别于其他商品而使用的商品的称谓。一般分为通用名称和特定名称。商品的通用名称(general name)，是指为公众所熟知的商品的一般名称，如：电视机、裤子、椅子等。商品的特定名称(specific name)，是指对特定商品的称呼，如：茅台酒、21 金维他等。商标和商品名称的区别主要表现在以下几个方面：

(1)独占性(Exclusiveness)

商标具有专有性和独占性，未经商标所有人许可，他人不得擅自使用；而商品名称具有大众性(popularity)，为公众所有，一般情况下不受法律保护，只有知名商品的名称，才能获得《反不正当竞争法》的保护。

(2)功能(Functions)

商标的最基本功能是商品来源的标示。② 企业之所以使用商标，就是为了使自己的商品或服务能和其他企业的类似商品或服务区分开来；而商品的名称是用来区别不同种类的商品或者同种类商品中的特定商品，但无法区别不同商品的生产者和销售者。

(3)认定条件(Identification)

商标必须经过申请核准(application and approval)后，才能成为注册商标(registered trademark)；而商品的名称是自然产生(naturally occurring)，无须办理任何手续。应当注意的是，如果商标的所有人对商标的使用不当、保护不当，商标则有可能会自然转化成家喻户晓的商品名称。例如：尼龙、阿司匹林等。

3. 商标与商品装潢(Trademark and Commodity Decoration)

商标装潢(trade decoration)，是指商品包装物(packaging)或其他附着物上的装饰设计(decorative design)，具有美化商品，提高商品品位的作用。③ 商标与商品装潢的相同之处是：商标是商品包装装潢的一部分，二者同时使用于商品包装上。二者的区别在于：

① 郭禾．知识产权法(第二版)[M]．北京：中国人民大学出版社，2005：192.

② 吴汉东．知识产权基本问题研究[M]．北京：中国人民大学出版社，2005：509.

③ 吴汉东．知识产权基本问题研究[M]．北京：中国人民大学出版社，2005：508.

(1)使用目的不同(Different Using Purposes)

商标的作用是区别商品的不同生产者或经营者；而装潢是为了美化商品，吸引消费者注意，以求达到推销商品的目的。

(2)受保护的方式不同(Protected by the Different Law)

商标是由《商标法》(*The Trademark Law*)来调整；而商品装潢可以作为美术作品受著作权法保护，知名商品的装潢还可以受《反不正当竞争法》(*The Anti-unfair Competition Law*)保护。

4. 商标与企业名称(Trademarks and Business Names)

A business name is a name under which a business operates. Registration serves as a means of identifying the owners of the business and is obtained under state or territory legislation.

If trading occurs in more than one state or territory, the business name must be registered respectively. Registration of a business name is compulsory and must be completed before the business starts trading.

A trademark is used to distinguish the goods or services of one trader from others. Registration of a trade mark gives the registered owner exclusive use of the trade mark throughout nationwide.

商标和企业名称两者虽均系商业标志(commercial marks)，但两者有着巨大的区别，主要表现在以下几个方面：

(1)构成要素不同(Different Elements)

企业名称(business names)一般由行政区划名称、字号、行业或经营特点、组织形式组成。商标(trademarks)只能由与他人提供的服务区别开来的显著部分构成。

(2)表现形式不同(Different Forms)

商标的表现形式可以是文字，还可以是图形或者是文字与图形的组合，甚至是三维标志①；而企业名称只能用文字表示。

(3)作用不同(Different Functions)

商标仅能区别不同的服务出处，而企业名称则可以识别不同企业的经营范围，包括服务和商品。一个企业可以有多个服务或商品的商标，但企业名称一般只能拥有一个。如宝洁公司，拥有"飘柔"、"潘婷"、"沙宣"等多个商品的商标。

(4)专用权范围不同(The Different Scope of the Exclusive Right)

商标一经核准注册，在全国享有专用权。企业名称仅在规定的区域内享有专用权。

(5)适用的法律程序不同(Different Legal Proceedings)

商标只要不违反《商标法》所禁用的条款，不侵犯他人商标专用权，不经注册就可使用，只是没有专用权(exclusive right)。而企业名称则必须经国家指定的主管机关经过核准登记、注册(approval registration and registered)，才能使用。

---

① 刘春田. 知识产权(第三版)[M]. 北京：高等教育出版社，北京大学出版社，2007：245.

二、商标的特征(The Features of Trademark)

(一)显著性(Distinctiveness)

商标既区别于具有叙述性(descriptive)、公知公用性质的标志，又区别于他人商品或服务的标志，从而便于消费者识别。

A trademark submitted for registration shall bear(具有)noticeable characteristics(显著的特征) and be readily distinguishable(便于识别), and it may not conflict with the legitimate rights obtained by others earlier.

(二)独占性(Exclusiveness)

使用商标的目的是为了区别与他人的商品来源或服务项目，便于消费者识别。所以，注册商标所有人对其商标享有专用权、独占权(exclusive rights)，未经注册商标所有人许可，他人不得擅自使用，否则，即构成侵犯注册商称所有人的商标权，违反我国商标法律的规定。

(三)价值性(Value)

商标代表着商标所有权人生产或经营的质量信誉、企业信誉和形象(reputation, quality and business image)，商标所有人通过商标的创意、设计、申请注册、广告宣传及使用，使商标具有了价值，也增加了商品的附加值。此外，商标可以有偿转让(paid transfer)，也可以经商标所有权人同意，许可(licensing)他人使用。

(四)竞争性(Competitiveness)

生产经营者的竞争就是商品或服务质量与信誉的竞争，其表现形式就是商标知名度(popularity)的竞争，商标知名度越高，其商品或服务的竞争力就越强。

(五)基本特性(Basic Features)

1. 识别性(Recognition)

识别性是商标最基本的功能，商标的特殊性质和特殊作用决定了商标必须具备独特的个性(unique personality)，使大众能够轻易地辨别出不同的商标所对应的商品或服务。

2. 传达性(Conveyance)

商标如同信号一样，只有个性特色越鲜明，视觉表现感染力就越强，刺激的程度才能越深。而且商标不仅仅只是商品的标记，同时还表达一定的含义，如企业的经营理念，产品性能用途等。

3. 适应性(Adaptability)

商标的表现形式必须适应不同材质、不同技术、不同条件的挑战，无论黑白彩色，放大缩小如何变化，都要遵从系统化和标准化的规定。

4. 时代性(Temporal Spirit)

商标必须适应时代的发展，在适当的时候进行合理的调整，以避免被时代所淘汰。

三、商标的作用(The Function of Trademarks)

(一)区别商品或服务的出处(The Origin of Goods or Services)

The trademark performs the role of identifying the goods or services of a particular manufacturer or service provider and gives an indication of its origin, or establishes a connection in the course of trade.

Trademark serves to keep lines of communication clear between sellers and buyers. In a world without trademarks, buying would be more difficult. If a buyer wanted to buy a phone but could not rely on the reputation of the seller, she would have to test the Phone (or car or database software or ...) herself. Consumers deal with far too many products to assess each one individually. Rather, consumers rely on the reputation of sellers: their experience with the seller's product or service, what others have told them about the seller, what *Consumer Reports* has to say, what's been said online or on the playground.

(二)促使生产者或经营者提高商品或服务的质量(Encouraging Producers or Operators to Improve the Quality of Goods or Services)

The seller can establish a brand, which allows her to capture the value from positive associations (created by marketing, consumer experience with the product, etc.). That can allow her to compete, both against others in the market and against potential entrants. A trademark is a very valuable asset. So trademark law provides incentives for sellers to build goodwill.

(三)有利于市场竞争和广告宣传(Conducive to Market Competition and Advertising)

A trademark advertises the product and creates an image in the mind of the ultimate purchaser. 一种商品要打开销路，为广大消费者所认识，除保证质量的可靠性(reliability)外，还必须通过商标这一焦点进行广告宣传，刺激消费者的购买欲望，使消费者以最快捷的途径认识商品。所以从这一角度上讲，商标是开拓市场的先锋。

Today, in contrast to the historical function of the mark, it actually sells the goods. The mark has become the "silent salesman", the conduit through which direct contact between the trademark owner and the consumer is assured.

(四)无形的财产，信誉的载体(Intangible Assets of Reputation)

商标作为一种直接面向消费者的信息，其传播速度会远远快于其他与商品有关的信息。只要商标能以可靠的产品质量为基础，其声名必将远播，其价值也必将不断上升，进而使企业的经济效益越来越好。因此，从这个意义上讲，注册商标是无价之宝，是一种无形的财富。

第二节 商标的分类
Ⅱ The Classification of Trademarks

商标作为商品的标志，附着在商品或商品包装上，以区别同类商品。随着市场经济的发展，商品的品种越来越多，商标的使用也越来越广泛。那么，商标到底有多少种类？如何划分？在学术上，我们也可以从不同的角度，用不同的标准划分商标的种类并进行研究。以商标的识别对象、形态、功能、使用者、知名程度等几个标准可以进行不同的划分和归类。

一、以商标的识别对象为标准分类(Classification Based on Objects)

(一)商品商标(Goods Mark)

A goods mark is a symbol used by a person to identify and distinguish his/her goods from those manufactured or sold by others and to indicate the source of the goods. "Goods" are any type of product. They include typical consumer goods such as so soft drinks (COCA-COLA), food(EDO, Kjeldsens), and toys (LEGO, TONKA).

(二)服务商标(Service Mark)

A trademark identifies a source of goods, and a service mark identifies a source of services, like PICC, KFC, and so on. Indeed, this book often uses "trademark" to refer to both goods mark and service marks.

我国 1982 年的《商标法》没有对服务商标予以规定，1993 年第一次修改的《商标法》增加了对服务商标的保护内容，进一步完善了我国的商标法律制度。根据《商标注册用商品和服务国际分类尼斯协定》(*Nice Agreement Concerning the International Classification of Goods and Services for the Purposes of the Registration of Marks*(简称《尼斯分类)》)的规定，把商品和服务分为 45 大类，其中服务占 11 类，服务商标所使用的对象有：广告销售；金融地产；建筑维修；通信服务；运输旅游；材料处理；教育娱乐；设计开发；餐饮住宿；医疗美容；法律服务。自 2017 年 1 月 1 日起，我国开始启用《尼斯分类(第十一版)》。

(三)商品商标与服务商标的区别(The Difference between Goods Marks and Service Marks)

1. 商标的识别对象不同(Different Identifications)

商品商标是特定商品的识别标志，标示的是有形的(tangible)、看得见的(visible)商品，表明商品的质量与特征；而服务商标表明的是服务项目本身，是区别不同服务项目提供者的专有标记，标示的是为他人提供的劳务活动(service activities)，表明服务的质量和特征。

2. 使用的领域不同(Different Use Areas)

商品商标可适用于所有商品领域，凡生产、加工、拣选、销售(production, processing, selection, sales)商品的行业均可使用商品商标；但是服务商标的适用领域则受到一定的限制，只能适用于服务行业(service industry)。

3. 使用的方式不同(Different Using Methods)

商品商标除广告宣传(advertising)外，还可直接附着(directly attached)在商品上，随着商品的出售达到宣传的目的；而服务商标只能通过服务项目的提供者所进行的服务行为来显示，通过广告宣传或其他方式来使用。

4. 使用的宣传效果不同(Different Effect of Publicity)

商品商标可以随着商品的出售和使用而广为传播，使消费者易于识别、认购(identification, subscription)；而服务是无形的，不像商品那样可以流通，服务商标表明服务出处和保证服务质量的作用不如商品商标之于商品那么强烈。这就决定了服务商标在某种程度上主要是依赖于广告宣传来扩大商标的知名度(popularity)。

二、以商标构成要素为标准的分类(Classification Based on the Constitutional Elements of the Trademark)

(一)文字商标(Character Trademark)

文字商标(character trademark),是指纯粹使用文字构成的商标。包括中文(汉字或拼音)商标、外文商标和数字商标。在商标的“家族”中,文字商标的使用率是最高的。它的优点是直观(intuitive)、易记(easy to remember)又便于宣传(facilitate to promotion),所以文字商标成为许多企业设计商标的首选。在文字商标设计时,应注意以下几点:

1. 中文商标(Trademark in Chinese)

中文商标中的文字,包括汉字、汉语拼音和少数民族的文字。除法律明确规定不得使用的文字外,企业可以自由选择文字作为商标,包括企业名称(company name)或其缩写、具有含义的字和词甚至包括不具有特定含义而杜撰的。但是少数民族的文字在申请注册商标时,应附加说明是何种文字及相应的含义,否则,均按相近似的中文含义解释或作无含义解释。此外,文字的字体,可以是印刷体、书写体或美术体等,当文字字体以某种图案形式变形表达时,这种商标就已脱离了文字商标的本来面目而成为图形商标(device trademark)。

2. 字母商标(Trademark in Letter)

字母(letter)是指用拼音文字或注音符号的最小书写单位,包括拼音文字(alphabetic writing)、外文字母(foreign letters)如英文字母、拉丁字母等所构成的商标。一般来说,由于单个的字母或者数字缺乏显著性,所以在世界上大多数采取审查制度的国家都是不能注册的,因此,必须有两个以上的字母或数字才可以用做文字商标。字母商标虽然简洁易记(simple and easy to remember),但是缺乏表意性(expressive)。我国原《商标法》未明确规定对字母商标的保护,但是由于实践中存在一定数量的字母商标,因此,我国在第二次修改《商标法》的时候,增加了对字母商标保护的规定。

3. 数字商标(Trademark in Number)

数字商标,是指由用阿拉伯数字(Arabic numbers)、罗马数字(roman numerals)或者是中文大写数字(Chinese capital number)所构成的商标。数字商标虽然简单、特别,但是容易与商品或服务的型号混淆(confusion),所以数字商标的注册长期受到限制。但在实践中,也有个别数字由于长期使用,获得了较高的显著性和知名度,最后被接受注册,如著名的4711香水。我国原《商标法》并未明确规定对数字商标的保护,但为了对实践中存在的少数数字商标进行保护,我国第二次修改的《商标法》增加了对数字商标的保护内容。

(二)图形商标(Device Trademark)

图形商标,是指由不含任何文字,只由图形构成的商标。对于“图形”的含义,我们可以作广义理解,即把那些有线条或者色块构成的图案都称为图形。①这类商标的优点是直观(intuitive)、艺术性(artistic)强,并富有感染力(appeal),而且不受语言的限制,不论哪国人讲何种语言,一般都可以看懂,可以给人留下较深的印象。但是,一些比较抽象的

① 郭禾.知识产权法(第二版)[M].北京:中国人民大学出版社,2005:209.

图形商标，因没有具体的称谓，有碍人们的口头交流，不便于广告宣传，所以单独使用图形商标者日渐减少。

(三)组合商标(Associated Trademark)

组合商标，即是由上述各种要素组合而成的商标。这种商标图文并茂，其设计一般以图形为主，文字为辅；既表形，又表意。在我国及国际上，组合商标的使用最为普遍。

(四)声音商标(Sound Trademark)

声音商标，与其他可以作为商标的要素(文字、数字、图形、颜色等)一样，具备能够将某一产品或服务与其他企业的产品或服务区别开来的基本功能，便于消费者识别。

声音商标在市场营销领域应用得比较早，但是由于声音商标有别于传统意义上的商标，具有不可视的特点，在大部分国家并不被作为商标看待。Article 15 of TRIPS provides that：Any sign，or any combination of signs，capable of distinguishing the goods or services of one undertaking from those of other undertakings，shall be capable of constituting a trademark.

可见，此规定为各成员国注册不可视标志提供了依据。我国在《商标法》第三次修正前也不支持声音商标注册，2013 年通过并于 2014 年 5 月 1 日施行的新《商标法》增加了可以注册的商标要素，规定声音可以作为商标注册。“中国国际广播电台广播节目开始曲”成为第一个在中国获得授权的声音商标。

(五)气味商标(Smell Trademark)

气味商标就是以某种特殊气味作为区别不同商品和不同服务项目的商标。如在美国销售的一种散发着“夹竹桃花香味”的绣花线和纱线，这种香味便是这种绣花线和纱线使用的注册商标。目前对这种特殊形态商标提供注册保护的国家为数极少，但是这类商标的出现也是经济发展和科技进步的必然产物，对这一特殊形态商标实施保护的国家也会越来越多。

三、以其功能为标准的分类(Classification Based on the Functions)

(一)联合商标(Joint Trademark)

联合商标，是指同一个商标所有人(trademark owner)在相同或类似商品上使用的若干个近似商标(similar mark)。在这些近似的商标中，首先注册或主要使用的商标为正商标，其余商标为该商标的联合商标。例如，某一企业的正商标为“娃哈哈”，又以“娃娃哈”、“娃哈娃”、“哈哈娃”注册了联合商标。注册联合商标的目的是为了保护主商标，防止他人使用和注册商标近似商标，防止消费者误认。我国《商标法》未规定联合商标，但是允许同一个申请人注册两个以上相近的商标，其中任一商标的使用视为其他商标也在使用。联合商标作为一整体，不得分开转让，必须全部一同转让或许可他人使用。

(二)防御商标(Defensive Trademark)

防御商标，是指同一商标所有人(trademark owner)在不同类别的商品上注册使用同一个驰名商标(well-known mark)。最先创设的商标为正商标，后在不同类别商品上使用的统一商标为防御商标。我国《商标法》对防御商标没有规定，但允许企业就同一商标在不同类别里注册。如海尔，不仅在空调、冰箱等产品上，还在其他商标和服务类别上注册了同一商标。注册防御商标，目的在于保护驰名商标的信誉，因为如果他人在非类似商品上使用该商标，也会造成消费者的误认和原商标所有人利益的损害。

（三）证明商标（Certification Trademark）

证明商标，又称保证商标（guarantee trademark），是指由对某种商品或者服务具有监督能力的组织所控制，而由该组织以外的单位或者个人使用，用以证明该商品或者服务的原产地、原料、制造方法、质量或者其他特定品质的标志。证明商标的内容恰恰是一般商标所不允许包含的内容，即不符合一般商标的构成要件，因而其商标注册人（trademark holders）一般是具有商品质量检验能力的商会或其他组织机构，而不是该商标的实际使用人。A certification mark is not used by the owner of the mark. Rather, persons other than the owner use the mark to certify to potential purchasers that their goods or services meet the standards set by the mark's owner.

A certification mark allows the potential purchaser to rely on a third party which is the owner of the certification mark, for information about a seller's goods or services. A certification mark could certify the regional origin of goods, the materials (such as the grade of wool), the mode of manufacture, or other characteristics of the goods or services. Certification marks are used in diverse ways, such as certifying compliance with environmental protection, with religious rules governing food preparation（绿色食品）, and with professional qualification standards.

Because consumers rely on the owner's approval of the mark's use, the owner of the mark shall fulfill certain requirements to obtain the certification mark.

使用证明商标，须经商标所有人许可。凡符合证明商标使用管理规则条件的，在履行注册人所规定的手续后，可以使用该注册商标，注册人不得拒绝其使用。证明商标的功用在于提供质量证明，打开商品销路，使商品对消费者产生吸引力。目前，国际上流行的纯羊毛标志、欧共体采用的"担保商标"等，都是一种证明商标。

（四）等级商标（Grade Trademark）

等级商标，是指在商品质量、规格、等级不同的一种商品上使用的同一商标或者不同的商标。这种商标的使用往往同公司的司标或厂标配套使用。司标或厂标为主商标，表示商品的生产厂家，等级商标为副商标，表示商品的档次。如在丰田主商标下，不同等级的汽车分别使用了"皇冠"、"锐志"、"凯美瑞"、"花冠"、"威驰"、"雅力士"，等等。但是，到目前为止，只有极少数国家的商标法对该种商标作了明文规定，我国商标法中也没有这一方面的规定。

四、以使用者为标准的分类（Classification Based on Users）

（一）制造商标（Manufacture Trademark）

制造商标，亦称生产商标，是指商品制造者（producers）所使用的商标。例如，南京熊猫电子集团公司在生产的收录机上使用的"熊猫"商标；重庆啤酒集团股份公司在自己生产的啤酒上使用的"山城"商标。制造商标的功用，不仅在于区别不同的生产厂家，而且能在销售经营中突出表示制造者。若生产厂商在自己生产出来的商品上不使用自己的制造商标，而让销售商仅使用自己的销售商标（business trademark），就可能使消费者认为此种商品是销售者自己生产出来的，从而只知道此种商品的销售商，而不知道商品的生产厂家，这样就会使销售商独得其利。因此，制造厂商在自己生产的商品上，使用自己的制造商标，则完全可以避免销售商对自己经济利益的损害。

(二)销售商标(Business Trademark)

销售商标，又称商业商标，是指销售者在自己经销的商品上使用的商标。例如，贸易公司、百货公司等商业企业在其销售的商品上所使用的标志。使用销售商标的目的在于宣传商业企业的经营，使其销售的商品与其他经销商销售的同类商品展开商业竞争。

(三)集体商标(Collective Trademark)

Collective mark refers to a trademark or service mark used by the members of a group or organization. For collective marks, the requirement that the mark be associated with specific goods or services is somewhat relaxed. The term includes marks indicating membership in a union, an association, or other organization. The mark maybe used to distinguish the goods and services of members of the group from nonmembers.

另外，我国《商标法实施条例》规定，以地理标志(geographic mark)作为证明商标注册的，其商品符合使用该地理标志条件的自然人、法人或者其他组织可以要求使用该证明商标，控制该证明商标的组织应当允许。

集体商标虽然也表示商品来源，但它并不是标示某一特定厂家，而是代表由若干企业组成的集体组织。一般来说，集体商标不允许转让，使用该商标的意义在于表明若干企业所生产的同一商品具有相同的质量和规格。

五、以知名度为标准的分类(Classification Based on the Popularity)

(一)驰名商标(Well-known Trademark)

A "well-known trademark" is a trademark that is "widely known to the pertinent public and enjoys a relatively high reputation." 驰名商标与非驰名商标的界定，不是以注册与否为准，而是商标在市场上的公信力（credibility）和相关公众的熟知度（familiarity），也即注册的商标未必都是驰名商标，驰名商标未必都经注册。对未注册的驰名商标可以按"使用原则"予以保护。①

(二)普通商标(Ordinary Trademark)

普通商标，也称非驰名商标。任何驰名商标在它"驰名"之前，都属于普通商标，不享受特殊保护。在商场上，绝大部分的商标都属于普通商标。

(三)普通商标与驰名商标的区别(The Difference between Common Trademark and Well-known Trademark)

1. 认定条件不同(Different Conditions on the Designation)

普通商标只要经过商标局核准注册，就受国家法律的保护；而驰名商标的认定，则需

① 刘春田．知识产权法(第三版)[M]．北京：高等教育出版社，北京大学出版社，2007：318.

考虑下列因素：(1)相关公众对该商标的知晓程度；(2)该商标使用的持续时间；(3)该商标的任何宣传工作的持续时间、程度和地理范围；(4)该商标作为驰名商标受保护的记录；(5)该商标驰名的其他因素。

2. 保护范围不同(Different Scope of Protection)

普通商标的保护范围，限定在与注册商标所核定使用商品相同或类似的商品上使用的与注册商标相同或近似的商标。① 但为了更有效地保护驰名商标，法律扩大了对驰名商标的保护范围。不仅在相同或类似的商品上禁止他人使用与驰名商标相同或近似的商标，而且在不同类别的商品上，也不允许使用。

The Special Protection for Well-known Trademarks lies in：

The owner of a well-known but not yet registered trademark may prevent others from registering trademarks that are the same as, or similar to, the well-known trademark in identical or similar categories of goods or services；

The owner of a well-known registered trademark may prevent others from registering trademarks that are the same as, or similar to, the well-known trademark in all categories of goods or services；

The owner of a well-known registered trademark may prevent others from incorporating the well-known trademark in the name of their enterprises；

The owner of a well-known registered trademark is not restricted by the five-year time limit for bringing cancellation actions against trademarks registered in bad faith, while such five-year time limit applies to ordinary trademarks；and

In infringement cases, courts or administrative bodies tend to grant larger awards to owners of well-known trademarks, and subject infringers to more severe punishment.

第三节 商标制度的产生与发展
Ⅲ The Origin and Development of Trademark System

一、商标制度的产生(Emergence of the Trademark System)

(一)商标制度在中国的产生(Origin of Trademark in China)

中国商标制度的产生过程，可以大致划分为4个阶段：早期的萌芽阶段；被动接纳阶段；计划经济体制下的社会主义商标制度；中国商标制度走向成熟阶段。

1904年6月，清政府在西方列强的影响下，颁布了《商标注册试办章程》。该章程是我国历史上第一部成文的商标法。该章程中参考了西方国家商标法中的一些做法。

进入民国时期，当时的北洋政府于1923年5月4日颁布了《商标法》及《商标法施行细则》并真正付诸实施。在之后的10余年里，民国政府又对该法进行了3次修改。在这段

① 刘春田．知识产权法(第三版)[M]．北京：高等教育出版社，北京大学出版社，2007：318.

时期里，中国尽管有了自己的《商标法》，但它是被迫产生的，保护的主体主要是外国人，具有强烈的半殖民地、半封建的色彩。

1949 年中华人民共和国成立，废除了民国政府时期的所有有关商标的法律。1950 年颁布了《商标注册暂行条例》及《商标注册暂行条例施行细则》。1954 年，又颁布了补充性的《未注册商标暂行管理办法》。然而，随着社会主义经济的进一步发展，国家出现了各种极左的思潮，具体体现在商标制度上，便是 1963 年国家颁布的《商标管理条例》。该条例的明显特征是，将重心转移到监督企业商品质量上。全国的所有商标不再采取自愿注册(voluntary registration)，而是必须全面强制性注册(comprehensive mandatory registration)，以便加强对企业产品的管理。到了“文革”时期，中国的商标制度基本上是名存实亡。

改革开放带来中国商标制度全新时代。当国门第一次打开时，我们意识到自己在不知不觉中已被世界甩在了后面。中国的最高决策层决定再建并完善知识产权制度。在 1979 年颁布的《中华人民共和国刑法》中，第一次对假冒注册商标(counterfeiting registered trademarks)犯罪以及保护商标专用权(exclusive right)作出了明确规定。

In China, the *Trademark Law* was enacted in 1983; the "principle of registration", "first-to file rule" and "principle of examination by examiner" were formally established. China is the member of *Paris Convention*, *Nice Agreement*, *TRIPS Agreement*, *Trademark Law Treaty*, and *Madrid Protocol*. The Chinese trademark Law has amended for two times and rived once, the revision of 2001 of trademark law has great change and refers to the many provisions. Concerning to the law system, the judicial examination system is adopted in the administrative procedure of conferring trademark rights.

《商标法》施行至今，国内的企业对知识产权(Intellectual Property)的认识也有了极大的提高。人们开始认识到商标对于企业的重要性，开始纷纷创建自己的品牌。为了适应我国经济发展的需要，并在一些做法上符合我国加入的国际公约(international convention)的相关规定，我国已对《商标法》进行过两次重大修改。1993 年，第七届全国人大常委会第 30 次会议对《商标法》作出 9 条修订，其中最重要的修订是增加服务商标的注册与保护(the registration and protection of service trademark)，这也对我国在这之后 10 余年的服务业发展，起到了极为重要的影响。2001 年，为了适应加入 WTO 的需要，第九届全国人大常委会第 24 次会议审议通过了对《商标法》的又一次重大修改。随着我国市场经济体系的不断完善和全球经济一体化发展的趋势，为了进一步贯彻落实《国家知识产权战略纲要》的要求，充分发挥商标制度作用，2003 年国家工商行政管理总局启动了《商标法》第三次修改工作，并于 2013 年 8 月 30 日第十二届全国人大常委会第四次会议表决通过了《全国人民代表大会常务委员会关于修改〈中华人民共和国商标法〉的决定》，该决定自 2014 年 5 月 1 日起施行。2014 年 4 月 29 日国务院令第 651 号修订《商标法实施条例》并与修改后的《商标法》同日施行。《商标法》的修改内容主要包括：

1. 完善商标注册、审查、续展制度，便利商标权利人

一是扩大可以申请注册商标的标志范围，将声音商标纳入到商标可申请的范围。二是完善注册商标显著性的规定。三是优化注册商标申请、审查程序制度，允许跨类申请和电

子申请，恢复审查意见书制度，明确注册商标申请、复审的审查时限，提高商标注册的效率。四是扩展办理注册商标续展的时间，允许商标期满前 12 个月即可进行续展。

2. 简化商标异议程序，维护商标权利的稳定

一是限定提出异议的主体和理由，并将异议理由分为“绝对理由”和“相对理由”两大类。二是简化程序，以解决商标异议程序冗长而使得商标权长时间内难以确定的问题。

3. 制止恶意注册商标，保护商标在先使用者

一是增加了诚实信用原则的有关内容，明确界定并禁止了商标抢注行为，为打击恶意抢注，维护公平竞争的市场秩序提供了法律依据。二是完善驰名商标保护制度，厘清了驰名商标的保护制度，引导驰名商标回归其立法本意。驰名商标不是荣誉称号，而是一个法律概念，驰名商标认定是对驰名商标扩大商标保护范围而设立的特别保护制度，因而不允许把驰名商标作为一种广告宣传的手段。三是禁止抢注商业合作伙伴在先使用的商标。四是赋予商标在先使用者先用抗辩权，强化商标代理机构的诚信义务。

4. 加强注册商标专用权保护

一是增加了商标侵权行为的种类，规定了对商标侵权行为的法定从重处罚情节，并根据涉案金额进一步规范了工商行政管理部门行政处罚的标准。二是引入了惩罚性赔偿规定，将法定赔偿额上限从 50 万元提高到 300 万元，加强了惩罚性赔偿规定，将法定赔偿额从 50 万元提高到 300 万元，加大侵权人的违法成本。三是减轻商标权利人举证责任，有效防止因权利人“举证难”导致损害赔偿数额偏低的现象。

至此，我国也已参加了几乎世界上所有重要的国际条约和公约。我国通过立法以及行政执法和司法执法(legislation, administrative enforcement, judicial enforcement)，已经建立了一套既符合中国国情又与国际接轨的商标制度。

(二)商标制度在外国的产生(Origin of Trademark System Overseas)

1. 美国的商标制度(Trademark System in United States)

Congress enacted the first federal trademark statute in 1870, providing a system of federal registration for all trademarks used within the United States, regardless of whether they were used in interstate commerce. In 1879, however, the U. S. Supreme Court held the law unconstitutional due to a conflict with the provision on patents in the U. S. Constitution. It was therefore abolished. In its place, a trademark law was enacted on March 3, 1881 that targeted trademarks used in interstate commerce (and in the commerce with Indian tribes) based on the interstate commerce clause in the U. S. Constitution (art. 1, sec. 8, and cl. 3). This law, however, was unable to accommodate the development of the American economy and underwent a major amendment in 1905. It underwent further partial revisions occasionally later. Finally, Congress undertook a major overhaul of federal trademark law in the *Lanham Trademark Act*(《兰哈姆法》) of 1946.

值得我们注意的是：美国长期不加入《马德里协定》。究其原因，一是因为该协定有一些不利于美国利益的条款，二是因为《马德里协定》有 18 个月的审查时限(review time limit)要求，美国当时还达不到这样的审查速度。直到 2003 年，美国才加入了《马德里议

定书》，而始终未加入《马德里协定》。

2. 欧盟的商标制度(The Trademark System in European Union)

为了加快建立欧洲内部市场，扫清商品自由流通的障碍，欧盟于 1988 年制定了协调各成员国商标立法的一号指令《缩小成员国商标法差别的指令》，力促各成员国的商标法趋于一致。该指令要求各成员国最迟于 1992 年年底前，按设定的目标修改国内法律、条例和行政规章，使之与该指令相符，并付诸实施。尽管一些成员国未能按时完成修改任务，但最终都相继按指令的要求对商标法规、政策进行了大刀阔斧的修订。终于，欧盟于 1994 年开始实施《欧共体商标条例》，同时组建了位于西班牙的内部市场协调局，来管理商标注册工作。2004 年欧盟又以国际组织的身份加入了《马德里议定书》，实现了与国际商标注册体系的全面对接。

3. 日本的商标制度(The Trademark System in Japan)

The first Japanese trademark law was enacted in the form of trademark regulations in 1884, and consisted of 24 articles and additional rules. It was simple, but contained all the fundamental systems that shaped modern Japanese trademark law.

日本现行《商标法》制定于 1959 年，至今已修改 6 次，且修改频率越来越快。而且不断修改和完善以《商标法》为核心的商标法规政策体系，有力地配合了其“技术立国”、“科技立国”、“知识产权立国”战略的实施。

与美国一样，日本长期不加入马德里体系，也是因为《马德里协定》的一些条款不利于日本国家利益，而且一时达不到《马德里协定》规定的 18 个月审查时限要求。条件成熟后，日本于 2000 年加入了《马德里议定书》。

为实施知识产权战略，加强知识产权管理和保护，日本于 2003 年 3 月成立了知识产权本部。这是个联系各部门的高层机构，设在内阁，负责统一制定并实施有关知识产权创造、保护及应用的政策和规划，协调相关部门的工作，下设推进事务局。为了加强海外知识产权保护，日本政府于 2004 年在 196 个驻外使馆设立了知识产权对策官员，负责支援知识产权保护工作。

二、商标制度的发展(Development of the Trademark System)

(一)商标制度要顺应国情变化而变化(Trademark System Should Adapt to National Conditions)

美国和日本由于一些条款对国家利益不利而长期不加入《马德里协定》，解决自身问题和提高管理水平后，它们分别于 2003 年、2000 年加入了《马德里议定书》，而始终未加入《马德里协定》。应该说，他们加入马德里体系也是出于国家利益(country interests)考虑，如果不加入，该国商标权人要在国外获得保护，就需要在这些国家逐个使用该国的语言和货币，分别递交申请，其麻烦是显而易见的，对该国企业争夺国际市场非常不利。

商标制度要适应当时的经济社会发展状况，只有顺应国情的变化，才能真正促进经济的健康发展。

(二)根据实践活动及时调整商标管理工作(Adjusting the Management of Trademarks According to the Practice Timely)

创造商标和使用商标的活跃程度与市场活动紧密相关，从而对商标管理工作提出不同的要求。商标管理工作应随着工作情况变动而及时调整。

(三)根据不同地区和行业，适度调整各项措施(Adjusting Every Measures According to the Different Regions and Industries)

在统一的法规、政策框架下，允许发达地区和优势行业采取更严格的商标管理和保护措施。我国是一个幅员辽阔的国家，地区间和行业间商标发展水平差距较大，在国家统一的法规、政策框架下，应允许一些发达地区和优势行业根据实际需要先走一步，采取更加严格的商标管理和保护措施。

(四)加强保护力度，严厉打击侵权假冒行为(Strengthening the Protection of Trademark, Cracking down on Infringement and Counterfeiting Severely)

法律应规定完善的保护措施，如被侵权者不仅可以收回诉讼费用和实际损失的补偿，还可以得到被告人从侵权活动中获得的利润。同时，严厉打击侵权行为，依法取缔造假商家。

【英语词汇】

Associated trademark　组合商标
cancellation　*n.* 撤销
character trademark　文字商标
credibility　*n.* 公信力
distinctiveness　*n.* 显著性
grade trademark　等级商标
popularity　*n.* 知名度
service mark　服务商标
trade decoration　商标装潢
trade name　商品名称
voluntary registration　自愿注册
business trademark　销售商标
certification trademark　证明商标
collective trademark　集体商标
defensive trademark　防御商标
general name　通用名称
joint trademark　联合商标
restrict　*v.* 约束，限制
specific name　特定名称
trademark holder　商标权人
uniqueness　*n.* 独特性
well-known mark　驰名商标

【英语句型】

1. A trademark, trade mark, or trade-mark is a distinctive sign or indicator used by an individual, business organization, or other legal entity to identify that the products or services to consumers with which the trademark appears originate from a unique source, and to distinguish its products or services from those of other entities.

"distinguish...from..."是指"区别，不同于"。

译文：商标是自然人、企业或其他法律组织用于区分自己的产品和服务与其他外形相似产品的一个特殊标志或指示物。

2. The principle of territoriality means that the protection of a trademark in a certain country depends exclusively on the law of that country.

“depends on”是指“取决于，随……而定”。

译文：属地原则是指一个商标在某国的保护完全取决于该国的法律。

【阅读资料】

第十三章　商标注册与商标管理

Chapter 13　Trademark Registration and Administration

【引言】与著作权(copyright)不同，商标权(trademark right)的取得并不是自动产生的。商标权的取得可以经过两种途径，一是使用取得(through use)，二是注册取得(through registration)。而我国与世界上大多数国家的商标法一样，采取注册获得商标权的方式。中国《商标法》及《商标法实施细则》和其他关于商标的行政法规，规定了详细的商标注册申请、核准及管理的条件与程序。

【学习目的与要求】商标注册申请、核准及管理的问题不仅仅是程序性(procedural)的问题，而且也涉及很多实体性(substantive)的规定。以商标注册与管理的程序为线索，注意重点掌握商标注册需要满足的条件，关注社会现实中商标注册与管理出现的种种现象。

第一节　商标注册的原则

Ⅰ　Principles of Trademark Registration

一、申请在先的原则(Prior Application Rule)

(一)申请在先原则的含义(Meaning of Prior Application Rule)

Prior application rule means that if two or more applicants apply to register identical(相同的) or similar trademarks for use on the same kind of goods or similar goods, the trademark office shall first conduct examination of, give approval to and announce(审查、核准并公告) the trademark whose registration is applied for earlier than the rest.

(二)申请日的确定(The Date of Application)

The filing date of an application for trademark registration shall be the date on which the application documents are received by the Trademark Office.

当事人向商标局提交申请文件，直接递交的，以递交日为准；邮寄的，以寄出的邮戳日为准；邮戳日不清晰或者没有邮戳的，以商标局实际收到日为准，但是当事人能够提出实际邮戳日证据的除外。通过邮政企业以外的快递企业递交的，以快递企业收寄日为准；收寄日不明确的，以商标局实际收到日为准，但是当事人能够提出实际收寄日证据的除外。以数据电文方式提交的，以进入商标局或者商标评审委员会电子系统的日期为准。

Where the application formalities for trademark registration are completed, the application documents are filled in as required, and the fees are paid, the Trademark Office shall accept the application and notify the applicant in writing; where the application formalities are not completed, the application documents are not filled in as required or the fees are not paid, the Trademark Office shall not accept the application and shall notify the applicant in writing and give the reasons. Where the application formalities are basically completed or the application documents are basically in compliance with the provisions, but supplements or amendments are necessary, the Trademark Office shall notify the applicant of the supplements or amendments to be made, requiring him to make supplements or amendments to the specified items and send them back to the Trademark Office within 30 days from the date of receipt of the notification. Where the supplements or amendments are made and sent back to the Trademark Office within the specified time limit, the filing date shall be reserved(保留). Where no supplements or amendments are made at the expiration of the specified time limit, or the supplements or amendments are not made as required, the Trademark Office shall not accept such application and shall notify the applicant in writing.

(三)申请在先原则的运用(Application of Prior Application Rule)

In the light of first-to-file principle, proprietary rights in relation to a trademark may be established through registration of the mark, regardless whether the trademark is actually used in business. Even if someone uses the trademark without registration beforehand, other people may be granted for the trademark right through application for the identical or similar mark, thereby the prior user is excluded from using the trademark.

意识到申请在先原则的客观存在，对市场经济中竞争激烈的各门商家而言是至关重要的，商家应当注意及时或尽早注册商标。① 当然，申请在先原则并不是绝对的。这主要体现在两个方面。

一方面是对同一天商标申请的处理。《商标法》规定，两个或者两个以上的商标注册申请人，在同一种商品或者类似商品上，以相同或者近似的商标申请注册的，初步审定并公告申请在先的商标；同一天申请的，初步审定并公告使用在先的商标，驳回其他人的申请，不予公告。

This article indicates that in China trademark rights can be established through either use or register, or both, and the first-to-file principle plays the leading role while the first-to-use acts as a supplementary one.

Where two or more applicants apply respectively on the same day for the registration of an identical or similar trademark in respect of the same or similar goods, both or all of the applicants shall, within 30 days from the date of receipt of the notification of the Trademark Office, submit evidence of prior use of such trademark before the application is filed. Where the use of the trademark was on the same day or no one has put it into use, both or all of the applicants may, within 30 days from the date of receipt of the notification of the Trademark Office, negotiate on their own and submit a written agreement to the Trademark Office; where the applicants are reluctant to negotiate or fail to reach an agreement through negotiation, the Trademark Office shall

---

① 吴汉东．知识产权法[M]．北京：北京大学出版社，2009：283.

notify both or all of the applicants that there will be a lot drawing to determine one of them as the applicant, and the applications filed by others shall be refused. Where any applicant notified by the Trademark Office fails to participate in the lot drawing, the application filed by such applicant shall be considered abandoned, and the Trademark Office shall notify in writing the applicant who fails to participate in the lot drawing.

另一方面，我国商标法在坚持申请在先原则的同时，还强调使用在先的正当性(legitimacy)，防止不正当的商标抢注行为(preemptively register)。

No applicant for trademark application may infringe upon another person's existing prior rights(在先权利), nor may he, by illegitimate means(不正当手段), rush to register(抢注) a trademark that is already in use by another person and has certain influence. 该条强调商标的申请在先必须符合诚实信用原则(the principle of good faith)。一是对他人现有的在先权利(prior rights)的保护。这里他人现有的在先权利与下节提到的商标注册的非冲突性是一致的，主要指商标申请注册不得损害他人的著作权(copyright)、肖像权(portraiture right)等。二是对他人使用在先并具有一定影响力的未注册商标予以保护。这也是我们常说的制止商标"抢注"行为。①

Hereon, the owner of an unregistered trademark shall prove that the trademark has been used and of certain reputation. Meanwhile he shall prove that other people register the trademark with subjective malice(主观恶意) and through improper means. Regarding to the end and effect of preemptive registration, the trademark preemptively registered has established certain reputation as a result of the manpower and resources the prior user put into business operations. It is unfair to the prior user and a violation of the principle of good faith that someone is granted for the proprietary rights of the trademark through first to file, which is abusing the business performance of other people. Hence it is necessary to restrain(约束) preemptive registration.

二、自愿注册原则(Principle of Voluntary Registration)

(一)自愿注册原则的含义(Meaning of Principle of Voluntary Registration)

自愿注册原则，是指商标使用人是否申请商标注册取决于其自己的意愿的原则。商标作为私权，因而是否取得权利应当充分体现意思自治的精神。

In accordance with this principle, the trademark registrant has exclusive rights on a registered trademark, which shall be protected by law. Unregistered trademark is allowed to use in commercial activities, but the user has no exclusive rights and has no right to ban other people from using a trademark that is identical with or similar to the trademark.

(二)我国关于商标注册原则的变化(Development of Voluntary Registration in China)

As for the subject of adopting the voluntary registration in trademarks, legislations in China are inconsistent in different historically.

1950 年颁布的《商标注册暂时条例》采用的是自愿注册原则。而到了 1963 年的《商标

① 郑成思. 知识产权论(第三版)[M]. 北京：法律出版社，2003：307.

管理条例》，则改为采用“全面注册”的原则，即所有的商标都必须先注册才能使用。这与当时的计划经济体制(the planned economy system)以及通过商标管理商品质量的思路是相适应的。改革开放以后，为顺应国际商标保护的趋势，又恢复了自愿注册的原则，这反映在1983年开始实施的《商标法》中。在实行自愿注册原则的同时，我国规定了在极少数商品上使用的商标实行强制注册原则，作为对自愿注册原则的补充。①

Where registered trademark is required to be used for some goods by laws or administrative regulations, an application for trademark registration shall be made. No such goods may be marketed without an approved and registered trademark.

在一开始，必须使用注册商标的商品是人用药品(medicines for human beings)与烟草制品(tobacco product)。目前必须使用注册商标的商品只有烟草制品，包括卷烟、雪茄烟和有包装的烟丝。使用未注册商标的烟草制品，禁止生产和销售。

(三)自愿注册原则的运用(Application of Principle of Voluntary Registration)

采用商标自愿注册原则，并不排除通过使用获得商标权，这就是未注册商标的保护。这就提供给商家根据其自己具体的经营情况进行选择的机会。

As for those trademarks to be used for a long run, one may acquire the trademark rights through registration and benefit from the protection by law. For those used only in goods on trial sale, he may use them in commercial activities without registration, which will be protected by laws like *Unfair Competition Law*, or be specifically protected by the *Trademark Law* after becoming well-known.

而从权利人的角度，获得注册的商标，不仅在全国范围内有通告的作用，而且在遇到侵权纠纷时也易于举证，这是未注册商标所不具有的好处。②

三、优先权原则(Principle of Priority Right)

(一)优先权原则的含义(Meaning of Principle of Priority Right)

优先权原则，是《保护工业产权巴黎公约》(*Paris Convention for the Protection of Industrial Property*)所规定的商标申请的基本原则之一，是指任何人或其权利继承人(successor in title)，在《巴黎公约》的某一成员国首次提出某项商标注册申请或使用相关商标的商品首先是在国际性展览会上展出，从该申请日算起的6个月内，再向其他巴黎公约的成员国提出这项商品商标注册申请，其在后申请可视同最先提出申请的日期提出的原则。该商标注册申请人享有的这种优先于其他商标申请人的权利被称为商标申请的优先权(the priority right)。

The Convention priority right is probably the most widely known priority right, which is defined by its Article 4 A. (1) of the Paris Convention for the Protection of Industrial Property of 1883: “Any person who has duly filed an application for a patent, or for the registration of a utility model, or of an industrial design, or of a trademark, in one of the countries of the Union,

① 李明德. 知识产权法[M]. 北京：社会科学文献出版社，2007：333.

② 郑成思. 知识产权论(第三版)[M]. 北京：法律出版社，2003：307.

or his successor in title, shall enjoy, for the purpose of filing in the other countries, a right of priority during the periods hereinafter fixed." Article 4 B. of the Paris Convention describes the effects of the priority right: "Consequently, any subsequent filing in any of the other countries of the Union before the expiration of the periods referred to above shall not be invalidated by reason of any acts accomplished in the interval, in particular, another filing, the publication or exploitation of the invention, the putting on sale of copies of the design, or the use of the mark, and such acts cannot give rise to any third-party right or any right of personal possession."①

The right of priority offers great practical advantages to the applicant desiring protection in several countries. The applicant is not required to present all applications in several countries at the same time, because he has six months to decide in which countries to request protection.

(二)优先权的产生(Sources of Priority Right)

There are two kinds of priority in trademark application.

One is that the priority arise from the initial application(首次申请). According to article 25 of *Trademark Law*, if an applicant, within six months from the date he applies for registration of his trademark for the first time in a foreign country, again applies in China for registration of one and the same trademark for the same kind of goods, he may, in accordance with any agreement concluded between the foreign country concerned and the People's Republic of China or any international treaty to which both countries are parties, or on the basis of the priority principle mutually accepted, enjoy priority.

The other is that the priority arise from the initial exhibition(首次展出). Article 26 of *Trademark Law* provides: the applicant for registration of a trademark that is used for the first time on goods displayed at an international exhibition organized or recognized by the Chinese Government may, within six months from the date the said(上述的) goods are placed on exhibition, enjoy priority.

(三)优先权申请(Application of Priority)

无论是因首次申请还是因首次展览而产生的优先权，都不是自动产生的。

Relevant applicant shall make a writing statement filing the application for the trademark registration, and submit, within three months, a copy of the application documents he first filed for the registration of the trademark or the name of the exhibition, evidence supporting the use of the trademark on the goods displayed, documents proving the date the exhibition, etc.; if the applicant fails to make the claim in writing or submit the copy of the documents within the time limit, the claim shall be deemed not to have been made for the right of priority.

具体而言，主张首次申请而产生优先权的，须提交第一次提出的商标注册申请文件的副本。该副本应当经受理该申请的商标主管机关证明，并注明申请日期和申请号；主张首次展览而产生优先权的，须提交展出其商品的展览会名称、在展出商品上使用该商标的证据、展出日期等证明文件。这些文件应当经国务院工商行政管理部门规定的机构认证，但

① Article 4 of *Paris Convention for the Protection of Industrial Property*.

展出其商品的国际展览会是在中国境内举办的除外。

(四)诚实信用原则(The Principle of Good Faith)

In order to reduce the phenomenon of malicious registration of trademarks, the third revision of the *Trademark Law* of China has increased one provision that "the principle of good faith shall be upheld in the application for trademark registration and in the use of trademarks".

诚实信用原则要求自然人、法人和其他组织在申请商标注册和使用商标的过程中，必须意图诚实、守信，行使权利时不得侵害社会的利益。把诚实信用原则作为商标注册和使用具体条款的基础，具有弥补具体条款漏洞的功能。此外，在 2013 年《商标法》的修改中，专门增加了代理机构的规定，要求代理机构应当遵循诚实信用原则，以保护委托人的合法权益，规范商标代理机构的行为。

Trademark agencies shall uphold the principle of good faith, comply with laws and administrative regulations, apply for trademark registration or deal with other trademark-related matters as entrusted(委托) by the principals, and keep confidential the principals' trade secrets that come to their knowledge during the agency process.

Where a trademark entrusted by a principal for registration application may fall under the circumstances prescribed by this Law under which registration is not allowed, the trademark agency shall explicitly so inform the principal. A trademark agency shall not apply for registration of trademarks other than the ones entrusted to it.

第二节 商标注册的条件
Ⅱ Conditions of Trademark Registration

商标作为区别不同商品或服务来源的标志，但并不是任何标志都可以申请为注册商标。在中国，申请注册商标除了必须具有合格的主体以及履行必要的申请手续，用于申请商标的标志还必须符合法定构成要素、显著性、合法性、非功能性。

As soon as the conditions mentioned above are violated, the application of trademark will be rejected(驳回), or will be unable to register due to opposition(异议), or may be canceled(撤销) even if registered.

一、商标具备法定的构成要素(Statutory Component Elements)

It follows from the purpose of the trademark that virtually any sign that can serve to distinguish goods from other goods is capable of constituting a trademark. But countries may set limits on registrability for practical purposes. The majority of countries allow the registration only of signs that can be represented graphically, since only they can be physically registered and published in a trademark journal to inform the public of the registration of the trademark.

In China, according to the *Trademark Law*, any signs, including words, graphs, letters, numbers, three-dimensional symbols, color combinations, sound or any combination thereof, that are capable of distinguishing the goods of a natural person, legal person or other organization from those of others may be applied for registration as trademarks.

In fact, any distinctive sign like smell or invisible signs(隐形标记) which is capable of distinguishing goods and services of one business from those of others and has certain connection with specific objects may be registered as trademark in some foreign countries. The United States of America is the first country to have recognized the registrability of a smell mark-fresh floral fragrance reminiscent of Plumeria blossoms(鸡蛋花香味) for sewing thread and embroidery yarn (缝纫线和绣花纱线)，将气味或者触觉作为商标予以保护，会牵涉到注册受理以及保护的一些实际问题，比如如何描述气味或触觉等。因此，目前也只是极少数国家对这些标志予以商标的保护。

(一)平面商标(Graphic Trademarks)

Graphic trademark is a basic form of trademarks, including any word(文字), design(图形), letters of an alphabet(字母), numerals(数字), and their combination.

文字是最常见的商标的构成要素，如"美的"、"长虹"、"怡宝"等。其中，作为商标的文字，可以是中国文字(含简化字、繁体字及少数民族文字)也可以是外国文字。图形商标也是比较常见的。比如奥迪汽车商标中的四个圆环图形。字母商标大多指的是外文字母，如英文、法文、俄文字母等。常见的如松下电器的"Panasonic"、宝马汽车的"BMW"等。数字商标在我们日常生活中也很常见。如"999"胃泰、"555"牌电池等。

(二)三维商标(Three-dimensional Trademarks)

A three-dimensional trademark, or stereoscopic trademark(立体商标), is comprised of three-dimensional visual marks, which is more visual and directly perceived than graphic trademark, and produces strong visual effects, such as the shape of a Coca-Cola bottle, and the clown of McDonald's.

三维商标在我们日常生活中并不多见，主要有两个原因。一是三维标志缺乏内在的显著性，难以作为商标保护。显著性是下文会提到的商标注册条件之一，指的是商标必须具备能够将商品或服务的不同来源区别的性质。而三维标志因缺乏内在显著性，本身难以指示商品或服务的来源。只有当三维标志获得市场上的第二含义后，能够指示商品或服务的来源，才可以作为商标受到保护。二是很多三维标志，尤其是产品的外形，往往与产品的功能性要素结合。① 商标法并不保护商标的功能性要素，以三维标志注册商标的，必须具备非功能性，下文会详细阐述这个问题。

(三)颜色组合商标(Trademark of Combination of Colors)

颜色组合商标，是指由两种或两种以上的彩色排列、组合而成的商标。单色的(monochrome)商标不属于颜色组合商标，按照中国目前的商标法，单色商标即使能够区别不同商品或服务的来源，也不能获得注册与保护；而文字、图案加颜色所构成的商标，也不是颜色组合商标，只是作为一般的平面商标而受到商标法的保护。Trademarks of combination of colors are widely used in gas stations, because for drivers at night, colors are more eye-catching and striking than words or designs and are much better in prompting. For example,

---

① 李明德. 知识产权法[M]. 北京：社会科学文献出版社，2007：332.

the trademark of Shell is a typical combination of two colors, i. e. red and yellow.

(四)声音商标(Sound Trademark)

A sound trademark is a trademark where sound is used to perform the trademark function of uniquely identifying the commercial origin of products or services.

Two typical categories of sound marks can distinguished, namely those that can be transcribed in musical notes or other symbols and others (the cry of an animal).

A sequence of notes(音符) can of course be registered as a trademark, but that registration does not normally give protection to the actual musical phrases so expressed. What is protected is the sequence of notes, as registered, against the use of similar sound.

Sound marks clearly can serve as trademarks. The United States of America, for example, allows the registration of sound marks. In practical terms, this means that the sound must be recorded and the cassette (磁带) submitted to the U. S. Patent and Trademark Office for registration. ①

声音由于不具有可视性的特点，有别于传统意义上的商标，一直被排除在商标类型之外。但随着时代的进步以及商品、服务种类的不断丰富，将声音作为商标表现形式之一的优势日益凸显。与其他类型的商标相比，声音商标更能够引起消费者的关注，便于区别商品和服务的来源，例如听到苹果或者诺基亚手机的铃声就能让消费者迅速识别其代表的品牌，看电影的时候听到狮子的吼声，很快就可以识别到这部电影出自米高梅公司。2013年，我国在《商标法》第三次修订中明确声音可以作为商标注册。以五线谱或者简谱对声音加以描述并附加文字说明，无法以五线谱或者简谱描述的，应当使用文字进行描述。

二、显著性(Distinctiveness)

A trademark with distinctiveness is able to distinguish the goods or services of a party, will not confuse consumers about the relationship between one party and another, and will not otherwise deceive consumers to the qualities of the product.

商标具有显著性是取得商标法律保护的必要条件，缺乏显著性的标记由于没有可能起到商标的区别不同来源的作用，则不能作为商标得到注册和保护。《商标法》就规定，申请注册的商标，应当有显著特征，便于识别。同时，商标法又规定，仅有本商品的通用名称、图形、型号的；仅仅直接表示商品的质量、主要原料、功能、用途、重量、数量及其他特点的；缺乏显著特征的，不得作为商标注册。而这些标志经过使用取得显著特征，并便于识别的，可以作为商标注册。

For instance, computers attached to the brand "Apple", are able to distinguish from those produced by other brands, which means that "Apple" for computers is distinctive. Yet to apply the brand "Apple" for apples, i. e. to adopt the common name as a trademark is not allowed, for

---

① WIPO. WIPO Intellectual Property Handbook (Second Edition)[M]. New York: WIPO Publication, 2008: 70-71.

it is not capable of serving the essential trademark function of distinguishing the products or services of a business from those of other businesses, and will confuse consumers about the relationship between one producer and another.

商标的显著性问题实际是一个程度强度问题，同时也是一个不断发展变化的因素，既可能会从无到有，由弱变强，也可能从有到无，由强变弱，发生商标侵权的可能性也会相应地不断发生变化。① American Courts have categorized marks according to their level of distinctiveness. Marks in the highest category-arbitrary（任意的），fanciful（臆造的），and suggestive（暗示的）marks—are deemed inherently distinctive（固有显著的）. Inherently distinctive marks receive protection immediately upon use, and the greatest degree of protection against infringement. Marks in the middle category—descriptive marks—are not viewed as inherently distinctive, but they are capable of becoming distinctive if they are used as marks sufficiently to acquire secondary meaning（named acquired distinctiveness，获得显著性）. Words and symbols in the final category—generic marks—are incapable of becoming distinctive, and cannot be the subject of mark ownership rights. ②

Fanciful marks convey no meaning at all, other than their trademark meaning. Examples include newly coined words, and combinations of letters and numbers, such as "Kodak" for photo papers, "Haier" for refrigerators.

Arbitrary marks is usually a common word, but does not describe the product or service it identifies or any of its characteristics, e. g. "Apple" for computers.

Suggestive marks are marks that indirectly describe the product or service they identify. The consumer must engage in a mental process of his or her own in order to associate the mark with a description of the product or service. For example the mark "penguin" for refrigerators is suggestive. The consumer must think that refrigeration effect of this refrigerator is very good.

Descriptive marks（描述性标记）can be protected if they acquire secondary meaning. The term maybe deemed to be merely descriptive if it identifies anything about the product: its purpose, size, color, ingredients, intended users, origin, or anything else. A merely descriptive term is not inherently distinctive. The consuming public would likely interpret the term to describe the product, not to denote the source of the product. But a descriptive mark can acquire distinctiveness if it acquires secondary meaning. A mark acquires secondary meaning when, in the minds of the public; the primary significance of the mark is to identify the source of the product rather than the product itself. ③

A generic word or symbol is the common descriptive name of the good or service The generic name（通用名称）of a good or service, by definition, cannot serve as a valid mark for that good

① 黄晖．商标法[M]．北京：法律出版社，2004：56.

② Abercrombie & Fitch Co. v. Hunting world, Inc., 537 F. 2d. 4 (2d Cir. 1976).

③ Inwood Laboratories v. Ives Laboratories, 456 U. S. 844, 851, n. 11 (1982).

or service, because it cannot identify those goods coming from a particular merchant and distinguish them from other merchants' goods of the same kind. ①例如“家具”(用在桌子、桌子上)。

If a sign is not distinguishable, it cannot function as a trademark and its registration should be refused.

Therefore the strength of the mark refers to its distinctiveness (along the spectrum of generic—descriptive—suggestive—arbitrary—fanciful) and to its commercial strength (how strong it is in the relevant market). The more distinctive the mark, the more likely its use by others would confuse potential buyers. Accordingly, the more distinctive the mark, the stronger it is. Inherently distinctive marks are the strongest; descriptive marks are deemed weaker.

三、非冲突性(Non-conflicts)

(一)不得与特定官方标记、地名相同或近似(Not Identical or Similar to a Particular Official Mark or Place Name)

我国《商标法》第10条规定，下列标志不得作为商标使用，包括：(1)同中华人民共和国的国家名称、国旗、国徽、国歌、军旗、军徽、军歌、勋章等相同或者近似的，以及同中央国家机关的名称、标志、所在地特定地点的名称或者标志性建筑物的名称、图形相同的；(2)同外国的国家名称、国旗、国徽、军旗等相同或者近似的，但经该国政府同意的除外；(3)同政府间国际组织的名称、旗帜、徽记等相同或者近似的，但经该组织同意或者不易误导公众的除外；(4)与表明实施控制、予以保证的官方标志、检验印记相同或者近似的，但经授权的除外；(5)同“红十字”、“红新月”的名称、标志相同或者近似的。

上述前四项禁用标志是我国依照《巴黎公约》应承担的国际义务，是国际上的通行做法，各国商标法都作了相应的规定，目的是为了维护政府、国际组织的尊严，同时防止误导消费者。如果准予使用这些标志作为商标运用在商品上或者准许未经许可使用与官方标志、检验印记相同或者近似的标志，消费者容易认为该商品来源于政府或者国际组织的批准而生产销售的，或者误认为该商品已经达到了国家或者国际组织认可的质量要求。另外，“红十字”和“红新月”是医疗机构的标志，根据《日内瓦公约》的规定，带有这些标志的医疗机构在战争期间可以受到特定保护，因此不能随意将其作为商标进行注册和使用。

(二)不得违反公序良俗(Not against Public Order and Good Faith)

Trademarks, which are attached to goods or services and are widely known through advertising, have the function of information dissemination. Therefore, signs used as trademarks shall be in accordance with public order and good customs, and shall not be detrimental to socialist morals or customs, or having other unhealthy influences.

根据我国《商标法》第10条的规定，带有民族歧视性的；带有欺骗性，容易使公众对

---

① Margreth Barrett. Intellectual Property (Emanuel Law Outlines) (Third Edition) [M]. New York: Wolters Kluwer Law & Business, 2012: 503-513.

商品的质量等特点或者产地产生误认的；有害于社会主义道德风尚或者有其他不良影响的标志不得作为商标使用。

如将“印第安人”用在卫生洁具商品上，可能使消费者对印第安人产生不雅的联想，因而不允许使用和注册，但有明确的其他含义或者不会产生民族歧视性的除外，如将“印第安人”用在婴儿全套衣上；又如将“24K”用在仿金饰品上，会使消费者误认为是纯金而购买，带有欺骗性，因而也不允许注册。

Objective standards, i. e. recognition of consumers and social public order at that time, shall be adopted in determining whether or not a sign is against public order and good customs, rather than the subjective intentions of trademark registrants in choosing trademarks.

(三)不得与在先合法权利相冲突(No Conflict with Any Prior Right)

不得与在先合法权利相冲突要求商标申请人应当遵循诚实信用原则(the principle of good faith)，在选择相关标志时应当顾及他人的合法利益，有助于商标确权的公平、公正与合理。①

Trademarks usually conflict with prior rights of other people such as names, portraits, works, designs, etc., which can be registered and used as trademarks. However, using names, portraits, works, and designs of other people shall take lawful rights into consideration and acquire permission of the owner; otherwise it may result in infringement of prior rights.

四、非功能性(Non-functionality)

商标注册的非功能性，是指用于商标注册申请的标志不得具有商品功能性的直接表示。As with copyright law, trademarks do not protect functional matter. There are three ways that a feature can be deemed functional②:

(1) It is essential to the use or purpose of the device; or

(2) It affects the cost or quality of the device; or

(3) Its exclusive use by one seller would put competitors at a significant nonreputation-related(与声誉无关的) disadvantage.

Article 12 of the *Trademark Law* in China made special restrictions on the three-dimensional symbol that where the sign merely indicates the shape inherent in the nature of the goods concerned, it may not be granted as a trademark , for example, the shape of apple for fruit; or where the sign is only dictated by the need to achieve technical effects or the need to give the goods substantive value, it may not be granted as a trademark , for example, blade of an electric razor(电动剃须刀的刀片), a diamond design which improves its perceived softness and bulk and reduces nesting and ridging.

---

① 刘春田．知识产权法(第二版)[M]．北京：高等教育出版社，2003：253.

② Stephen M. McJohn. Intellectual Property (Fifth Edition) [M]. New York: Wolters Kluwer, 2014: 492.

第三节 商标注册的申请
Ⅲ Application of Trademark Registration

一、申请人(Applicant)

在申请人的问题上，自然人、法人或者其他组织(any natural person, legal entity or other organization)都可以向商标局提出商标申请注册。法律对申请人的商业性质不作要求，使不具有商业性质的团体、协会或其他组织(non-commercial bodies, associations or other organizations)在商标法上的地位得到了明确，对于集体商标(collective marks)、证明商标(certification marks)、地理标志(geographical marks)的保护具有重要意义。

Two or more natural persons, legal entities or other organizations may jointly file an application for the registration for the same trademark with the Trademark Office, and jointly enjoy and exercise the exclusive right to use the trademark.

A party may apply for trademark registration or handle trademark-related matters on its own or by entrusting(委托) a trademark agency (商标代理机构) established according to the law. Where an agent or representative(代表人), without authorization of the client, seeks to register in its own name the client's trademark and the client objects, the trademark shall not be registered and its use shall be prohibited.

Any foreign person or foreign enterprise intending to apply for the registration of a trademark in China shall file an application in accordance with any agreement between the People's Republic of China and the country to which the applicant belongs, or according to the international treaty to which both countries are parties, or on the basis of the principles of reciprocity(对等原则). Meanwhile, any foreign person or foreign enterprise intending to apply for the registration of a trademark or for any other matters concerning a trademark in China shall appoint any of such organizations as designated by the State to act as its or his agent.

二、申请文件(Application Documents)

提出商标注册申请，提交完整而详细的申请文件是关键步骤之一。根据《商标法》及《商标法实施细则》的规定，每一件商标注册申请应当向商标局提交的文件主要有：《商标注册申请书》(Application of Trademark Registration)1份、商标图样(the reproduction of the trademark)1份、申请人身份证明文件(identity document of the applicant)。需要注意的是，申请商标注册或者办理其他商标事宜，应当使用中文。If the various certificates, documents and proofs submitted under the *Trademark Law* and these Regulations are in a foreign language, the Chinese translation thereof shall be attached; if the Chinese translation is not attached, the certificates, documents and proofs shall be deemed not to have been submitted.

(一)《商标注册申请书》(Application of Trademark Registration)

《商标注册申请书》是商标局提供的一种格式文件，主要填写申请人与商标的基本情况，并加盖申请人的印章或签字。申请书式的格式或位置不能随意改变或改动。如果申请人改变或改动申请书式的格式或位置，商标局不予受理。在填写的过程中，最重要的是申请书中“类别”及“商品/服务项目”的填写，应根据申请人自己经营的商品或提供的服务，参照《商标注册用商品和服务国际分类》(《尼斯分类》第十一版)以及商标局根据上述国际分类表修改的《类似商品和服务区分表》来填写。商标可以使用在成千上万种商品和服务上，实行商标注册制的国家为了确保注册能够产生商标专有权，均规定商标需按类别进行注册，在相同或类似的商品或服务上，一般情况下不允许相同或类似的商标掌握在不同的主体中。只有按照既定的商品和服务分类表进行注册，商标局才能按照类别进行检索和审查，防止在同类商品或服务上出现两个相同或相似的注册商标分属于不同主体。

《商标法》于2013年修订之后，允许申请人通过一份申请就多个类别的商品申请注册同一商标。例如，申请在第24类(洗涤手套)和第25类手套(不含特种手套)上注册同一商标时，以往必须按照两个商品类别提出两件申请，现在则可以通过一份申请同时在第24类和第25类商品上申请注册同一商标，从而简化了商标注册的手续。

(二)商标图样(The Reproduction of Trademark)

The reproduction of a trademark shall be clear, easy to paste, and printed on smooth and durable paper(光洁耐用的纸张) or be replaced by photographs, and the length and width of the reproduction shall be not more than 10 centimeters and not less than 5 centimeters respectively.

商标图样方面，若商标指定颜色(color is claimed)的，并应当提交着色图样，并提交黑白稿1份；以三维标志申请注册商标的，应当在申请书中予以声明，并提交能够确定三维形状的图样，提交的商标图样应当至少包含三面视图；以颜色组合申请注册商标的，应当在申请书中予以声明，并提交文字说明商标使用方式；以声音标志申请商标注册的，应当在申请书中予以声明，提交符合要求的声音样本，对申请注册的声音商标进行描述，说明商标的使用方式。对声音商标进行描述，应当以五线谱或者简谱对申请用做商标的声音加以描述并附加文字说明；无法以五线谱或者简谱描述的，应当以文字加以描述；商标描述与声音样本应当一致。

(三)申请人身份证明文件(Identity Document of the Applicant)

When filing an application for the registration of a trademark, the applicant shall submit a copy of effective certificate capable of proving his identification(能够证明其身份的有效证件的复印件). The name of the applicant for trademark registration shall be consistent with the certificate submitted.

申请人为企业的，申请人的地址应与营业执照(business license)中的地址一致。An party entrusting a trademark agency with the filing of an application for trademark registration or attending to other trademark matters shall submit a Power of Attorney(代理委托书).

Where an application is jointly filed for registration of a trademark, or when proceeding to other matters concerning a jointly owned trademark, a representative(代表人) shall be designated in the application; where no representative is designated, the person named first in the application shall be taken as the representative.

若申请注册集体商标、证明商标的，应当在申请书中予以声明，并提交主体资格证明文件和使用管理规则。当事人委托商标代理组织申请商标注册或者办理其他商标事宜，还应当提交代理委托书。

The Power of Attorney shall indicate such contents and competence(权限) as authorized; the Power of Attorney from a foreign person or foreign enterprise shall, in addition, indicate the nationality of the entruster(委托人). Notarization(公证) and legalization(认证) of the Power of Attorney and other relevant certificates from a foreign person or enterprise shall be done based on the principle of reciprocity(对等原则).

三、申请的提出(Filing of an Application)

按照相关规定，商标注册申请人可以直接向商标局提出申请。但在实践中，许多申请人对商标注册的法律规定和程序并不是很熟悉，所以一般情况下还是委托专门从事商标注册的代理机构代办商标注册申请等事宜。

Any foreign person or enterprise intending to apply for the registration of a trademark or for any other matters concerning a trademark in China shall appoint any of such organizations as designated by the State to act as its or his agent.

在提出商标注册申请时，除了提交必要的文件外，还应按照国家工商行政管理总局商标局的规定缴纳申请费(application fee)、注册费(registration fee)。对于其他一些特殊情形的商标注册申请，我们也应当予以适当的关注，以维护自身的权益。(1) If the sign of a registered trademark is to be altered, a new registration shall be applied. (2) If, after the registration of a trademark, the name, address or other registered matters concerning the registrant change, an application regarding the change(变更申请) shall be filed. (3) If an applicant changes his name, address, agent, or deletes or reduces designated goods(删减指定的商品), he may go through the formalities for the change with the Trademark Office. An applicant who assigns(转让) his application for trademark registration shall go through the formalities for the assignment with the Trademark Office.

第四节　商标注册的审核
Ⅳ　Examination of Trademark Registration

一、形式审查(Formal Examination)

商标申请的形式审查，是指商标局对申请人提交的相关文件进行格式上的审查，对申请文件是否填写完整、证件或图样是否齐全等进行审查，并确定申请日(date of application)。由于我国商标注册采取的是“申请在先原则”，申请日的确定是商标权获得的重要依据。The filing date of an application for trademark registration shall be the date on which the application documents are received by the Trademark Office.

形式审查内容主要涉及申请人是否具备申请资格、申请书和图样是否符合要求、是否符合分类申请原则，以及是否缴纳了申请费等。如果商标局在审查中发现了形式问题，会通知申请人予以补正，限其自收到通知之日起 30 日内，按照指定内容补正并交回。若在规定期限内补正并交回商标局的，保留申请日期；若期满未补正的，视为放弃申请，商标局应当书面通知申请人。

In addition, anyone claiming the right of priority(优先权) shall make a statement in writing when it or he files the application for the trademark registration, otherwise the claim shall be deemed not to have been made for the right of priority.

二、实质审查(Substantive Examination)

商标申请的实质审查，是对申请案中的商标是否符合商标注册的条件进行审查，包括对商标注册的绝对条件(absolute conditions)与相对条件(relative conditions)的审查。商标注册的绝对条件是指申请案中的商标是否具备法定的构成要素，满足显著性及非功能性，不违反公共道德等要求。商标注册的相对条件是指申请案中的商标是否与他人的在先权利相冲突，是否与已注册的商标构成相同或近似。

通过实质审查，申请的商标如果符合有关规定，商标局予以初步核准并予以公告；对于虽不符合关规定，但可以修正的，通知在规定的时间内修正；如果未在规定的期限内修正或修正后不符合规定的，则驳回申请；若不符合有关规定，并且存在实质性缺陷，无法通过修正使其符合规定的，直接驳回。

Where an application for trademark is rejected and no preliminary review announcement is to be made, the trademark office shall so notify the trademark registration applicant concerned in writing.

Where the applicant disagrees to the result, he may, within 15 days from the date he receives the notice, apply to the Trademark Review and Adjudication Board(商标评审委员会) for a second review.

The Trademark Review and Adjudication Board shall, within nine months upon receipt of the application, make a decision and notify the applicant in writing. Where it is necessary under special circumstance, an extension of three months may be granted upon approval by the administrative department for industry and commerce of the State Council.

Where the applicant disagrees to the decision of the Trademark Review and Adjudication Board, he may, within 30 days from the date he receives the notice, bring a lawsuit to a people's court.

三、初步审定与公告异议 (Preliminary Approval and Opposition against Publication)

(一)初步审定 (Preliminary Approval)

The trademark office shall issue a preliminary review announcement if the said application is in compliance with the relevant provisions of this Law. 此时，该商标尚未正式注册，也未取得商标专用权。商标局公告初步审定的商标，将商标注册置于公众的监督下，征求社会公众的意见，提高商标注册的准确性。

(二)公告异议(Opposition against Publication)

按照规定，对于初步审定的商标，自公告之日起3个月内，任何人都可以向商标局提出异议。对商标局初步审定予以公告的商标提出异议的，异议人应当向商标局提交商标异议书(the Application for Trademark Opposition)一式两份(in duplicate)。商标异议书应当写明被异议商标刊登《商标公告》的期号及初步审定号。

The Application for Trademark Opposition shall contain the specific requests, facts and grounds, with relevant proofs and certificates attached.

商标局应当将商标异议书副本及时送交被异议人，限其自收到商标异议书副本之日起30日内答辩。被异议人不答辩的，不影响商标局的异议裁定。当事人需要在提出异议申请或者答辩后补充有关证据材料的，应当在申请书或者答辩书中声明，并自提交申请书或者答辩书之日起3个月内提交；期满未提交的，视为当事人放弃补充有关证据材料。

If an opposition is filed against the trademark that has, after examination, been preliminarily approved and published, the Trademark Office shall hear both the opponent (异议人) and applicant state facts and grounds, and shall, after investigation and verification, make a decision (裁定).

当事人不服的，可以自收到通知之日起15日内向商标评审委员会申请复审，由商标评审委员会作出裁定，并书面通知异议人和被异议人。当事人对商标评审委员会的裁定不服的，可以自收到通知之日起30日内向人民法院起诉。人民法院应当通知商标复审程序(the trademark reexamination proceeding)的对方当事人作为第三人(a third party)参加诉讼。当事人在法定期限内对商标局作出的裁定不申请复审或者对商标评审委员会作出的裁定不向人民法院起诉的，裁定生效(take effect)。

四、核准注册(Approval of Registration)

If no opposition has been filed after the expiration of the time limit from the publication(公告期满), or the opposition cannot be established upon adjudication(经裁定), the registration shall be approved, a certificate of trademark registration (商标注册证) shall be issued and the trademark shall be published; If the opposition is established upon adjudication, the registration shall not be approved.

异议成立，商标注册申请不予核准。异议在部分指定商品上成立的，在该部分指定商品上的商标注册申请不予核准。被异议商标在异议裁定生效前已经刊发注册公告的，撤销(cancel)原注册公告，经异议裁定核准注册的商标重新公告。

注册商标的有效期(the period of validity)为10年，自核准注册之日(the date of approval of the registration)起计算。但经裁定异议不能成立而核准注册的，商标注册申请人取得商标专用权的时间自初审公告3个月期满之日起计算。经异议裁定核准注册的商标，自该商标异议期满之日起至异议裁定生效前，对他人在同一种或者类似商品上使用与该商标相同或者近似的标志的行为不具有追溯力(retroactive effect)；但是，因该使用人的恶意(bad faith)给商标注册人造成的损失，应当给予赔偿。

第五节　商标管理
V　Trademark Administration

商标申请注册只是获得了商标专用权，获得了法律保护的基础。商标作为市场经营的主要构成部分，商标能否给经营者乃至整个国家的经济带来良好的经济效益，主要取决于商标管理的水平。商标管理有广义与狭义之分。广义的商标管理包括国家主管机关和企业对商标注册与使用的管理；而狭义的商标管理则仅指国家主管机关对商标注册与使用的管理，不包括企业商标管理。我国商标法规定的商标管理指的是狭义的商标管理。

一、商标管理机关(Administrative Authority of Trademark)

我国商标管理实行集中注册、分级管理(centralized registration and level-to-level administration)的制度，建立了国家工商行政管理总局商标局与地方各级工商行政管理局两级管理的商标管理机构体制。

(一)商标局(The Trademark Office)

国务院工商行政管理部门商标局(Trademark Office of the Administrative Authority for Industry and Commerce under the State Council)隶属于国家工商行政管理总局(State Administration for Industry and Commerce of the People's Republic of China)，承担商标注册与管理等行政职能，具体负责全国商标注册和管理工作，依法保护商标专用权和查处商标侵权行为(trademark infringement)，处理商标争议(trademark disputes)事宜，加强驰名商标(well-known trademark)的认定和保护工作，负责特殊标志(special marks)、官方标志(official marks)的登记、备案和保护，研究分析并依法发布商标注册信息，为政府决策和社会公众提供信息服务，实施商标战略(trademark strategy)等工作。

(二)商标评审委员会(The Trademark Review and Adjudication Board)

商标评审委员会是依据《商标法》的有关规定，在国家工商行政管理总局设立的负责商标评审(trademark review and adjudication)与争议的专门行政执法机构，依法对商标评审事宜行使裁决权；当事人对商标评审委员会的决定不服的，可以向人民法院提起诉讼。根据《商标法》的规定，国务院工商行政管理部门商标局主管全国商标注册和管理的工作。国务院工商行政管理部门设立商标评审委员会，负责处理商标争议事宜。商标评审委员会主要负责办理商标评审事宜，其与商标局的工作既相互关联、又相互制约，构成了我国商标授权、确权和商标保护的行政体系。

商标评审委员会依法对商标评审事宜独立行使裁决权。商标评审委员会以事实为根据、以法律为准绳(take facts as the basis and laws as the criterion)处理商标评审事宜。商标评审委员会处理商标评审事宜，采取合议形式(panel discussion)并实行委员投票表决制(voted by all members of the committee)，遵循少数服从多数的原则(the rule of majority)。商标评审委员会对商标评审事宜实行书面审理(written hearing)。商标评审委员会设立专家咨询小组(advisory specialist group)，就商标评审事宜中的有关问题征求意见。专家咨询小组由知识产权法学界专家若干人组成，其成员由商标评审委员会聘任。

(三) 地方各级工商行政管理局(The Administrative Authorities for Industry and Commerce at Different Levels)

省(自治区、直辖市)、地(市)、县(市、区)各级商标行政管理机关为地方各级工商行政管理局，主要负责本辖区内的商标管理工作，职责范围主要包括监督注册商标的商品质量，对商标标识的印制与使用进行管理，对未注册商标进行管理，宣传商标法规与制度，查处商标侵权行为。

二、商标使用管理 (Administration of Use of Trademarks)

(一)注册商标的使用管理(Administration of Use of Registered Trademarks)

1. 对商标注册标记的管理 (Administration of Marks of Trademark Registration)

If a registered trademark is used, it may carry the indication of "Registered Trademark" or the registration signs of the goods, packaging or description or other attachments of the goods. 注册标记包括(注外加○)和(R 外加○)。使用注册标记，应当标注在商标的右上角或者右下角。商标主管机关应严格检查商标使用者是否正确使用商标注册标记，对不当标示商标注册标记的行为予以纠正与处理。

2. 对《商标注册证》的管理 (Administration of Certificate of Trademark Registration)

Where a Trademark Registration Certificate is lost or damaged, an application for reissuance of the Trademark Registration Certificate shall be filed with the Trademark Office. Where a Trademark Registration Certificate is lost, a statement of loss shall be published in the Trademark Gazette(《商标公告》). A damaged Trademark Registration Certificate shall be returned to the Trademark Office when the application for reissuance is filed.

Whoever forges (伪造) or alters (变造) a Trademark Registration Certificate or other trademark certifications shall be investigated for criminal liability in accordance with the provisions of the Criminal Law on the crime of forging or altering certificates of State organs or on other crimes.

Reinforcing administration of Certificate of Trademark Registration will contribute to reducing and handling promptly trademark disputes, and maintaining the order of trademark administration.

3. 对强制注册商标的管理 (Administration of Compulsory Registered Trademarks)

目前我国仅要求在烟草制品(tobacco product)上必须使用注册商标。使用未注册商标生产、销售烟草制品的，地方工商行政管理部门可以责令停止生产、销售、责令期限申请注册，还可以并处罚款。

4. 对商标期满续展的管理 (Administration of Renewal of Expired Trademarks)

The period of validity of a registered trademark shall be 10 years, counted from the day the registration is approved.

If a trademark registrant intends to continue using the registered trademark upon expiry of the validity period of registration, the trademark registrant shall go through the renewal procedure within 12 months prior to the expiry date in accordance with relevant provisions; where the registrant fails to do so during the said time limit, an extension of six months may be granted.

Each renewal of registration shall be valid for ten years calculating from the date immediately following the expiry date of the last validity period of the trademark. If no application for renewal is filed upon expiry of the extension period, the registered trademark shall be cancelled.

5. 对不当使用注册商标的行为的管理（Administration of Malpractice of Registered Trademarks）

不当使用注册商标的，由商标局责令限期改正(rectify within a specified period)或者撤销其注册商标。依据《商标法》的相关规定，这些行为主要有以下几种情形：

(1)自行改变注册商标、注册人名义、地址或者其他事项的

A trademark registrant that, without authorization, makes alternations with respect to the registered trademark, the name or address of the registrant or other registration items during the use of the registered trademark shall be ordered to make correction within at a limit by the relevant local administrative department for industry and commerce. If it fails to make correction within the prescribed time limit, the trademark office shall cancel the registered trademark thereof.

When applying for modification of his name, address or other registration matters, the registrant shall file an Application for Modification with the Trademark Office. The Trademark Office shall, upon examination and approval, issue the trademark registrant the relevant certificates, and make an announcement. If the application is not approved, the Trademark Office shall notify the applicant in writing and explain the reason.

变更商标注册人名义的，还应当提交有关登记机关出具的变更证明文件(modification certificate)。未提交变更证明文件的，可以自提出申请之日起 30 日内补交；期满不提交的，视为放弃变更申请，商标局应当书面通知申请人。

(2)自行转让注册商标的(if the registered trademark is assigned unilaterally)

Where a registered trademark is assigned, both the assignor(转让人) and the assignee(受让人) shall jointly file an Application for Assignment of the Registered Trademark to the Trademark Office. The assignor and the assignee shall jointly go through the formalities for the application for assignment of the registered trademark.

转让注册商标时，商标注册人对其在同一种或者类似商品上注册的相同或者近似的商标，应当一并转让；未一并转让的，由商标局通知其限期改正；期满不改正的，视为放弃转让该注册商标的申请，商标局应当书面通知申请人。对可能产生误认(mislead)、混淆(confuse)或者其他不良影响(adverse effects)的转让注册商标申请，商标局不予核准，书面通知申请人并说明理由。

(3)连续 3 年停止使用注册商标的(if the use of the registered trademark has ceased for three consecutive years)

Where a registered trademark has not been put in use for three consecutive years(连续 3 年) without a justifiable reason, any entity or individual may apply to the trademark office for revocation(撤销) of the registered trademark.

The justifiable reasons prescribed above include following four circumstances: force majeure (不可抗力); restrictions imposed by government policy (政府政策性限制); bankruptcy liquidation(破产清算); and other justifiable reasons not attributable to the trademark registrant.

商标局应当通知商标注册人，限其自收到通知之日起 2 个月内提交该商标在撤销申请提出前使用的证据材料或者说明不使用的正当理由；期满不提供使用的证据材料或者证据材料无效并没有正当理由的，由商标局撤销其注册商标。其中，证据材料包括商标注册人使用注册商标的证据材料和商标注册人许可他人使用注册商标的证据材料。

6. 对使用注册商标的商品进行商品质量管理(Quality Control of Goods Using Registered Trademark)

对注册商标的质量管理主要涉及三个方面：

(1)The user of a trademark shall be responsible for the quality of the goods on which the trademark is used. The administrative departments for industry and commerce at all levels shall, through the administration of trademarks, put an end to any practice that deceives consumers.

(2)The assignee shall guarantee the quality of the goods on which the registered trademark is used.

(3)The licensor shall supervise the quality of the goods on which the licensee uses his registered trademark, and the licensee shall guarantee the quality of the goods on which the registered trademark is to be used.

7. 对商标转让、许可使用及移转进行管理(Administration of Assignment, Licensing and Transferring of Trademarks)

If a registered trademark is assigned(转让), the assignor and assignee shall conclude a contract for the assignment, and jointly file an application with the trademark Office. The assignment of a registered trademark shall be published after it has been approved, and the assignee enjoys the exclusive right(专用权) to use the trademark from the date of publication.

The owner of a registered trademark may, by concluding a trademark licensing contract, authorize another person to use his registered trademark.

If any person is authorized to use the registered trademark of another person, the name of the licensee and the origin of the goods shall be indicated on the goods that bear the registered trademark.

A licensor who licenses others to use his registered trademark shall submit the trademark licensing to the trademark office for file(备案), and the trademark office shall announce the trademark licensing. Without filing, the trademark licensing shall not be used against a bona fide third party(善意第三人).

8. 对注册商标无效程序的管理(Administration of Invalid Procedure of Registered Trademarks)

商标获得核准注册，在法律程序上而言商标权人仅仅是获得了一种推定合法有效的权利，如果发现商标无效理由，利害关系人可以依法申请商标行政管理机关撤销已经注册的商标。商标法没有使用“无效”的字眼，而是将无效程序纳入“撤销”程序之中。依法被撤销的商标，其商标专用权视为自始即不存在(non-existent)。注册商标被撤销的，自撤销或者注销之日起 1 年内，商标局对与该商标相同或者近似的商标注册申请，不予核准。

根据《商标法》相关规定，注册商标无效的理由分为注册商标无效的绝对理由与相对理由。

(1)注册商标无效的绝对理由(absolute invalidity)

已经注册的商标，违反《商标法》第10条、第11条、第12条的规定，或者是以欺骗手段或者其他不正当手段取得注册的，由商标局宣告该注册商标无效；其他单位或者个人可以请求商标评审委员会宣告该注册商标无效。无论何时发现，一律撤销。

(2)注册商标无效的相对理由(relative invalidity)

①就相同或者类似商品申请注册的商标是复制、摹仿或者翻译他人未在中国注册的驰名商标，容易导致混淆的；就不相同或者不相类似商品申请注册的商标是复制、摹仿或者翻译他人已经在中国注册的驰名商标，误导公众，致使该驰名商标注册人的利益可能受到损害的。

②未经授权，代理人或者代表人以自己的名义将被代理人或者被代表人的商标进行注册。

③商标中有商品的地理标志，而该商品并非来源于该标志所标示的地区，误导公众的。

④申请注册的商标，不符合商标法有关规定或者同他人在同一种商品或者类似商品上已经注册的或者初步审定的商标相同或者近似的。

⑤注册商标与他人现有的在先权利相冲突。

A registered trademark conflicts with any prior right acquired by another person.

符合上述五种情况的注册商标，利害关系人可以在该商标核准注册之日起的5年内，启动注册商标的无效程序。如果过了这5年时间，有关商标就会成为不可争议的商标。须注意的是，对于驰名商标，如果他人是恶意注册的，驰名商标所有人不受5年的时间限制。

(二)未注册商标的使用管理(Administration of Unregistered Trademark)

我国实行的是商标自愿注册原则，未注册商标和注册商标一样被允许作为商标公开使用，以区别不同商品或服务的来源。

Misuse of unregistered trademarks may result in conflicts and disputes of trademarks, and mislead the public and cause confusion, moreover is likely to create prejudice to the interests of the well-known mark registrant.

因此，未注册商标的使用也应当依法进行，我国《商标法》及《商标法实施条例》都对未注册商标使用的管理做了具体的规定。

1. 未注册商标不得冒充注册商标

Unregistered trademark shall not be falsely represented as registered.

未注册商标不得擅自在商品、商品包装、说明书或者其他附着物上标明“注册商标”或者注册标记。将未注册商标冒充为注册商标，损害了市场竞争的正常秩序，蒙骗了广大的消费者，属于不正当竞争行为，应当制止。

2. 未注册商标不得违反公序良俗或使用其他禁止用做商标使用的标志

Unregistered trademark shall not be detrimental to socialist morals or customs, or use signs that shall not be used as trademarks.

商标可以未注册而使用，但不得违反公序良俗或使用其他禁止用做商标使用的标志，否则工商行政管理机关将禁止其作为商标使用，封存或收缴其商标标识，并根据情况予以通报，处以罚款。

3. 使用未注册商标的商品不得粗制滥造，以次充好，欺骗消费者

Regarding commodities using unregistered trademark, the manufacture shall not be qualified, or superior quality shall not be replaced by inferior quality, so that consumers are deceived.

尽管不同商标代表的商品或服务的质量品质不同，但商标有着保证商品恒定品质的特征。使用注册商标的商品必须保证其商品的质量达到核定的标准。而未注册商标同样也起着区别不同商品或服务来源的作用，因此使用未注册商标的商品也不得粗制滥造，以次充好，欺骗消费者，扰乱正常的市场秩序。

三、商标印制管理（Administration of the Printing and Production of Trademarks）

我国除声音商标外，都是可视性商标，因此商标标识的印制成为商标使用与管理中的重要组成部分。加强商标印制管理，可以从源头堵塞商标使用管理中的漏洞，防范不合法和不合格的商标标识进入市场，有助于打击商标假冒行为（counterfeit registered trademarks），切实保护注册商标专用权，维护广大消费者的利益与社会经济秩序。我国对商标印制管理的规定几经修改，目前实施的是国家工商行政管理局于 2004 年 9 月公布的《商标印制管理办法》。

（一）对商标印制委托人的管理（Administration of the Entrusting Party of Trademarks Printing and Production）

商标印制委托人委托商标印制单位印制商标的，应当出示营业执照副本（duplicate of business license）或者合法的营业证明（certification of lawful business operations）或者身份证明（certification of identity）。若委托印制的是注册商标，委托人还应当出示商标注册证或者由注册人所在地县级工商行政管理局签章的商标注册证复印件，并另行提供一份复印件。签订商标使用许可合同使用他人注册商标，被许可人需印制商标的，还应当出示商标使用许可合同文本并提供一份复印件；商标注册人单独授权（separately authorize）被许可人印制商标的，除出示由注册人所在地县级工商行政管理局签章的商标注册证复印件外，还应当出示授权书并提供一份复印件。

委托印制未注册商标的，商标印制委托人提供的商标图样还应当符合下列要求：所印制的商标不得违反《商标法》第 10 条的规定；所印制的商标不得标注“注册商标”字样或者使用注册标记。

（二）对商标印制单位的管理（Administration of the Trademarks Printing and Production Entity）

“商标印制单位”是指依法登记从事商标印制业务的企业和个体工商户。商标印制单位应当对商标印制委托人提供的证明文件和商标图样进行核查（verify）。商标印制单位承印符合商标印制业务的，商标印制业务管理人员应当按照要求填写《商标印制业务登记

表》(*The Trademark Printing and Production Business Register Form*)，载明商标印制委托人所提供的证明文件的主要内容，《商标印制业务登记表》中的图样应当由商标印制单位业务主管人员加盖骑缝章(affixed with a cross-page seal)。

商标标识印制完毕，商标印制单位应当在15日内提取标识样品(samples of trademark signs)，连同《商标印制业务登记表》、商标注册证复印件、商标使用许可合同复印件、商标印制授权书复印件等一并造册存档(keep as archives)。商标印制单位应当建立商标标识出入库制度，商标标识出入库应当登记台账。废次标识(the discarded and inferior signs)应当集中进行销毁，不得流入社会。商标印制档案及商标标识出入库台账(the account of ins and outs of trademark signs)应当存档备查(preserved for inquiry)，存查期为2年。

【英语词汇】

acquired distinctiveness　获得显著性
adjudication　*n.* 裁定
arbitrary mark　任意性标志
assignee　*n.* 受让人
assignor　*n.* 转让人
a third party　第三人
bad faith　恶意
confiscate　*v.* 收缴
descriptive marks　描述性标记
fanciful mark　臆造性标志
fulfill　*v.* 履行，满足
generic name　通用名称
graphic trademarks　平面商标
identical　*adj.* 相同的
monochrome　*adj.* 单色的
note　*n.* 音符
notarization　*n.* 公证
portraiture right　*n.* 肖像权
preliminarily approve　初步审定
prior right　在先权利
power of attorney　授权委托书
principle of reciprocity　对等原则
sound trademark　声音商标
suggestive marks　暗示性标记
the principle of good faith　实信用原则
three-dimensional trademarks　三维商标
trademark agency　代理机构
trademark review and adjudication board　商标评审委员会

【英语句型】

1. Signs used as trademarks shall be in accordance with public order and good customs, and shall not be detrimental to socialist morals or customs.

"be detrimental to..."意思是"对……不利"。

译文：用做商标的标志应当符合公共秩序与善良风俗的要求，不得违反国家的公共秩序和社会的一般道德。

2. Anyone claiming the right of priority shall make a statement in writing when it or he files the application for the trademark registration, otherwise the claim shall be deemed not to have been made for the right of priority.

"be deemed not to..."意思是"不被视为……"。

译文：申请人若需要主张优先权，还应当注意在提交申请时一并提出优先权的申请，否则将视为未要求优先权。

3. If a trademark, before its being approved for registration, has been the object of opposition and decision, no application for adjudication may be filed based on the same facts and grounds.

"on the ground of..."意思是"以……为依据"。

译文：对核准注册前已经提出异议并经裁定的商标，不得再以相同的事实和理由申请撤销商标的裁定。

4. Whoever forges or alters a Trademark Registration Certificate or other trademark certifications shall be investigated for criminal liability in accordance with the provisions of the Criminal Law on the crime of forging or altering certificates of State organs or on other crimes.

"be investigated for..."表示"追究……"。

译文：伪造或者变造商标注册证的，依照刑法关于伪造、变造国家机关证件罪或者其他罪的规定，依法追究刑事责任。

【阅读资料】

第十四章　商标权的利用、限制与保护
Chapter 14　The Utilization, Limitation and Production of Trademark

【引言】商标权(trademark right)是商标法(trade law)的核心内容，商标的申请(application)、注册(registration)及商标权的取得(acquisition)、利用以及保护都是围绕着商标权进行的。商标权的利用主要包括注册商标(registered trademark)的禁止使用、注册商标的许可和转让(licensing and assignment)等。与著作权和专利权一样，法律对注册商标的保护也不是绝对的。在特定情形下，他人对与商标相同标志的使用并不构成侵权，如表示商品的特性、说明商品或服务的用途以及商标权用尽后的使用等。

【学习目的与要求】掌握注册商标权的具体内容、商标权的含义，法律对未注册商标和注册商标的保护及不同条件和方式。掌握注册商标的使用许可和转让的有关规定，熟悉商标质押的基本内容和有关法律规定。掌握对注册商标的限制和法律保护，尤其是对商标的合理使用和权利用尽等内容。

第一节　商标权的内容
Ⅰ　The Contents of Trademark Rights

一、商标权的概念和特征(The Concept and Characteristics of Trademark Rights)

(一)商标权的概念(The Concept of Trademark Rights)

1. 商标权(Trademark Right)

商标权，是指基于商标(trademark)而产生的权利(right)。理论上也可以将商标权称为商标权人(trademark owner)对其拥有的商标所享有的权利，广义上包括注册商标所有人(registered trademark owner)对其注册商标(registered trademark)所拥有的权利、合法受许可人(licensee)对受许可人使用之注册商标所享有的权利，还包括了商标持有人(trademark holders)对未注册商标(unregistered trademarks)所享有的权利。

2. 商标专用权(Exclusive Right of Trademark)

我国商标法并没有规定"商标权"的概念，而是以"商标专用权"代之。我国《商标法》规定，经商标局核准注册的商标为注册商标，商标注册人享有商标专用权，受法律保护。Registered trademarks refer to trademarks that are registered with the approval of the trademark office, including trademarks for goods and services, collective trademarks and certification trademarks, collective trademarks and certification trademarks. The owner of a registered trademark shall enjoy the exclusive right(专用权) to the use of the trademark, which shall be protected by law. 可见，我国商标专用权的取得除法律另有规定外，采取注册原则，只有注册才是确定商标专用权的法律依据，只有经商标局核准注册的商标，才享有商标专用权并依法得以保护。

Article 56 of *Trademark Law* provides that the exclusive right to the use of a registered trademark shall be limited to trademarks which are registered upon approval(核准注册的商标) and to goods or services the use of a trademark on which is approved(核定使用的商品). 即“商标专用权”(exclusive right of trademark)仅仅限定了商标权人可排他性使用商标的界限。商标权人自己仅有“在核定使用的商品上使用核准注册的商标”的“专用权”①，而在未核准使用的其他商品类别上则没有“专用权”。“核准注册的商标”与“核定使用的商品或服务”共同限定了商标专用权的范围，在这一范围之内，商标注册人得以独占性地使用注册商标，使注册商标与其指定的商品或服务之间建立起固定的、唯一的联系，以便消费者实现“认牌购物”，避免对商品或服务来源产生混淆。如果他人未经许可在相同商品上使用与注册商标相同的商标，一般情况下会导致消费者误将该商品认为来源于商标注册人，因此构成商标侵权。② 另外为了防止对消费者的欺骗和对商标权人商业利益与信誉的损害，《商标法》还规定商标权人对于某些其本人并不享有专用权的行为，有禁止他人实施的权利。

A trademark right is granted when a trademark is registered in the Office. The grantee of the trademark right is permitted to use the trademark continuously (known as a “use right”). He has the right to prohibit the use of the same trademark, or a similar trademark, for the same or similar goods (the “prohibitive right”). Moreover, the grantee can request damages or sue a person for intentionally infringing his trademark right.

There are exceptional cases, however, in which unregistered trademarks are protected. If the trademark is well known or famous, it is subject to additional protection under the Unfair Competition Prevention Law.

(二)商标权的特征(The Characteristics of Trademark Rights)

商标权(trademark right)与著作权(copyright)、专利权(patent)统称为知识产权(intellectual property)，商标权具有知识产权的一般特征，即专有性(exclusiveness)、时间性(timeliness)和地域性(territoriality)；同时，相对于著作权和专利权而言，又有自己的特征。

1. 禁止性效力大于专用性(Prohibition is Greater Than Exclusiveness)

注册商标的禁止权(prohibitive right)涉及的是对抗他人非法使用(illegal use)注册商标的问题，即他人未经注册人许可(license)，不得在同一种商品(identical products)上或类

① 专用权，以核准注册的商标和核定使用的商品为限。

② 王迁．知识产权法教程(第四版)[M]．北京：中国人民大学出版社，2014：438.

似商品(similar product)上使用与注册商标相同或近似(same or similar)的商标；而注册商标的专有使用权(exclusive use right)涉及的是注册人如何使用自己的注册商标的问题，即以核准注册的商标和核定使用的商品为限。因此，注册商标禁止权的效力范围(effective range)远远大于专有使用权的效力范围。①

Any of the following acts shall constitute an infringement on the exclusive rights to the use of a registered trademark:

(1) Using a trademark that is identical with a registered trademark on the same kind of goods without obtaining licensing from the registrant of the registered trademark;

(2) Using a trademark that is similar to a registered trademark on the same kind of goods, or using a trademark that is identical with or similar to the registered trademark on similar goods without obtaining licensing from the registrant of the registered trademark, and is likely to cause confusion;

(3) Selling goods that infringe on the exclusive right to the use of a registered trademark;

(4) Counterfeiting (伪造), or making without authorization, representations of another person's registered trademark, or selling such representations;

(5) Altering a registered trademark without permission of its owner and selling goods bearing such an altered trademark on the market;

(6) Providing, intentionally (故意地), convenience for such acts as infringe upon others, exclusive right of trademark use, to facilitate others to commit infringement on the exclusive right of trademark use;

(7) Impairing in other manners another person's exclusive right to the use of its registered trademark.

2. 相对永久性(Relative Permanence)

商标权作为一种知识产权，其保护期也有时间的限制，但是这种限制不同于著作权和专利权的期限限制。The period of validity of a registered trademark shall be ten years, counted from the day the registration is approved.

If a registrant needs to continue to use the registered trademark after the period of validity expires, an application for renewal of registration shall be made within twelve months before the expiration. If the registrant fails to make such an application within that period, an extension period of six months may be granted. If no application has been filed before the extension period expires, the registered trademark shall be cancelled. The period of validity for each renewal of registration shall be ten years.

我国商标法规定的商标权保护期为10年，商标注册到期可以续展，续展的次数不受限制(unlimited)。但著作权和专利权的保护期一旦届满，其进入公有领域(public

① 韩松主编. 知识产权法(第二版)[M]. 北京：中国人民大学出版社，2006：306.

domain)，权利人就永久丧失了专用权。

二、商标权的主要内容(The Contents of Trademark Rights)

(一)专用权(Exclusive Right)

专用权，是指商标权人对其注册商标享有完全独占使用(completely exclusive use)的权利。商标的专用权，是商标权人最基本的权利。专用权即排他权，商标专用权意味着只有权利人能够在特定的范围内使用注册商标，其他人未经商标权人许可不得使用注册商标。

The exclusive right is given to the owner of the trademark to use it exclusively and prohibit others from similar marks. 根据我国《商标法》的规定，"商标专用权"(exclusive right of trademark)专门用来描述注册商标(registered trademark)受保护的法律后果(legal consequences)和状况。"商标专用权"即"注册商标专用权"，所提供的保护无法及于那些未注册的商标。对于注册商标来说，使用"商标专用权"还是"商标权"，似乎并无实质性区别；但对于未注册商标而言，由于不享有"商标专用权"，故而"商标权"这一概念似乎更有法律意义。赋予注册商标所有人独占使用权的目的，是为了通过注册建立起来特定商标(certain trademarks)与特定商品(specific product)的固定联系，从而促使生产经营者保持商品声誉(product reputation)，保证消费者能够避免混淆并能接受到准确无误的商品来源信息。① 商标权人除了自己使用商标外，也可以将注册商标转让(transfer)给他人或许可(license)他人使用。

(二)转让权(Transfer Right)

1. 转让权的概念(The Concept of Transfer Right)

转让权，是指注册商标所有人(registered trademark owner)有将其对注册商标的所有权(ownership)转移给他人所有的权利。商标权转让的对象是注册商标。商标权作为一种财产权(property)，可以作为转让的标的(the subject of transfer)。注册商标所有权转让后，原商标权人的商标权随之消失，受让人成为该注册商标的所有人。

2. 注册商标转让的原则(The Principles of Assignment of Registered Trademark)

关于商标权的转让，国外不同的商标立法采取不同的转让原则，即连同转让原则和自由转让原则。

(1) 连同转让原则(Principle of Together-transfer)

连同转让原则是指转让注册商标时必须连同商标所属的企业一起转让，不能单独转让注册商标，美国、瑞典、德国等少数国家采用该原则。They provide that a trademark serves to tell consumers the source of the goods or services. If the trademark is sold to another seller who provides completely different goods and services, consumers might be misled. Likewise, if the trademark owner licenses the mark to numerous sellers who have different standards for the relevant goods or services, the trademark fails to serve its function. Accordingly, if a trademark is sold, it must be sold with the associated goodwill of the business.

(2) 自由转让原则(Principle of Unrestrained-transfer)

---

① 黄晖. 商标法[M]. 法律出版社，2004：113.

自由转让原则是指注册商标既可以连同商标所属的企业一起转让，也可以分开转让。分开转让即商标权可以脱离所属企业单独转让，有利于商标权的充分行使。随着贸易和物流的发展，消费者更关心的是商品或服务本身的质量，而不是商品的生产者或服务的提供者，只要商品或服务质量没有变化，即使改变了生产者，消费者也同样予以认可，因而目前大部分国家均采用自由转让原则。

In Article 6 of *Paris Convention*, when, in accordance with the law of a country of the Union, the assignment of a mark is valid only if it takes place at the same time as the transfer of the business or goodwill to which the mark belongs, it shall suffice for the recognition of such validity that the portion of the business or goodwill located in that country be transferred to the assignee, together with the exclusive right to manufacture in the said country, or to sell therein, the goods bearing the mark assigned.

我国《商标法》第42条未明确规定采用哪项原则，但要求转让注册商标的，转让人和受让人应当签订转让协议，并共同向商标局提出申请。受让人应当保证使用该注册商标的商品质量。对容易导致混淆或者有其他不良影响的转让，商标局不予核准，书面通知申请人并说明理由。

(3)注册商标转让的限制(The Limitations on Assignment of Registered Trademark)

根据我国《商标法》和《商标法实施细则》的有关规定，注册商标转让的限制性规定，主要有：

①用于两种类似商品的商标，不得单独转让(The trademark which is used on identical or similar trademarks cannot be transferred separately)

允许此类商标分割移转，就会违反《商标法》的规定，造成同一商标在类似商品上有两个商标注册人同时使用，从而发生不同厂家商品混淆。

②联合商标不能分割转让(The transfer of joint trademarks cannot be divided)

联合商标(joint trademarks)是同一商标所有人基于经营需要而使用的系列商标，它具有标记近似特征。如果允许将联合商标中的某一个单独转让，也会发生两个商标所有人在同一种商品上使用近似商标的情况，造成商品来源混淆。

③未经共有人同意不得自行转让(The trademark cannot be transferred without the consent of the co-owner)

④转让注册商标未履行法定程序的，其转让无效(The trademark's transfer non-compliant with statutory procedures is invalid)

在转让注册商标时，应依法定程序(due course of law)进行。转让权(transfer right)是商标所有人对其注册商标最重要的一种处分方式。转让注册商标应由双方当事人签订合同(sign a license contract)，并应共同向商标局(trademark office)提出申请(application)，经商标局核准公告(approve and notice)后方生效。未经商标局核准公告的，注册商标的转让不产生对抗第三人(the third parties)的效力。

(三)许可权(The Right of Licensing)

许可权，是指注册商标所有人(registered trademark owner)有将其对注册商标的专用权(exclusive right)许可(license)他人行使的权利。许可他人使用注册商标是商标所有人利用商标权的一种重要方式。使用许可能够促进商品生产和商品流通，对促进经济发展具有积极意义，也是许可证贸易的一种重要形式。许可合同一般为有偿合同，被许可方(licensee)支付一定的使用费取得在约定的时间和地域范围内的商标使用权，商标所有权仍由注册人享有，主体未发生变更，注册商标所有权未发生转移。

A licensor who licenses others to use his registered trademark shall submit the trademark licensing to the trademark office for file, and the trademark office shall announce the trademark licensing. Without filing, the trademark licensing shall not be used against a bona fide third party.

可见，我国对商标许可采取的是登记对抗主义，即商标使用许可合同未经备案的，不影响该许可合同的效力，但不得对抗善意第三人。

与专利许可制度一样，根据注册商标使用许可合同中许可人和被许可人之间的权利义务不同，注册商标的许可分为以下三种形式：

1. 独占使用许可(Monopoly Use License)

独占使用许可，是指商标注册人在约定的期间、地域和以约定的方式，将该注册商标仅许可一个被许可人使用，商标注册人依约定不得使用该注册商标。

在发生注册商标专用权侵权(registered trademark infringement)案件时，独占使用许可合同的被许可人可以向人民法院提起诉讼。独占使用许可合同的被许可人享有独立的诉权(independent right of appeal)。

2. 排他使用许可(Exclusive Use License)

排他使用许可，是指商标注册人在约定的期间、地域和以约定的方式，将该注册商标仅许可一个被许可人使用，商标注册人依约定可以使用该注册商标但不得另行许可他人使用该注册商标。

在发生注册商标专用权被侵害时，排他使用许可合同的被许可人可以和商标注册人共同起诉(class action)，也可以在商标注册人不起诉的情况下，自行提起诉讼。

3. 普通使用许可(Ordinary Use License)

普通使用许可，是指注册商标权人将其注册商标在约定的期间、地域范围、使用方式授权他人使用的一种注册商标许可使用方式。

在发生注册商标专用权被侵害时，普通使用许可合同的被许可人经商标注册人明确授权(expressly authorized)，可以提起诉讼。由此可见，普通使用许可合同的被许可人不具有独立的诉权。在发生商标侵权案件时，普通使用许可合同的被许可人不能自行提起诉讼，而应向商标注册人说明情况，由商标注册人向人民法院提起诉讼。在取得商标注册人明确授权的情况下，普通使用许可合同的被许可人也可以提起诉讼。

4. 分许可使用(Sub-licensing)

分许可使用，是指注册商标许可合同的被许可方依据合同规定，除了取得在规定的范围内使用许可方的注册商标外，还可以许可第三方(the third parties)使用许可方的注册商标。分许可使用的范围，不能超出许可方与被许可方约定的地域和时间范围，并必须取得许可方的许可方能使用。

(四)禁止权(Right of Prohibition)

禁止权，是指商标权人有禁止他人未经许可使用其注册商标的权利。The owner of trademark right has the right to prohibit the following act: using a trademark which is identical with or similar to the registered trademark on the same kind of commodities or similar commodities without permission.

禁止权的效力范围及于"类似商品"和"近似商品"，而使用权的范围以核准注册的商标和核定使用的商品为限，禁止权的效力范围大于专用权的效力范围。这样的规定更有利于保护商标权人的利益。

三、商标权的期限、续展和终止(The Term, Renewal and Termination of Trademark)

(一)商标权的期限和续展(The Term and Renewal)

1. 商标权的保护期(The Duration of Protection of Trademark Rights)

商标权的保护期，是指注册商标所有人享有的商标专用权的有效期限(valid term)。各国商标法对注册商标的有效期都有不同的规定。According to the *Chinese Trademark Law*, the period of validity of a registered trademark shall be ten years, counted from the day the registration is approved. 因此，商标权的法律特征之一是时间性(timeliness)，即商标权只在合法注册之后的法定期间(legal term)内受保护。商标权人所享有各项商标权利的期间与注册商标的有效期相同。

2. 商标权的续展(The Renewal of Trademark)

(1)商标权续展的概念及有关规定

商标权的续展，是指注册商标所有人在商标注册有效期届满前后的一段时间内，依法办理一定的手续，延长其注册商标有效期的制度。

The term of a trademark can be renewed upon filing a request. Without such a request, a trademark will be terminated. Therefore, trademark rights are regarded as continuing semi-permanently(半永续性).

According to the *Chinese Trademark Law*, if a registrant wants to continue to use the registered trademark after the period of validity expires, an application for renewal registration shall be made within twelve months before the expiration. If the registrant fails to make such an application within that period, an extension period of six months may be granted. If no application has been filed before the extension period expires, the registered trademark shall be cancelled.

每次续展注册的有效期为10年，即每续展一次商标权的有效期延长一个10年，自该商标上一个有效期届满次日算起。The period of validity for each renewal shall be ten years. 另外，《商标法》规定，基于商标权人的合法续展，其商标受法律保护的期限可以不断延长。对于申请续展的次数，法律没有限制性规定(restrictions)，即商标权人可以根据自己的意志来确定是否续展和续展。只要商标权人按照规定及时办理续展注册手续，商标权就永远存在，换言之，商标权就成为一种相对的永久权。

(2)商标权续展的程序(The Procedures of Trademark's Renewal)

申请商标续展注册，应履行法定程序。凡申请商标续展注册的，申请人应向商标局提交《商标续展注册申请书》以及申请人经盖章或者签字确认的主体资格证明文件复印件。申请书应填写注册商标的编号、商品的类别等，同时缴纳续展注册费。如果委托代理机构的，要提交《代理委托书》在宽展期内申请的，还应交续展延迟费。商标局收到申请经审查认为不合规定的，将不予续展；如果申请符合法律规定，续展申请核准后，商标局发给申请人续展证明，并对申请续展的商标予以公告。

(二)商标权的终止(The Termination of Trademark Rights)

商标权的终止，是指由于出现了法定原因(legal reasons)导致商标权丧失(extinguishment)，不再受法律保护。

Extinguishment of a trademark right means that a trademark right loses effect due to the occurrence of certain events. The events that cause extinguishment shall include: (i) expiration of the term; (ii) cancellation of registration, or a ruling for such cancellation; (iii) non-existence of an heir and (iv) surrender.

If a trial decision that the trademark registration is to be invalidated has become final and conclusive, the trademark right shall be deemed never existed, or not existed from the time when any extinguishing event occurred.

根据我国商标法的规定，导致商标权终止的原因主要有两种情形：

1. 商标权因注销而终止(Terminated Due to Cancellation)

商标的注销(the cancellation of trademark)，是指商标局对注册商标所有人自愿放弃或因故不能使用注册商标的事实之确认行为。注销注册商标须由商标局备案，并予以公告。导致注册商标注销的具体缘由有以下几种：

(1)注册商标有效期届满未申请续展注册(The term of registered trademark is expiration and not filing for renewal)

注册商标有效期届满，宽展期(grace period)已过，商标所有人仍未提出续展申请的；或者虽然提出续展申请而被商标局驳回(reject)的。

Although a trademark right is, in effect, semi-permanent, the term is fixed for a certain period; namely, ten years from the date of registration, with the intent to dispose of unused rights, and the trademark right remains in effect on the assumption that its term may be renewed upon expiration of the current term. Should the procedure for renewal not be taken, the trademark right is extinguished upon expiration of the term.

(2)自动放弃(Voluntary Surrender)

注册商标所有人在商标注册期间自愿申请放弃其商标权，并向商标局办理注销手续的情形。

Because a trademark right is a proprietary right(所有权), it may be surrendered. A portion of a trademark connected to certain designated(特定的) goods or services may be surrendered. If there is an exclusive licensee(专有特许持有人), pledgee(质押权人), or non-exclusive licensee, a person who has the right to the trademark may surrender his trademark right only with the consent of other such persons so as not to harm interested persons by the surrender.

(3)商标注册人消亡(Trademark Registrant Withers Away)

注册商标有效期内,因注册商标所有人被撤销(revocation)、解散(dissolution)、破产(bankruptcy)及其他原因而关闭,或者因注册商标所有人死亡而在法定期限内无人继承(non-existence of an heir)的,由商标局注销其注册商标。商标注册人死亡或者终止,自死亡或者终止之日起1年期满,该注册商标没有办理移转手续的,任何人都可以向商标局申请注销该注册商标。

2. 商标权因撤销而终止(Terminated Due to Cancellation)

商标权因撤销(cancellation)而终止,是指因商标获得注册后,未依法使用而导致其注册商标权消灭。具体包括以下几种具体的缘由:

(1)不按规定使用的

A trademark registrant that, without authorization, makes alternations with respect to the registered trademark, the name or address of the registrant or other registration items during the use of the registered trademark shall be ordered to make correction within a time limit by the relevant local administrative department for industry and commerce. If it fails to make correction within the prescribed time limit, the trademark office shall cancel the registered trademark thereof.

(2)连续3年不使用的

Where a registered trademark has become the generic name of the goods for which its use is approved or a registered trademark has not been put in use for three consecutive years without a justifiable reason, any entity or individual may apply to the trademark office for revocation of the registered trademark, and the trademark office shall make a decision within nine months upon the receipt of the application. Whereat is necessary under special circumstances, an extension of three months may be granted for making a decision upon approval by the administrative department for industry and commerce of the State Council.

四、商标权人的义务(Obligations of the Trademark Owner)

根据我国现行《商标法》及《商标法实施条例》的有关规定,商标权人在行使其注册商标专用权时负有如下义务:

(一)缴纳各项费用的义务(The Obligation of Payment)

商标权人应当按照《商标法》以及《商标法实施条例》的规定缴纳注册商标的各项费用,包括商标申请费(Application Fees)、转让注册费(Transfer Fees)、续展注册费(Renewal Fees)等。

(二)保证商品或服务质量的义务(Obligations to Guarantee the Quality of Goods or Services)

The user of a trademark shall be responsible for the quality of the commodities on which the trademark is used.

保证商品或服务的质量是商标权人必须履行的一项义务,这是对消费者负责的具体表现,也是维护商标信誉,扩大商品和服务知名度的关键。在商标许可使用中,商标权人也要慎重选择被许可人，并对使用其商标的产品和服务质量实施监督。

(三)依法使用注册商标的义务(The Obligation of Legal Use of Registered Trademarks)

商标权人应当依法使用其注册商标。商标注册人在使用注册商标的过程中，自行改变注册商标、注册人名义、地址或者其他注册事项的，由地方工商行政管理部门责令限期改正；期满不改正的，由商标局撤销其注册商标。注册商标成为其核定使用的商品的通用名称或者没有正当理由连续3年不使用的，任何单位或者个人可以向商标局申请撤销该注册商标。商标局应当自收到申请之日起9个月内作出决定。有特殊情况需要延长的，经国务院工商行政管理部门批准，可以延长3个月。

第二节 商标权的限制
Ⅱ The Limitations on Trademark Rights

商标权的限制(the limitations on trademark rights)，是指在某些情况下，注册商标所有人享有的权利因与他人正当权利和公众利益(legitimate rights and public interest)产生冲突，为了协调权利人与社会公众利益之间的关系，而对商标权的行使和保护作出的必要约束。

Mark law does not give mark owners absolute control over others' use of the words or symbols constituting their marks. As long as another person's use of a trademark causes no likelihood of consumer confusion, that person will not be liable for trademark infringement.

商标权利限制主要分为权利用尽、合理使用和非商业性使用。大部分国家的法律都只规定了商标的合理使用。非商业性使用的法律依据为商标法意外的法律，如宪法关于言论自由的规定，市场竞争法保障商品正常流通的基本理念等。

一、商标权的权利用尽(Exhaustion of Trademark Rights)

Exhaustion of trademark rights (sometimes called the doctrine of first sale) provides that once a mark owner sells or authorizes sale of goods bearing its mark, it has no authority to prevent subsequent owners from reselling those goods with the mark. However, subsequent owners' use of the mark in the resale must be truthful, and not misleading: the resale must not lead to a likelihood of consumer confusion about the immediate source of the goods (for example, if the immediate seller has changed the goods), or mislead consumers about the nature of the goods (for example, mislead consumers into thinking that the goods are new when they are used, or that they are in their original state when they have been materially changed).

商标用尽的理论基础在于防止商标权人利用商标权进行市场分割，保障商品贸易的正常流通，获取不合理的垄断利润(unreasonable monopoly profits)。不过，《欧共体商标条例》第13条在规定商标权利用尽的同时，指出商标权人有正当理由的，例如商品在投放市场后商品质量有变化或者损坏的，可以反对商品的进一步流通。此外，如果商品被重新包装的，也构成商标用尽的例外。例如，激光打印机中的打印鼓，有人回收之后灌装碳粉再行出售的行为，就构成侵权。购买他人带有注册商标的商品，对该注册商标进行排斥性处理转而加贴上自己的商标出售的商业行为，不适用商标权用尽，而是属于不正当竞争(unfair competition)的行为。①

二、注册商标的合理使用(Fair Use of Registered Trademark)

(一)合理使用的概念(The Conception of Fair Use)

合理使用，是指他人在经营活动中以善意、正当的方式使用描述性商标的，不视为侵犯商标专用权的行为。允许经营者对描述性商标进行使用，是现代商标法权利限制中最为常见的一种。

Most trademarks are adapted from words or symbols already common to the culture, as Apple Computer is from apple, instead of being invented by the mark owner (such as Kodak). Courts have recognized that ownership in the mark cannot prevent others from using the word or symbol in these other senses, such as if the trademark is a descriptive word or symbol such as a pine tree. This means that the less distinctive or original the trademark, the less able the trademark owner will be to control how it is used.

A no owner(非所有人) may also use a trademark nominative—to refer to the actual trademarked product or its source. In addition to protecting product criticism and analysis, United States law actually encourages nominative usage by competitors in the form of comparative advertising.

Members may provide limited exceptions to the rights conferred by a trademark, such as fair use of descriptive terms, provided that such exceptions take account of the legitimate interests of the owner of the trademark and third parties.

所谓说明性词汇(descriptive terms)，又称叙述性词汇，实践中常常是表示商品质量、主要原料、用途等因素的普通文字，或者是地名。这些词汇本为公用，虽然商标权人经过使用而使得其获得显著性，但是公众仍可以善意正当的方式进行非商业性的使用。《欧共体商标条例》，以及现行的英国、日本的商标法也有类似规定。

Article 59 of Chinese *Trademark Law* provides that the holder of the exclusive right to use a registered trademark shall have no right to prohibit others from properly using the generic name (通用名称), graphics or models of a commodity contained in the registered trademark, or such information as directly indicates the quality, main raw materials (主要原料), functions, purposes, weight, quantity or other features of the commodity, or the names of the geographical locations as contained therein.

(二)合理使用的分类

我国《商标法》没有规定合理使用的问题。国家工商管理局在1999年的《关于商标行政执法中若干问题的意见》第9条中规定了两种类型的使用与注册商标相同或者近似的文字、图形但不属于商标侵权的行为：善意地使用自己的名称或者地址；善意地说明商品或

① 马强．商标权权利穷竭研究[DB/OL]．[2017-05-07]．法律教育网，http：//www.chinalawedu.com/new/21604_5300_/2009_10_13_zh88318510131019002512.shtml.

者服务的特征或者属性，尤其是说明商品或者服务的质量、用途、地理来源、种类、价值及提供日期。此外，新闻媒体基于事实对商标进行的客观报道和评论，也属于合理的使用。

1. 名称或地址的合理使用(The Fair Use of Name or Address)

地名商标(geographical names as trademark)，是指将行政区划的地理名称或其他地理区域的名称、历史地名作为商标内容或商标主要组成部分的商标，如北京饭店、青岛啤酒等。

由于地名商标或直接表现为地名，其在与商品或服务结合使用时，消费者往往会将此地名词汇误认为产地的名称，从而将该商品或服务与特定的地域联系起来，而不是与特定的厂商联系起来。换言之，地名商标识别商品或服务特定出处的作用较弱，即商标的显著性较弱。也正因为如此，各国商标法对地名注册为商标普遍采取了一种限制的态度。欧共体一号指令和德国商标法均规定，只要可能被用来作为产源的标记就不能注册为商标。美国的做法与此相近，原则上纯粹的地名不得注册，但经使用取得第二含义的则不在限制之列。我国商标法也有类似规定。根据我国商标法的规定，一般情况下，没有其他含义的县级以上行政区划名称及公众知晓的外国地名不能被注册为商标的。但对已经注册的地名商标继续承认其合法性，同时允许地名作为证明商标、集体商标组成部分，对县级以下行政区划的地名和不是行政区划名称的地名注册为商标则未予禁止。由此可以推断出，有其他含义的县级以上行政区划名称、县级以下行政区划名称以及不是行政区划名称的地名注册为商标在我国不存在法律上的障碍。

2. 叙述性商标的合理使用(The Fair Use of Descriptive Trademarks)

叙述性商标(descriptive trademarks)通常由直接表示商品质量、主要原料、功能、用途等通用名称的普通词汇构成。商标法赋予商标权利人使用商标的专用权，同时也赋予其排除他人妨害其商标权的权利。但这种排除妨害的范围仅限于禁止他人将商标用于标志商品来源的作用，也就是说，本身不具有显著性的商标，经过使用具有了第二含义，因而获得了显著性特征，就应该受到保护。但这种保护仅仅限制在第二含义的范围内，并不能阻止他人以第一含义的方式使用该文字、图形或者记号。

一般可从以下几方面判断是否属于善意正当使用(proper use of good faith)：除使用与他人商标相同或近似的文字、图形外，是否加注了其他说明性文字；所使用的文字、图形是否作为商标使用，或者该文字或图形是否足以标志、区别商品来源；使用该说明性文字是否突出强调经商标所有人长期使用而具有的显著性特征，也就是该商标的第二含义；是否同时突出使用自己的商标，消费者对产品的来源是否产生混淆等。

因此，对叙述性商标应当进行有必要的权利限制，否则会妨碍其他经营者对公共资源的使用，商标法上的获得显著性规则也就因此而失去存在的合理性。叙述性使用作为商标权利的例外，就是允许商标权利人以外的经营者对叙述性商标做善意、正当的使用。

3. 指示性商标的合理使用(The Fair Use of The Indicative Mark)

指示性合理使用，是指为了使一般公众了解与商品和服务有关的真实信息，而在生产经营活动中使用他人注册商标以指称他人商品或服务的行为。允许指示性使用主要考虑到消费者对于与产品有关的真实信息的需要，以及某些行业惯例。指示性使用多见于零配件销售、保养维修(汽车、电子消费者的维修服务)，例如，“奥迪汽车维修”、“索尼电脑专营店”，这种店铺名称或服务招牌中使用商标是为了表明本店经营的零部件、电子耗材等，属于指示性使用。与对地名商标和描述性商标合理使用不同的是，在指示性合理使用的情形下，被控侵权人使用原告的商标是用来指代原告的商品或者服务，而非指代被控侵权人自己的商品或服务，尽管最终仍是为了描述被控侵权人自己的商品或服务。而在地名商标和描述性商标合理使用中，被控侵权人使用原告商标均是用来说明或描述被控侵权人自己的产品或服务。

第三节　商标权的保护
Ⅲ　The Protection of Trademark Rights

一、商标权的保护及其意义(Trademark Protection and Its Significance)

The protection of trademarks has long been accepted internationally. In most countries, rights are initially secured by registration and maintained by later use in the country. Generally speaking, use without registration does not provide trademark protection. Only the United States and a few other nations require use of the mark before registration (e. g. , Canada and the Philippines) or give some priority of rights based solely on use (e. g. , in addition to the United States, common law countries such as Australia, Canada and the United Kingdom).

(一)商标权保护的界定和意义(Definition and Meaning of Trademark Protection)

商标权的保护，是指以法律手段制裁侵犯他人注册商标专用权(infringement of exclusive rights of registered trademark)的行为，以保护商标权人对其注册商标所享有的专有权利。保护注册商标专用权在宏观层面来讲是健全商标法制的中心环节，是我国商标法的立法宗旨，也是商标管理机关和司法机关的重要任务。在微观层面，商标权的保护不仅有利于保护企业的无形资产，商标专用权的保护愈彻底，商标的信誉价值就愈高，企业的竞争实力就愈强；而且也有利于保护消费者的利益，减少假冒伪劣商品，构建公平有序的市场秩序。

(二)商标权的保护范围(The Scope of Trademark Protection)

1. 商标权保护的范围

我国商标法以注册商标(registered trademark)的专用权为保护对象。注册商标的专用权，以核准注册的商标和核定使用的商品为限。这是区别和判断侵权与否的一条重要界限。即注册人使用的商标应当与核准注册的商标在文字、图形、字母、数字、三维标志、颜色组合和声音等或者其他构成要素上相一致，不得自行改变注册商标。同时，注册商标专用权以核定使用的商品为限，即商标权人使用注册商标的商品应当和国家商标局核定使用的商品相一致。而商标权的保护范围是指权利人有权禁止他人在相同或类似的商品上使用与自己注册的商标相同或者相近似的商标。可见，商标权保护范围比商标专用权的范围要大很多，即商标权的保护范围扩大到了类似的商品和近似的商标，商标权人有权禁止他人在相同或类似的商品上使用与注册商标相同或近似的商标。

2. 商标权保护的期限(Duration of Trademark Protection)

商标权保护的期限，是指注册商标专用权受法律保护的有效期限(valid term)。我国注册商标的有效期为10年，自核准注册之日起计算。注册商标有效期满可以续展；商标权的续展是指通过一定程序，延续原注册商标的有效期限，使商标注册人继续保持其注册商标的专用权。我国商标法规定，注册商标有效期满需要继续使用的，应当在期满前12个月内申请续展注册。每次续展注册的有效期为10年。续展注册经核准后，予以公告。

二、商标侵权行为及其法律保护(Infringement of Trademark and Its Legal Protection)

(一)商标侵权行为的概念和构成条件(The Concept of Trademark's Infringement)

商标侵权行为，是指违反商标法规定，假冒或仿冒他人注册商标，或者从事其他损害商标权人合法权益的行为。

Infringement occurs when someone else using a trademark that is same as or similar to your registered trademark for the same or similar goods/services. Trademark infringement claims generally involve the issues of likelihood of confusion(混淆之虞), counterfeit marks(伪造商标) and dilution of marks(稀释商标).

Uses that do not infringe a famous mark (because there is no likelihood of confusion) may still be prevented if they are likely to dilute the mark by blurring or by tarnishment. Dilution protects the distinctiveness of a famous mark. The more distinctive a mark, the greater power the mark owner has to enforce it. Beyond legal rights, the more distinctive and well known the marks, the greater value it has as an asset.

(二)商标侵权的表现形式(The Manifestations of Infringements)

根据我国《商标法》第57条和《商标法实施条例》第75、76条以及最高人民法院的相关司法解释，商标侵权的行为主要有以下几种表现形式：

1. 假冒或仿冒注册商标行为(Acts of Forgery or Counterfeiting a Registered Trademark)

假冒或仿冒注册商标行为，是指未经商标注册人的许可，在同一种商品或者类似商品上使用与其注册商标相同或者近似的商标。这类行为会混淆商品来源，损害消费者及商标权人利益，具体包括以下四种：

(1)在同一种商品上使用与他人注册商标相同的商标。

(2)在同一种商品上使用与他人注册商标相近似的商标。

(3)在类似商品上使用与注册商标相同的商标。

(4)在类似商品上使用与他人注册商标相近似的商标。

第一种行为是假冒行为(act as passing off)，其余三种是仿冒行为(counterfeit)。假冒注册商标是最严重的侵害商标专用权的行为，情节严重的，还要依法追究刑事责任(criminal responsibility)。

“相同商标”(identical trademark)是指被控侵权的商标与原告的注册商标相比较，二者在视觉上基本无差别。“近似商标”(similar trademark)是指被控侵权的商标与原告的注册商标相比较，其文字的字形、读音、含义或者图形的构图及颜色，或者其各要素组合后的整体结构相似，或者其立体形状、颜色组合近似，易使相关公众对商品来源产生误认或者认为其来源与原告注册商标的商品有特定的联系。

Infringement does not require use of identical mark; use of a similar mark may suffice. But the greater the similarity, the more likely that consumers will be confused. Courts look to the "sight, sound, and meaning" of the two marks in assessing similarity. If a mark is FISH, then similar marks could be FnSH (similar on sight), PHYTCH (sound), or TRAWL (meaning) — or a picture of a fish (meaning again). Courts consider the marks as they appear in the marketplace. The placement of the marks, colors, typeface, and other design elements may affect he likelihood of confusion. Factors beyond the mark itself, such as the use of additional trademarks, may tend to dispel possible confusion. The prominent use of the maker of the product may dispel any confusion as to source. Likewise, even close similarity may be negated by sufficiently prominentise disclaimers. ①

"类似商品"(similar/proximity goods)是指在功能、用途、生产部门、销售渠道、消费对象等方面相同，或者相关公众一般认为其存在特定联系、容易造成混淆的商品。在认定商品或者服务是否类似时，应以相关公众对商品或者服务的一般认识综合判断，《商标注册用商品和服务国际分类表》、《类似商品和服务区分表》可以作为判断类似商品或者服务的参考。

The more similar the goods and services (or their marketing), the more like the confusion. Infringement does not require use by a competitor or even by someone who sells related goods and services. Courts look to the actual nature of the goods and services (are parties selling the same thing?), channels of marketing (do they sell through the same media?), market segments (do they target the same buyers?), geographical trading area, and any other ways in which the relevant product so or do not share a market. "Proximity/similar" can be quite literal—the products do or do not share a market. "Proximity" can be quite literal—the products might sit near each other on store shelves. But it may also come through other modes of marketing. If the products are different in nature but are marketed through similar channels, confusion is more likely. If the goods are in a different market but are in a category that is closely related to the plaintiff's goods, consumers may still be likely to infer that the goods are produced or endorsed by the mark owner. ②

对商标的使用，包括将商标用于商品、商品包装或者容器以及商品交易文书上，或者将商标用于广告宣传、展览以及其他商业活动中。

2. 销售侵犯注册商标专用权的商品(Selling Goods that Infringe on the Exclusive Right to the Use of a Registered Trademark)

---

① Stephen M. McJohn. Intellectual Property (Fifth Edition) [M]. New York: Wolters Kluwer, 2014: 540-541.

② Stephen M. McJohn. Intellectual Property (Fifth Edition) [M]. New York: Wolters Kluwer, 2014: 541.

这是一种流通领域的侵权行为，即是商品销售者实施的一种侵犯商标专用权行为，它以其他侵权事实的存在为其存在的前提条件。这类侵权行为虽然没有直接非法使用他人的注册商标，但在客观上为直接侵权人实现其侵权目的，谋取非法利益提供了条件，其行为也侵害了商标权人的利益，应追究其侵权责任。此类侵权行为的主体是商品经销商(commodity dealers)，不管行为人主观上是否有过错，只要实施了销售侵犯注册商标专用权的商品的行为，都构成侵权，属于直接侵权行为。只是在行为人主观上是善意时，可以免除其赔偿责任。

If a party is unaware of the infringing nature of such products and is able to prove that the products are obtained by legitimate means and can provide information on the suppliers of the products, it shall be ordered to stop selling the products by the administrative department for industry and commerce , and shall not bear the liability for compensation.

3. 伪造、擅自制造他人注册商标标识或者销售伪造、擅自制造的注册商标标识(Counterfeiting, or Making without Authorization, Representations of Another Person's Registered Trademark, or Selling such Representations)

商标标识是指用于商品上的商标载体，是独立于被标志商品上的商标物质表现形式。如酒类商品上的瓶贴、自行车上的标牌、服装上的织带等。伪造是指未经注册商标权人许可，模仿其注册商标进行印制商标标识的行为。仿造的形式很多，如模仿商标标识刻制印模而进行印制、复印、手工描绘等。擅自制造是指未经注册商标权人同意而印制确实是注册商标的商标标识。

这种侵权行为是商标标识侵权问题，包括“制作”和“销售”两种行为。行为人一般为从事商标印刷的企业和个体工商户(enterprises and individual business)，他们实施的行为专为制假售假行为提供条件。具体包括四种情况：一是伪造他人注册商标标识；二是未经商标权人授权和委托而制造其商标标识；三是虽有商标权人的授权或委托，但超出授权或委托的范围，制造其注册商标标识；四是销售他人注册商标标识。

4. 反向假冒(Reverse Passing off)

反向假冒，又称为逆假冒，是指未经商标注册人同意，更换其注册商标并将该更换商标的商品又投入市场的行为，也称为商标的反向假冒行为。根据对商品变更程度的不同，商标反向假冒行为的表现形式呈现以下两种：整体反向假冒，即保持所涉及商品的原样，对其本身不做任何变更，而只是作了商标的替换；部分反向假冒，即对所涉及商品作了拆分，只利用该商品的局部，或者将该商品的局部应用到自己商品之上另外构成一个整体，然后在自己商标名下予以出售。

反向假冒这一概念最早见于1946年美国成文商标法即《兰哈姆法》(*Lanham Act*)第43条(a)款，此外加拿大、意大利、葡萄牙等国对此也有不同的法律进行了规定。

In reverse passing off, the originator of the misidentified product is involuntarily deprived of the advertising value of his name and the goodwill, and the consumer is deprived of knowing the true source of the product, and may even be deceived about the source.

Reverse passing off falls into two categories, express reverse passing off and implied reverse passing off. In express reverse passing off, the infringer replaces the original mark with his mark and sells the product. In implied reverse passing off, the infringer only removes the mark prior to selling the unbranded product.

我国《商标法》第 57 条第 5 款规定，“未经商标注册人同意，更换其注册商标并将该更换商标的商品又投入市场的”(Altering a registered trademark without permission of its owner and selling goods bearing such an altered trademark on the market)，属侵犯注册商标专用权行为。

我国《反不正当竞争法》第 2 条第 1、2 款作了如下规定：“经营者在市场交易中，应当遵循自愿、平等、公平、诚实信用的原则，遵守公认的商业道德。”“本法所称的不正当竞争，是指经营者违反本法规定，损害其他经营者合法权益，扰乱社会经济秩序的行为。”商标反向假冒行为直接违反了我国《反不正当竞争法》第 2 条之规定。

5. 故意为侵犯他人商标专用权行为提供便利条件，帮助他人实施侵犯商标专用权行为(Providing, Intentionally, Convenience for such Acts as Infringe upon Others' Exclusive Right of Trademark use, To facilitate others to Commit Infringement on the Exclusive Right of Trademark Use)

商标侵权行为往往不是孤立进行的，它经常需要借助第三人的帮助、参与和支持。随着科技的发展，知识产权侵权的成本不断降低，导致侵权行为越来越分散化，权利人追究直接侵权者的责任有时不但费时费力，而且很难得到充分的补偿。如果直接侵权者不在法院管辖范围内，权利人甚至无法起诉。为了加强对商标的保护，很多国家在商标法中均规定引诱他人实施侵权行为或明知他人准备从事侵权行为，为其提供实质性帮助的，构成间接侵权。如我国《商标法》第 57 条第 6 款规定，故意为侵犯他人商标专用权行为提供便利条件，帮助他人实施侵犯商标专用权行为的，属侵犯注册商标专用权行为。

An act of providing such facilities as storage, transport, mailing, printing, concealing, business premises, or an online goods trading platform for infringing upon another person's exclusive right to use a registered trademark constitutes an act of providing convenience for infringement.

当然，间接侵权要求主观状态是明知或者应当知道，如果确实不知情，不构成间接侵权。

6. 给他人的注册商标专用权造成其他损害的行为(Impairing in Other Manners Another Person's Exclusive Right to the Use of Its Registered Trademark)

根据《商标法实施条例》和《最高人民法院关于审理商标民事纠纷案件适用法律若干问题的解释》等规定，下列行为属于“给他人的注册商标专用权造成其他损害”的商标侵权行为：

(1)在同一种或者类似商品上，将与他人注册商标相同或者近似的标志作为商品名称或者商品装潢使用，误导公众的。

(2)将与他人注册商标相同或者相近似的文字作为企业的字号在相同或者类似商品上突出使用，容易使相关公众产生误认的。

(3)复制、模仿或者翻译他人注册的驰名商标或其主要部分在不相同或者不相类似商品上作为商标使用，误导公众，致使该驰名商标注册人的利益可能受到损害的。

(4)将与他人注册商标相同或者相近似的文字注册为域名，并且通过该域名进行相关商品交易的电子商务，容易使相关公众产生误认的。

(三)注册商标侵权的法律责任(The Legal Liability of Trademark Infringement)

依法核准注册的商标，商标注册人享有该商标的专用权，受法律保护。伪造、擅自制造、销售侵犯注册商标专用权的行为，根据《商标法》、《商标法实施条例》、《民法通则》和《刑法》的规定，侵犯他人的注册商标的，需要承担民事责任、行政责任和刑事责任。

1. 民事责任(Civil Liability)

(1)停止侵权、消除影响、恢复名誉

根据我国《民法总则》《商标法》《商标法实施条例》的规定，商标专用权人在其商标权受到不法侵害时，有权要求人民法院依法责令侵权人停止侵害(stopping the infringement)、消除影响(eliminating the effects)、恢复名誉(rehabilitating the reputation)、赔偿损失(compensation for the losses)及承担其他民事责任。

因侵权行为给商标权人或利害关系人造成损失的，侵权人应当给予赔偿。根据我国《商标法》第 63 条规定，侵犯商标专用权的赔偿数额，按照权利人因被侵权所受到的实际损失(actual losses)确定；实际损失难以确定的，可以按照侵权人因侵权所获得的利益(illegal profits)确定；权利人的损失或者侵权人获得的利益难以确定的，参照该商标许可使用费的倍数合理确定。对恶意侵犯商标专用权，情节严重的，可以在按照上述方法确定数额的 1 倍以上 3 倍以下确定赔偿数额。赔偿数额应当包括权利人为制止侵权行为所支付的合理开支。

人民法院为确定赔偿数额，在权利人已经尽力举证，而与侵权行为相关的账簿、资料主要由侵权人掌握的情况下，可以责令侵权人提供与侵权行为相关的账簿、资料；侵权人不提供或者提供虚假的账簿、资料的，人民法院可以参考权利人的主张和提供的证据判定赔偿数额。

权利人因被侵权所受到的实际损失、侵权人因侵权所获得的利益、注册商标许可使用费难以确定的，由人民法院根据侵权行为的情节判决给予 300 万元以下的赔偿。

The compensation for infringing upon the right to exclusive use of a trademark shall be the proceeds obtained from the infringement during the period of infringement, or the losses suffered by the infringed due to the infringement during the period of being infringed, including the reasonable expenses paid by the infringed to stop the acts.

商标只有在实际使用中才能发挥识别作用并累计商誉，如果商标在注册后并未实际使用，则他人未经许可使用的行为也不可能导致消费者混淆，也不涉及不正当利用他人商誉而给商标权人造成损失，因此在确定赔偿数额过程中，如果被控侵权人以注册商标专用权人未使用注册商标提出抗辩的，人民法院可以要求注册商标专用权人提供此前 3 年内实际使用该注册商标的证据。注册商标专人不能证明此前 3 年内实际使用过该注册商标，也不能证明因侵权行为受到损失的，被控侵权人不承担赔偿责任。另外如果销售不知道是侵权注册商标专用权的商品，能证明该商品是自己合法取得的并说明提供者的，不承担赔偿责任。

2. 行政责任(Administrative Liability)

商标侵权行为除了对商标权人的民事权利构成侵害之外，还可能破坏正常的市场经济秩序，阻碍社会经济健康发展，损害广大消费者的切身利益。根据我国《商标法》第60条的规定，侵犯注册商标专用权行为，引起纠纷的，由当事人协商解决；不愿协商或者协商不成的，商标注册人或者利害关系人可以向人民法院起诉，也可以请求工商行政管理部门处理。工商行政管理部门处理时，认定侵权行为成立的，责令立即停止侵权行为，没收、销毁侵权商品和专门用于制造侵权商品、伪造注册商标标识的工具，违法经营额5万元以上的，可以处违法经营额5倍以下的罚款，没有违法经营额或者违法经营额不足5万元的，可以处25万元以下的罚款。对5年内实施两次以上商标侵权行为或者有其他严重情节的，应当从重处罚。销售不知道是侵犯注册商标专用权的商品，能证明该商品是自己合法取得并说明提供者的，由工商行政管理部门责令停止销售。

对侵犯商标专用权的赔偿数额的争议，当事人可以请求进行处理的工商行政管理部门调解，也可以依照我国《民事诉讼法》向人民法院起诉。经工商行政管理部门调解，当事人未达成协议或者调解书生效后不履行的，当事人可以依照我国《民事诉讼法》向人民法院起诉。此外，对于侵犯注册商标专用权的行为，工商政管理部门有权依法查处。

3. 刑事责任(Criminal Liability)

刑事责任是指人民法院依照《刑法》对假冒注册商标的犯罪行为所作的刑事制裁。《刑法》第213条、第214条和第215条分别规定了“假冒注册商标罪”、“销售假冒注册商标的商品罪”和“非法制造、销售非法制造的注册商标标识罪”。

(1)假冒注册商标罪(Crime of counterfeiting a registered trademark)

未经注册商标所有人许可，在同一种商品上使用与其注册商标相同的商标，情节严重的，处3年以下有期徒刑或者拘役，并处或者单处罚金；情节特别严重的，处3年以上7年以下有期徒刑，并处罚金。销售明知是假冒注册商标的商品，销售金额数额较大的，处3年以下有期徒刑或者拘役，并处或者单处罚金；销售金额数额巨大的，处3年以上7年以下有期徒刑，并处罚金。

最高人民法院和最高人民检察院于2004年颁布的《关于办理侵犯知识产权刑事案件具体应用法律若干问题的解释》(以下简称《刑事司法解释》)第1条将以下两种情形规定为“情节严重”：①非法经营数额在5万元以上或者违法所得数额在3万元以上的；②假冒两种以上注册商标，非法经营数额在3万元以上或者违法所得数额在2万元以上的。同时，该《刑事司法解释》将以下两种情形解释为“情节特别严重”：①非法经营数额在25万元以上或者违法所得数额在15万元以上的；②假冒两种以上注册商标，非法经营数额在15万元以上或者违法所得数额在10万元以上的。其中“非法经营数额”，是指行为人在实施侵犯商标权行为过程中，制造、储存、运输、销售侵权产品的价值。已销售的侵权产品的价值，按照实际销售的价格计算。制造、储存、运输和未销售的侵权产品的价值，按照标价或者已经查清的侵权产品的实际销售平均价格计算。侵权产品没有标价或者无法查清其实际销售价格的，按照被侵权产品的市场中间价格计算。

(2)销售假冒注册商标商品罪(Crime of selling commodities carrying counterfeit registered trademark)

销售明知是假冒注册商标的商品，销售金额数额较大的，处3年以下有期徒刑或者拘役，并处或者单处罚金；销售金额数额巨大的，处3年以上7年以下有期徒刑，并处罚金。根据《刑事司法解释》的规定，具有下列情形之一的，就可以认定销售者“明知”被销售的是假冒注册商标的商品：①知道自己销售的商品上的注册商标被涂改、调换或者覆盖的；②因销售假冒注册商标的商品受到过行政处罚或者承担过民事责任，又销售同一种假冒注册商标的商品的；③伪造、涂改商标注册人授权文件或者知道该文件被伪造、涂改的。

(3)伪造、擅自伪造他人注册商标标识罪(Crime of forging, manufacturing without authorization the marks of a registered trademark)

伪造、擅自制造他人注册商标标识或者销售伪造、擅自制造的注册商标标识，情节严重的，处3年以下有期徒刑、拘役或者管制，并处或者单处罚金；情节特别严重的，处3年以上7年以下有期徒刑，并处罚金。

【英语词汇】

bankruptcy *n.* 破产

cancellation *n.* 注销

dissolution *n.* 解散

identical *adj.* 相同的

licensor *n.* 许可人

together-transfer 连同转让

prohibit *v.* 禁止

renewal *n.* 续展

revocation *n.* 撤销

semi-permanently *n.* 半永续性

trademark holder 商标持有人

voluntary surrender 自动放弃

business reputation *n.* 商誉

damage *v./n.* 损害

exhaustion of trademark right 商标权穷竭

licensee *n.* 被许可方

limitation *n.* 限制

unrestrained-transfer 自由，转让

registered trademark 注册商标

reverse passing off 反向假冒

registration antagonism 登记对抗主义

successive assignment 继受转让

valid term 有效期限

【英语句型】

1. The trademark registrant is entitled to use the trademark in respect of the goods and service approved and uses it in relevant business.

“is entitled to...”是指“有资格做……”，“in respect of ”是指“在……方面”。

译文：商标注册人有权在核准的商品、服务以及相关业务中使用该注册商标。

2. Extinguishment of a trademark right means that a trademark right that has come into effect loses effect due to the occurrence of certain events.

“due to...”是指“由于，因为……”。

译文：商标权的消失是指商标权因为特定事件的出现而丧失效力。

【阅读资料】

第十五章　驰名商标的特殊法律保护制度
Chapter 15　Specific Protection of Well-Known Trademarks

【引言】社会上的商业广告宣传以及商品上的商标，其知名度(reputation)并不完全一样。一个好的品牌之商品，通常质量较好且价格也相对比较高。正如人们所说的"人怕出名猪怕壮"，品牌产品屡屡被假冒(counterfeit)。因此，对于驰名商标(well-known trademark)的法律保护，无论在国际相关的公约上还是在商标法中，均已作出了较为特殊的规定。

【学习目的与要求】驰名商标的问题不仅涉及商业的宣传广告，而且涉及商业竞争行为和法律保护的基本原理和制度，要真正地把握好这一章的内容，应了解驰名商标特殊法律保护制度的起源、发展，理解认定机构、认定条件和反淡化理论在驰名商标特殊法律保护中的作用，关注社会现实中出现的与驰名商标有关的纷争，了解相关的立法和司法解释。

第一节　驰名商标特殊保护制度的起源与发展
Ⅰ　The Origin and Development of Specific Protection of Well-Known Trademarks

一、驰名商标的特性及其作用(Features and Functions of Well-Known Trademarks)

(一)驰名商标的概念(Definition of Well-Known Trademark)

驰名商标，又称为周知商标、著名商标、高信誉商标、世所共知商标等，通常是指那些在市场上享有较高声誉、为相关公众广为熟知，并具有较强竞争力的商标。

Although well-known trademarks are presented in international conventions such as *Paris Convention for the Protection of Intellectual Property* and TRIPS, and are set in the trademark laws and unfair competition laws in many countries, there is still no agreed definition of well-known trademark.

In the United States, laws like trademark law and unfair competition laws do not give the definition of "famous trademark" (i. e. well-known trademark), but list factors which a court may consider in determining whether a mark is distinctive and famous:

(A) the degree of inherent or acquired distinctiveness of the mark;

(B) the duration and extent of use of the mark in connection with the goods or services with which the mark is used;

(C) the duration and extent of advertising and publicity of the mark;

(D) the geographical extent of the trading area in which the mark is used;

(E) the channels of trade for the goods or services with which the mark is used;

(F) the degree of recognition of the mark in the trading areas and channels of trade used by the marks' owner and the person against whom the injunction is sought;

(G) the nature and extent of use of the same or similar marks by third parties; and

(H) whether the mark was registered under the Act of March 3, 1881, or the Act of February 20, 1905, or on the principal register.

根据《日本商标法》以及1999年日本特许厅公布的《关于周知商标、著名商标的保护的审查标准》，日本认定的驰名商标其知晓范围是“相关公众”，且不以商标注册为前提，驰名商标的认定也不以本国驰名为必需条件。

德国、法国、希腊通过本国的商标法或反不正当竞争法对驰名商标进行保护，对驰名商标的概念也都没有作出明确的界定。

我国修订后的《商标法》明确将驰名商标纳入商标法保护范围，并由国家工商总局于2014年7月3日发布了《驰名商标认定和保护规定》，从而使我国驰名商标的认定和管理工作法制化、规范化，对其保护程度达到了国际先进水平。我国驰名商标是指在我国为相关公众所熟知的商标。

(二)驰名商标的特性(Features of Well-Known Trademarks)

1. 广为人知性(Popularity)

驰名商标具有区别于一般商标的特性在于其广为人知。在某种程度上，驰名商标已经超越了一定的地域范围并跨越了相应的时间。For example, “Coca-Cola” has established a reputation all over the world, and has become a household term.

2. 显著性(Distinctiveness)

尽管注册商标也要求申请注册的商标必须具有显著性，但是驰名商标的显著性不仅仅表现在符合注册条件的显著性，而且在所有商标乃至所有标识中均体现出了其极强的显著性。So to say the relevant public is able to distinguish a well-known trademark, and will not be confused about the relationship between one party and another.

3. 巨额经济价值性(Huge Economic Value)

驰名商标所具有的经济价值，不仅仅表现在驰名商标本身，而且还表现在其所蕴含着的商誉。In a manner of speaking, a well-known trademark with worldwide influence, the economic value of which is beyond measure. 根据国际品牌咨询公司Interbrand发布的《2016年全球最佳品牌》显示，苹果连续第4年成为全球最有价值品牌，该公司品牌价值达到了1780亿美元，同比去年增长了5%。①

4. 商誉性(Goodwill)

---

① 创业资讯.2016年全球最佳品牌榜单出炉 苹果连续四年登榜[DB/OL].[2017-06-12]. 腾讯·大楚网，http://hb.qq.com/a/20161008/017401.htm.

尽管说驰名商标就是一个识别标志，只不过知道的人多一点儿而已。《商标法》只调整“标”的问题，“誉”不是《商标法》直接调整的对象。《商标法》只能通过对“标”的保护间接地涉及“誉”。① That a well-known trademark is popular among the public, implies the public recognition of the enterprise. 当一个企业的产品或者其服务出现了质量问题而得不到有效解决的时候，其驰名商标也会连带受累，甚至会波及与该商标有关的产品乃至整个企业或者行业的商业信誉。②

(三)驰名商标的作用(Functions of Well-Known Trademarks)

1. 宣传影响(Advertising)

在当今的“眼球经济社会”中，从“不认识”到“知道”发展到“重视”而最终“选择”，消费者的消费行为受到品牌广告宣传的重大影响。驰名商标背后隐含着的经济实力、商誉、产品质量和售后服务，给广大的消费者以相应的信心。For this reason, many hypermarkets choose to introduce brands as an advertisement to show their strong economic strength.

2. 经济实力(Economic Strength)

“驰名商标——实力——质量——信誉”之间形成了紧密的关联性。在现代的经济社会中，质量相差不大的产品，商标是否驰名往往产生了价格的巨大反差。From certain point of view, a developed country usually possesses numerous well-known trademarks, which have become an economic business card of a country or region. 一个国家没有自己的民族工业，其经济安全就成为问题，而民族工业需要民族品牌为外在的标志来表示，驰名商标往往又成为民族品牌的代表。

3. 市场竞争力(Competitiveness)

现代经济社会中，拥有驰名商标的大型企业乃至跨国企业集团(international conglomerate)，专利技术成为其竞争的内核，驰名商标则成为其竞争的外在形式。A well-known trademark means a competitive advantage in market competition. Therefore, well-known trademarks, as important intangible assets of intellectual property, are becoming more significant, the protection of which will be further strengthened.

“形成一批拥有自主知识产权和知名品牌、国际竞争力较强的优势企业”是我国“十一五”时期经济社会发展战略目标中的一项重要内容。

尽管驰名商标所具有的特性以及作用已经为社会各界尤其是企业的重视，但是驰名商标制度本身是出于维护市场竞争秩序而设，故不重视产品质量、罔顾消费者权益的“做秀”以求“政绩”、“为驰名而驰名”的“异化”现象值得注意。由于没有正确认识驰名商标的功能，某些政府的行政机关将本地区获得驰名商标的数量单纯地作为经济发展的标杆，因此使驰名商标制度发生了“异化”。③

---

① 郭禾．驰名商标和商誉无关[J]．电子知识产权，2009(8)：18.

② 问题婴幼儿奶粉事件[DB/OL]．[2017-05-28]．新浪新闻中心，http：//news. sina. com. cn/z/video/wtnfyesjs/index. shtml.

③ 程永顺．驰名商标被异化的两个主要原因[J]．电子知识产权，2009(8)：16.

二、驰名商标特殊法律保护制度的起源(Origin of Specific Protection of Well-Known Trademarks)

自有商标以来，以商标的知名度为标准就可以划分出一般商标与驰名商标。如果说对驰名商标的认识属于一种事实判断的话，那么对驰名商标的特殊法律保护则是一种带有价值取向的制度性安排。

1925 年修订的《巴黎公约》首次在世界范围内将驰名商标作为正式的法律术语，并作出了对驰名商标保护的规定，拉开了国际上保护驰名商标的序幕。在 1925 年海牙大会上，《巴黎公约》增补了保护驰名商标的第 6 条之 2，现行有效的文本是 1958 年里斯本外交大大会形成的文本：

The Paris Convention provides a protective principle for well-known trademarks in Article 6 bis:

(1) The countries of Union undertake, ex officio(当然)if their legislation so permits, or at the request of an interested party, to refuse or to cancel the registration, and to prohibit the use, of a trademark which constitutes a reproduction, an imitation(仿造), or a translation, liable to create confusion, of a mark considered by the competent authority (主管当局) of the country of registration or to use to be well known in that country as being already the mark of a person entitled to the benefits of this Convention and used for identical or similar goods. These provisions shall also apply when the essential part of the mark constitutes a reproduction of any well-known mark or an imitation liable to create confusion therewith.

(2) A period of at least five years from the date of registration shall be allowed for requesting the cancellation of such a mark. The countries of the Union may provide for a period within which the prohibition of use must be requested.

(3) No time limit shall be fixed for requesting the cancellation or the prohibition of the use of marks registered or used in bad faith.

除了《巴黎公约》以外，世界范围内保护驰名商标较有影响的公约就是 TRIPS 协议，在《巴黎公约》的基础上对驰名商标保护作了重要补充，第 16 条第 2、3 款作了如下规定：

Article 6 bis of the *Paris Convention* (1967) shall apply, mutatis mutandis(作必要的修正), to services. In determining whether a trademark is well-known, Members shall take account of the knowledge of the trademark in the relevant sector of the public, including knowledge in the Member concerned which has been obtained as a result of the promotion of the trademark.

Article 6 bis of the *Paris Convention* (1967) shall apply, mutatis mutandis, to goods or services which are not similar to those in respect of which a trademark is registered, provided that use of that trademark in relation to those goods or services would indicate a connection between those goods or services and the owner of the registered trademark and provided that the interests of the owner of the registered trademark are likely to be damaged by such use.

驰名商标的保护虽已在国际公约中确定下来，但是两个国际公约仅对驰名商标的认定作了原则性规定。《巴黎公约》第 6 条之 2 规定了对驰名商标的保护，规定各缔约方在认定商标是否驰名时，不以实际使用为条件，不以是否注册为前提条件，既包括已注册的驰名商标，也包括已使用未注册的驰名商标。与《巴黎公约》相比，TRIPS 协议在保护驰名商标方面又有了新的进步：首先，它明确将驰名商标的保护延伸到服务商标上；其次，是否驰名应当以相关公众知晓程度为准；最后，驰名商标的保护范围扩展到不相类似的商品或服务上，即"跨类保护"；对如何认定驰名商标作了原则性规定，具体由各国主管机关依照《巴黎公约》及 TRIPS 协议有关驰名商标保护的原则确定。①

驰名商标的特殊法律保护制度，已经成为了世界贸易组织成员国应当建立的制度，也逐渐演变成为了一个世界范围内的商标法律保护问题。

三、驰名商标特殊法律保护制度在中国的发展(Development of Specific Protection of Well-Known Trademarks)

(一)相关的立法与行政规章、知识产权战略的颁布(Publication of Relevant Laws and Administrative Regulations, and Strategy of Intellectual Property)

China began to protect well-known trademarks since its signing of *Paris Convention* in 1985.

1996 年，国家工商局根据《商标法》、《商标法实施细则》制定并发布了《驰名商标认定和管理暂行规定》(国家工商局 56 号令)，这是中国明确保护驰名商标的第一部法律性文件。

2001 年修订的《商标法》和随后颁布的《商标法实施条例》从法律法规的层面正式建立了我国驰名商标的保护制度，体现了两个国际公约的基本精神，为驰名商标的认定和保护提供了明确的法律依据。

为贯彻 2001 年修订的《商标法》和其后颁布的《商标法实施条例》有关对驰名商标予以保护的规定，2003 年 4 月 17 日，国家工商总局公布了《驰名商标认定和保护规定》(国家工商总局 5 号令)，对驰名商标的认定和保护作出了具体的规定，从而使我国驰名商标的行政认定和管理法制化、规范化。

为规范驰名商标认定工作，完善驰名商标认定工作程序，经国家工商总局审定，国家工商总局商标局和商标评审委员会于 2004 年 2 月下发《驰名商标认定工作规则》(内部规程)，对有关驰名商标的认定工作程序作出了具体规定。

2008 年 6 月，国务院发布的《国家知识产权战略纲要》将"支持企业实施商标战略，在经济活动中使用自主商标，引导企业丰富商标内涵，增加商标附加值，提高商标知名度，形成驰名商标"作为国家实施知识产权战略的任务之一。

2013 年通过的《商标法》第三次修正案又将行政执法和司法保护中有关驰名商标保护的成熟经验以法律的形式规定下来。为了落实《商标法》第三次修正案的相关规定，国家工商行政管理总局于 2014 年修订了《驰名商标认定和保护规定》，废止了 2003 年颁布的规章。

---

① 杨巧．知识产权法学(第二版)[M]．北京：中国政法大学出版社，2016：334.

（二）司法解释（Judicial Interpretation）

早在 2001 年 7 月 17 日，最高人民法院就公布了《最高人民法院关于审理涉及计算机网络域名民事纠纷案件适用法律若干问题的解释》，2002 年 10 月 12 日又公布了《最高人民法院关于审理商标权民事纠纷案件适用法律若干问题的解释》，规定了人民法院在审理商标、域名等知识产权纠纷案件中，按照个案认定、被动认定和根据案件需要认定的原则，在查明事实的基础上，严格按照《商标法》的规定，对涉案注册商标是否驰名依法作出认定并给予强有力的保护。

2009 年 4 月，最高人民法院公布了《最高人民法院关于审理涉及驰名商标保护的民事纠纷案件应用法律若干问题的解释》，对加强驰名商标的司法保护以及遏制驰名商标的“异化”等方面作出了较为详细的解释。

第二节　驰名商标的认定
Ⅱ　Identification of Well-Known Trademarks

一、认定主体(Bodies of Identification)

Paris Convention does not specify measures for protection of well-known trademarks or their recognition procedures, leaving room for each signatory country to decide how it wishes to address these matters.

世界贸易组织 TRIPS 第 16 条第 2 款对驰名商标的认定原则作了相应的规定，并在条文表述中有意识地回避了认定机关，突破了《巴黎公约》中由商标注册国或使用国主管机关认定驰名商标的规定：“In determining whether a trademark is well-known, Members shall take account of the knowledge of the trademark in the relevant sector of the public, including knowledge in the Member concerned which has been obtained as a result of the promotion of the trademark. ”①

TRIPS 的这一规定，实际是将驰名商标的认定机构的确定问题交由各国立法所决定，根据“司法最终审定原则”，为驰名商标的司法认定打开了一扇“方便之门”。因此，各国普遍规定由司法部门或行政主管部门来认定驰名商标。依照我国《驰名商标认定和保护规定》的规定，对驰名商标的认定机构为国家工商行政管理总局商标局及其商标评审委员会和人民法院。在我国驰名商标的认定机构及范围包括：

(1)在审查商标注册、工商行政管理部门查处商标违法案件过程中，当事人依照《商标法》第 13 条规定主张权利的，商标局根据审查、处理案件的需要，可以对商标驰名情况作出认定。

(2)在商标争议处理过程中，当事人依照《商标法》第 13 条规定主张权利的，商标评审委员会根据处理案件的需要，可以对商标驰名情况作出认定。

(3)在商标民事、行政案件审理过程中，当事人依照《商标法》第 13 条规定主张权利

---

① Article 16 (2) of *TRIPS*.

的，最高人民法院指定的人民法院根据审理案件的需要，可以对商标驰名情况作出认定。

二、认定程序(Procedures of Identification)

驰名商标的认定方式有两种，即主动认定与被动认定。主动认定是指国家有关主管机关对当事人的商标是否驰名依职权认定，又称事前认定。被动认定是指应当事人的请求，由商标主管机关或司法部门依职权对商标是否驰名做出认定，又称事后认定。

从20世纪90年代开始，国家商标局分4批共认定了293个全国驰名商标，囊括了36个行业或商品领域，但文教、电信、皮革雨具制品、安全、服务等9个行业或商品领域以前从未认定过驰名商标。①

There are malpractices in appraisement through comparison by the list of government departments, which the competition between enterprises on the list and those not is unequal and that it may result in power-for-money deals.

2003年6月1日开始实施的《驰名商标认定和保护规定》，结束了驰名商标政府行政批量认定的做法，实行个案认定、被动认定与保护的基本原则。即商标局或商标评审委员会在商标注册、商标评审或者查处商标违法案件过程中，可以根据当事人的请求对所涉商标是否为驰名商标进行认定。同时，人民法院在审理商标纠纷案件中，可以根据当事人的请求对所涉商标是否为驰名商标进行认定。但商标局、商标评审委员会和人民法院不能在当事人没有提出请求的情况下，主动依职权去认定驰名商标。

Article 14 of *Trademark Law* clearly provides that a well-known trademark shall be recognized as a fact that needs to be ascertained in dealing with a trademark-related case upon request by the party concerned.

1. 行政个案认定的程序(Procedures of Identification in Administrative Individual Cases)

当事人在商标异议案件中、在商标不予注册复审案件和请求无效宣告案件中提出驰名商标保护请求时，商标局、商标评审委员会应当在《商标法》第35条、第37条、第45条规定的期限内及时作出处理。

涉及驰名商标保护的商标违法案件由市(地、州)级以上工商行政管理部门查处时，工商行政管理部门应当对投诉材料予以核查，依照《工商行政管理机关行政处罚程序规定》的有关规定决定是否立案。决定立案的，工商行政管理部门应当对当事人提交的驰名商标保护请求及相关证据材料是否符合《商标法》第13条、第14条，《商标法实施条例》第3条和《驰名商标认定和保护规定》第9条的规定进行初步核实和审查。经初步核查符合规定的，应当自立案之日起30日内将驰名商标认定请示、案件材料副本一并报送上级工商行政管理部门。经审查不符合规定的，应当依照《工商行政管理机关行政处罚程序规定》的规定及时作出处理。

省(自治区、直辖市)工商行政管理部门应当对本辖区内市(地、州)级工商行政管理部门报送的驰名商标认定相关材料进一步进行核实和审查。经核查符合规定的，应当自收

① 驰名商标将实行申请认定，不再由政府批量认定[DB/OL].[2017-08-04].中国鞋业互联网，http://www.chinashoes.com/AllNews/2007/09/10/176420.shtml.

到驰名商标认定相关材料之日起 30 日内，将驰名商标认定请示、案件材料副本一并报送商标局。经审查不符合规定的，应当将有关材料退回原立案机关，由其依照《工商行政管理机关行政处罚程序规定》的规定及时作出处理。

商标局经对省(自治区、直辖市)工商行政管理部门报送的驰名商标认定相关材料进行审查，认定构成驰名商标的，应当向报送请示的省(自治区、直辖市)工商行政管理部门作出批复。

立案的工商行政管理部门应当自商标局作出认定批复后 60 日内依法予以处理，并将行政处罚决定书抄报所在省(自治区、直辖市)工商行政管理部门。省(自治区、直辖市)工商行政管理部门应当自收到抄报的行政处罚决定书之日起 30 日内将案件处理情况及行政处罚决定书副本报送商标局。

2. 司法审判实践中的个案认定(Identification in Individual Cases of Judicial Practice)

2009 年 4 月 23 日，最高人民法院公布了《最高人民法院关于审理涉及驰名商标保护的民事纠纷案件应用法律若干问题的解释》，对驰名商标的概念(definition of well-known trademark)、驰名商标司法认定适用的范围(scope of judicial identification of well-known trademark)、认定的因素(elements of identification)、举证责任(burden of proof)、保护要求(protection requirement)5 个方面进行规范，为人民法院在审理涉及驰名商标保护的民事纠纷案件中进一步明确标准、严格适用条件和范围、统一司法尺度、加强对驰名商标的司法保护提供了法律依据。

(1)不同情形的划分(Demarcation of Different Situations)

①无须认定驰名商标之情形(Situations Dispensed with Identification of Well-Known Trademarks)

对于注册商标，商标专用权人指控被告侵犯其商标专用权的案件，由于有注册商标的存在，且被指控的标识使用在注册商标被核准使用的同类商品或者服务上，故无论原告的注册商标是否驰名，对案件中被告之行为是否构成侵权的判断没有任何的实质性意义。故，无论原告是否请求认定其注册商标为驰名，均无须对原告之商标是否属于驰名商标加以认定。Therefore, there is no need to identify no matter whether the plaintiff asks for an identification of well-known trademark of the registered trademark.

②需要认定驰名商标之情形(Situations Under Which Identification of Well-Known Trademark is Required)

如果原告的商标为未注册商标，被告在同类商品或服务上使用了与原告的商标相同或者相似的标识，被告之行为是否构成侵权，则需要对原告之商标是否驰名进行认定。With non-famous marks, the owner of the mark must show that the allegedly infringing use creates a likelihood of confusion as to the source of the product or service being identified by the allegedly infringing use. With non-famous marks, it is unlikely a likelihood of confusion will be found if the products or services are in unrelated markets.

如果原告的商标为注册商标，被告在原告注册的商品或者服务类别之外使用了与注册商标相同或者相类似的标识时，则需要对原告之商标是否驰名加以认定，从而确定被告的行为是否正当。However, with famous marks, any use by another person of the mark has the potential for confusion since a famous mark is so well-known among the public that people will assume affiliation with the owner of the mark regardless of the product or service being sold under the infringing use.

如果被告未经原告之许可，将原告之商标当成自己的商号使用，或者将他人的商标使用在域名上，又或者将他人的商标予以“淡化”等，则需要对原告的商标是否驰名予以认定。

(2)司法认定驰名商标的相关规则(Relevant Rules of Judicial Identification of Well-Known Trademark)

The People's Court shall determine whether the trademark is well-known strictly in accordance with related specifications of relevant laws and regulations and on the basis of facts.

If the identification of trademarks is required, the party concerned shall carry the burden of proof.

被诉侵犯商标权或者不正当竞争行为发生前，曾被人民法院或者国务院工商行政管理部门认定驰名的商标，被告对该商标驰名的事实不持异议(opposition)的，人民法院应当予以认定。被告提出异议的，原告仍应当对该商标驰名的事实负举证责任(burden of proof)。

人民法院对于商标驰名的事实，不适用民事诉讼证据的自认规则(rule of confession)。即使原告自认其商标为驰名商标，被告或者其他当事人对此不持异议的，也不能直接予以认定。人民法院应当对于商标使用时间长短(time for use of the mark)、行业排名(ranking in the industry)、市场调查报告(report of market research)、市场价值评估报告(assessment report of market value)、是否曾被认定为著名商标(whether it was identified as a well-known trademark)等证据，人民法院应当结合认定商标驰名的其他证据，客观、全面地进行审查。

(3)司法认定驰名商标之表现(Representations of Judicial Identification of Well-Known Trademark)

Identification of well-known trademarks through judicial proceedings must be used for preventing unfair competition, if registered trademarks cannot be directly protected by the *Trademark Law*, rather than merely an identification of well-known trademarks. In judicial proceedings, the court shall make a thorough investigation of the defendant's behavior, i. e. whether the infringement of well-known trademark is by directly infringing upon the exclusive right to use registered trademark or by means of unfair competition.

对驰名商标的司法认定，实质上是通过对驰名商标的认定来维护正常之竞争秩序，最终要落实到被告行为是否合法的判断，而非原告的商标是否属于驰名的判决。因此，人民法院的民事判决书中，应当对原告之商标是否驰名在“本院认为”部分予以阐述，仅作为案件事实和判决理由，不写入判决主文；以调解方式审结的，在调解书中对商标驰名的事实不予认定。

三、认定条件(Conditions of Identification)

A well-known trademark enjoys higher reputation than general trademarks; hence it produces huge economic benefits of the owner, and provides competitiveness for the enterprise. Therefore, an enterprise expects the trademark to be well known out of its concern for reputation and requirement for market competition. In the meantime, the well-known trademarks are usually counterfeited.

然而对驰名商标的提供特殊保护，首先要解决的问题是什么样的商标可以被认定为是驰名商标。可以说，驰名商标的认定是整个驰名商标特殊法律保护的基础。

(一)通常的条件(General Conditions)

根据我国《商标法》的规定，认定驰名商标应当考虑下列因素：

1. 相关公众对该商标的知晓程度(Publicity of the mark to the relevant public)

“相关公众”，通常是指与商标所标识的某类商品或者服务有关的消费者和与前述商品或者服务的营销有密切关系的其他经营者。根据商品的普及性可以将商品划分为普通商品(general merchandise)和专用商品(exclusive merchandise)，对于普通商品的商标，一般的消费者对诸如饮料的“可口可乐”商标都有所认识；而对于某些特定的商品，如钢琴、小提琴等，则并非全社会所有的人都对其相关的商标有所认知。

Therefore, in determining whether the specific trademark is famous, the scope of relevant public shall be taken into consideration.

Reputation is a matter of uncertainty involving the extent, number of people and depth of awareness. It is generally determined by general consumers in a relevant field.

2. 该商标使用的持续时间(Time of duration for continued use of the mark)

商标的培育与商誉的积累有关，一个商标不可能在一夜之间就成为驰名商标。从另一个角度来分析，一枚商标附属在其商品或者服务上流传了一个多世纪，是否驰名已经成为了不言而喻的事实。但是，在具体的时间上，很难说需要有多长的时间。

3. 该商标宣传工作的持续时间、程度和地理范围(Consecutive time, extent and geographical area of advertisement of the mark)

A well-known trademark shall be widely known, for this reason the consecutive time, extent and geographical area of advertisement of the mark are important factors in determining its reputation. 在信息时代的今天，无法想象一枚从未做过任何形式广告宣传的商标能广为人知。

4. 该商标作为驰名商标受保护的记录(Records of protection of the mark as a well-known mark)

由于驰名商标本身所具有的经济价值，驰名商标往往成为被假冒的对象；而出于对自身商誉的保护需要，出现了假冒行为时，权利人会依法寻求保护(行政保护或者司法救济)。

Records of protection of the mark as a well-known mark means it used to be identified as a well-known trademark by administrative authorities or through judicial practice, thus makes it one of the factors of identification of a well-known trademark.

5. 该商标驰名的其他因素(Other factors relevant to the reputation)

商标局、商标评审委员会以及人民法院在认定驰名商标时，应当综合考虑以上各项因素，但不以该商标必须满足该条规定的全部因素为前提。

（二）证明商标驰名的相关证据材料（Certification Materials of a Well-Known Trademark）

1. 证明相关公众对该商标知晓程度的有关材料（Relevant materials evidencing the extent that the relevant public knows the trademark）

通常，社会咨询调查机构，通过随机（random）的方式进行消费者调查，以了解公众对某一商标的知晓程度。但“相关公众”是一个相对模糊的概念，而由谁来界定这一模糊的范围也将成为一个重要的问题。

2. 证明该商标使用持续时间的有关材料（Relevant materials evidencing the lasting time of the trademark）

商标的驰名培育需要有一个过程。从一枚普通的商标演变成为驰名商标，权利人不但投入了巨额的广告宣传费用，而且为了维护其商誉通常在其商品或者服务的质量以及相关的售后服务等方面下了不少的功夫。

Therefore, the materials involving the history and scope of the use and registration of the trademark can be used as materials that can evidence the lasting time of the trademark.

3. 证明该商标的任何宣传工作的持续时间、程度和地理范围的有关材料（Relevant materials that can evidence the lasting time, extent and geographic scope of any publicity work）

在各种传媒上所发布的广告宣传和促销活动的方式、地域范围、宣传媒体的种类以及广告投放量（the quantity of advertisements）等有关材料，都是证明商标宣传的材料。

4. 证明该商标作为驰名商标受保护记录的有关材料（Relevant materials that can indicate that this trademark has been protected as a famous one）

该商标曾在中国或者其他国家和地区作为驰名商标受保护的有关材料以及要求行政查处假冒、侵权，他人申请商标注册因自己的商标驰名而将之驳回注册等相关资料，均属于驰名商标受保护的资料。

5. 证明该商标驰名的其他证据材料（Other evidential materials that can indicate the trademark is famous）

有关使用该商标的主要商品近 3 年的产量（output）、销售量（sales）、销售收入（profit）、利税（tax turnover）、销售区域（sales territory）等有关材料。

四、认定的效果（Effects of Identification）

驰名商标的认定效力仅限于个案，即认定驰名商标的目的是判断在具体案件中他人的使用行为是否侵权。如果日后商标权人对他人在其他的商品和服务上使用商标的行为提起诉讼，以前法院或商标局的认定没有当然的效力。只要对方当事人提出异议，商标局或法院就应当重新根据商标权人提出的证据对是否驰名商标进行重新认定。既然驰名商标认定的效力仅限于个案，就不能将个案认定的结果作为宣传的手段。

Therefore, no manufacturers and business operators may indicate the words “well-known trademark” upon the goods, the packaging or the containers of the goods, nor may they use the same for advertising, exhibition or other commercial activities.

第三节 驰名商标的特殊法律保护
Ⅲ Specific Protection of Well-Known Trademarks

一、商标制度本身之局限性与客观现实(Limitation and Reality of Trademark System)

(一)未注册商标受保护的局限性(Limitation on the Protection of Unregistered Trademarks)

根据自愿注册的商标注册原则，除特殊商品烟草制品外，一般商品和服务是否使用商标以及商标是否注册，均由商品生产者、销售者或者服务提供者根据现实需要考虑。因此，从这个意义上说，商标专用权是指注册商标的专用权。

According to the *Trademark Law*, the exclusive right to use the trademark is based on a registered trademark, while the user of unregistered trademark does not have the exclusive right. In terms of theory using the unregister trademark of other people is not regarded as infringement. Cases of preemptive registration of trademarks(抢注商标) usually happen.

(二)注册商标保护范围的非跨类性限制(Limitation on Scope of Registered Trademarks Protection)

立足于商标法的领域，根据注册商标的保护范围限于“核准注册的标识”与“核定使用的范围”之基本原理，注册商标权人无权禁止他人在其他类别上注册该相同或相似的商标，也无权排斥他人在其他类别上使用与该注册商标相同或者相似的商标。对此种跨类别使用商标的现象，按照商标法的原理和制度是难以解决的，而根据反不正当竞争法的原理分析，则属于不正当竞争行为。

(三)超越商标范围使用商标标识的无奈(Use in Excess of the Scope of Trademarks)

The *Trademark Law* protects any right attached to the trademark, yet is unable to deal with problems of use in excess of the scope of trademarks such as using in a trade name(商号) or realm name(域名).

2001年6月，最高人民法院颁布了《关于审理涉及计算机网络域名民事纠纷案件适用法律若干问题的解释》，明确列举了四种最为常见的情形：第一，为商业目的将他人驰名商标注册为域名的；第二，为商业目的注册、使用与原告的注册商标相同或近似的域名，故意造成与原告提供的产品、服务或者原告网站的混淆，误导网络用户访问其网站或其他在线站点的；第三，曾要约高价出售、出租或者以其他方式转让该域名获取不正当利益的；第四，注册域名后自己不使用也未准备使用，而有意阻止权利人注册该域名的。

二、对驰名商标给予特殊法律保护的表现(Representations of Special Legal Protection of Well-Known Trademarks)

对驰名商标的特殊法律保护，实质上是给予驰名商标在一定范围内的扩展性特殊保护。

(一)不受理他人关于驰名商标的注册，撤销抢注(Canceling the Preemptive Registration)

Where the trademark of an identical or similar kind of goods is a reproduction, imitation or translation of another person's well-known trademark not registered in China and is liable to cause public confusion, no application for its registration may be granted and its use shall be prohibited.

他人凡是与驰名商标相同或者相似商标的注册申请，而且不论该申请的商标是否属于与驰名商标使用在同类商品或服务项目上，有关国家的商标管理机关均应拒绝给予注册。如果已经得到注册的，驰名商标权利人得以在他人商标注册后5年内向商标评审委员会请求予以撤销，而对于恶意注册的则不受5年的时间限制。

(二)禁止使用他人的驰名商标(Prohibiting the Use of Others' Well-known Trademarks)

对于一般的商标，他人只要使用在非注册商标核定的使用范围内，就算商标相同或者相似，因无商标专用权，故不构成商标侵权。但是由于驰名商标具有的影响力和公众对其特有的关注，他人虽未将驰名商标注册于其他类别的商品或服务项目上取得专用权，但是使用在其他类别的商品上或者其他的服务类时，使用者这种有意识地暗示驰名商标与自己的商品或服务存在某种必然的联系，欺骗消费者、导致消费者的错误认识，从而增加销售额。

If a trademark in respect of which the application for registration is filed for use for non-identical or dissimilar goods is a reproduction, imitation or translation of that of another person that has been registered in China, misleads the public and is likely to create prejudice to the interests of the well-known mark registrant, it shall be rejected for registration and prohibited.

(三)降低对驰名商标申请注册商标的显著性要求(Reducing the Requirement for Distinctiveness)

显著性是商标的注册的积极条件之一。原本不具有显著性的商标，通过长期大范围使用而弥补了设计该商标时显著性不足之缺陷。例如，"555"香烟，由于其使用的纯数字组合，本身不具有显著性，不能获得注册，但是经过在特定的范围内长期、反复地使用而驰名，使得该商标标识在社会相关公众中有较大的认知度，从而具有了相应的显著性。

(四)反驰名商标的"淡化"(Preventing from Trademark Dilution)

淡化(dilution)，是指一个逐渐被稀释和冲淡的过程。反淡化理论不要求淡化行为者与驰名商标所有人之间存在竞争关系，不以是否产生混淆、误认为前提。

Trademark law is generally focused on the need for consumer protection. Consequently, trademark law traditionally concerned itself with situations if an unauthorized party sold goods that are directly competitive with or at least related to those sold by the trademark owner. Trademark dilution is giving the owner of a famous trademark standing to forbid others from using that mark in a way that would lessen its uniqueness.

反淡化理论最早起源于德国判例，后被美国学者所继承，并在法、日等国家的判例中被引用。反淡化的理论通常被认为是美国斯科特1927年在《哈佛法律评论》发表的《商标保护的理论基础》中创立的，其认为通过把驰名商标用于非竞争性的商品上，以至逐渐消磨或分散其识别性，影响商标(或商号)在公众中的形象之行为属于淡化行为。禁止使用在非竞争性的商品上。

In most cases, trademark dilution involves an unauthorized use of another's trademark on products that do not compete with, and have little connection with, those of the trademark owner. For example, a famous trademark used by one company to refer to hair care products might be diluted if another company began using a similar mark to refer to breakfast cereals or spark plugs.

正如美国律师协会知识产权分会主席汤姆斯·E. 史密斯(Thomas E. Smith)对斯凯特的理论作了进一步阐述和发展所指出的："如果法院容许或者放任'劳斯莱斯'餐馆、'劳斯莱斯'自助餐厅、'劳斯莱斯'裤子、'劳斯莱斯'糖果存在的话，那么，不出10年，'劳斯莱斯'商标的所有人就将不再拥有这个世界驰名商标。"①

Therefore a trademark is diluted when the use of similar or identical trademarks in other non-competing markets means that the trademark will lose its capacity to signify a single source.

1947年美国马萨诸塞州率先将斯科特的理论在立法中予以体现，通过了第一部州的反淡化法，之后其他州也陆续通过了自己的反淡化法，1995年美国通过《联邦商标反淡化法》明确了"不管驰名商标权利人与他人之间是否存在竞争关系，或者存在混淆、误解或欺骗的可能性，减少、削弱驰名商标对其商品或服务的识别性和显著性能力的行为"。

In other words, unlike ordinary trademark law, dilution protection extends to trademark uses that do not confuse consumers regarding the producer. Instead, dilution protection law aims to protect trademarks from losing their singular association in the public mind with a particular product, perhaps imagined if the trademark were to be encountered independently of any product.

反淡化成为保护驰名商标的另一途径被多国采纳。对驰名商标的"淡化"通常有弱化、丑化和退化三种表现形态。

1. 弱化(Blurring)

弱化，是指驰名商标与特定商品或服务本应具有的直接对应性减弱之表现。弱化和分为直接弱化和间接弱化两种。

(1)直接弱化(Direct Blurring)

将他人的驰名商标使用在与该商标所标志的商品或服务不相同、不相似的商品或服务上，为传统的直接商标侵权形态所不能概括。驰名商标蕴涵了巨大的市场声誉，相对固定地向消费者表达了某种具备优良品质商品或服务与驰名商标的关联性，并使驰名商标作为一种标志成为了该商品或服务的信誉保障。

When consumers purchase a trademarked product, they are choosing it for a particular reason such as perceived corporate responsibility or quality. If a competing company uses a similar mark, this can undermine consumer confidence. A prime example may be the past involvement of Coca-Cola in clothing lines.

如消费者看到"可口可乐"商标就会联想到碳酸饮料，见到"麦当劳"商标就会联想到

① [美]苏珊·瑟拉德. 美国联邦商标反淡化法的立法与实践[J]. 外国法译评，1998(4)：2.

快餐。可见，驰名商标与其关联商品或服务在思维上的关联性是唯一和直接的，如果放任“可口可乐”商标用在饮料以外的商品上使用，则不可避免地破坏了“可口可乐”商标与饮料在思想上唯一和直接的关联性。同样，如允许他人将“万宝路”使用在服装、鞋帽、包袋等类别的商品上，就割裂了“万宝路”与香烟之间的关联，甚至产生了无端的关联性，从而会冲淡驰名商标原有的特定、明确之标示。

驰名商标的弱化行为，不恰当地利用了驰名商标与商品或服务之间的关联性，这犹如在一盏明亮的灯旁边悬挂了另一盏灯(无论该灯泡的瓦数大小)，都将会使原本的灯光弱化。因此，弱化行为应当受到禁止。

(2)间接弱化(Indirect Blurring)

“Blurring” is defined as “association arising from the similarity between a mark or trade name and a famous mark that impairs(损害) the distinctiveness of the famous mark.”

In determining whether a mark or trade name is likely to cause dilution by blurring, the court may consider all relevant factors, including the following:

(i) The degree of similarity between the mark or trade name and the famous mark.

(ii) The degree of inherent or acquired distinctiveness of the famous mark.

(iii) The extent to which the owner of the famous mark b engaging substantially exclusive use of the mark.

(iv) The degree of recognition of the famous mark.

(v) Whether the user of the mark or trade name intended to create association with the famous mark.

(vi) Any actual association between the mark or trade name and the famous mark.

在相同类别商品或服务商使用与驰名商标相似的商标，如将与驰名商标“金利来”相似的“全利来”、“金利莱”商标使用在领带上的行为，也属于弱化行为。

2. 丑化(Tarnishment)

丑化，通常是指将他人的驰名商标进行恶意、贬义性(in derogatory sense)的使用或者在使用中产生不良影响的行为。

Dilution may be used to protect the reputational value of a mark: not just its distinctiveness but also its connotations(内涵). For famous mark holders, this may prove to be a more valuable tool than the core protection against dilution by blurring. Blurring threatens only harm at the margin of the mark's commercial value by possibly reducing its ability to trigger an association with some consumers. But tarnishment, in theory at least, threatens to change the very meaning of the mark itself by loading disreputable meaning to the mark's associations.

In the instance of tarnishment, a company's mark may be associated with an unsavory or poor quality product. As a result, consumers develop a negative image of it. 如“百威”有经典的广告词——“哪里有生活，哪里就有百威(bud)”。而一个杀虫剂的生产商也做了类似的广告——“哪里有生活，哪里就有臭虫(bug)”。之后的广告将讨厌的臭虫与前面广告中的“百威”产生了不正当的联系，从而破坏了驰名商标的良好形象和信誉。

3. 退化(Degeneration)

退化，又称为曲解(misinterpretation)，是指由于权利人对驰名商标的不当使用或他人以间接的方式，将驰名商标曲解为核定使用的商品或服务的普通名称的行为。

A trademark is said to be generalized when it began as distinctive but has changed in meaning to become generic. A trademark typically becomes "generalized" when the products or services with which it is associated have acquired substantial market dominance or mind share such that the primary meaning of the generalized trademark becomes the product or service itself rather than an indication of source for the product or service to such an extent that the public thinks the trademark is the generic name of the product or service.

商标与商品应当有紧密的关联，但是这种关联却又不能使之直接地相等。否则，会割裂商标与其对应的商品在思想上的关联性，破坏商标与商品的区分功能。

If such a mark becomes synonymous with that product or service to the extent that the trademark owner can no longer enforce its proprietary rights, the mark becomes generic. The users may not realize that the term is a brand name rather than a medical term. 如"吉普"一开始是一个商标，经过长期的使用逐渐成为了驰名商标，其与商品——越野车在思想上的关联性是唯一和直接的。而当越野车的销售商和消费者长期将"吉普"与越野车等同使用时，慢慢地"吉普"就被沦为越野车的代名词，从而丧失了其显著性。"阿斯匹林"作为一种治头疼药的驰名商标，但是却逐渐演变成为了治头疼的通用药品名称；"氟里昂"也曾是驰名商标，现沦为氟制冷剂的通用名称。

(五)禁止他人在非商标领域的不合理使用(Prohibiting Irrational Use by Another Person Outside the Scope of Trademark)

根据企业名称登记的有关规定，只要在特定工商行政管理辖区的地域范围内、在同行业内申请的名称与已经存在的企业名称不相同，一般都会获得登记认可。由于企业名称登记与商标注册属于两个不同的审查登记系列，而且所规定的条件也不尽相同。事实上就存在着一些企业有意或无意地将他人的驰名商标或者驰名商标中的一部分作为自己企业的名称使用。

Whoever uses a registered trademark or an unregistered well-known trademark of another party as the trade name in its enterprise name and mislead the public, which constitutes unfair competition, shall be dealt with in accordance with the *Anti-unfair Competition Law* of the People's Republic of China.

驰名商标权利人认为他人将其驰名商标作为企业名称登记，可能欺骗公众或使公众造成误解的，可以向企业名称登记机关申请撤销该企业名称登记。

企业名称登记主管机关应当依照《企业名称登记管理规定》处理。1999年的保护工业产权巴黎联盟大会和世界知识产权组织大会《关于驰名商标保护规定的联合建议》第3条也规定与商标发生冲突的域名亦在驰名商标的"排除权"之列；第6条还进一步规定如果某域名或该域名的主要部分至少构成对驰名商标的复制、模仿、翻译或音译，且该域名是恶意注册或使用的，即应认为该域名与该驰名商标发生冲突。对于将他人驰名商标作为域名登记或者使用的，驰名商标权利人有权要求其停止，并有权要求相关部门予以撤销。

(六)不得对驰名商标进行其他的损害行为(Prohibiting Any Prejudice to Well-known Trademarks in other Respects)

Any act that may cause, in other respects, prejudice to the reputation of well-known trademarks, shall be prohibited. The owner of well-known trademarks may require prohibition according to the *Contract Law*, the *Trademark Law* or the *Unfair Competition Law*.

1. 侮辱性使用 (Insulting Use)

在展览带有驰名商标的商品时，应当尊重他人的驰名商标。如果将他人的驰名商标之标识、带有驰名商标的包装进行侮辱性、诽谤性使用(画上红色交叉等)，或者损毁性展示(破烂不堪等)，产生不良影响的，也将构成对驰名商标权利之侵害。

2. 有意歪曲 (Intended Misinterpretation)

有意识地将驰名商标之文字或者图案进行歪曲性使用，将会使驰名商标的接触者产生错误认识，割裂了驰名商标应有的显著性和应有之特征，也将构成对驰名商标的损害。

3. 损坏现状维持 (Maintaining the Current Situation of Damage)

户外广告宣传画或者客户宣传画册中涉及他人驰名商标的，无论是被人为还是出于自然现象，对损毁部分(如霓虹灯广告中灯管之“缺胳膊少腿”现象等)不及时修复，都会产生对损害驰名商标的不良宣传效果。

【英语词汇】

at random　*adv.* 随机
certification　*n.* 证据
generic　*adj.* 类的，一般的
degeneration　*n.* 退化
imitation　*n.* 摹仿
identification in individual cases　个案认定
preemptive registration　抢注
sales volume　*n.* 销售量
tarnishment　*n.* 丑化
blur　*v.* 使模糊不清
competitiveness　*n.* 竞争力
goodwill　*n.* 商誉
identification　*n.* 认定
identification in batches　批量认定
misinterpret　*v.* 曲解
realm name　*n.* 域名
trademark dilution　商标淡化
well-known trademark　驰名商标

【英语句型】

1. If the pertinent functionaries engaged in the identification of famous trademarks neglect their duties, abuse their powers, seek private interests, seek improper profits, violate the law in the identification of famous trademarks, they shall be given an administrative punishment in accordance with the law; and those who constitute crimes shall be subject to the criminal responsibilities in accordance with the law.

“engaged in…”的意思是“从事于……”。

译文：参与驰名商标认定工作的有关人员，滥用职权、徇私舞弊、牟取不正当利益，违法办理驰名商标认定有关事项，依法给予行政处分；构成犯罪的，依法追究刑事责任。

2. The identification of the plaintiff's trademark by the court is a finding of facts for court

decision of the case, rather than an administrative assessment, neither does it produce any effect of judicial precedent.

"neither do..."引导的是一个倒装句，意思是"也不会……"。

译文：人民法院对原告之商标驰名的认定，仅为本案提供一个判决结果的事实认定支持，并非一种行政性的评定结果，也不产生司法判例之效果。

3. If a trademark in respect of which the application for registration is filed for use for non-identical or dissimilar goods is a reproduction, imitation or translation of the well-known mark of another person that has been registered in China, misleads the pub1ic and is likely to create prejudice to the interests of the well-known mark registrant, it shall be rejected for registration and prohibited from use.

"in respect of..."的意思是"涉及……"。

译文：就不相同或者不相类似商品申请注册的商标是复制、摹仿或者翻译他人已经在中国注册的驰名商标，误导公众，致使该驰名商标注册人的利益可能受到损害的，不予注册并禁止使用。

【阅读资料】

第五编　知识产权的反不正当竞争制度

PART FIVE　The System Against Unfair Competition of Intellectual Property

第十六章　其他主要的知识产权
Chapter 16　Other Main Types of Intellectual Property

【引言】除了专利权(patent right)、商标权(trademark right)、著作权(copyright)这种对知识产权的传统划分外，广义的知识产权还包括一切人类智力创作的成果(creation of the mind)所享有的权利，也即《建立世界知识产权组织公约》(*Convention Establishing the World Intellectual Property Organization*)中所划定的范围。对这一范围，在学术上至今仍存在较大争议；在各国立法中，真正把世界知识产权组织所称为“知识产权”的内容都当作知识产权保护的国家并不多。但由于已经有100多个国家参加了这一公约，故应认为大多数国家原则上同意该公约为广义知识产权所划定的范围。① 我国于1980年也参加了该公约。本章涉及的集成电路布图设计权(rights of layout-design of integrated circuits)、商业秘密权(rights of trade secrets)、地理标记权(rights of geographical indications)、植物新品种权(rights of new varieties of plants)、商号权(rights of trade names)、域名权(rights of domain names)等均属于这一广义的划分。

【学习目的与要求】随着人类智力创作成果的不断发展，集成电路布图设计权、商业秘密权、地理标记权、植物新品种权、商号权、域名权等知识产权越来越受到人们的关注。因此，本章学习的目的是了解这些知识产权的基本概念、权利的取得以及立法保护，其中要重点关注这些知识产权的基本概念。

第一节　集成电路布图设计权
Ⅰ　Layout-Designs of Integrated Circuits

一、集成电路布图设计概述(Overview on Layout-Designs of Integrated Circuits)

(一)集成电路概念和特征(Concept and Features of Integrated Circuits)

1. 集成电路的概念(Concept of Integrated Circuits)

集成电路，是指以蚀刻工艺技术将特定模型置于两层以上金属的绝缘物或半导体的涂层之上，并使其发挥电子电路技术功能的电子产品。

According to the 1989 *Treaty on Intellectual Property in Respect of Integrated Circuits*(《关于集成电路的知识产权条约》), also called *Washington Treaty*(《华盛顿条约》), “integrated

① 郑成思．知识产权法论[M]．北京：法律出版社，2003：58.

circuit" means a product, in its final form or an intermediate form, in which the elements, at least one of which is an active element(有源元件), and some or all of the inter-connections are integrally formed in and/or on a piece of material and which is intended to perform an electronic function.

我国自2001年10月1日起施行的《集成电路布图设计保护条例》对"集成电路"的定义为："集成电路，是指半导体集成电路，即以半导体材料为基片，将至少有一个是有源元件的两个以上元件和部分或者全部互连线路集成在基片之中或者基片之上，以执行某种电子功能的中间产品或者最终产品。"关于集成电路的定义，虽然有不同的描述，但基本含义大致相同。

2. 集成电路的特征(Features of Integrated Circuits)

集成电路的特征主要包括：

(1)技术成果的综合性(Comprehensiveness)

集成电路是一种综合技术成果，它包括布图设计(layout-design)和工艺技术(process engineering)。迄今为止，各国在以法律手段保护集成电路时，主要保护的是体现集成电路设计原理与技术的反映各层材料之间各元件三维配置(three-dimensional disposition)的图像。

(2)技术成果的原创性(Originality)

集成电路的技术成果必须具有原创性，才能受到法律的保护。如果集成电路的技术成果只是对他人的布图设计进行仿制或简单修改，或属于在集成电路中经常应用的显而易见的常规设计，则不能受到法律的保护。

(二)布图设计的概念(Concept of Layout-Designs)

集成电路中的布图设计，并非集成电路本身。布图设计(layout-designs)，是指附着于各种载体上的电子元件和连接这些元件的连线的有关布图设计。在美国称之为"掩膜作品"(mask work)，欧洲国家称之为"半导体产品拓扑图"，日本及我国称之为"布图设计"。

Washington Treaty gives the following definition that a "layout-design (topography)" means the three-dimensional disposition, however expressed, of the elements, at least one of which is an active element, and of some or all of the interconnections of an integrated circuit, or such a three-dimensional disposition prepared for an integrated circuit intending for manufacture. 我国《集成电路布图设计保护条例》也将集成电路布图设计定义为："集成电路布图设计(以下简称布图设计)，是指集成电路中至少有一个是有源元件的两个以上元件和部分或者全部互连线路的三维配置，或者为制造集成电路而准备的上述三维配置。"

尽管布图设计是无形的，但可以通过掩膜版、芯片、磁带、磁盘等方式表现出来。这些掩膜版、磁盘、磁带、芯片等，都是布图设计的载体。布图设计是在这些载体上所反映出来的电子元件和连接这些元件的连线的布图设计。

在集成电路产品的开发中，布图设计的完成是关键。据统计，布图设计的开发成本一般占集成电路开发总成本的50%以上。① 集成电路的设计和制造是一项十分艰巨的技术工

① 李颖怡．知识产权法[M]．广州：中山大学出版社，2005：253.

作，需要大量的资金和智力的投入。因此各国立法都是通过保护布图设计来保护集成电路的。

Since they bring about enormous economic interests, piracy of integrated circuits increasingly occurs, resulting in damage to the developer's lawful rights, and causes adverse effect on the research and development of new products as well. Layout-designs of integrated circuits are the key to the completion of integrated circuits, and integrated circuits are protected through the legal protection of layout-designs.

(三)集成电路布图设计的立法(Legislation of Layout-Designs of Integrated Circuits)

1958 年世界上第一块集成电路在美国研制成功后，集成电路技术得到了飞快的发展。集成电路是微电子技术的核心，是现代电子信息技术的基础，它首先引起了计算机技术的巨大变革。由于计算机的逻辑部件，特别是中央处的集成化，微型计算机才应运而生。此外，因为集成电路具有体积小、重量轻、功能多、能耗低、可靠性高等优点，已被广泛运用于社会生产生活之中。从我们日常生活中的仪器仪表、通信工具、电视机、音响设备到导弹、卫星等几乎所有的电子产品都离不开集成电路。而集成电路的研制开发是一个复杂的过程，需要耗费大量的人力、物力和财力。一般而言，开发一种普通的超大规模集成电路动辄需要投入数百万美元以上，花费 2~3 年的时间。但与此同时，仿制上述集成电路一般仅需几个月，成本也就数万美元。许多企业为了节省研发费用，纷纷仿制他人的集成电路，牟取暴利，甚至还形成了专门的行业。由于仿制产品的成本极低，使得前期投入昂贵研发费用的集成电路研制开发者血本无归，这就极大地挫伤了这些研发者的积极性，实际上侵犯了研发者的智力成果。为了维护集成电路研发者的智力劳动成果，保障集成电路研制生产的正常开展，所以，需要加强集成电路的法律保护，禁止集成电路的非法仿制。①

As intangible products, layout-designs of integrated circuits combine the features of both copyright and patent right, yet possess its own features in many respects. Traditional intellectual property is unable to provide effective protection for layout-designs of integrated circuits; therefore it is necessary to establish a new type of legal form for implementing special protection, which is widely accepted by more and more countries and put into practice.

美国国会于 1984 年 11 月 8 日通过了世界上第一部保护集成电路布图设计的专门立法——《半导体芯片保护法》(*Semiconductor Chip Protection Act*)，开创了以专门法律保护集成电路布图设计的先河。随后，日本于 1985 年 5 月 31 日通过了《半导体集成电路的电路布局法》，欧共体于 1986 年 12 月 16 日通过了《关于半导体产品布图设计法律保护的理事会指令》。瑞典、英国、德国、法国、意大利、俄罗斯、韩国等也相继制定了自己的集成电路布图设计保护法。

在国际上，1989 年 5 月 26 日，世界知识产权组织在华盛顿召开的关于集成电路知识产权的外交会议上通过了《关于集成电路的知识产权条约》(简称《华盛顿条约》)。我国也已在《华盛顿条约》和《与贸易有关的知识产权协议》上签字，承担着保护集成电路布图设

① 杨巧．知识产权法学[M]．北京：中国政法大学出版社，2016：344.

计的国际义务。2001 年 3 月 28 日我国通过了《集成电路布图设计保护条例》，并制定了《集成电路布图设计保护条例实施细则》。

二、我国对集成电路布图设计的保护(Protection of Layout-Designs of Integrated Circuits in China)

(一)集成电路布图设计权的主体及客体(Subject and Object of Layout-Designs of Integrated Circuits)

1. 集成电路布图设计权的主体(Subject of Layout-Designs of Integrated Circuits)

集成电路布图设计权的主体，是指对布图设计享有权利和承担义务的人或组织。按照《集成电路布图设计保护条例》的规定，布图设计权的主体范围包括中国的自然人、法人或其他组织和外国人。

2. 集成电路布图设计权的客体(Object of Layout-Designs of Integrated Circuits)

集成电路布图设计权的客体，是指符合法定保护条件的集成电路布图设计，并非集成电路本身。并非所有的集成电路布图设计都能取得专有权，只有那些具备法定的必要条件的布图设计，才能作为布图设计专有权的客体。

集成电路布图设计既具有知识产权客体的一般特征，也具有其独特的特征。

Article 3(2) of the *Washington Treaty* provides that the obligation referred to in paragraph (1)(a) shall apply to layout-designs (topographies) that are original in the sense that they are the result of their creators' own intellectual effort and are not commonplace among creators of layout-designs (topographies) and manufacturers of integrated circuits at the time of their creation.

A protected layout-design shall possess originality, That is, the layout-design is the intellectual achievement of the creator himself, and it is not commonplace among creators of layout-designs and manufacturers of integrated circuit at the time of its creation.

(1)布图设计具有无形性(Intangibility)

布图设计是集成电路中所有元器件的配置方式，这种"配置方式"本身是抽象、无形的，它没有具体的形体，可以用不同载体表现。如：以编码方式存在于磁盘、磁带中。

(2)布图设计具有可复制性(Reproducibility)

当载体为磁盘、磁带时，可以通过拷贝的方法复制布图设计。当载体为掩膜版时，布图设计以图形方式存在，这时可以通过对模版的翻拍复制布图设计。

(二)集成电路布图设计权的归属(Ownership of Layout-Designs of Integrated Circuits)

除《集成电路布图设计保护条例》另有规定外，布图设计专有权属于布图设计创作者。由法人或者其他组织主持，依据法人或者其他组织的意志而创作，并由法人或者其他组织承担责任的布图设计，该法人或者其他组织是创作者。由自然人创作的布图设计，该自然人是创作者。

If two or more natural persons, legal entities or other organizations have jointly invented a layout-design, the exclusive rights therein are owned according to what is agreed upon by the co-operating persons or parties; if no agreement is reached or the agreement does not clearly specify, the exclusive rights are shared by the co-operating persons or parties.

The exclusive rights of a layout-design invented by entrustment are owned according to the agreement concluded between the entrusting and entrusted parties(委托人和受托人); if no agreement does reached or the agreement is not clearly specify, the exclusive rights are shared by the entrusted party.

布图设计专有权属于自然人的，该自然人死亡后，其专有权在本条例规定的保护期内依照《继承法》的规定转移。

(三)集成电路布图设计权的取得(Acquisition of Layout-Designs of Integrated Circuits)

集成电路布图设计专有权因登记而取得。我国《集成电路布图设计保护条例》规定，布图设计专有权经国务院知识产权行政部门登记产生。未经登记的布图设计不受本条例保护。布图设计自其在世界任何地方首次商业利用之日起2年内，未向国务院知识产权行政部门提出登记申请的，国务院知识产权行政部门不再予以登记。

中国自然人、法人或其他组织创作的布图设计的专用权的取得只需以登记为要件。

Any layout-design created by a foreigner shall, where it is first commercially exploited in the territory of the People's Republic of China, be accorded the exclusive rights of layout-design in accordance with these Regulations.

Any layout-design created by a foreigner shall be accorded the exclusive rights of layout-design in accordance with these Regulations, if the country to which the foreigner belongs has concluded an agreement with China to protect layout-design or the country to which the foreigner belongs and China are both parties to an international treaty concerning the protection of layout-design.

(四)集成电路布图设计权的内容(Contents of Layout-Designs of Integrated Circuits)

集成电路布图设计权的内容主要包括复制权和商业利用权。

1. 复制权(Rights of Reproduction)

复制权，是指对受保护的布图设计的全部或者其中任何具有独创性的部分进行复制的权利。

应当注意的是，这里所讲的复制与版权法中的复制的含义是不同的。对布图设计的复制是通过以下步骤实现的：首先，将含有布图设计的半导体芯片通过化学方法把半导体材料溶解，使体现在上面的布图设计暴露出来；其次，用特制的照相机将各个涂层上的布图设计拍摄下来进行放大处理，再将照片输入到计算机中进行处理，然后制成布图设计的掩膜板；最后，按照集成电路的制作过程将版图体现在集成电路上，成为布图设计。

布图设计权人通过行使复制权，才能对布图设计进行利用，才能获取经济效益。由于日益猖獗的非法复制活动，严重损害了创作者的权益，因而，各国都在立法中明确保护布图设计复制权。权利人既可以自己行使复制权，也可以许可给他人。除法律规定的合理使用、反向工程的情况以外，任何人不经许可，不得以商业目的复制受保护的布图设计，否则即构成侵权，要承担法律责任。

2. 商业利用权(Rights of Commercial Exploitation)

商业利用权，是指为商业目的进口、销售或者以其他方式提供受保护的布图设计、含有该布图设计的集成电路或者含有该集成电路的物品的行为。商业利用权就是将上述物品投入商业利用的权利。

Article 6 of Washington Treaty provides that the act of importing, selling or otherwise distributing for commercial purposes a protected layout-design (topography) or an integrated circuit in which a protected layout-design (topography) is incorporated.

Article 36 of TRIPS provides that members shall consider unlawful the following acts if performed without the authorization of the right holder: importing, selling, or otherwise distributing for commercial purposes a protected layout-design, an integrated circuit in which a protected layout-design is incorporated, or an article incorporating such an integrated circuit only in so far as it continues to contain an unlawfully reproduced layout-design.

可见，《华盛顿条约》中规定的商业利用权的范围比 TRIPS 协议的规定略窄，不包含对含有专有权的布图设计的集成电路构成的物品的商业利用。我国《集成电路布图设计保护条例》第 2 条第 5 项规定，商业利用，是指为商业目的进口、销售或者以其他方式提供受保护的布图设计、含有该布图设计的集成电路或者含有该集成电路的物品的行为。我国有关集成电路商业利用的范围，和 TRIPS 一样，包括含有专有权的布图设计的集成电路构成的物品的商业利用。

（五）集成电路布图设计权的限制（Limitation on Layout-Designs of Integrated Circuits）

1. 合理使用（Fair Use）

合理使用，是指为个人目的或者单纯为评价、分析、研究、教学等目的而复制受保护的布图设计的，可以不经布图设计权利人许可，不向其支付报酬而使用。

A layout-design may be used without the authorization of its right holder and without any payment of remuneration, when a third patty reproduces the protected layout-design for private purposes or for the sole purpose of valuation, analysis, research or teaching.

2. 反向工程（Reverse Engineering）

反向工程，是指在对他人的布图设计进行评价、分析的基础上，创作出具有独创性布图设计的研究。由于反向工程有利于新产品的开发，促进技术进步，各国法律大多承认其合法性，行为人可以不经布图设计权利人许可，不向其支付报酬。

A layout-design may be used without the authorization of its right holder and without any payment of remuneration, when a third patty creates a layout-design with originality on the basis of the evaluation or analysis of the protected layout-design.

3. 独立创作（Independent Creation）

独立创作，是指对自己独立创作的与他人相同的布图设计工作。创作者对自己独立创作的作品进行复制或者将其投入商业利用的，可以不经布图设计权利人许可，不向其支付报酬。

A layout-design may be used without the authorization of its right holder and without any payment of remuneration, when a third patty reproduces or commercially exploits a layout-design made independently by oneself that is identical with a layout-design of another person.

4. 权利穷竭(Exhaustion of Rights)

权利穷竭，也称权利穷尽或权利用尽，是指受保护的布图设计、含有该布图设计的集成电路或者含有该集成电路的物品，由布图设计权利人或者经其许可投放市场后，其权利已经实现，他人再次商业利用的，可以不经布图设计权利人许可，并不向其支付报酬。

For any protected layout-designs, integrated circuits in which the layout-designs are incorporated, or articles incorporating such integrated circuits, so long as they have been put on the market by the right holders of the layout-designs or with their authorization, anyone may exploit them for commercial purposes without the authorization of, nor payment of remuneration made to, the right holders of the layout-designs.

权利穷竭原则能够限制权利人对布图设计产品的控制，防止权利人滥用权利而妨碍布图设计产品的正常流转，避免法律的过度保护而损害公共利益。

5. 善意的商业利用(Commercial Exploitation in Good Faith)

善意的商业利用，是指行为人在获得含有受保护的布图设计的集成电路或者含有该集成电路的品时，不知道也没有合理理由应当知道其中含有非法复制的布图设计，而将其投入商业利用的，不视为侵权。前述的行为人得到其中含有非法复制的布图设计的明确通知后，可以继续将现有的存货或者此前的订货投入商业利用，但应当向布图设计权利人支付合理的报酬。

6. 强制许可(Compulsory License)

强制许可，或称非自愿许可(non-voluntary license)，是指在不经权利人同意的情况下由有关主管部门直接发放的使用许可。根据我国《集成电路布图设计保护条例》的规定，在下列情况下可以发放强制许可：

(1)紧急状态之强制许可(Compulsory License Required by the State of Emergency)

在国家出现紧急状态或者非常情况时，或者为了公共利益的目的，或者经人民法院、不正当竞争行为监督检查部门依法认定布图设计权利人有不正当竞争行为而需要给予补救时，国务院知识产权行政部门可以给予使用其布图设计的强制许可。

(2)公共目的之强制许可(Compulsory License Required by the Public Interests)

国务院知识产权行政部门作出给予使用布图设计强制许可的决定，应当及时通知布图设计权利人。给予使用布图设计强制许可的决定，应当根据强制许可的理由，规定使用的范围和时间，其范围应当限于为公共目的非商业性使用(non-commercial exploitation)，或者限于经人民法院、不正当竞争行为监督检查部门依法认定布图设计权利人有不正当竞争行为(act of unfair competition)而需要给予的补救(remedies)。强制许可的理由消除并不再发生时，国务院知识产权行政部门应当根据布图设计权利人的请求，经审查后作出终止使用布图设计强制许可的决定。

(3)获得强制许可后的限制(Limitation on Compulsory License)

取得使用布图设计强制许可的自然人、法人或者其他组织不享有独占的使用权，并且无权允许他人使用。

(六)集成电路布图设计权的保护期限(Protection Duration of Protection of Layout-Designs of Integrated Circuits)

关于布图设计权的有效期,《华盛顿条约》要求至少为 8 年,TRIPS 协议则规定为 10 年,并允许其缔约方规定自布图设计作出之日起 15 年以后保护终止。目前,世界上大多数国家都将布图设计权的保护期限规定为 10 年。

我国《集成电路布图设计保护条例》的规定,布图设计专有权的保护期为 10 年,自布图设计登记申请之日或者在世界任何地方首次投入商业利用之日起计算,以较前日期为准。但是,无论是否登记或者投入商业利用,布图设计自创作完成之日起 15 年后,不再受本条例保护。

(七)侵犯集成电路布图设计权的行为及法律责任(Acts and Legal Liability of Infringement of Layout-Designs of Integrated Circuits)

1. 侵权行为的表现(Infringing Acts)

根据《集成电路布图设计保护条例》的规定,侵犯集成电路布图设计权的行为主要有以下两种:

(1)未经布图设计权利人许可,复制受保护的布图设计的全部或者其中任何具有独创性的部分的。

(2)未经布图设计权利人许可,为商业目的进口、销售或者以其他方式提供受保护的布图设计、含有该布图设计的集成电路或者含有该集成电路的物品的。

2. 法律责任(Legal Liability)

(1)民事责任(Civil Liability)

If a dispute is caused by any exploitation of a layout-design without the authorization of the holder of right, namely an infringement of his or its exclusive rights in the layout-design, it shall be settled through consultation between the interested parties. If the parties are unwilling to consult or fail in the consultation, the holder of right or an interested party may institute legal proceedings in the People's Court. The Court shall make a decision according to the law, and order the infringer to stop immediately his infringing act and bear liability for damages.

侵犯布图设计专有权的赔偿数额,为侵权人所获得的利益或者被侵权人所受到的损失,包括被侵权人为制止侵权行为所支付的合理开支。

布图设计权利人或者利害关系人有证据证明他人正在实施或者即将实施侵犯其专有权的行为,如不及时制止将会使其合法权益受到难以弥补的损害的,可以在起诉前依法向人民法院申请采取责令停止有关行为和财产保全的措施。

(2)行政责任(Administrative Responsibility)

For the infringement of layout-designs, the holder of right or an interested party may institute legal proceedings in the People's Court or request the intellectual property administrative authority under the State Council to handle the matter. When the intellectual property administrative authority under the State Council handles the matter and it decides the infringement is constituted (侵权行为成立), the intellectual property administrative authority under the State Council may order the infringer to immediately desist, confiscate(没收) and destroy(销毁) the infringing products or material.

当事人对行政处罚不服的，可以自收到处理通知之日起 15 日内依照《中华人民共和国行政诉讼法》向人民法院起诉；侵权人期满不起诉又不停止侵权行为的，国务院知识产权行政部门可以请求人民法院强制执行(compulsory enforcement)。

第二节 商业秘密权
Ⅱ Trade Secret Rights

一、商业秘密的概念及范围(Concept and Scope of Trade Secrets)

(一)商业秘密的概念(Concept)

A trade secret is information that derives actual or potential economic value from the fact that it is not known or readily ascertainable by others, and is subject to reasonable efforts to maintain its secrecy.

商业秘密是国际上通用的法律术语，法国、德国等国家称之为工商秘密。TRIPS 并没有提到“商业秘密”这个术语，只是提到“未披露过的信息”(undisclosed information)。但从 TRIPS 给“未披露过的信息”下的定义来看，它主要就是指商业秘密，而不是指与个人的“隐私权”等有关的秘密信息。①

商业秘密的法律保护方式并不是仅有反不正当竞争法一种，合同法、侵权责任法以及某些国家的商业秘密专门立法，都从不同的侧面对商业秘密提供了保护。但反不正当竞争法可以综合各种法律手段，对商业秘密提供更为周密和可靠的法律保护，这也是世界上多数国家将商业秘密纳入反不正当竞争法保护的主要原因。②

Trade secret protection promotes two public policies: (1) it gives an incentive to businesses to invest in the development of technical “know-how,” ideas, and compilations of information by prohibiting certain unauthorized uses by others; and (2) it promotes state interests in maintaining basic standards of ethical conduct by marketplace actors. On the other hand, trade secret protection has the potential to interfere with competition and employees’ freedom to advance in their professions if applied too strictly to prevent employees from moving from one place of employment to another.

(二)商业秘密的范围(Scope)

商业秘密的范围非常广泛，工业、农业、商业等几乎所有领域与经营有关并具有经济价值的信息，都属于商业秘密。我国《反不正当竞争法》规定的商业秘密的范围包括技术信息和经营信息两大类。

1. 技术信息(Technical Information)

技术信息，又称技术秘密，是指未公开过，与产品生产和制造有关的技术诀窍或秘密技术。如：生产方案、产品设计、工艺流程、配方、质量控制等方面的技术知识等。Any

① 郑成思．知识产权法[M]．北京：法律出版社，2003：396.

② 韩松．知识产权法[M]．北京：中国人民大学出版社，2003：363.

information or technical expertise that is undisclosed and confers some sort of economic benefit on the owner of the right, and is safeguarded from disclosure by reasonable steps taken by a business, is seen to be technical information.

2. 经营信息(Operational Information)

经营信息，又称经营秘密，是指能够为经营者带来经济利益的保密信息。如：未公开的产品推销计划、顾客名单、进货渠道、销售网络、管理方法、产品价格、市场调查资料、标底、标书内容等。

目前，商业秘密的保护范围有逐步扩大的倾向。早期商业秘密的保护仅指技术信息，随着经济的不断发展，逐步扩大到经营信息。随着世界经济一体化的展开，加之世界贸易组织《与贸易有关的知识产权协议》以及世界知识产权组织《反不正当竞争保护的示范法》的影响，各国在商业秘密保护范围的认识上的差距正逐渐缩小。目前，大多数国家都接受了商业秘密的保护范围包括技术信息和经营信息。

二、商业秘密的构成要件(Constitutive Requirements of Trade Secrets)

In United States, the court listed the following six factors to "be considered in determining whether given information is one's trade secret."

(1) the extent to which the information is known outside of his business;

(2) the extent to which it is known by employees and others involved in his business;

(3) the extent of measures taken by him to guard the secrecy of the information;

(4) the value of the information to him and to his competitors;

(5) the amount of effort or money expended by him in developing the information;

(6) the ease or difficulty with which the information could be properly acquired or duplicated by others.

根据我国《反不正当竞争法》对商业秘密的规定，商业秘密的构成要件包括三个方面。

(一)秘密性(Secrecy)

秘密性，是指作为商业秘密的技术信息和经营信息必须是未公开的，是不为公众所知晓的。这是构成商业秘密的核心条件，也是商业秘密区别于专利技术和公知技术的最显著特征。

Absolute secrecy is not required, however. Trade secrets may be revealed to agents, employees, and others ordinarily entrusted with such information, so long as it is understood that the information is confidential and disclosure is forbidden. At the same time, keeping information strictly confidential does not make it a trade secret unless the information is useful or valuable. Information that is common knowledge will receive no protection as a trade secret. Information must rise to a sufficient level of originality, novelty, or utility before a court will recognize it as a commodity.

(二)价值性(Value)

价值性，是指作为商业秘密的技术信息和经营信息能够给权利人带来经济利益并具有实用性。The idea or information must be valuable to the owner and give it an advantage over competitors who do not have it. The value to the owner must be commercial in nature. Religious or spiritual value, for example, will not suffice.

这一要件包括两方面的要求：

1. 能为权利人带来经济利益（Capable of bringing economic benefits to the owners of the rights）

因为只有能为权利人带来经济利益，才有作为商业秘密保护的价值。是否能为权利人带来经济利益是商业秘密与隐私的区别之一。

2. 具有实用性（Practicability）

具有实用性，就是可以在商业活动中实际应用。实用性是商业秘密具有价值性的基础，如果没有实用性，不能付诸实践，也就谈不上价值性。

（三）保密性（Confidentiality）

保密性，是指权利人不仅要有将商业秘密加以保护的主观意识，还应当在客观上采取了保密措施。The owner of trade secret should take reasonable precautions to ensure that the information remains a secret. It should anticipate ways in which others might be expected to obtain the information and take reasonable measures to prevent access. For example, if the secret can be ascertained by observing the production process in the owner's factory, the owner may be required to restrict public access to that part of the factory. However, the claimant will not be required to make unreasonable expenditures to protect secrecy.

保密措施有多种形式，根据国家工商行政管理局《关于禁止侵犯商业秘密行为的若干规定》的内容来看，保密措施包括了订立保密协议，建立保密制度以及采取其他合理的保密措施。该规定实质上将保密措施分为两类，一类是制度措施，如订立保密合同、制定保密规章、加强保密教育等；另一类是合理的实际措施，这一类的范围较广，凡是适当、合理的保密措施都可以归入该类，如划定保密区域、设置保卫人员、为计算机加密、在资料上标明秘密标志、将资料放入保险柜等。

三、商业秘密权的概念及内容（Concept and Content of Trade Secret Rights）

（一）商业秘密权的概念（Concept）

商业秘密权，是指商业秘密的所有人依法对其商业秘密享有的权利。

我国《反不正当竞争法》确认了商业秘密所有人对其商业秘密享有权利，并确认了商业秘密的财产属性，规定了侵权人负有赔偿责任，这说明商业秘密是一种无形财产权。

At present, trade secrets are protected in many jurisdictions through legal protection of intellectual property rights. 我国刑法将侵犯商业秘密罪纳入侵犯知识产权罪中，这说明我国也将商业秘密权视为知识产权的一种。

（二）商业秘密权的内容（Content）

1. 占有权（The Right of Possession）

占有权，是指权利人有权对商业秘密进行控制、管理，防止他人采取不正当手段获取、泄露、使用等。

2. 使用权（The Right of Use）

使用权，是指权利人有权将自己的商业秘密付诸工商业活动并从中受益。

3. 处分权（The Right of Disposition）

处分权，是指权利人有权处分自己的商业秘密，包括转让、赠与、放弃、无偿公开等。

4. 许可使用权（The Right of Licensing）

许可使用权，是指权利人有权允许他人使用其商业秘密并有权获得报酬。

四、商业秘密权的保护(Protection of Trade Secrets)

(一)侵犯商业秘密的行为(Acts Infringing Trade Secrets)

根据我国《反不正当竞争法》的规定，侵犯商业秘密的行为包括以下四种：

1. 以不正当手段获取商业秘密(Obtaining Trade Secrets by Illegitimate Means)

以不正当手段获取商业秘密，是指行为人以盗窃、利诱、胁迫或其他不正当手段获取权利人的商业秘密。这一规定明确了不正当获取商业秘密的行为本身即属于违法，不管是否披露、使用非法获取的商业秘密。

2. 披露、使用或允许他人使用以不正当手段获取的商业秘密（Disclosing, Using or Allowing Others to Use the Trade Secrets Obtained by Illegitimate Means）

披露(disclose)，是指行为人将以不正当手段获取的商业秘密向他人扩散，使公众知晓该商业秘密的内容。不仅包括向不特定的人公开商业秘密，也包括向特定的人透露商业秘密。

使用，是指行为人将以不正当手段获取的商业秘密用于自己的生产经营。

允许他人使用，是指行为人将以不正当手段获取的商业秘密以有偿或无偿的方式提供给第三人使用。

3. 负有保密义务者披露、使用或允许他人使用其所掌握的商业秘密（Disclosing, Using or Allowing Others to Use the Trade Secrets that It Has Obtained by Breaking an Engagement or Disregarding the Requirements of the Owner of the Right to Preserve the Trade Secrets）

与前两种行为不同的是，侵犯商业秘密的行为人获取和掌握权利人的商业秘密的手段是合法的。行为人往往是通过合同或者工作关系等正当途径获得权利人的商业秘密，但是行为人却违反了所负的保密义务，将商业秘密披露、使用或允许他人使用，这种行为同样是侵害商业秘密的行为。

4. 第三人因故意或重大过失侵犯权利人的商业秘密（Infringing the Trade Secrets of the Right Owner by the Third Party Due to His Intentional Behavior or Gross Negligence）

我国《反不正当竞争法》规定，第三人明知或者应知向其提供商业秘密的一方具有违法行为，仍然获取、使用、披露该商业秘密的，视为侵犯商业秘密。

这里的第三人是指对商业秘密没有保密义务或者没有不正当获取商业秘密的人。由于第三人对商业秘密不负保密义务又未直接侵害商业秘密，因此第三人只有在故意(明知)或者重大过失(应知)的情况下才构成侵权。该规定要求第三人应承担合理的注意义务。如果第三人不可能知道存在违法行为而善意取得、使用、披露权利人的商业秘密的，不构成侵犯商业秘密的行为。

(二)侵犯商业秘密行为的法律责任(Legal Liability of Infringement of Trade Secrets)

1. 民事责任(Civil Liability)

侵犯商业秘密的民事责任主要有停止侵害和赔偿损失，如果因侵权行为给权利人造成不良影响的，还应赔礼道歉、消除影响、恢复名誉。

(1)停止侵害(Cessation of Infringements)

对侵害商业秘密的行为，人民法院可以经权利人申请，责令侵权行为人停止侵权行为，包括禁止使用、扩散、责令保密等。

(2)赔偿损失(Compensation for the Loss)

侵权人侵犯商业秘密的行为给权利人造成损害的，应当承担损害赔偿责任，赔偿权利人的损失。

侵权人进行损害赔偿时，赔偿额有两种计算方法：一是权利人的实际损失加上权利人因调查侵权行为所支出的合理费用(reasonable fees)；二是侵权人的利润加上权利人因调查侵权行为所支出的合理费用。当权利人的损失难以计算时适用第二种方式。

当侵权人与权利人之间发生侵权行为与违约行为的竞合，此时，权利人可以要求其承担违约责任或者侵权责任，但二者只能选其一。

(3)赔礼道歉、消除影响、恢复名誉(Extending a Formal Apology, Eliminating Ill Effects, Rehabilitating One's Reputation)

侵犯商业秘密常常会给他人造成信用损害，如利用他人商业秘密制造劣质产品出售，此时可以要求侵权人赔礼道歉、消除影响、恢复名誉。

2. 行政责任(Administrative Responsibility)

对侵害商业秘密的行为，监督检查部门可以实施以下行政处罚：

(1)责令停止侵权行为(Order to Desist from the Infringing Acts)

如责令侵权人销毁使用权利人商业秘密生产的、流入市场将会造成商业秘密公开的产品。

(2)罚款(Imposing a Fine)

监督检查部门可以根据情节，可处以1万元以上20万元以下的罚款。

3. 刑事责任(Criminal Responsibility)

根据《中华人民共和国刑法》的规定，侵犯商业秘密，给商业秘密权利人造成重大损失的，处3年以下有期徒刑或者拘役，并处或者单处罚金；造成特别严重后果的，处3年以上7年以下有期徒刑，并处罚金。

第三节 地理标记权
Ⅲ Geographical Indication Rights

一、地理标记与地理标记权的概念(Concepts of Geographical Indications and Rights of Geographical Indications)

(一)地理标记的概念(Concept)

地理标记，又称地理标志、地理标识，是指用来表示产品或服务的地理来源的名称、标记或符号。A geographical indication is a name or sign used on certain products which corresponds to a specific geographical location or origin (e. g. a town, region, or country). The use of a geographical indication may act as a certification that the product possesses certain qualities, or enjoys a certain reputation, due to its geographical origin. 地理标记又可作广义和狭义的划分。广义的地理标记包括来源地标志(indications of source)和原产地名称(appellations of origin)，世界知识产权组织(WIPO)及其管理的国际公约就是从广义上使用这一概念的。而狭义的地理标记仅指原产地名称。原产地名称与《与贸易有关的知识产权协议》(以下简称《知识产权协议》)中规定的地理标志的概念是一致的。① 为了与《知识产权协议》相一致，我国商标法对地理标记的概念采取了狭义说。

来源地标志，又称货源标记、产源标记，是指表示一种产品来源于某个国家、地区或地方的说明标记，通常由名称、标记或符号组成。Indications of source are direct or indirect reference of the geographical source of goods or services. 如"Made in China"、"上海制造"等都属于来源地标志。《保护工业产权巴黎公约》(以下简称《巴黎公约》)首次规定了对来源地标志的保护，1891 年《制裁商品来源的虚假或欺骗性标志协定》(*Madrid Agreement for the Repression of False or Deceptive Indications of Source on Goods*)则是一个专门保护来源地标志的国际协定。

原产地名称，又称原产地标志，是指标示某商品来源于某地区，该商品的特定质量、信誉或者其他特征主要由该地区的自然环境因素或者人文因素所决定的标志。如"贵州茅台酒"、"西湖龙井茶"、"波尔多葡萄酒"等。原产地名称便于相关国家发挥自己在生产经营方面的独到之处，可以说是借助地区优势，促进生产发展和经济增长的一种有效手段。目前，1958 年缔结的《保护原产地名称及其国际注册里斯本协定》(*Lisbon Agreement on the Protection of Appellations of Origin and Their Registration*，以下简称《里斯本协定》)是保护原产地名称最主要的国际条约。

An appellation of origin is the name of a region, a specific place or a country (hereinafter referred to as region) used for goods originating in that region, whose quality or other characteristics are essentially or exclusively given by a particular geographical environment with its

① 郑成思．知识产权法[M]．北京：法律出版社，2003：196.

inherent natural and human factors and whose processing, production and preparation takes place in a delimited geographical region. Traditional geographical and non-geographical appellations are also considered as original agricultural products of foodstuff, provided that such goods fulfill other conditions according to this regulation.

(二)地理标记权的概念(Concept)

地理标记权，是指原产地内符合条件的商品生产者对原产地名称所拥有的权利。地理标记权虽然归类于工业产权，但并不完全具备该类权利的基本特征。

1. 非个体专有独占性(Non-Exclusiveness by Individuals)

第一，来源地标志或原产地名称不允许有个人独自注册，若独家作为商标注册则势必剥夺该地区内其他生产经营者的使用权。我国《商标法》规定，县级以上的行政区域名称和公众知晓的外国地名不得用做商标注册。但地名具有其他含义的除外。

第二，在盗用、假冒来源地标志或原产地名称的行为发生时，任一权利人均可提起诉讼。

According to *Paris Convention*, any producer, manufacturer, or merchant, whether a natural person or a legal entity, engaged in the production or manufacture of or trade in such goods and established either in the locality falsely indicated as the source, or in the region where such locality is situated, or in the country falsely indicated, or in the country where the false indication of source is used, shall in any case be deemed an interested party(有关当事人).

2. 不具有时间性(Timelessness)

该项权利无保护期间的限制，是一项永久性的财产权利；商标权因有效期届满而未续展，依法将丧失专用权；商业秘密权虽然无保护期限限制，但一旦泄密即丧失权利；商号权虽具有永久性特征，但必须以企业存续为前提条件。

Relatively speaking, indications of source or appellations of origin are attached to geographical indications, and is associated with producers; hence it is a permanent right with no legal basis of extinction.

3. 不可转让性(Non-Transferability)

该项权利虽然具有财产意义，但使用这一标记的任何生产经营者都不得转让或许可使用，这是由权利客体即地理标记的本源性决定的。如果允许来源地标志或原产地名称转让使用，则会造成商品地域来源的混淆，扰乱社会经济秩序，从而也就丧失了地理标记的原有功能和作用。

二、原产地名称与来源地标志的区别(Distinction between Appellations of Origin and Indications of Source)

原产地名称与来源地标志虽然都起到标识商品或服务的地理来源之作用，但二者也存在明显的区别。

1. 范围不同(Different Scope)

来源地标志是用于标识产品或服务产于某个国家、地区或特定地方的表示或标记，这种表示或标记通常与货物质量无关；而原产地名称除了标识产品或服务产于某个国家、地区或特定地方外，还表明其特有的品质完全或基本上取决于该地域的包括自然的、人文的或两者兼具的因素在内的地理环境。

2. 联系不同(Different Relation)

作为原产地名称要求产品与其出产的地区存在质量上的联系，这种质量上的联系包括该产品的特殊品质完全或主要归因于该地理来源的特殊气候、土壤或传统生产方式等特殊因素。作为来源地标志，只要该产品出产于其所标识的地区即可。从某种意义上说，原产地名称也是一种特殊的来源地标志，但在一般情况下，来源地标志仅表示那些不能被当作原产地名称使用的地理来源。

三、地理标记权的法律保护(Legal Protection of Geographical Indications)

(一)国际公约对地理标记权的协调保护①(Legal Protection of Geographical Indication by International Conventions)

In the present expanding global economy geographical indications are significantly emerging as an important intellectual property. Countries and trade organizations increasingly recognize that geographical indications are valuable as "marketing tools" in the global economy. Geographical Indications prevent misuse of designation or presentation of a product, which indicates that the product originates in a place different from where it actually originates. An example is the word "Champagne" that is claimed exclusively by the Champagne region of France, which is the geographical region where the wine derives its world fame. No other wine, even if it is made from the same grape variety, by the same method, and is identical in taste, aroma and other qualities, can be called "Champagne". However, the exceptions to protections are if the geographical indication becomes generic or semi-generic that is if the name of a place is used as the designation of a kind of product, rather than an indication of the place of origin of that product, this term no longer functions as a geographical indication.

世界知识产权组织管理下的保护地理标记的国际公约主要有：《巴黎公约》、《制裁商品来源的虚假或欺骗性标志协定》以及《保护原产地名称及其国际注册里斯本协定》(以下简称《里斯本协定》)。《知识产权协议》也专门规定了地理标记的保护。

1.《巴黎公约》的有关规定(Relevant Provisions of *Paris Convention*)

《巴黎公约》中涉及来源地标志和原产地名称的条款主要有：第1条第(2)项规定了来源地标志和原产地名称；第10条规定了对来源地标志的保护；第9条规定了对假冒来源地标志行为的制裁；第10条之3规定了来源地标志受到侵害是的救济手段。虽然在《巴黎公约》第9条和第10条中仅规定了来源地标志的保护，但由于原产地名称也属于特殊的来源地标志，因此这几条规定也适用于原产地名称。

不过，对地理标记的保护而言，《巴黎公约》的重要意义在于将地理标记的保护扩展到了整个《巴黎公约》成员国的范围内。但《巴黎公约》并没有解决一些地理标记在原属国之外被当作通用标识使用的问题。《巴黎公约》仅规定了禁止使用虚假来源地标志，并未

① 韩松．知识产权法[M]．北京：中国人民大学出版社，2003：377.

对地理标志提供全面的保护。这些问题都留给了其他国际公约，如《制裁商品来源的虚假或欺骗性标志协定》和《里斯本协定》加以解决。

2.《制裁商品来源的虚假或欺骗性标志协定》的有关规定(Relevant Provisions of *Madrid Agreement for the Repression of False or Deceptive Indications of Source on Goods*)

《制裁商品来源的虚假或欺骗性标志协定》是第一个关于地理标记的专门性国际条约。该协定没有区分来源地标志和原产地名称，仅提到了来源地标志。但是由于原产地名称也属于特殊的来源地标志，因此，本协定对原产地名称也适用。

该协定的第 1 条至第 4 条规定了对来源地标志的实质性保护措施。All goods bearing a false or deceptive indication by which one of the countries to which this Agreement applies, or a place situated therein, is directly or indirectly indicated as being the country or place of origin shall be seized on, or prohibited from importation into any of the member countries, or taken other actions and remedies.

按照该协定第 4 条的规定，通用名称不得作为来源地标志受到协定的保护，各国法院有权决定通用名称的范围，但葡萄产品的产地名称不在此列。也即葡萄产品的产地名称受到本协定的绝对保护。

3.《里斯本协定》的有关规定(Relevant Provisions of *the Lisbon Treaty*)

The Lisbon Treaty was signed by the EU member states on 13 December 2007, and enacted on 1 December 2009. It amends the Treaty on European Union and the Treaty establishing the European Community.

《里斯本协定》是一个专门规定原产地名称保护的国际条约。该协定不仅规定了原产地名称保护的实质内容，而且对原产地名称的国际注册进行了规定。

The stated aim of the treaty was to complete the process started by the *Treaty of Amsterdam* and by the *Treaty of Nice* with a view to enhancing the efficiency and democratic legitimacy of the Union and to improving the coherence of its action.

按照《里斯本协定》的规定，原产地名称系指一个国家、地区或地方的地理名称，用于指示一项产品来源于该地，且其质量和特征完全或主要取决于包括自然人和人文因素在内的地理环境。《里斯本协定》对原产地名称的保护比较宽泛，任何盗用或模仿原产地名称的行为，即使是为了标明产品的真实来源，或者以翻译的方式使用原产地名称，或者使用诸如“类”、“型”、“式”、“仿”之类的标识，都属于禁止之列。

4.《知识产权协议》的有关规定(Relevant Provisions)

虽然《制裁商品来源的虚假或欺骗性标志协定》和《里斯本协定》已经对地理标记的保护进行了比较全面的规定，但这两个国际条约参加国较少，因而所起到的作用也比较有限。而《知识产权协议》由于其成员的广泛性，对地理标记的国际保护起到了积极的作用。

《知识产权协议》中讲的原产地标记，是从它含有的无形财产权的意义上讲的。尤其对于酒类商品，原产地标记有着重要的经济意义。《知识产权协议》从总体上讲是禁止使用原产地标记作商标使用的，但如果已经善意取得了这种标记的商标注册，又不会在公众中引起误解的，则可以不撤销其注册，不禁止其使用。我国的“茅台”酒、“泸州”老窖等，均属于这种善意而又不至于引起混淆的"原产地标记型"商标。①

Protection of Geographical Indications:

1. Geographical indications are indications which identify a good as originating in the territory of a Member, or a region or locality in that territory, where a given quality, reputation or other characteristic of the good is essentially attributable to its geographical origin.

2. In respect of geographical indications, Members shall provide the legal means for interested parties to prevent:

(a) the use of any means in the designation or presentation of a good that indicates or suggests that the good originates in a geographical area other than the true place of origin in a manner which misleads the public as to the geographical origin of the good;

(b) any use which constitutes an act of unfair competition within the meaning of Article 10 bis of *the Paris Convention* (*1967*).

3. A Member shall, ex officio if its legislation so permits or at the request of an interested party, refuse or invalidate the registration of a trademark which contains or consists of a geographical indication with respect to goods not originating in the territory indicated, if use of the indication in the trademark for such goods in that Member is of such a nature as to mislead the public to the true place of origin.

4. The protection under paragraphs 1, 2 and 3 shall be applicable against a geographical indication which, although literally true as to the territory, region or locality where the goods originate falsely represents to the public that the goods originate in another territory. ②

Each Member shall provide the legal means for interested parties to prevent use of a geographical indication identifying wines for wines not originating in the place indicated by the geographical indication or identifying spirits for spirits not originating in the place indicated by the geographical indication, even if the true origin of the goods is indicated or the geographical indication is used in translation or accompanied by expressions such as "kind", "type", "style", "imitation", etc. ③

除上述规定外,《知识产权协议》还在第23条中规定了对葡萄酒和白酒地理标记的补充保护。第23条第1款规定,每一成员方应为各利益方提供法律手段,以阻止不产自于某一地理标志所指地方的葡萄酒或烈性酒使用该地理标志,即使在标明了商品真正原产地或在翻译中使用了该地理标志或伴以"种类"、"类型"、"风味"、"仿制"等字样的情况下也不例外。

(二)国内法中对地理标记权的法律保护(Domestic Legal Protection of Geographical Indications)

我国对地理标记权的法律保护是通过《商标法》、针对地理标记的专门立法和《反不正

① 郑成思. 知识产权法[M]. 北京: 法律出版社, 2003: 196.

② Article 22 of *TRIPS*.

③ Article 23 of *TRIPS*.

当竞争法》这三个方面加以保护。

1. 地理标记权的《商标法》保护(Geographical Indications in the *Trademark Law*)

根据《商标法》的规定，地理标志(geographical indications)，是指标示某商品来源于某地区，该商品的特定质量、信誉或者其他特征，主要由该地区的自然因素或者人文因素所决定的标志。《商标法实施条例》规定，《商标法》所规定的地理标志，可以依照商标法和本条例的规定，作为证明商标(certification mark)或者集体商标(collective marks)申请注册。

根据《商标法》的规定，集体商标，是指以团体(group)、协会(association)或者其他组织名义注册，供该组织成员在商事活动中使用，以表明使用者在该组织中的成员资格(membership)的标志。证明商标，是指由对某种商品或者服务具有监督能力的组织所控制，而由该组织以外的单位或者个人使用于其商品或者服务，用以证明该商品或者服务的原产地、原料、制造方法、质量或者其他特定品质的标志。从《商标法》规定的集体商标和证明商标的功能来看，二者都可以起到指示商品或者服务来源的作用，因而可以成为保护地理标记的手段。

中华人民共和国工商行政管理局于《集体商标、证明商标注册和管理办法》中规定了可以将地理标记作为集体商标、证明商标注册登记。

2. 地理标记的专门立法保护(Special Legislative Protection of Geographical Indications)

除了通过《商标法》对地理标记进行保护外，国家质量技术监督局于1999年8月17日发布的《原产地域产品保护规定》、国家出入境检验检疫局于2001年3月5日发布《原产地标记管理规定》和《原产地标记管理规定实施办法》，都从原产地的角度对地理标记提供了保护。目前，国家质量技术监督局和出入境检验检疫局已合并为国家质量监督检验检疫总局。上述涉及的原产地标记保护工作由国家质量监督检验检疫总局负责。

3. 地理标记的《反不正当竞争法》保护(Geographical Indications in *Law for Countering Unfair Competition*)

反不正当竞争法是从虚假表示(false representation)或者虚假宣传(false propaganda)的角度保护地理标记的。我国《反不正当竞争法》将“伪造产地，对商品质量做引人误解的虚假表示”作为一种不正当竞争行为加以禁止。

值得注意的是，《反不正当竞争法》中规范的产地是在商品产出地意义上加以使用的，与《巴黎公约》中的货源标记(indication of source)含义相同。本节所涉及的地理标记属于产地标志的特殊类型，也可以得到《反不正当竞争法》的保护。

第四节 植物新品种权
Ⅳ New Varieties of Plants

一、植物新品种与植物新品种权的概念(Concepts of New Varieties of Plants and Rights of New Varieties of Plants)

植物新品种(new varieties of plants)，是指经过人工培育或者对发现的野生植物加以开发，具备新颖性、特异性、一致性和稳定性并有适当生命的植物品种。Plant variety is a legal term, following the International Union for the Protection of New Varieties of Plants (UPOV) Convention.

植物新品种权，是指新品种所有权人(以下简称品种权人)对其授权的品种所享有的排他性的独占权。Plant breeders' rights, also known as plant variety rights, are rights granted to the breeder of a new variety of plant that give him exclusive control over the propagating material (including seed, cuttings, divisions, tissue culture) and harvested material (cut flowers, fruit, foliage) of a new variety for a number of years. ①

This "variety" should not be confused with the international taxonomic rank of "variety", or with the term "cultivar". Some horticulturists use "variety" imprecisely; for example, viticulturists almost always refer to grape cultivars as "grape varieties". ②

优良的植物品种是重要的农、林业生产资料，是获得农、林产品高产、优质的内在因素，具有巨大的社会效益和经济效益。然而，植物新品种的开发和培育是十分艰巨和复杂的技术工作，需要投入大量资金和智力。因此，许多国家制定保护植物新品种的法律法规，以此保护育种人的合法权益，推动植物新品种的研究和推广工作，促进科研进步和农业发展。

二、植物新品种权的国际保护(International Protection of New Varieties of Plants)

目前，多数国家通过专门立法对植物新品种进行保护，将植物新品种的保护排除在专利法之外。其理由是植物新品种是有生命之物，具有自身生长繁殖的特性，难以套用工业产品发明的模式保护。

The United States of America passed the Plant Patent Act in 1930 at the urging of such notable figures. Plant patents provided a special form of patent protection, which relaxed certain requirements of the utility patent law as applied to asexually reproduced varieties of plants. In 1957, the French Government held a conference in Paris concerned with the protection of new varieties. This led to the creation of the *International Union for the Protection of New Varieties of Plants* (UPOV) in 1961. ③

Convention for the Protection of New Varieties of Plants (UPOV) was established by the International Convention for the Protection of New Varieties of Plants. The Convention was adopted in Paris in 1961 and revised in 1972, 1978 and 1991. The objective of the Convention is

① Plant Breeders' Rights [DB/OL]. [2017-05-03]. Wikipedia, http: //en.wikipedia.org/wiki/Plant_breeders'_rights.

② Plant Variety (Law) [DB/OL]. [2017-05-03]. Wikipedia, http: //en.wikipedia.org/wiki/Plant_variety_(law).

③ Plant Breeders' Rights [DB/OL]. [2017-05-13]. Wikipedia, http: //en.wikipedia.org/wiki/Plant_breeders'_rights.

the protection of new varieties of plants by an intellectual property right. By codifying intellectual property for plant breeders, UPOV aims to encourage the development of new varieties of plants for the benefit of society. ① The purpose of the Convention was to ensure that the member states party to the Convention acknowledges the achievements of breeders of new plant varieties by making available to them an exclusive property right, on the basis of a set of uniform and clearly defined principles. ②我国于 1999 年 3 月加入该公约，采用 1978 年文本，成为国际植物新品种保护联盟第 39 个成员国。③

根据该公约的规定，成员国可以自由选择专门立法或专利法或者二者并用对植物新品种给予保护；受保护的植物品种的范围可以适用于一切植物属和种；育种者权利的核心是享有为商业目的的生产、销售其品种的繁殖材料的专有权；一般情况下，植物专有权的保护期不少于 15 年；取得植物新品种的保护须申请，申请人在任何一个成员国第一次提出申请后，12 个月内可在公约其他成员国享有优先权；同一个植物新品种在不同成员国所受的保护相互独立。此外，该公约还对授予品种权的条件、育种者权利的限制、品种权的无效和终止等内容作了明确的规定，确立了国际植物新品种知识产权保护体系的基本框架。

此外，《知识产权协议》第 27 条规定，各成员应规定通过专利或一种有效的特殊制度或通过这两者的组合来保护植物品种。④ 本项的规定应在《知识产权协议》生效之日起 4 年后进行审议。这一规定进一步加强了对植物新品种的国际保护，并对世界各国立法产生了巨大影响。

三、我国对植物新品种权的保护(Protection of New Plants Varieties in China)

我国对植物新品种并没有通过专利法保护，根据《专利法》的规定，植物新品种不属于专利法的保护对象。我国是通过专门立法对植物新品种进行保护。国务院于 1997 年 3 月 20 日发布了《植物新品种保护条例》，并于 1997 年 10 月 1 日起施行。

(一)植物新品种权保护的条件(Protection Conditions of New Varieties of Plants)

根据我国《植物新品种保护条例》的规定，植物新品种必须具备新颖性、特异性、一致性和稳定性等条件。

1. 新颖性(Novelty)

Novel means that it must not have been previously marketed in the country where rights are applied for. A variety is new if it has not been commercialized for more than one year in the

① International Union for the Protection of New Varieties of Plants [DB/OL]. [2017-05-23]. Wikipedia, http://en.wikipedia.org/wiki/International_Union_for_the_Protection_of_New_Varieties_of_Plants.

② Plant Breeders' Rights [DB/OL]. [2017-05-23]. Wikipedia, http://en.wikipedia.org/wiki/Plant_breeders'_rights.

③ 李颖怡. 知识产权法[M]. 广州：中山大学出版社，2005：261.

④ 《与贸易有关的知识产权协议》[DB/OL]. [2017-05-23]. 中华人民共和国国家知识产权局网站，http://www.sipo.gov.cn/zcfg/flfg/qt/gjty/200804/t20080403_369216.html.

country of protection.

在中国境内销售该品种繁殖材料未超过1年；在中国境外销售藤本植物、林木、果树和观赏树木品种繁殖材料未超过6年，销售其他植物品种繁殖材料未超过4年。此处的新颖性与专利法中不同，其强调的是申请日之前未经商业销售。

2. 特异性(Specificity)

Specificity means the new plant must be distinct from other available varieties. A variety is distinct if it differs from all other known varieties by one or more important botanical characteristics, such as height, maturity, color, etc.

3. 一致性(Consistency)

Consistency means that the plants must display homogeneity. The plant in same variety must appear the same nature after reproduce. A variety is uniform if the plant characteristics are consistent from plant to plant within the variety.

4. 稳定性 (Stability)

Stability refers to the trait or traits unique to the new variety must be stable so that the plant remains true to type after repeated cycles of propagation. A variety is stable if the plant characteristics are genetically fixed and therefore remain the same from generation to generation, or after a cycle of reproduction in the case of hybrid varieties.

(二)植物新品种权的内容及归属(Contents and Ownership of New Varieties of Plants)

1. 植物新品种权的内容(Contents of New Varieties of Plants)

根据《植物新品种保护条例》的规定，品种权所有人享有以下权利：

(1)排他独占权(Exclusive Rights)

The entity which or the person who has accomplished the breeding has an exclusive right in their protected variety. Except otherwise provided in these Regulations, no other entity or person shall, without the consent of the holder of the variety rights, produce or sell for commercial purposes the propagating material of the said protected variety, or use for commercial purposes the propagating material of the protected variety in a repeated manner in the production of the propagating material of another variety. ①

(2)依法转让权(Assignment Rights)

植物新品种的申请权和品种权可以依法转让。中国的单位或者个人就其在国内培育的植物新品种向外国人转让申请权或者品种权的，应当经审批机关批准。国有单位在国内转让申请权或者品种权的，应当按照国家有关规定报经有关行政主管部门批准。转让申请权或者品种权的，当事人应当订立书面合同，并向审批机关登记，由审批机关予以公告。

① Article 6 of *Regulations on the Protection of New Varieties of Plants*.

2. 植物新品种权的归属(Ownership of New Varieties of Plants)

根据《植物新品种保护条例》的规定，品种权的归属由于育种的性质的不同而有所不同。

(1)职务育种(Service Breeding)

In the case of job-related breeding accomplished by any person in undertaking tasks for the entity to which he belongs, or primarily by using the facilities of that entity, the right to file an application for variety rights in respect of the new plant variety shall belong to the entity in question. ①

(2)非职务育种(Non-Service Breeding)

For breeding that is not job-related, the right to file such an application shall belong to the person accomplishing the breeding. Upon approval of the application, the variety rights shall belong to the applicant. ②

(3)委托育种或合作育种(Commissioned Breeding or Jointly Conducted Breeding)

For commissioned breeding or jointly conducted breeding, the ownership of the variety rights shall be agreed upon by the parties in a contract; failing such an event, the variety rights shall belong to the entity or person commissioned to conduct or jointly conduct breeding. ③

(三)植物新品种权的期限、终止和无效(Term, Termination and Nullity of New Varieties of Plants)

1. 植物新品种权的期限(Term of New Varieties of Plants)

The term of protection of variety rights, counted from the date of grant thereof, shall be 20 years for vines, forest trees, fruit trees and ornamental plants and 15 years for other plants. ④

品种权人应当自被授予品种权的当年开始缴纳年费，并且按照审批机关的要求提供用于检测的该授权品种的繁殖材料。

2. 植物新品种权的终止(Termination of New Varieties of Plants)

Variety rights shall be terminated prior to the expiration of the term thereof in any of the following cases:

(a) Where the variety rights holder makes a written statement renouncing his variety right;

(b) Where the variety rights holder has not paid the annual fees as prescribed;

(c) Where the variety rights holder has not furnished, in the manner required by the examining and approving authorities, such propagating material of the protected variety necessary for control;

(d) Where, on control, the protected variety no longer conforms to the features, and

① Article 7 of *Regulations on the Protection of New Varieties of Plants.*

② Article 7 of *Regulations on the Protection of New Varieties of Plants.*

③ Article 7 of *Regulations on the Protection of New Varieties of Plants.*

④ Article 34 of *Regulations on the Protection of New Varieties of Plants.*

characteristics that existed when the variety rights were granted.

The termination of the variety rights shall be registered and published by the examining and approving authorities. ①

3. 植物新品种权的无效（Nullity of New Varieties of Plants）

自审批机关公告授予品种权之日起，植物新品种复审委员会可以依据职权或者依据任何单位或者个人的书面请求，对不符合新颖性、特异性、一致性和稳定性的植物新品种，宣告品种权无效；对不符合名称规定的，予以更名。宣告品种权无效或者更名的决定，由审批机关登记和公告，并通知当事人。当事人对植物新品种复审委员会的决定不服的，可以自收到通知之日起3个月内向人民法院提起诉讼。

被宣告无效的品种权视为自始不存在。宣告品种权无效的决定，对在宣告前人民法院作出并已执行的植物新品种侵权的判决、裁定，省级以上人民政府农业、林业行政部门作出并已执行的植物新品种侵权处理决定，以及已经履行的植物新品种实施许可合同和植物新品种权转让合同，不具有追溯力；但是，因品种权人的恶意给他人造成损失的，应当给予合理赔偿。依照上述规定，品种权人或者品种权转让人不向被许可实施人或者受让人返还使用费或者转让费，明显违反公平原则的，品种权人或者品种权转让人应当向被许可实施人或者受让人返还全部或者部分使用费或者转让费。

（四）侵犯植物新品种权的法律责任（Legal Liability of Infringing New Varieties of Plants）

1. 侵犯植物新品种权的法律责任（Legal Liability of Variety Right Infringements）

未经品种权人许可，以商业目的生产或者销售授权品种的繁殖材料的，是侵犯植物新品种权的行为。对于该侵权行为，品种权人或者利害关系人可以请求省级以上人民政府农业、林业行政部门依据各自的职权进行处理，也可以直接向人民法院提起诉讼。

The administrative departments of agriculture and forestry of the governments at provincial level or above may, according to their respective competence and based on the principle of free will of the parties, mediate the compensation of damages caused by the infringement. Where accord has been reached through mediation, it should be executed by the parties concerned; where no accord has been reached through mediation, the variety rights holder or the party having an interest therein may file a suit with the Court according to civil action procedures. In handling cases of infringement of variety rights in accordance with their respective competence, the administrative departments of agriculture and forestry of the governments at provincial level or above may, for the purposes of safeguarding the public interest of the society, order the infringe to stop the infringing act, confiscate the unlawful earnings and punish him with a fine five times more than the unlawful earnings. ②

2. 假冒授权品种行为的法律责任（Legal Liability of Counterfeiting Protected Variety）

① Article 36 of *Regulations on the Protection of New Varieties of Plants*.

② Article 40 of *Regulations on the Protection of New Varieties of Plants*.

Where any new plant variety is counterfeited, the administrative departments of agriculture and forestry of the Governments at county level or above shall order the party concerned to stop the counterfeiting act, confiscate the unlawful earnings and the propagating material of the plant variety, and punish him with a fine at least one but not exceeding five times more than the unlawful earnings; where the circumstances of the case are so serious as to constitute a crime, the party concerned shall be subjected to criminal liability investigation in accordance with the law. ①

省级以上人民政府农业、林业行政部门依据各自的职权在查处品种权侵权案件和县级以上人民政府农业、林业行政部门依据各自的职权在查处假冒授权品种案件时，根据需要，可以封存或者扣押与案件有关的植物品种的繁殖材料，查阅、复制或者封存与案件有关的合同、账册及有关文件。

3. 销售授权品种未使用其注册登记的名称的法律责任（Legal Liability of Selling Protected Variety without Using Its Registered Denomination）

销售授权品种未使用其注册登记的名称的，由县级以上人民政府农业、林业行政部门依据各自的职权责令限期改正，可以处 1 000 元以下的罚款。

第五节 商号权
V Trade Name Rights

一、商号权概述（Overview of Trade Name Rights）

（一）商号的概念（Concept of Trade Names）

商号，又称厂商名称、字号或商业名称，是经营者在经营活动中用于标示自己并区别于其他经营者的文字标志。A trade name may be the actual name of a given business or an assumed name under which a business operates and holds itself out to the public. 经营者将商号应用于商品或其包装以及广告媒体上，起到区别其他不同经营者的商品或服务的作用。社会公众则通过商号对众多经营者进行识别，对特定经营者的商品和服务进行评价。因此，商号和商标都属于识别性商业标识的范畴，是企业信誉和声誉的载体，是经营者重要的无形资产。如我国的“全聚德”、“同仁堂”、“六必居”等商号就深受消费者信赖，在市场中具有较强的竞争优势。

（二）商号与企业名称的区别（Distinction between Trade Names and Corporate Names）

商号与企业名称是容易相混淆的一组概念。依较为通行的观点认为，商号是企业名称中的字号，即经营者特定化、人格化的标志，是企业名称中具有区别性的部分。如“珠海

① Article 40 of *Regulations on the Protection of New Varieties of Plants*.

格力电器股份有限公司”这一企业名称，是由行政区划(珠海)、字号(格力)、行业(电器)、组织形式(股份有限公司)依次组成的，其中的“格力”就是这个企业的商号，或叫字号。

Trade name regulation derives from the Common Law of Unfair Competition. Trade dress is used by competitors to distinguish their products by visual appearance, including size, shape, and color, while service marks are used by competitors to distinguish their services from each other. Gradually, the law of trade dress and service marks has evolved into separate causes of action, independent from the law of trade name infringement. ①

(三)商号权的概念及特征(Concept and Features of Trade Name Rights)

1. 商号权的概念（Concept of Trade Name Rights）

商号权，又称厂商名称权，是指企业对依法核准登记的名称在一定地域范围内享有的独占使用权。

商号是一种具有识别作用的商业标志，能具体标示出商品的经营者或服务项目的提供者。授予企业对其核准登记的商号享有独占使用权，禁止他人假冒，是保护经营者和消费者合法权益的需要，也是制止不正当竞争、维护社会正常经济秩序的需要。

Trade name regulation serves four purposes. First, the law seeks to protect the economic, intellectual, and creative investments made by businesses in distinguishing their trades. Second, the law seeks to preserve the good will and reputation that are often associated with a particular trade name. Third, the law seeks to promote clarity and stability in the marketplace by encouraging consumers to rely on a merchant's trade name when evaluating the quality of its merchandise. Fourth, the law seeks to increase competition by requiring businesses to associate their own trade names with the value and quality of their goods and services. ②

2. 商号权的特征（Features of Trade Name Rights）

(1)专有性(Exclusiveness)

只有作为权利主体的经营者对自己核准登记的名称才依法享有使用权，同行业的其他企业不得使用，否则构成侵权。

When obligee owns the common law rights to a trade name, he will have exclusive protectable rights in his geographic commercial area.

(2)地域性(Regionalism)

企业对核准登记的企业名称中的商号在登记机关辖区内享有独占使用权，该地域内的同行业商号不得与之相同或近似。经国家工商管理局核准的商号在全国范围内受到法律保

① Trade Name [DB/OL]. [2017-06-12]. The Free Dictionary, http://legal-dictionary.thefreedictionary.com/trade+name.

② Trade Name [DB/OL]. [2017-06-12]. The Free Dictionary, http://legal-dictionary.thefreedictionary.com/trade+name.

护，而省、市、县工商行政管理局核准的商号则只能在本行政区域内受法律保护。

(3)唯一性(Unique)

One enterprise shall be granted only one set of trade name rights. In this point, it is quite different with trademark.

(4)终身性(Lifelong Time)

商号权的使用一般不受期限的限制，这一点与其他知识产权不同，只要经营者依法使用，原则上可以终身享有。因为，商号的时间积累往往代表着极大的信誉，历史悠久的老字号的商号往往对消费者更有吸引力。

(5)程序性(Procedural)

According to the article 8 of *Paris Convention*, a trade name shall be protected in all the countries of the Union without the obligation of filing or registration, whether or not it forms part of a trademark. ①

二、商号权的内容(Contents of Trade Name Rights)

商号权的内容主要包括以下几个方面：

1. 设定权(Rights of Setting)

经营者可以在法律规定的范围内自由决定其商号。但由于商号的选定关系到社会公共利益和社会公德问题，因而法律也对商号权的设定作出了一定的限制。这些限制性的规定主要体现在《企业名称登记管理规定》及《企业名称登记管理实施办法》。

Trade name is a simple type of registration that informs the public who you are and what kind of business you are in, as well as giving you some degree of name protection. This type of registration is commonly used by sole proprietorships, association of individuals, or other entities that want to do business under a different name. But the name must be limited to certain proper legal domain under consideration of social morals, public interests and legal clauses.

2. 专用权(Exclusive Rights)

When competitors share deceptively similar trade names, a cause of action for infringement may exist. The law of unfair competition forbids competitors from confusing consumers through the use of identifying trade devices that are indistinguishable or difficult to distinguish. Actual confusion need not be demonstrated to establish a claim for infringement, so long as there is likelihood that consumers will be confused by similar identifying trade devices.

3. 转让权(Rights of Assignment)

As a private right, trade name right has the attributes of property right, which contribute to its assignable targets. The name of enterprise may be assigned with the transfer of enterprise or

① Article 8 of *Paris Convention for the Protection of Industrial Property*.

part of it.

三、商号权的法律保护(Legal Protection of Trade Name Rights)

(一)商号权的国际保护(International Protection of Trade Name Rights)

商号的国际保护起源于《巴黎公约》。《巴黎公约》第1条第2项关于工业产权客体的规定中明确把商号包括在内。公约的第8条还规定了各成员国保护商号的最低标准，商号应在本同盟国一切成员国内受到保护，无须申请或注册，也不论其是否为商标的组成部分。公约第9条规定了对假冒商号行为的制裁。公约第10条之3规定了商号受到侵害时的救济手段。但《巴黎公约》仅仅为商号保护建立了一个基本框架，对于商号保护的具体制度则缺乏清晰、全面的规定。

(1) All goods unlawfully bearing a trademark or trade name shall be seized on importation into those countries of the Union where such mark or trade name is entitled to legal protection.

(2) Seizure shall likewise be affected in the country where the unlawful affixation occurred or in the country into which the goods were imported.

(3) Seizure shall take place at the request of the public prosecutor, or any other competent authority, or any interested party, whether a natural person or a legal entity, in conformity with the domestic legislation of each country.

(4) The authorities shall not be bound to effect seizure of goods in transit.

(5) If the legislation of a country does not permit seizure on importation, seizure shall be replaced by prohibition of importation or by seizure inside the country.

(6) If the legislation of a country permits neither seizure on importation nor prohibition of importation seizure inside the country, then, until such time as the legislation is modified accordingly, these measures shall be replaced by the actions and remedies available in such cases to nationals under the law of such country.

在《巴黎公约》之后，世界知识产权组织为发展中国家制定了《商标、商号及反不正当竞争示范法》。这一文件比较清晰全面地规定了商号保护的具体制度。对商号的设定、商号的转让、商号保护的范围以及禁止用做商号的名称等都进行了规定。

除上述文件外，在世界知识产权组织1996年《关于反不正当竞争保护的示范规定》中，还规定了对商号的反不正当竞争保护。该规定中不仅对假冒他人商号造成混淆的行为加以禁止，而且对于淡化商号识别性、损害商号声誉的行为也规定为不正当竞争行为，从而更加丰富了商号的保护方式。①

(二)商号权的国内保护(Domestic Protection of Trade Name Rights)

我国对商号权的保护并无统一立法，但在其他法律规范中加以规定。目前，涉及商号权保护的国内法律规范主要有：《民法通则》《商标法》《反不正当竞争法》以及相关的商事登记管理法规，如《企业名称登记管理规定》及《企业名称登记管理实施办法》。其中，《民

---

① 韩松．知识产权法[M]．北京：中国人民大学出版社，2003：373.

法通则》规定，法人(legal persons)、个体工商户(individual businesses)、个人合伙(individual partnerships)享有名称权。因此，民法更侧重于对商号人格属性(personality attributes)的保护；有关商事登记的法规主要是侧重于对企业名称(cooperate name)的行政监管，对企业名称的设定(setting)、变更(alteration)、转让(assignment)等事宜加以规定；《商标法》也可以对商号提供保护。由于《商标法》可以提供更为周全的保护，因此，使用商标(trademark)作为商号(trade name)，或者将商号注册为商标(registered trademark)，已经成为许多企业增强商号保护的共同选择；《反不正当竞争法》主要是通过对假冒商号(counterfeit trademark)等不正当竞争行为加以禁止，对商号提供保护。

第六节　域名权
Ⅵ　Domain Name Rights

一、域名概述(Overview of Domain Names)

(一)域名的概念(Concept of Domain Name)

域名，是指为了方便用户访问互联网而设置的，与 IP 地址具有对应关系的网络地址。根据 2004 年 12 月 20 日起施行的《中国互联网络域名管理办法》的规定，“域名：是互联网络上识别和定位计算机的层次结构式的字符标识，与该计算机的互联网协议(IP)地址相对应。中文域名：是指含有中文文字的域名。顶级域名：是指域名体系中根节点下的第一级域的名称。”

A domain name is an identification label that defines a realm of administrative autonomy, authority, or control in the Internet. Domain names are hostnames that identify Internet Protocol resources such as web sites. Domain names are formed by the rules and procedures of the Domain Name System. ①

(二)域名的结构(Structure of Domain Names)

为了便于大家进一步了解域名的实质，有必要在这里谈谈域名的体系结构。域名是由原点隔开的多个代码段构成的字符串，如从中国互联网信息中心 WWW. CNNIC. NET. CN 这个域名来看，它是由几个不同的部分组成的，这几个部分彼此之间具有层次关系。其中最后的 . CN 是域名的第一层，. NET 是第二层，. CNNIC 是真正的域名，处在第三层，当然还可以有第四层，如：INNER. CNNIC. NET. CN，至此我们可以看出域名从后到前的层次结构类似于一个倒立的树型结构。其中第一层的 . CN 叫做地理顶级域名。

A domain name consists of one or more parts, technically called labels that are conventionally concatenated, and delimited by dots, such as example. com.

The right-most label conveys the top-level domain; for example, the domain name www. example. com belongs to the top-level domain com.

---

① Domain Name [DB/OL]. [2017-05-03]. Wikipedia, http://en. wikipedia. org/wiki/Domain_name.

The hierarchy of domains descends from the right to the left label in the name; each label to the left specifies a subdivision, or subdomain of the domain to the right. This tree of labels may consist of 127 levels. Each label may contain 1 up to and including 63 octets. The empty label is reserved for the root node. The full domain name may not exceed a total length of 253 characters. In practice, some domain registries may have shorter limits.

A hostname is a domain name that has at least one associated IP address. For example, the domain names www. example. com and example. com are also hostnames, whereas the com domain is not. However, other top-level domains, particularly country code top-level domains, may indeed have an IP address, and if so, they are also hostnames.

Hostnames impose restrictions on which characters may be used in the domain name. A valid hostname is also a valid domain name, but a valid domain name is not necessarily valid as a hostname.

目前互联网上的域名体系中共有两类顶级域名：一类是地理顶级域名，共有243个国家和地区的代码。例如．CN代表中国，．JP代表日本，．UK代表英国等；另一类是类别顶级域名，共有7个：．COM(公司)，．NET(网络机构)，．ORG(组织机构)，．EDU(美国教育)，．GOV(美国政府部门)，．ARPA(美国军方)，．INT(国际组织)。由于互联网最初是在美国发展起来的，所以最初的域名体系也主要供美国使用，所以．GOV，．EDU，．ARPA虽然都是顶级域名，但却是美国使用的。只有．COM，．NET，．ORG成为供全球使用的顶级域名。相对于地理顶级域名来说，这些顶级域名都是根据不同的类别来区分的，所以称之为类别顶级域名。随着互联网的不断发展，新的顶级域名也根据实际需要不断被扩充到现有的域名体系中来。新增加的顶级域名是．BIZ(商业)，．COOP(合作公司)，．INFO(信息行业)，．AERO(航空业)，．PRO(专业人士)，．MUSEUM(博物馆行业)，．NAME(个人)。在这些顶级域名下，还可以再根据需要定义次一级的域名，如在我国的顶级域名．CN下又设立了．COM，．NET，．ORG，．GOV，．EDU以及我国各个行政区划的字母代表如．BJ代表北京，．SH代表上海等。①

2009年10月30日，全球互联网管理机构国际互联网名称和编号分配公司(ICANN)批准，国际互联网可使用中文、阿拉伯文和韩文等非拉丁字母文字注册域名。2009年11月16日，中国互联网信息中心(CNNIC)正式向ICANN提交有关中文全球顶级域名“．中国”的正式国际申请。自2010年年初，全球华语网民都可在地址栏中直接输入例如“北京商报．中国”这样的中文域名来访问网站了。②

根据CNNIC的规定，中国互联网络域名体系在顶级域名“CN”之外设“中国”、“公司”、“网络”、“政务”和“公益”等中文顶级域名。其中，“中国”适用于在中国境内的单位；“公司”适用于工商企业等营利性单位；“网络”适用于拥有或利用网络设施提供服务

① 丁春燕．域名监管制度研究[M]．北京：中国政法大学出版社，2016：12.

② 我国正式递交“．中国”域名国际申请[DB/OL]．[2017-06-20]．腾讯网，http：//tech. qq. com/a/20091117/000010. htm.

的单位；“政务”适用于党政群机关、政务部门等；“公益”适用于非营利性单位。①

(三)域名的注册(Registration of Domain Names)

根据《中国互联网络域名管理办法》的规定，域名注册服务应遵循“先申请先注册”原则。为维护国家利益和社会公众利益，域名注册管理机构可以在报请信息产业部备案后，对部分保留字进行必要保护。

任何组织或个人注册和使用的域名，不得含有下列内容：反对宪法所确定的基本原则的；危害国家安全，泄露国家秘密，颠覆国家政权，破坏国家统一的；损害国家荣誉和利益的；煽动民族仇恨、民族歧视，破坏民族团结的；破坏国家宗教政策，宣扬邪教和封建迷信的；散布谣言，扰乱社会秩序，破坏社会稳定的；散布淫秽、色情、赌博、暴力、凶杀、恐怖或者教唆犯罪的；侮辱或者诽谤他人，侵害他人合法权益的；含有法律、行政法规禁止的其他内容的。违反上述规定，构成犯罪的，依法追究刑事责任；尚不构成犯罪的，由国家有关机关依照有关法律、行政法规的规定予以处罚。

域名注册申请者应当提交真实、准确、完整的域名注册信息，并与域名注册服务机构签订用户注册协议。域名注册完成后，域名注册申请者即成为其注册域名的持有者。注册域名应当按期缴纳域名运行费用。

Registries and registrars usually charge an annual fee for the service of delegating a domain name to a user and providing a default set of name servers. Often this transaction is termed a sale or lease of the domain name and the registrant may sometimes be called an “owner”, but no such legal relationship is actually associated with the transaction, only the exclusive right to use the domain name. More correctly, authorized users are known as “registrants” or as “domain holders”.

二、域名权争议及其解决途径(Disputes and Settlements of Domain Name Rights)

(一)域名权的概念(Concept of Domain Name Rights)

域名权，是指域名持有人对其先申请先注册的域名所享有的权利。域名权之所以引起知识产权法的重视，主要是因为域名与传统知识产权，尤其是与商业标识之间容易发生冲突。如何认识和解决域名权与传统知识产权之间的冲突是我们研究域名权首先要解决的问题。

A domain name is a contractual right to use a particular web address. With so many modern businesses actively involved in e-commerce, a website is a valuable component of a business and is often its main portal to new customers. Having a domain name that reflects a business's goodwill and brand image is therefore extremely important.

---

① 中华人民共和国信息产业部关于中国互联网络域名体系的公告[DB/OL].[2017-06-20].中国互联网络信息中心网站，http://www.cnnic.net.cn/html/Dir/2006/02/27/3619.htm.

(二)域名权争议的类型(Types of Disputes over Domain Name Rights)

1. 域名权与受保护的商业标记权之间的冲突(Disputes between Domain Names and Protected Commercial Marks)

All commercial marker rights may be conflict with domain name rights. But at present what concerns most is that conflict between domain name rights and trademark rights.

域名权与商标权的冲突可分为两类：第一类是受法律保护的商标权人对注册域名提出的争议，认为域名持有人将与其商标相同或近似的文字注册为域名，侵害了其合法权益。这是近年来最受人关注，而且发生争议最多的一类。第二类是在先注册的网络域名持有人对在后使用或注册的商标提出的争议，认为商标使用人将与其所有的域名相同或相似的标识作为商标使用或注册，侵害其合法权益。这类争议的数量目前还不多，而且并未造成具有全社会意义的影响，因而还不是人们广泛关注的焦点问题。①

2. 域名之间的权利冲突(Conflicts of Rights between Domain Names)

所谓域名之间的权利冲突，是指不同的域名所有人(registrants)将相同或相似的自身代码(self-code)注册在不同的顶级域名(top level domain)之下而产生的冲突。

As some domain names already been treated as business properties, the same or similar domain name with their code may cause confusion to relevant public. Therefore, the conflict between the domain names is still essentially conflict between domain names and commercial marks.

3. 域名与其他受保护的利益之间的冲突(Conflicts of Interests of Domain Names and Other Protected Interests)

除了商业标识以外，域名与个人姓名及其他的名称标识也可能发生冲突，如地名。

In addition to the conflict between domain name and commercial marks, the name of natural person and other identification may also cause conflicts with domain name, such as place names.

(三)域名权争议的解决途径(Settlement of Disputes over Trade Name Rights)

与解决其他民事纠纷的途径一样，传统上域名权争议的解决途径有四种方式：协商(negotiation)、调解(mediate)、仲裁(arbitration)和诉讼(lawsuit)。其中，协商解决域名权纠纷的情况大量发生在民间，争议双方当事人通过协商，以有价或无价的方式转让域名。

In case of non-malicious domain preemptive registration(非恶意抢注), the compromise settlement is most common and effective way. Although mediation is the main mode of civil dispute solution, not very frequent used in dispute over trade name rights. Arbitration has an applied limitation that evolved parties have to reach an agreement prior to it. Litigation is the ultimate means the parties settle disputes, but due to the inconvenience of cross-regional, cross-border and problems of jurisdiction and law applicable, it is often not so realistic or convenient. In addition, lawsuits over domain rights are length process and highly cost.

---

① 唐广良. INTERNET 域名争议及其解决[M]//郑成思. 知识产权文丛(第4卷). 北京：中国政法大学出版社，2000：78.

除了传统上的争议解决途径外，根据《中国互联网络域名管理办法》的规定，域名注册管理机构可以指定中立的域名争议解决机构解决域名争议。任何人就已经注册或使用的域名向域名争议解决机构提出投诉，并且符合域名争议解决办法规定的条件的，域名持有者应当参与域名争议解决程序。域名争议在人民法院、仲裁机构或域名争议解决机构处理期间，除域名受让方以书面形式同意接受人民法院裁判、仲裁裁决或争议解决机构裁决约束的以外，域名持有者不得转让有争议的域名。

There is now a Uniform Domain Name Dispute Resolution Policy (UDRP) (统一域名解决政策) which allows anyone to lodge a complaint with an approved dispute resolution service provider (such as the World Intellectual Property Organization "WIPO") against the registration of a domain name which is identical or confusingly similar to a trade mark (including an unregistered trade mark) owned by them. To succeed in a dispute, the complainant must establish that the respondent has no legitimate interest of his own in the name (e. g. it is not his personal name) and has registered and used it in bad faith. This procedure allows unregistered trade mark owners to protect their marks without having to bring an expensive "passing off" or defamation action in the courts.

Once a complaint is lodged, a panel of one or three independent adjudicators will decide whether the conditions above have been established and if so, will order the registrar to transfer or cancel the domain name registration. A decision will normally take between 30 and 60 days. Anyone registering a domain name with a registered provider will have signed a registration agreement to the effect that he will comply with any future judgment of a UDRP panel. Accredited registrars are obliged to implement the panel's decision but some do not always comply.

域名争议解决机构作出的裁决只涉及争议域名持有者信息的变更。而且，域名争议解决机构作出的裁决与人民法院或者仲裁机构已经发生法律效力的裁判不一致的，域名争议解决机构的裁决服从于人民法院或者仲裁机构发生法律效力的裁判。

【英语词汇】

appellation of origin　原产地名称
breeding　*n.* 育种
commercial exploitation in good faith　善意的商业利用
commissioned breeding　*n.* 委托育种
confiscate　*v.* 没收
consistency　*n.* 一致性
desist　*v.* 停止，中止
geographical indication　地理标记
jointly conducted breeding　合作育种
layout-design　*n.* 布图设计
mask work　掩膜作品
mark of origin　产地标记
new variety of plants　植物新品种
process engineering　*n.* 工艺技术
reverse engineering　*n.* 反向工程
right of domain names　域名权
service breeding　*n.* 职务育种
stability　*n.* 稳定性
trade secret　商业秘密

【英语句型】

The right to use a domain name is delegated by domain name registrars who are accredited by the Internet Corporation for Assigned Names and Numbers (ICANN), the organization charged with overseeing the name and number systems of the Internet.

"be delegated by..."意思是"由……授权……"。

译文：域名权是由监管网络名称和数字的互联网名称与数字地址分配机构认可的登记部门授权的，组织指控监督的名字和电话系统的因特网。

【阅读资料】

第十七章　知识产权的竞争法保护与规制
Chapter 17　The Protection and Regulation of Competition Law on Intellectual Property

【引言】知识产权保护的“力度”(intensity)与“密度”(density)，很大程度上影响了知识产权本身的价值。因此知识产权的保护除了著作权法(Copyright Law)、专利权法(Patent Law)、商标权法(Trademark Law)等提供的保护外，还有反不正当竞争法(Anti-unfair Competition Law)、反垄断法(Antitrust Law)提供的竞争法保护。知识产权法与竞争法的关系是交叉(cross)、互补(complementary)关系。经营者违反诚实信用原则(bona fides)而实施的“商业假冒(counterfeit)、虚假宣传(misleading propaganda)、诋毁商誉(slander goodwill)”等不正当竞争行为(unfair competition)，以及经营者滥用知识产权，而实施的“搭售、独家交易、一揽子许可”等排除、限制竞争(restraint of competition)的行为，都不利于公平与效率(justice and efficiency)兼顾的市场秩序的构建，都具有违法性和应受惩罚性。竞争法应当对其进行规范和控制，以在保护知识产权的同时，限制知识产权滥用。

【学习目的与要求】通过本章的学习，应当了解我国反不正当竞争法、反垄断法对知识产权进行保护的背景知识，掌握知识产权法与竞争法之间的关系，熟悉知识产权领域的不正当竞争与滥用知识产权的界限，明确知识产权领域不正当竞争行为与限制竞争行为的构成与种类，并具体把握其特征与责任。

第一节　知识产权法与竞争法的关系
Ⅰ　Relations between Intellectual Property Law and Market Competition Law

一、市场竞争与竞争法(Market Competition and Competition Law)

(一)竞争、竞争行为、竞争法的定义(Definitions of Competition, Competitive Behavior and Competition Law)

竞争是指在两个或更多地追求同一目标的人之间形成的冲突、争斗与对抗，它是现代市场经济运行和发展的推动力。现代意义的竞争行为是指市场主体在市场经济条件下行使竞争权利而实施的行为的总称。

竞争权利滥用行为，从国际竞争法法理上分析，包括不正当竞争行为和限制竞争行为。而相应地由反不正当竞争法与反限制竞争法(反垄断法)加以规制，这已是当今大多数国家所采取的通例。由此可见，由“反不正当竞争法”与“反垄断法”构成的竞争法是在市场失灵背景下，为维护正常的竞争秩序而对市场主体的竞争行为进行规制的法律规范的总称。从调整对象上看，竞争法调整竞争关系和竞争管理关系。从法律地位上看，竞争法已经成为现代市场经济国家调整国民经济的基本法律之一，其中的反垄断法在西方甚至有“经济宪法”之称。

Competition law, known in the United States as antitrust law, has three main functions. Firstly, it prohibits agreements aimed to restrict free trading between business entities and their customers. Secondly, competition law can ban the existence or abusive behavior of a firm dominating the market. One case in point could be a software company who through its monopoly on computer platforms makes consumers uses its media player. Thirdly, to preserve competitive markets, the law supervises the mergers and acquisitions of very large corporations. Competition authorities could for instance require that a large packaging company give plastic bottle licenses to competitors before taking over a major PET producer. In this case (as in all three), competition law aims to protect the welfare of consumers by ensuring business must compete for its share of the market economy. ①

(二)我国竞争法立法现状与适用范围(Legislation and Applicability)

我国竞争法在1982年国务院颁布的《广告管理暂行条例》中最先使用“禁止广告的垄断与不正当竞争”的提法。而我国的竞争法律，则是从20世纪90年代才开始逐步确立。从我国竞争立法的形式与适用的范围上看：

首先，为保障市场经济健康发展、鼓励和保护公平竞争、制止不正当竞争行为、保护经营者和消费者的合法权益，我国于1993年9月颁布、并于同年12月开始生效的《中华人民共和国反不正当竞争法》第2条第2款对“不正当竞争”作了定义性规定：“经营者违反本法规定，损害其他经营者的合法权益，扰乱社会经济秩序的行为”，并在第二章规定了11种不正当竞争行为的具体表现形式。由此，从我国立法上看，我国反不正当竞争法所适用的范围是特定的，其规制的是“不正当竞争行为”。“不正当行为”从定义上看包含三层含义：

(1)不正当竞争的主体是经营者。The subjects of unfair competition are those individuals, legal persons and other economic organizations who engage in commodity business or profit-making service.

(2)行为具有违法性。The meaning of “illegal behavior of unfair competition” is understood comprehensively under the competition law and in combination with other relevant legal provisions.

(3)行为具有损害他人合法权益，扰乱社会秩序的危害性。The acts have perniciousness in harming others’ legitimate rights and interests and disturbing social order.

其次，为了预防和制止垄断行为、保护市场公平竞争、提高经济运行效率、维护消费者利益和社会公共利益、促进市场经济健康发展，我国又于2007年8月颁布、并于次年8月正式施行了《中华人民共和国反垄断法》。该法第3条规定：垄断行为包括“经营者达

① Competition [DB/OL]. [2017-06-12]. Wikipedia, http://en.wikipedia.org/wiki/Competition.

成垄断协议”、“经营者滥用市场支配地位”和“具有或者可能具有排除、限制竞争效果的经营者集中”三种。以上三种垄断行为的主体仍然是“经营者”，即从事商品生产、经营或者提供服务的自然人、法人和其他组织。三种垄断行为都有违法性和应受处罚性。由此，从我国立法上看，我国反垄断法所适用的范围亦是特定的，其规制的“垄断行为”，从定义上看：

(1)垄断协议。The “monopoly agreements” are agreements reached between the operators, aiming at eliminating or restricting competitive effect, or coming up to other collaborative consistent decisions.

(2)市场支配地位。The “dominant market position” refers to the market position of one or several operators as a whole who are able to control commodity prices, quantity, other trading terms, or block access to the relevant market.

(3)经营者集中。The “concentration of operator” refers to the operator has control power to other operators through merger or other methods.

综而观之，我国的《反不正当竞争法》是通过对违反诚实信用原则(bona fides)的不正当竞争行为的责任落实，来实现对竞争秩序破坏的“事后补救”。而我国的《反垄断法》则是通过规制垄断优势滥用(antitrust regulation)和规范兼并行为(merger regulation)，以实现对可能破坏竞争秩序的行为进行“事前防范”。二者从两个方向切入竞争秩序的保护，从而在保障实力不同的竞争者都有公平的竞争权的基础上保证可持续发展和社会整体利益。

而从知识产权的视角来看竞争法，我们认为：知识产权领域的不正当竞争，是在经营者之间因知识产权行使不当而实施的有害竞争秩序并违反竞争法的行为总称。而知识产权领域的垄断行为，则是经营者因滥用知识产权的合理垄断权而实施的有害竞争秩序并违反垄断法的行为总称。当然，鉴于竞争法作为经济法的部门法，是政府干预经济之法，是限制经济自由之法，因此其在一定程度上应突破传统民商法和知识产权法的概念。比如，许多形式上的不正当竞争、垄断由于受国家宏观经济政策的影响以及出于国家、社会公共利益的长期考虑，而依法享受豁免。由此，某些知识产权的垄断成了垄断法中的除外性规定。这也恰恰体现了知识产权法与竞争法之间的复杂关系。

二、知识产权法与竞争法的关系(Relations Between Intellectual Property Law and Competition Law)

知识经济是以现代科学技术为基础，建立在知识和信息的生产、分配、使用和消费基础上的经济。为了给知识穿上“权利”的外衣，建立相应的赋权与限权机制，于是产生了知识产权法。

(一)知识产权法与反不正当竞争法的关系(Relations Between Intellectual Property Law and Law Against Unfair Competition)

一般认为，知识产权法是“以促进文艺和科技领域的著作权、计算机软件等智力成果以及工商业领域的商标、专利、植物新品种(new varieties of plants)、集成电路布图设计(layout-designs of integrated circuits)等工商业标记(industrial designs)和成果的保护与利用为宗旨的法律法规的总称”①。虽然知识产权法与竞争法调整的主要是平等主体之间的财产关系，二者联系紧密，但并没有融为一体。因为前者是对私权进行保护的民商法，而后者是关注社会整体利益的经济法。在知识产权的保护上，二者是相辅相成、交叉互动关系：

1. 相辅相成的关系：前者是主导(dominance)后者是补充(supplement)

知识产权法对知识产权的保护起主导作用，是保护知识产权的基本法，而反不正当竞争法主要调整知识产权法没有调整的那一部分知识产权，对传统知识产权法起着弥补空白的作用。② 结合我国的司法实践，反不正当竞争法对知识产权的“补充性保护”③可以归纳为：

(1)保护那些不受知识产权法保护的客体。Protect those object beyond the intellectual property protection, such as commodity design (商品的装潢), title of works.

(2)保护那些虽然可以受到知识产权法保护，但是尚未取得授权的客体。Protect those objects although under the protection of intellectual property, has not been authorized. Since before granted patent certificate by the Patent Office, the technical invention is under anti-unfair competition law protection, if holder adopt confidentiality measures.

(3)保护那些权利期限已经届满的客体。After copyright protection duration expires, the cartoon, as a work, has become a well-known commercial image. Any fraud and abuse to the image causing confusion violate the protection against unfair competition.

(4)保护那些新型智力成果、工商业标记。其实，对此类新成果的保护大致有三种方式④：其一是扩大解释现有的知识产权特别法律，将其纳入现行知识产权保护的体制内。The protection of computer program works through redefining the concept of works in copyright law；其二是制定专门法加以保护。For example, the protection on semiconductor chips and new varieties of plants；其三，直接通过反不正当竞争法来保护。在第一、二种方式实现之前，反不正当竞争法常常可以提供过渡性的保护。For those data bases which don't have originality are not treated as compiled works, so they are beyond the protection of copyright law. In this case, anti-unfair competition law provides a very important protection.

2. 交叉互动的关系：法条竞合时优先适用(legal application)前者

鉴于反不正当竞争法对侵犯著作权、专利权、商标权等知识产权的行为予以法律制裁。⑤ 因此，侵犯知识产权的行为在许多情况下同时属于不正当竞争行为，在法律适用上存在竞合。鉴于各专门知识产权法对知识产权已经提供了特别保护，并且鉴于反不正当竞争法是规范市场竞争关系、保障交易公平的一项基本法律，它只是在知识产权法提供的特别保护之外为知识产权提供附加或者兜底的保护。因此，通常情况下，凡是知识产权法已

---

① 郑友德．知识产权法[M]．北京：高等教育出版社，2004：29.
② 冯晓青，杨利华．知识产权法学[M]．北京：中国大百科全书出版社，2008：431.
③ 郑友德．知识产权法[M]．北京：高等教育出版社，2004：336.
④ 廖柏明．论知识产权法与反不正当竞争法的逻辑关系[J]．社会科学家，2006(3).
⑤ 吴汉东．知识产权法学[M]．北京：北京大学出版社，2005：352.

经规范的侵权行为，应当直接适用知识产权法的规定。只有对那些缺乏特别法规范的不正当竞争行为，才适用反不正当竞争法进行判决。凡知识产权专门法已作穷尽性保护的，不能再在反不正当竞争法中寻求额外的保护。

由此可见，虽然知识产权法调整私权关系，属于私法(民商法)范畴，反不正当竞争法调整横向私权与纵向公权关系，属于社会法(经济法)范畴，但是知识产权法与反不正当竞争法的交叉现象明显：在知识产权领域，反不正当竞争主要集中在对工业产权领域权利的保护，如企业名称和知名商品的特有名称、包装、装潢与商标以及商业秘密等。它们在性质上非常接近由知识产权法调整的一些知识产权类型。

When encounter the anti-unfair competition infringement cases involved infringement judging and calculation methods, jurists can refer to the applicable(参照适用) of similar provisions in intellectual property right law and judicial explanation(司法解释).

(二)知识产权法与反垄断法的关系(Relations Between Intellectual Property Law and Anti-monopoly Law)

知识产权是一种专有权(exclusive right)，在一定意义上讲其自身就是一种合理的垄断权(monopoly right)。因此传统反垄断法一般将其作为反垄断法适用除外的对象。经济自由(economic freedom)与经济民主(economic democracy)之间有着相克又相生的关系：前者强调个人权利(individual rights)，后者强调多数决定(majority decision)。而自由主义的“产权绝对化”会导致“权利作弄财产”的弊病。竞争产生垄断(competition produce monopoly)、垄断产生专制(monopoly give rise to despotism)的逻辑，不利于多数人利益的经济民主。鉴于此，当前世界大部分国家反垄断法总体上是适用于知识产权行使行为的：“既不因为知识产权固有的垄断性而对知识产权行使进行特别规定，也不因为法律保护知识产权而对知识产权行使行为网开一面。”①总体来看，知识产权法与反垄断法的关系是既冲突又一致的关系：

1. 在直接目标上：冲突(Immediate Goal：Conflict)

Intellectual property is a kind of absolute right(绝对权) of private law.

知识产权法通过“专用权”作为“利益之油”，来彰显知识产品的“商品属性”，促使企业、个人为了获得合理垄断而进行积极的创新。然而，反垄断法从保护社会法益角度出发，弱化知识产权人的个人法益，彰显知识产品进入市场流转领域的“社会属性”，对知识产权的私权性和专用性进行界定，规制知识产权滥用，抵抗知识产权边界的无限扩大的同时遏制暴利。从这个角度来看，反垄断法是对知识产权法授予创新者或者知识产权所有者阶段性排他权利的“限制”。在直接目标上，包括专利权、商标权和版权在内的有关知识产权保护与反垄断法规制之间是存在内在矛盾的。

2. 在根本目标上：一致(Basic Goal：Consistent)

知识产权法和反垄断法的目的都是激发人们的竞争性活动，提高资源配置效率。只不过它们两者推动竞争的方式有不同：反垄断法是通过禁止限制竞争行为来推动竞争，知识

① 杨洁．知识产权的反不正当竞争保护与反垄断规制[M]//吴汉东．中国知识产权蓝皮书．北京：北京大学出版社，2007：347.

产权法则是通过保护权利人的专有权，即以某些限制竞争的方式，激发人们在知识经济领域开展竞争。①

Therefore, both of their abstract value(抽象价值) and general legal terms(一般性法律条款) have introduced the bona fides(诚实信用), good customs(善良风俗) and other business morals principles(工商业道德原则). Both need to give consideration to competitors interests(竞争者利益), consumer interests(消费者利益) and public interests(公共利益).

在专利权领域，专利许可、标准化和反垄断之间是动态的、不等边三角关系，专利许可的底线地位牢固、标准化边线向底线倾斜，使得专利权人地位强势。而反垄断边线则起到制衡作用。② 专利法与反垄断法的根本目标一致，是相互协调配合的。

3. 在法律适用上：私法与公法的交叉(cross)、互补(complementary)

The protection of intellectual property rights and the use of intellectual property rights (including licensing) are subject to both *Intellectual Property Law* and *The Anti-monopoly Law*.

反垄断法与知识产权各单行法相衔接的对接点就体现在对知识产权的合法垄断(legal monopoly)与非法垄断(illegal monopoly)的界定上：当知识产权与限制竞争行为结合在一起有害竞争时，就应由反垄断法进行规制。由此，在知识产权法与反垄断法的法律适用问题上，必须妥善处理私法与公法的交叉调整关系：一方面要强化私权保护意识，尊重当事人的意思自治(autonomy of the will)，通过保护私权实现激励创新；另一方面，私权保护又必须服从为维护竞争秩序所设定的强制性规范。凡属于反垄断法律法规禁止的事项，均应适用反垄断法。

总之，知识产权法与反垄断法的关系是经济自由(economic freedom)与经济民主(economic democracy)、知识产权人的合法垄断(legal monopoly)与公众的合理需求(reasonable request)、知识产品的商品属性(commercial characteristic)与其进入市场流转的社会属性(social characteristic)之间的对立统一关系(law of the unity of opposite)的体现。二者在效率与公平的二难选择中寻找契合点，在各自的适用前提下，互相补充，共同推动和保障市场竞争。

第二节 知识产权领域的反不正当竞争保护

Ⅱ Protection against Unfair Competition in Intellectual Property

一、不正当竞争主体的认定(Identification of the Subject)

Just like the general property rights, the most important characteristic of the intellectual property rights is exclusiveness. If intellectual property rights which the infringement violate are

① 王晓晔．知识产权滥用行为的反垄断法规制[DB/OL]．[2017-05-04]．中国社会科学院，http：//www.cass.net.cn/file/2005102850829.html.

② 张乃根．专利许可、标准化与反垄断的三角关系[M]//张乃根，陈乃蔚．技术转移与公平竞争．上海：上海交通大学出版社，2008：20.

specified in slip laws(单行法), the infringement shall be recognized and handled according to the civil infringement recognition and processing. However, when defining the unfair competition of intellectual property, its subject is the first definition to be narrow down.

市场主体资格有一般资格(general qualification)与特殊资格(specialized qualification)之分。一般资格是指各种主体进入市场都必备的资格，即民法所规定的一般民事主体资格。特殊资格指各种主体进入特定市场，即从事特定项目、行业、地域、场所等的交易与竞争资格。①

认定不正当竞争主体，除了要具备一般民事权利能力(capacity for civil rights)与行为能力(capacity for civil conduct)的构成要件以外，还要注意审查确定是发生在"竞争市场主体"之间的竞争关系(competitive relation)。具体体现为：

第一，反不正当竞争法所调整的竞争关系限于作为平等主体(equal subject)的市场经营者(market operator)之间，非市场经营者之间不存在竞争关系。而所谓经营者(operator)是指在竞争市场上从事提供商品(commodity)或服务(service)的法人、其他组织和自然人，其行为具有直接或间接的营利目的(seek profits)。

第二，竞争关系一般是指经营者经营同类(same species)商品或服务，或者其经营业务虽不相同，但行为违背了自愿(free will)、平等(equality)、公平(fair)、诚实信用(bona fides)的原则和公认的商业道德(commercial morality)(《反不正当竞争法》第2条)，也可以认定具有竞争关系。

第三，存在特定、具体的竞争关系亦是经营者提起不正当竞争诉讼的前提。

The specific and concrete competitive relation is the premise of civil litigation in opposing unfair competition. On this basis, some unfair competition causes damage of nonspecific operators (不特定的经营者). But as long as the infringer, infringement and damages are specific and concrete, jurists can deduce that the competitive relation between injured operators and specific infringer is specific and concrete. As a result, any impaired nonspecific operators can claim litigation in principle.

由此可见，不正当竞争行为是"平等主体"(经营者)间所实施的行为。不正当竞争行为已超过了一般民法行为性质，已不是单纯的私权侵犯，而是滥用私权侵犯了社会法益，必须依照反不正当竞争法对其进行规范和控制。

二、不正当竞争行为的种类(Classifications of Unfair Competition)

为了依法规范市场秩序、维护公平竞争和保护知识产权，我国《反不正当竞争法》第5条、第9条、第10条和第14条，对知识产权的不正当竞争行为进行了专门规定。此外，最高人民法院《关于审理不正当竞争民事案件应用法律若干问题的解释(2007)》，则明确了涉及仿冒、虚假宣传和侵犯商业秘密、商业诋毁等与知识产权有关案件审理的一些重要

① 王全兴．经济法基础理论专题研究[M]．北京：中国检察出版社，2002：607.

法律界限。综而观之，我国知识产权领域的不正当竞争行为主要有以下几种：

(一)假冒、仿冒行为(Counterfeiting)

根据《反不正当竞争法》的规定，经营者损害竞争对手的假冒仿冒行为表现为：

1. 假冒他人的注册商标(Counterfeiting Others' Registered Trademark)

即未经注册商标权利人的许可，在相同或类似的商品上使用与注册商标相同或近似的商标，以造成市场的误认、混淆(傍名牌)而获利的行为。此时会产生商标法与反不正当竞争法的适用竞合问题，根据《反不正当竞争法》的规定，应当优先适用《商标法》。

It is noteworthy that the protection here only limits to the registered trademark. If counterfeit the unregistered trademark, the infringement shall be handled as the name(名称), package(包装) and decoration(装潢) counterfeit of famous commodity(知名商品).

2. 仿冒知名商品特有的名称、包装、装潢(Counterfeit of Name, Package and Decoration of Famous Commodity)

即擅自使用知名商品特有的名称、包装、装潢，或者使用与知名商品近似的名称、包装、装潢，造成和他人的知名商品相混淆，使购买者误认为是该知名商品的行为。其中：

(1)所谓"知名商品"(famous commodity)是指在中国境内具有一定的市场知名度，为相关公众所知悉，并经过人民法院通过考虑该商品的销售时间(sales period)、销售区域(sales territory)、销售额(sales)和销售对象(target customer)，进行任何宣传的持续时间(duration)、程度(degree)和地域范围(territorial scope)，作为知名商品受保护的情况(protected as famous commodity before)等因素，进行综合判断而认定知名的商品；

(2)所谓"特有名称、包装"(specialized name and package)是指具有区别商品来源(source)的显著特征(marked feature)的商品的名称、包装。该名称与包装不能是商品的通用名称(common name)、图形(figure)、型号(model)，不能是仅仅直接表示商品的质量(quality)、主要原料(raw material)、功能(function)、用途(application)、重量(weight)、数量(quantity)及其他特点的商品名称，不能是仅由商品自身的性质产生的形状、为获得技术效果而需有的商品形状以及使商品具有实质性价值的形状；

(3)所谓"装潢"(decoration)是指由经营者营业场所(business site)的装饰、营业用具(business tool)的式样、营业人员(business staff)的服饰等构成的具有独特风格的整体营业形象(business image)；

(4)所谓"使用"(use)是指在中国境内进行商业使用，包括将知名商品特有的名称、包装、装潢用于商品、商品包装以及商品交易文书上，或者用于广告宣传、展览以及其他商业活动。

3. 假冒他人企业名称或姓名(Misrepresenting Names of Enterprises or Persons)

即擅自使用他人的"企业名称"(enterprise name)(具体指工商机关依法登记注册的企业名称，以及在中国境内进行商业使用的外国(地区)企业名称)或者"姓名"(natural person's name)(具体指具有一定的市场知名度、为相关公众所知悉的自然人的笔名、艺名)，引人误认为是他人的商品的行为。其中，所谓"使用"，具体指在中国境内进行商业使用，包括将企业名称、姓名用于商品、商品包装以及商品交易文书上，或者用于广告宣传、展览以及其他商业活动。

(二)虚假表示、虚假宣传行为(False Representation and Propaganda)

根据《反不正当竞争法》的规定，经营者的虚假表示、虚假宣传表现为：

1. 虚假表示行为(False Representation)

虚假表示，即经营者在商品上伪造或者冒用认证标志、名优标志等质量标志，伪造产地，对商品质量作引人误解的虚假表示行为。其可以细化为：

(1)伪造或者冒用质量标志。其中"认证标志"(certification mark)是指质量认证机构准许经其认证产品质量合格的企业在产品或包装上使用的质量标志。"Certification mark" refers to the quality sign stamped on certificated products or their package, which is granted by certification authority. 而"名优标志"(mark of famous brands and quality products)是指经国际或国内有关机构或社会组织评定为名优产品而发给经营者的质量荣誉标志。

(2)伪造产地。所谓产地(producing area)是指商品的制造(place of manufacture)、加工地(processing place)或者商品生产者地(place of commodity producer)。比如阳澄湖产的大闸蟹、青岛本地酿制的啤酒，因自然环境、特殊工艺而使其具有较高的商品声誉。所以为了制止产地假冒产生了商品原产地证明(certificate of origin)和地理标志证明(geographical indication certification)。

(3)产品质量的虚假表示(false representation)，是指经营者在商品上对商品质量的若干内容作虚假或引人误解的标注，使公众发生误认、误购的行为。

2. 虚假宣传行为(False Propaganda)

虚假宣传，即经营者利用广告或者其他方法，对商品的质量、制作成分、性能、用途、生产者、有效期限、产地等作引人误解的虚假宣传行为。而"引人误解的虚假宣传行为"具体表现为：

(1)对商品作片面宣传(one-sided propaganda)或者对比的(contrast propaganda)；

(2)将科学尚未定论的观点、现象等当作定论的事实用于商品宣传的；

(3)以歧义性语言(ambiguity)或者其他引人误解的方式(misconceive way)进行商品宣传的。当然，以明显的夸张方式宣传商品，不足以造成相关公众误解的，不属于引人误解的虚假宣传行为。The court may determine false propaganda according to the relevant public daily life experience, general attention of public, misleading facts and other actual situations.

需要注意的是，经营者作为广告主(advertiser)是虚假宣传的规制主体，广告的经营者(电视、广播、报纸、广告公司等)亦不得在明知或者应知的情况下，代理、设计、制作、发布虚假广告(方式既包括电视广播媒体、平面媒体、网络媒体的传媒手段，也包括召开新闻发布会、印制宣传小册子等)。

(三)侵犯商业秘密行为(Infringement on Trade Secrets)

在我国，商业秘密是不为公众所知悉、能为权利人带来经济利益、具有实用性并经权利人采取保密措施的技术信息和经营信息。

A trade secret is a formula, practice, process, design, instrument, pattern, or compilation of information which is not generally known or reasonably ascertainable, by which a business can obtain an economic advantage over competitors or customers. There are three factors that are common to all such definitions: a trade secret is information:

(1) that is not generally known to the public;

(2) That confers some sort of economic benefit on its holder (where this benefit must derive specifically from its not being generally known, not just from the value of the information itself);

(3) that is the subject of reasonable efforts to maintain its secrecy.

By comparison, under US law, "A trade secret, as defined under 18 U. S. C. § 1839(3)(A), (B) (1996), has three parts: ① information; ② reasonable measures taken to protect the information; and ③ which derives independent economic value from not being publicly known." ①

所谓"不为公众所知悉"是指有关信息不为其所属领域的相关人员普遍知悉和容易获得。以下信息不属于"不为公众所知悉"：(1)该信息为其所属技术或者经济领域的人的一般常识(common sense)或者行业惯例(trade usage)；(2)该信息仅涉及产品的尺寸、结构、材料、部件的简单组合等内容，进入市场后相关公众通过观察产品即可直接获得；(3)该信息已经在公开出版物或者其他媒体上公开披露(public disclosure)；(4)该信息已通过公开的报告会(public lecture)、展览(exhibition)等方式公开；(5)该信息从其他公开渠道可以获得；(6)该信息无须付出一定的代价而容易获得。

所谓"能为权利人带来经济利益、具有实用性"，是指有关信息具有现实的(actual)或者潜在的(potential)商业价值，能为权利人带来竞争优势(competitive edge)。

所谓"保密措施"，是指权利人为防止信息泄露(disclosure of information)所采取的与其商业价值等具体情况相适应的合理保护措施(reasonable protective methods)。人民法院可根据所涉信息载体的特性(natures of information carrier)、权利人保密的意愿、保密措施的可识别程度(identified degree of security)、他人通过正当方式获得的难易程度等因素，来认定权利人是否采取了保密措施。

根据《反不正当竞争法》的规定，经营者侵犯商业秘密的行为包括：(1)以盗窃、利诱、胁迫或者其他不正当手段获取权利人的商业秘密；(2)披露、使用或者允许他人使用以前项手段获取的权利人的商业秘密；(3)违反约定或者违反权利人有关保守商业秘密的要求，披露、使用或者允许他人使用其所掌握的商业秘密。当然，通过自行开发研制或者反向工程(指通过技术手段对从公开渠道取得的产品进行拆卸、测绘、分析等而获得该产品的有关技术信息)等方式获得的商业秘密，不应认定为侵犯商业秘密行为。

需要注意的是，第三人明知或者应知经营者有上述违法行为，仍获取、使用或者披露他人的商业秘密，亦被视为侵犯商业秘密，而不论其是企业还是自然人。

(四)商业诽谤行为(Business Defamation)

It is true that most defamation cases hitting the headlines involve the rich and famous. This

① Trade Secret [DB/OL]. [2017-06-18]. Wikipedia, http://en.wikipedia.org/wiki/Trade_secret.

doesn't mean that businesses do not take action when defamatory statements which could seriously affect their continued success (and in some cases may even result in the business going under) are made by rivals.

根据《反不正当竞争法》的规定，商业诽谤行为是指经营者故意捏造(fabricate)、散布(distribute)虚伪事实，损害竞争对手的商业信誉(commercial credit)、商品声誉(commodity reputation)的行为。其中“捏造、散布虚伪的事实”表现为向不特定的公众或特定的客户或同行经营者实施以下行为：(1)刊登对比性广告或声明性公告等，贬低竞争对手声誉；(2)唆使(instigate)或收买(bribe)某些人，以客户或消费者名义进行恶意投诉，败坏竞争对手声誉；(3)通过商业会议或者发布商业信息的方式对竞争对手的商品质量进行贬损。所谓“商业信誉”是指社会公众对某一经营者的经济能力(economic capability)、信用状况(credit status)等所给予的社会评价，即该经营者在经济生活中信用、名誉的地位。而所谓“商品声誉”是指社会公众对一经营者的商品性能(product performance)、品质所给予的社会评价，即该商品在经济生活中的地位。总之，商业诽谤是以侵犯同业竞争者的商业信誉、商品声誉的，旨在谋取竞争优势的不正当竞争行为。

三、不正当竞争行为的责任(Responsibility of Unfair Competition)

(一)行政责任(Administrative Responsibility)

根据《反不正当竞争法》的规定，县级以上工商部门有权采用询问当事人，查询、复制与不正当竞争行为有关的资料以及现场检查的方式，对经营者涉嫌不正当竞争的行为进行主动的监督检查。That is to say, the acts violate the anti-unfair competition law is mainly regulated by authorized specialized administrative departments(授权专门行政部门). The administrative departments always take the initiative intervene(主动干预) to realize the regulation.

不正当竞争行为一旦被工商部门认定，首先面临的是行政处罚，具体如下：

(1)经营者假冒他人的注册商标，擅自使用他人的企业名称(enterprise name)或者姓名(name of natural person)，伪造或者冒用认证标志(certificate mark)、名优标志(famous-and-excellent-product mark)等质量标志，伪造产地，对商品质量作引人误解的虚假表示的，依照《商标法》、《质量法》的规定处罚。

(2)经营者擅自使用知名商品特有的名称(name)、包装(package)、装潢(decoration)，或者使用与知名商品近似的名称、包装、装潢，造成和他人的知名商品相混淆(confusion)，使购买者误认为是该知名商品的，监督检查部门应当责令停止违法行为，没收违法所得，可以根据情节处以违法所得1倍以上3倍以下的罚款；情节严重的，可以吊销营业执照。

(3)经营者(广告主)的虚假广告行为(false advertising)，监督检查部门(department of supervision and inspection)应当责令停止违法行为，消除影响，还可根据情节处1万元以上20万元以下的罚款。广告的经营者，在明知或者应知的情况下，代理、设计、制作、发布虚假广告的，由监督检查部门责令其停止违法行为，没收违法所得，并依法处以罚款。

(4)侵犯商业秘密(trade secret)行为，由监督检查部门责令停止违法行为，还可根据情节处以1万元以上20万元以下的罚款。

(二)民事责任(Civil Liability)

根据《反不正当竞争法》的规定，经营者的合法权益受到不正当竞争行为损害的，可以提起民事诉讼追究侵权人的民事责任。该损害赔偿责任在落实的过程中，被侵害的经营者的损失难以计算的，赔偿额为侵权人在侵权期间因侵权所获得的利润，并应当承担被侵害的经营者因调查该经营者侵害其合法权益的不正当竞争行为所支付的合理费用。当然，除了赔偿方式之外，不正当竞争行为的民事责任承担方式还包括停止侵害、消除影响、赔礼道歉、恢复名誉(适用于诋毁商誉行为)以及修理、更换、退货(适用于虚假表示行为)等。

(三)刑事责任(Criminal Responsibility)

经营者实施假冒仿冒行为，生产、销售伪劣商品，构成犯罪的，依《刑法》第140、225条以“生产、销售伪劣产品罪”或“非法经营罪”追究刑事责任。经营者作为广告主，以及与广告主串通的广告经营者、广告发布者，对商品或服务做虚假表示、宣传，构成犯罪的，依《刑法》第222条以“虚假广告罪”追究刑事责任。此外，经营者侵犯权利人商业秘密，非法获取、披露、使用，情节严重的，依《刑法》第219条以“侵犯商业秘密罪”追究刑事责任。而经营者实施商业诽谤，捏造并散布虚伪事实，损害他人的商业信誉、商品声誉，给他人造成重大损失或者有其他严重情节的，则依《刑法》第221条以“损害商业信誉、商品声誉罪”追究刑事责任。

第三节　滥用知识产权的反垄断法规制
Ⅲ　Legal Regulation of Anti-monopoly Law

一、知识产权反垄断的适用前提(Application Premise of Antitrust Law)

Antitrust law seeks to make businesses compete fairly. Premised on the belief that free trade benefits the economy, businesses, and consumers alike, the law forbids several types of restraint of trade and monopolization. These fall into four main areas: agreements between competitors, contractual arrangements between sellers and buyers, the pursuit or maintenance of monopoly power, and mergers.

鉴于知识产权的专用性和合理垄断性，知识产权领域反垄断必须要有适用前提。反垄断的适用主体(subject)是从事商品生产、经营或者提供服务的自然人、法人和其他组织的“经营者”(operator)。并且该经营者在一定时期内就特定商品或者服务进行竞争的商品范围(commodity coverage)和地域范围(territorial scope)，即在“相关市场”(related market)有一定优势。该“优势”表现为经济优势(economic advantage)、身份优势(identical advantage)、市场环境优势(market environmental advantage)、交易条件的优势

(advantage of trade terms)及其他造成与相对人不平等的优势。只有该具有市场支配地位的优势经营者，在中华人民共和国境内滥用市场支配地位，实施排除、限制竞争行为的或者在中华人民共和国境外实施垄断行为，对境内市场竞争产生排除、限制影响的，才适用《反垄断法》。

应当划清法律上所禁止的“垄断”与日常用语中的“垄断”的界限(反垄断绝不是反大企业)。反垄断法意义上的“垄断”是与整体的市场竞争中“相关市场”①的界定相联系的。市场竞争中，拥有知识产权的经营者并不一定能在市场上占据支配地位，而且其即便拥有垄断地位，但只要没有实施垄断行为，没有对相关市场的竞争构成实质性损害，则不受反垄断法的规制(反垄断是反经营者滥用优势地位的行为)。因此，为了防止知识的异化(dissimilation of intellect)、规制知识产权权利滥用(abuse of intellectual property)，在具体的知识产权反垄断案件中，应当：“准确界定知识产权权利人和社会公众的权利界限，依法审查和支持当事人的在先权(prior right)、先用权(right of prior use)、公知技术(prior art)、禁止反悔(prosecution history estoppel)、合理使用(fair use)等抗辩事由；制止非法垄断技术、妨碍技术进步的行为，依法认定限制研发、强制回授、阻碍实施、搭售、限购和禁止有效性质疑等技术合同无效事由，维护技术市场的公平竞争；此外还要防止权利人滥用侵权警告和滥用诉权，完善确认不侵权诉讼和滥诉反赔制度。”②

二、知识产权滥用行为的类型(Types of Abuse of Intellectual Property)

为了预防和制止垄断行为，维护消费者利益和社会公共利益，我国《反垄断法》第55条对知识产权领域的反垄断进行了专门规定：“经营者依照有关知识产权的法律、行政法规规定行使知识产权的行为，不适用本法；但是，经营者滥用知识产权，排除、限制竞争的行为，适用本法。”鉴于该条是一条原则性规定，因此，依照《反垄断法》的规定，并结合法理和相关法律分析，我国知识产权领域的垄断行为主要表现为：

(一)垄断协议(Monopoly Agreements)

垄断协议是指排除、限制竞争的协议、决定或者其他协同行为。Agreements referred to this law are agreement, decision or concerted action which eliminate or restrict competition.

《合同法》第329条规定“非法垄断技术，妨碍技术进步”的技术合同无效。同时，最高人民法院司法解释《关于审理技术合同纠纷案件适用法律若干问题的解释》规定“非法垄断技术、妨碍技术进步”的垄断协议行为表现为：(1)限制当事人一方在合同标的(contract objects)技术基础(technological base)上进行新的研究开发或者限制其使用所改进的技术，或者双方交换改进技术的条件不对等。It includes one request the other party provide his own

① 丁春燕．论我国反垄断法适用中关于“相关市场”确定方法的完善——兼论SSNIP方法界定网络相关市场的局限性[J]．政治与法律，2015(3)：89.

② 曹建明．全国法院知识产权审判工作座谈会上的讲话——全面加强知识产权审判工作为建设创新型国家和构建和谐社会提供强有力的司法保障(2007)[DB/OL]．[2017-06-12]．北大法律信息网，http：//vip. chinalawinfo. com/newlaw2002/SLC/slc. asp？ db=chl&gid=110259.

improved technology gratuitously, having mutual beneficial transfer of their own improved technology(非互惠性转让给对方), free monopoly(无偿独占), or share the improved technology of intellectual property rights;(2)限制当事人一方从其他来源获得与技术提供方类似技术(similar technology)或者与其竞争的技术(competitive technology);(3)阻碍当事人一方根据市场需求,按照合理方式充分实施合同标的技术,包括明显不合理地(obviously improper)限制技术接受方实施合同标的技术生产产品或者提供服务的数量、品种、价格、销售渠道和出口市场;(4)要求技术接受方接受并非实施技术必不可少的附带条件,包括购买非必需的技术、原材料、产品、设备、服务以及接收非必需的人员等;(5)不合理地限制技术接受方购买原材料、零部件、产品或者设备等的渠道或者来源;(6)禁止技术接受方对合同标的技术知识产权的有效性提出异议或者对提出异议附加条件。

我国的《反垄断法》第13、14、15条对"具有竞争关系的经营者之间"以及"经营者与交易相对人之间"的非法垄断技术、妨碍技术进步的协议,遵循"原则上禁止,有条件豁免"原则。也就是说,一方面明确规定禁止各种垄断协议,另一方面考虑我国还处于经济转型期,同时规定豁免:即经营者能够证明所达成的协议属于为改进技术、研究开发新产品的;或为提高产品质量、降低成本、增进效率,统一产品规格、标准或者实行专业化分工的;或为提高中小经营者经营效率,增强中小经营者竞争力的;或为实现节约能源、保护环境、救灾救助等社会公共利益的;或因经济不景气,为缓解销售量严重下降或者生产明显过剩的;或为保障对外贸易和对外经济合作中的正当利益的,则不予禁止该协议的签订。

(二)滥用市场支配地位(Abuse of Market Ascendancy)

市场支配地位是指经营者在相关市场内具有能够控制商品价格、数量或者其他交易条件,或者能够阻碍、影响其他经营者进入相关市场能力的市场地位。认定经营者具有市场支配地位,可以参照的因素主要有:该经营者在相关市场的市场份额,其控制销售市场的能力,其财力和技术条件,其对该经营者在交易上的依赖程度以及其他经营者进入相关市场的难易程度等。知识产权人作为具有支配地位的经营者滥用其市场支配地位的行为包括:(1)垄断高价、掠夺性定价:以不公平的高价销售知识产权商品或者以不公平的低价购买知识产权商品;(2)低价倾销:没有正当理由,以低于成本的价格销售知识产权商品;(3)拒绝许可:没有正当理由,拒绝与交易相对人进行交易;(4)指定交易:没有正当理由,限定交易相对人只能与其进行交易或者只能与其指定的经营者进行交易;(5)搭售:没有正当理由搭售知识产权商品,或者在交易时附加其他不合理的交易条件;(6)价格歧视:没有正当理由,对条件相同的交易相对人在交易价格等交易条件上实行差别待遇。

(三)经营者集中(Concentration of Operators)

经营者集中,不仅指经营者进行合并或者通过取得股权或者资产的方式取得对其他经营者的控制权的行为,还包括经营者通过合同等方式取得对其他经营者的控制权或者能够对其他经营者施加决定性影响(也称联合限制竞争行为)。知识产权联营协议和相互许可协议，会形成较大的市场联合体，具有或者可能具有排除、限制竞争效果。因此按照《反垄断法》的规定，经营者集中达到国务院规定的申报标准的，经营者应当事先向国务院反垄断执法机构申报，未申报的不得实施集中。当知识产权联营或相互许可协议被用做限定价格、分割市场、强化协议联合体的市场支配地位以消除协议各方之间以及联合体与协议之外的竞争对手之间的竞争的(手段具体包括交叉许可、专利联营、多重许可、维持转售价格、销售区域分割条款、排他性交易、回授①)，并在限制条款中体现了对经营者集中对市场进入、技术进步，对消费者和其他有关经营者乃至国民经济有负面影响(该集中对竞争产生的不利影响明显大于有利影响)时，国务院反垄断执法机构依照《反垄断法》第27、28条的规定作出禁止该经营者集中的决定。

三、知识产权滥用行为的责任(Responsibility for Abusive Conducts)

(一)行政责任(Administrative Liability)

《反垄断法》第9、10条和第6章专章规定，国务院设立"反垄断委员会"(2008年8月成立)，其主要职责：研究拟定有关竞争政策；组织调查、评估市场总体竞争状况，发布评估报告；制定、发布反垄断指南；协调反垄断行政执法工作等。同时通过"国务院反垄断执法机构"(具体指三家部委"三驾马车、三足鼎立"：商务部负责"经营者集中"的反垄断审查；发改委负责"价格垄断行为"规制；工商总局负责垄断协议、滥用市场支配地位、滥用行政权力排除限制竞争方面的反垄断执法工作)，以上反垄断执法机构可以采取进现场检查、询问相关当事人、查阅复制有关资料、查封扣押相关证据乃至查询经营者的银行账户等调查措施，对涉嫌垄断行为进行调查。经认定：(1)经营者达成并实施垄断协议的，由相应反垄断执法机构责令停止违法行为，没收违法所得，并处上一年度销售额1%以上10%以下的罚款。尚未实施所达成的垄断协议的，可以处50万元以下的罚款。经营者有主动向执法机构报告有关情况并提供重要证据的，可以酌情减轻或者免除处罚；(2)经营者滥用市场支配地位的，由相应反垄断执法机构责令停止违法行为，没收违法所得，并处上一年度销售额1%以上10%以下的罚款；(3)经营者违法实施集中的，由相应反垄断执法机构责令停止实施集中、限期处分股份或者资产、限期转让营业以及采取其他必要措施恢复到集中前的状态，并可处50万元以下的罚款。反垄断执法机构确定具体罚款数额时，应当考虑违法行为的性质、程度和持续的时间等因素。

(二)民事责任(Civil Liability)

《反垄断法》规定，经营者实施垄断行为，给他人造成损失的，依法承担民事责任。因此涉及滥用知识产权的反垄断民事案件，应由各级法院负责知识产权案件审判业务的审判庭进行审理。鉴于反垄断法关于垄断行为民事责任的规定原则而抽象，因此其民事责任的承担方式可以参照民法及诉讼法的规定，具体可以包括赔偿损失(paying compensation or damages)、停止侵害(ceasing the infringing act)、消除影响(eliminating its ill effects)、赔礼

① 李建伟. 创新与平衡：知识产权滥用的反垄断法规制[M]. 北京：中国经济出版社，2008：167.

道歉(making a public apology)等。

(三)刑事责任(Criminal Responsibility)

经营者实施垄断协议(monopoly agreement)、滥用市场支配地位(abuse of market ascendancy)以及集中行为(centralized conduct)本身，并不能构成犯罪，也就不能因此行为而对经营者及相关责任人进行定罪量刑。但是在反垄断执法机构(antimonopoly execution authorities)对涉嫌垄断行为依法实施审查和调查过程中，经营者拒绝提供有关材料、信息，或者提供虚假材料、信息，或者隐匿、销毁、转移证据，或者有其他拒绝、阻碍调查行为的，构成犯罪的，则要依法追究刑事责任。并且，反垄断执法机构工作人员滥用职权(misuse of authority)、玩忽职守(dereliction of duty)、徇私舞弊(play favoritism and commit irregularities)或者泄露执法过程中知悉的商业秘密，构成犯罪的，亦应依法追究刑事责任。

【英语词汇】

absolute right　绝对权
antitrust　*adj.* 反垄断的
autonomy of the will　*n.* 意思自治
commodity design　商品的装潢
defamation　*n.* 诽谤
instigate　*v.* 唆使
misleading propaganda　*n.* 虚假宣传
restraint of competition　限制竞争
supplement　*v./n.* 补充
anti-unfair competition law　反不正当竞争
antitrust law　反垄断法
complementary　*adj.* 互补的
concentration of operator　经营者集中
fabricate　*v.* 捏造
market order　市场秩序
monopoly agreement　*n.* 垄断协议
slander　*v.* 诋毁
trade usage　行业惯例

【英语句型】

1. The legal protection of intellectual property can give instruction to operators for foreseeing the certain economic returns before technological development and innovation investment according to the legal exclusive degree beforehand, thereby, encouraging operators to enhance market competitiveness through technology innovation.

译文：对这种成果的知识产权保护，可以使经营者能够事先根据法律将会赋予的独占程度，比较确定地预期其技术开发和创新投资的经济回报，从而鼓励其通过技术创新增强市场竞争力。

2. The specific and concrete competitive relation is the premise of civil litigation in opposing unfair competition. On this basis, some unfair competition causes damage of nonspecific operators. But as long as the infringer, infringement and damages are specific and concrete, jurists can deduce that the competitive relation between injured operators and specific infringer is specific and concrete. As a result, any impaired nonspecific operators can claim litigation in principle.

译文：在此基础之上，某些不正当竞争行为导致受到损害，但只要侵权人、侵权行为和损害后果是特定、具体的，就可以认定在不特定的受损害的经营者与特定侵权人之间形成的竞争关系是特定、具体的，因此任何受损害的不特定的经营者原则上都可以主张诉权。

【阅读资料】

第六编　知识产权的国际协调保护制度

PART SIX　International Legal Protection System of Intellectual Property

第十八章　知识产权的国际协调保护

Chapter 18　International Protection of Intellectual Property

【引言】知识产权的国际保护问题自 19 世纪中叶开始日渐被放在重要的位置，随着《保护工业产权巴黎公约》(*Paris Convention for the Protection of Industrial Property*)、《保护文学艺术作品伯尔尼公约》(*Berne Convention for the Protection of Literary and Artistic Works*)等一系列保护知识产权的国际条约的诞生和世界知识产权组织以及世界贸易组织等与知识产权保护相关的国际组织的建立，知识产权的国际协调和保护越来越成熟和完善。

【学习目的与要求】了解知识产权国际协调保护的起源和发展，了解世界知识产权组织和世界贸易组织的相关知识，掌握 TRIPS 的宗旨、原则、意义等，了解《巴黎公约》等若干重要的有关知识产权的公约的基本知识。

第一节　知识产权国际协调保护的起源与发展

Ⅰ　The Origin and Development of International Protection of Intellectual Property

知识产权协调国际保护，是指以多边国际公约为基本形式，以政府间国际组织为协调机构，通过对各国国内知识产权法律进行协调并形成的相对统一的国际法律制度。知识产权国际保护有两个途径：一方面是缔结多边或双边的国际公约或协议；另一方面是成立知识产权保护的国际组织。Intellectual property in the international arena is a highly treaty-bound area, and one in which the international aspect goes largely toward enabling the enforcement of private rights across borders.

一、早期以国家为界的知识产权保护(Early National Protection)

(一)中国(China)

在我国，古籍中虽有北宋时期即开始保护图书印刷版式的记载，但是直到清末才有现代意义上的专利权和著作权的立法。新中国成立以后，由于各种原因，知识产权的保护制度迟迟未能建立。20 世纪 70 年代末改革开放以来，随着商品经济的蓬勃发展，智力成果的价值及其在生产力诸因素中的作用日益显著，客观上提出了保护知识产权的要求；同时，在对外经贸和文化交流过程中，我国的知识产权状况越来越为外商和贸易伙伴国所关注，成为影响他们在与我国进行贸易和文化交流过程中的一个决策因素。为此，我国于 1980 年 3 月批准加入了《世界知识产权组织公约》(*Convention Establishing the World Intellectual Property Organization*)，成为该组织的正式成员之一。

继参加世界知识产权组织之后，我国于 1985 年参加了《保护工业产权巴黎公约》(*Paris Convention on the Protection of Industrial Property*)，1989 年参加了《商标注册马德里协定》(*Madrid Agreement for International Registration of Trade Marks*)，1992 年参加了《保护文学艺术作品伯尔尼公约》(*Berne Convention for the Protection of Literary and Artistic Works*)、《世界版权公约》(*Universal Copyright Convention*)，1993 年参加了《保护录音制品制作者防止未经许可复制其录音制品公约》(*Convention for the Protection of Producers of Phonograms Against Unauthorized Duplication of Their Phonograms*，简称《录音制品公约》)、《专利合作条约》(*Patent Cooperating Treaty*)，1994 年参加了《商标注册用商品和服务国际分类尼斯协定》(*Nice Agreement Concerning the International Classification of Goods and Services for the Purpose of the Registration of Marks*)，1995 年参加了《国际承认用于专利程序的微生物保存布达佩斯条约》(*Budapest Treaty on the International Recognition of the Deposit of Microorganisms for the Purposes of Patent Procedure*)，等等。从以上不难看出，在相当短的时间内，我国在知识产权的国际保护方面做了大量的工作，取得了令人瞩目的成果，符合国际通例的知识产权国际协调保护制度已经初步形成。

(二)欧美国家(European Countries)

Modern usage of the term intellectual property goes back at least as far as 1867 with the founding of the North German Confederation whose constitution granted legislative power over the protection of intellectual property to the confederation. When the administrative secretariats established by the *Paris Convention* (1883) and the *Berne Convention* (1886) merged in 1893, they located in Berne, and also adopted the term intellectual property in their new combined title, the United International Bureau for the Protection of Intellectual Property. ①

在欧洲封建国家末期，原始著作权与专利权都是君主恩赐并作为特许权出现的，因此这种权利只可能在君主管辖地域内行使。随着近代资产阶级法律的发展，知识产权才最终脱离了封建特许权形式，成为法定的精神产权。但是，资本主义国家依照其主权原则，只对依本国法律取得的知识产权加以保护。在一国获得知识产权的权利人，如果要在他国受到法律保护，就必须按照该国法律规定登记注册或审查批准。从 19 世纪末起，随着科学技术的发展以及国际贸易的扩大，知识产权交易的国际市场也开始形成和发展起来。这样，为了适应知识产权的国际性需求，各国先后签订了一些保护知识产权的国际公约，成立了一些全球性或区域性的国际组织，在世界范围内形成了一套国际知识产权协调保护制度。

二、知识产权国际保护的起源(The Origin of International Protection)

19 世纪中后期，垄断资本主义不仅向国外输出资本和商品，还输出知识产品，这些知识产品往往附着着商标、专利等知识产权。然而知识产权保护的地域性导致各主权国家只保护依照本国法律法规取得的知识产权，不保护输出国的知识产权。随着科技的发展，

① Intellectual Property [DB/OL]. [2017-06-05]. Wikipedia, http://en.wikipedia.org/wiki/Intellectual_property#History.

贸易往来的增多，抢先申请专利、抢注商标的情况时有发生，作品被跨国使用的情况也越来越多。

1873 年奥地利邀请各国参加维也纳国际博览会，但各国都拒绝参加，其原因在于担心展览的技术得不到保护。为了保护知识产权权利人的利益，知识产品输出较多的国家急于寻求知识产权的国际合作，统一保护标准。1883 年，由比利时、西班牙、巴西、法国、意大利等 11 国发起，在巴黎签订了《保护工业产权巴黎公约》。1886 年，由英国、法国、德国、意大利、比利时等 10 国发起，在瑞士首都伯尔尼签订了《保护文学艺术作品伯尔尼公约》。1891 年，由法国、比利时、瑞士等国发起，在马德里缔结了《商标国际注册马德里协定》，作为对《巴黎公约》中关于商标国际保护的补充文件。100 多年来，经过各国政府的努力，知识产权的各个领域都有了国际公约，其中有些公约是对程序的规定，有些公约是对实质权利的规定。

三、知识产权国际保护的发展(The Development of International Protection)

知识产权国际协调保护制度现正处于知识经济的崭新时代。知识经济是以科学技术为第一生产力要素的智力经济，它的出现不仅对以往资源经济时代形成的价值观念(values)、分配原则(principle of distribution)、生活方式(life style)、管理机制(management mechanism)、政府政策(government policy)等带来冲击，而且会引起有关法律规范这一“游戏规则”在国际范围的重构。当代知识产权的国际协调保护，不仅凸显出基因专利(gene patent)、网络版权(network patent)、网络商标(network trademark)等对现行制度的改革，而且面临着崭新制度的突破(如传统知识、遗产资源)。科学技术革新频率高、技术进步速度快、边缘科学发展迅速、新科学技术门类不断衍生、新的高技术产业不断形成等特点，将进一步扩大知识产权保护范围。同时随着科学技术的发展和国际交往的日益频繁，知识产权国际协调保护也呈现出如下的发展的趋势：第一，保护知识产权的国际组织纷纷建立；第二，新的保护知识产权国际条约不断出现；第三，知识产权问题进入国际贸易领域，成为国际贸易谈判的中心问题。

(一)世界知识产权组织的成立(The Establishment of WIPO)

在知识产权国际协调保护制度的发展方面，世界知识产权组织发挥了积极作用。1996 年，世界知识产权组织主持制定了《世界知识产权组织版权条约》(以下简称 *WIPO Copyright Treaty*，《版权条约》)和《世界知识产权组织表演与录音制品条约》(以下简称 *WIPO Performance and Phonograms Treaty*，《表演与录音制品条约》)，这个以信息网络传播权为中心的“因特网条约”对各国立法产生了直接影响；1999 年，世界知识产权组织公布了关于国际因特网域名问题的最终研究报告，对全球域名系统的整体性改革提出了一系列的措施；2000 年，世界知识产权组织成立了“知识产权与遗传资源、传统知识和民间文学艺术”的政府间专门委员会，着手探索有别于现代知识产权的传统知识保护问题。对于这一问题，世界贸易组织也给予了高度重视，2001 年多哈会议的部长声明第 18 条与第 19 条已将传统知识保护问题列为下一次多边谈判考虑的议题。

(二)其他知识产权国际保护国际条约的出现(Other International Conventions)

除此之外，在有关人权、文化、贸易、粮农、土著权利、劳工标准、可持续发展、土地、环境与生物多样性等问题的国际论坛中，诸如联合国教科文组织(United Nations Educational Scientific and Cultural Organization，简称 UNESCO)、联合国环境计划署(United Nations Environmental Program，简称 UNEP)、联合国粮农组织(United Nations Food and Agriculture Organization，简称 UNFAO)、联合国贸易与发展会议(United Nations Conference on Trade and Development，简称 UNCTAD)、联合国开发计划署(United Nations Development Program，简称 UNDP)、世界卫生组织、世界粮食计划署等国际机构对传统知识和遗产资源的保护问题也都进行了广泛的讨论。

第二节　与知识产权有关的国际组织
Ⅱ　International Organizations Relevant to Intellectual Property

知识产权领域的国际组织，可以区分为地区性知识产权国际组织和全球性知识产权国际组织，也可以区分为政府间知识产权国际组织与非政府间知识产权国际组织。知识产权国际组织，特别是全球性的政府间国际组织，对知识产权法全球化的推动，具有举足轻重的作用。后面将主要介绍 WIPO、UNESCO、WTO 等全球性政府间国际组织。

一、世界知识产权组织(World Intellectual Property Organization—WIPO)

世界知识产权组织是一个致力于帮助确保知识产权创造者和持有人的权利在全世界范围内受到保护，从而使发明人和作家的创造力得到承认和奖赏的国际组织。它的成立标志着知识产权国际保护从分散走向了统一，形成了以 WIPO 为协调机构的统一的知识产权国际保护体系。中国于 1980 年 6 月 3 日加入《建立世界知识产权组织公约》，成为了 WIPO 一员。

The World Intellectual Property Organization (WIPO) is one of the specialized agencies of the United Nations (UN)(联合国) system of organizations. The "*Convention Establishing the World Intellectual Property Organization*"(《建立世界知识产权组织公约》) was signed at Stockholm(斯德哥尔摩) in 1967 and entered into force in 1970. However, the origins of WIPO go back to 1883 and 1886, with the adoption of the *Paris Convention*(《巴黎公约》) and the *Berne Convention*(《伯尔尼公约》) respectively.

《巴黎公约》的诞生对世界知识产权组织的成立有重大影响。《巴黎公约》于 1884 年生效后，当时的 14 个成员国成立了国际局来执行行政管理任务，诸如举办成员国会议等。

The *Berne Convention for the Protection of Literary and Artistic Works*, usually known as *the Berne Convention*, is an international agreement governing copyright, which was first accepted in Berne, Switzerland in 1886. 同《巴黎公约》一样，《伯尔尼公约》也成立了国际局来执行行政管理任务。

Both of these conventions provided for the establishment of international secretariats(国际秘书处), and both were placed under the supervision of the Swiss Federal Government(瑞士联邦

政府). The few officials who were needed to carry out the administration of the two conventions were located in Berne, Switzerland.

Initially there were two secretariats (one for industrial property, one for copyright) for the administration of the two conventions, but in 1893 the two secretariats united. The most recent name of the organization, before it became WIPO, was BIRPI, the acronym of the French, called United International Bureaux for the Protection of Intellectual Property(保护知识产权的联合国际局) in English. In 1960, BIRPI moved from Berne to Geneva(日内瓦).

基于知识产权保护国际协调的需要，1967 年，《巴黎公约》和《伯尔尼公约》的缔约国在斯德哥尔摩签订了《建立世界知识产权组织公约》(1970 年生效，1979 年有所修正)。

The Agreement marked a transition for WIPO from the mandate it inherited in 1967 from BIRPI, to promote the protection of intellectual property, to one that involved the more complex task of promoting technology transfer and economic development. ①

Long before the United Nations was established, BIRPl was the responsible intergovernmental organization in the field of intellectual property. WIPO, the successor(后继者) to BIRPI, became a specialized agency of the United Nations when an agreement was signed to that end between the United Nations and WIPO which came into effect on December 17, 1974.

(一)世界知识产权组织的组织机构(Institutional Framework of WIPO)

世界知识产权组织设立四个机构：大会、成员国会议、协调委员会和国际局。

1. 大会(General Assembly)

大会(General Assembly)是 WIPO 的最高权利机构(highest authority)，由参加《建立世界知识产权组织公约》(*Convention Establishing the World Intellectual Property Organization*)的各同盟的成员国组成。The General Assembly consists of all the States that are members of WIPO and also members of any of the Unions. 每个成员国政府(member state)应有一名代表(representative)，可辅以副代表(deputy representative)、顾问(council)和专家(specialist)。每个成员国在大会上只有一票的表决权(vote)。大会例会(regular meeting)每 3 年由总干事召开一次。大会特别会议应由总干事按协调委员会的请求，或者按大会四分之一的成员国的请求召开。

2. 成员国会议(Conference of State Members)

Unlike the General Assembly, the Conference consists of all the States which are members of WIPO, whether or not they are members of any of the Unions. The main functions of the Conference were originally divided into five groups.

Firstly, the Conference was to constitute a forum for exchanges of views between all States members of WIPO on matters relating to intellectual property, and in that context it was empowered, in particular, to make any recommendations on such matters, having regard to the competence and autonomy of the Unions.

---

① World Intellectual Property Organization[DB/OL]. [2017-06-05]. Wikipedia, http://en.wikipedia.org/wiki/World_Intellectual_Property_Organization.

Secondly, the Conference was to establish the biennial development cooperation program for developing countries and, thirdly, it was to adopt a budget for that purpose.

Thirdly, the Conference is also competent to adopt amendments to the Convention establishing WIPO. Proposals for the amendment of the Convention may be initiated by any State member of WIPO, by the Coordination Committee or by the Director General.

Fourthly, the Conference, like the General Assembly, was to determine which States and organizations would be admitted to its meetings as observers. ①

成员国会议由参加 WIPO 的国家组成，每个国家政府应有一名代表，可辅以副代表、顾问和专家。每个成员国在大会上只有一票的表决权。

3. 协调委员会(Coordination Committee)

协调委员会由担任巴黎同盟执行委员会(Paris Alliances Executive Board)委员或伯尔尼同盟执行委员会(Berne Alliances Executive Board)委员或者两委员会委员的 WIPO 参加国组成。协调委员会例会每年由总干事召开一次。其特别会议可由总干事以其个人名义提议或应协调委员会主席的请求或四分一的委员国的请求召开。

4. 国际局(International Bureau)

国际局为 WIPO 的秘书处(secretariat)，是 WIPO 的常设办事机构(permanent office)。国际局以总干事(secretary-general)为首，设两个以上副总干事(vice secretary-general)。国际局全体工作人员职责的性质是纯国际性的。总干事为 WIPO 的行政首脑，其任期不得少于 6 年，可以连任。初次任期和可能的连任以及其他任命条件由成员国大会规定。

(二)WIPO 的职权(Functions of WIPO)

The Agreement between the United Nations and the World Intellectual Property Organization notes in Article 2 that WIPO is responsible for promoting creative intellectual activity and for facilitating the transfer of technology related to industrial property to the developing countries in order to accelerate economic, social and cultural development, subject to the competence and responsibilities of the United Nations and its organs, particularly the United Nations Conference on Trade and Development, the United Nations Development Program and the United Nations Industrial Development Organization, as well as of the United Nations Educational, Scientific and Cultural Organization and of other agencies within the United Nations system.

促进旨在便利在全世界对知识产权的有效保护和协调各国有关这方面的法令的措施的发展；执行巴黎联盟及其有关专门联盟和伯尔尼联盟的行政任务；可同意担任或参加其他旨在促进知识产权保护的国际协定的行政工作；鼓励缔结旨在促进知识产权保护的国际协定；对请求知识产权方面的法律技术援助的国家给予合作；收集和传播有关知识产权保护的情报，从事并促进这方面的讲究，并公布这些研究的成果；提供促进知识产权国际保护的服务，并适当办理这方面的注册并公布有关注册的资料；采取其他适当的行动。

---

① WIPO Interllectual Property Handbook: Policy, Law and Use (Second Edition) [M]. WIPO Publication, 2008: 7.

二、联合国教科文组织（United Nations Educational, Scientific and Cultural Organization—UNESCO）

联合国教育、科学及文化组织属联合国专门机构，简称联合国教科文组织。1946 年 11 月正式成立，同年 12 月成为联合国的一个专门机构。总部设在法国巴黎。其宗旨是通过教育、科学和文化促进各国间合作，对和平和安全作出贡献。

联合国教科文组织是各国政府间讨论关于教育、科学和文化问题的国际组织，其主要机构有大会(assembly)、执行局(executive board)和秘书处(secretariat)。大会为该组织最高权力机构，每两年开会一次，决定该组织的政策、计划和预算。执行局为大会闭幕期间的管理和监督机构；秘书处负责执行日常工作，由执行局建议，经大会任命总干事领导秘书处的工作。联合国教科文组织的一项基本目标即是保护文学、艺术和科学作品。1946 年 11 月至 12 月，在巴黎举行的 UNESCO 大会第一届会议得出一个结论：各国之间自由传播和自由交流精神作品的主要障碍之一，是国际上实行的保护著作权的制度不完整和不适应现实需要。UNESCO 建议由起主持召开国际著作权会议，以达成一项协议，使各国能够加入一项旨在管理和促进著作权转移以及通过信息机构传播作品的新的国际公约。

UNESCO has 193 Member States and seven Associate Members. Most of the field offices are "cluster" offices covering three or more countries; there are also national and regional offices. UNESCO pursues its objectives through five major programs: education, natural sciences, social and human sciences, culture, and communication and information. Projects sponsored by UNESCO include literacy, technical, and teacher-training programs; international science programs; the promotion of independent media and freedom of the press; regional and cultural history projects; the promotion of cultural diversity; international cooperation agreements to secure the world cultural and natural heritage (World Heritage Sites) and to preserve human rights, and attempts to bridge the worldwide digital divide.

1952 年 9 月 6 日，在 UNESCO 的主持下，《世界版权公约》在日内瓦通过，并由 UNESCO 负责管理。此外，UNESCO 还主持或参与主持缔结了以下国际公约：(1)《罗马公约》(*Rome Convention for the Protection of Performers, Producers of Phonograms and Broadcasting Organizations*，简称 Rome Convention)，由 UNESCO、WIPO 和 ILO 共同管理；(2)《录音制品公约》(*Convention for the Protection of Producers of Phonograms Against Unauthorized Duplication of Their Phonograms*)；(3)《卫星公约》(*Convention on the International Maritime Satellite Organization*)；(4)《避免对版权使用费收入重复征税多边公约》(*Multilateral Convention for the Avoidance of Double Taxation of Copyright Royalties*)。

目前，UNESCO 在著作权方面的计划主要围绕三大目标：(1)鼓励加入现行的国际公约，并请各会员国采取立法措施，来促进翻译家权利，促进对民间创造的保护，提高艺术家的地位和促进对公有领域作品的保护；(2)发展著作权教学，在发展中国家大学的教学计划中纳入这一教学内容(这项活动包括为作者、各国的负责人和法官、新闻记者和图书管理员举办研讨会)；(3)用英文、西班牙文、法文和俄文等语言出版《著作权公报》，以此对专家和广大公众进行宣传。

三、世界贸易组织(World Trade Organization—WTO)

The World Trade Organization (WTO) officially commenced on January 1, 1995 under the Marrakech Agreement, replacing the General Agreement on Tariffs and Trade (GATT), which commenced in 1948. The organization deals with regulation of trade between participating countries; it provides a framework for negotiating and formalizing trade agreements, and a dispute resolution process aimed at enforcing participants' adherence to WTO agreements which are signed by representatives of member governments and ratified by their parliaments. Most of the issues that the WTO focuses on derive from previous trade negotiations, especially from the Uruguay Round. ①

(一)GATT 与乌拉圭回合谈判(GATT and Uruguay Round)

WTO 源自关税和贸易总协定(General Agreement on Tariffs and Trades, GATT),前者是后者的延伸和发展。GATT 在 1947 年由包括中国在内的 23 个国家共同签署。自 1948 年 1 月 1 日生效开始,GATT 适用了 40 余年,直至 1995 年 1 月 1 日才完成其历史使命。1986 年 9 月,GATT 在乌拉圭埃斯特角城举行缔约方部长级会议,决定发动第八轮多边贸易谈判,"乌拉圭回合"由此得名。这是 GATT 举行的最后一论全球性多边贸易谈判,也正是该轮谈判导致了 WTO 的建立。

(二)与贸易有关的知识产权问题的谈判(Negotiations on Trade-related Aspect of Intellectual Property)

1. 背景(Background)

20 世纪 70 年代末和 80 年代初关于国际知识产权制度的争论,突出了体现国家利益的知识产权观念的差异。发达国家认为,知识产权是一种私权利。应该受到像其他财产权那样的保护。发展中国家则认为,知识产权是一种公共物品,应当用于促进经济发展。正是基于这样一种认识上的差异,对知识产权国际协调保护是否纳入 GATT,发达国家和发展中国家持截然相反的态度。经过一番努力,在 1986 年 9 月,埃斯特角城部长级会议最终将知识产权问题列入乌拉圭回合的谈判议程。《乌拉圭回合部长宣言》声称,将对与贸易有关的知识产权问题,包括冒牌货贸易问题,进行讨论,并作出了三项授权。

由于发达国家与发展中国家对《乌拉圭回合部长级宣言》中关于知识产权的三项授权的理解和各方利益的冲突较大,致使乌拉圭回合谈判初期在知识产权问题的谈判上,几乎没有任何进步。直到 1990 年 12 月,在布鲁塞尔部长级会议上,各谈判方才基本认同进一步推进知识产权的谈判,也表示出一定的灵活性。1991 年 12 月,当时任 GATT 总干事的邓克尔提出了乌拉圭回合谈判的最后草案,其中包括了"与贸易(包括假冒商品贸易在内)有关的知识产权协议"草案,该知识产权协议草案基本获得了通过。包括《与贸易有关的知识产权协议》在内的乌拉圭回合谈判的最后文件,在 1994 年 4 月 15 日的马拉喀什部长级会议上由各方签署。自此,知识产权保护开始成为 WTO 关注的一个重要方面。

---

① World Trade Organization [DB/OL]. [2017-05-09]. Wikipedia, http://en.wikipedia.org/wiki/World_Trade_Organization.

2. 知识产权谈判的基本原则(Basic Principles of Intellectual Property Negotiation)

在乌拉圭回合谈判中，美国代表提出，有关知识产权规范的谈判，不能把世界知识产权组织的各项协定和世界版权协定作为唯一的基础，还应通过乌拉圭回合谈判在确立更有效而统一的原则方面达成一致。美国的这一立场得到了欧共体成员国、加拿大、日本、澳大利亚和新西兰等发达国家的支持。多数发展中国家对美国提出的原则立场态度表示不能接受。但出于政治上的考虑，以及从发展本国经济，从利用外资、引进技术、改善本国对外经济技术合作的长期利益目标出发，许多发展中国家终于转向支持。1989 年 4 月关贸总协定成员方部长们就知识产权谈判达成下列原则协议：

(1)关贸总协定基本原则和有关的国际知识产权方面的协议或条约的适用性；(2)为与贸易有关的知识产权的适用性、范围及使用确定标准和原则性条款；(3)拟定关于知识产权保护措施有效执行时，应考虑到各国的法律制度；(4)关于迅速而有效地防止和解决政府间争端的程序及有关条款(包括关贸总协定程序的适用性)；(5)为在最大范围内落实谈判成果而作的过渡安排。

The GATT still exists as the WTO's umbrella treaty for trade in goods, updated as a result of the Uruguay Round negotiations a long list of about 60 agreements, annexes, decisions and understandings was adopted in GATT. The agreements fall into a structure with six main parts:

(1) The Agreement Establishing the WTO;

(2) Goods and investment — the Multilateral Agreements on Trade in Goods including the GATT 1994 and the Trade Related Investment Measures;

(3) Services — the General Agreement on Trade in Services;

(4) Intellectual property — the Agreement on Trade-Related Aspects of Intellectual Property Rights (TRIPS);

(5) Dispute settlement (DSU);

(6) Reviews of governments' trade policies (TPRM). ①

3.《与贸易有关的知识产权协议》

The Agreement on Trade Related Aspects of Intellectual Property Rights (TRIPS) is an international agreement administered by the World Trade Organization (WTO) that sets down minimum standards for many forms of intellectual property (IP) regulation as applied to nationals of other WTO Members. TRIPS were negotiated at the end of the Uruguay Round of the *General Agreement on Tariffs and Trade* (GATT) in 1994. Its inclusion was the culmination of a program of intense lobbying by the United States, supported by the European Union, Japan and other developed nations.

乌拉圭回合知识产权谈判组于 1991 年 12 月提出了《与贸易有关的知识产权协议》(英文缩写 TRIPS)。TRIPS 的形成经历了缔约方多次的谈判交锋，在乌拉圭回合结束之际被各国接受而成为正式协议，成为乌拉圭回合谈判形成的最终文件之一，同时也是 WTO 的

① World Trade Organization [DB/OL]. [2017-05-09]. Wikipedia, http://en.wikipedia.org/wiki/World_Trade_Organization.

基本法律文件之一。以 TRIPS 为标志，知识产权的国际合作进入了新的历史时期，加速了各国知识产权法的全球化趋同化进程。

The TRIPS agreement introduced intellectual property law into the international trading system for the first time and remains the most comprehensive international agreement on intellectual property to date. In 2001, developing countries, concerned that developed countries were insisting on an overly narrow reading of TRIPS, initiated a round of talks that resulted in the Doha Declaration. The Doha declaration is a WTO statement that clarifies the scope of TRIPS, stating for example that TRIPS can and should be interpreted in light of the goal "to promote access to medicines for all."

TRIPS 的宗旨：(1)需要加强对知识产权实行有效和充分的保护，并确保实施知识产权的措施和程序不会成为贸易障碍；(2)建立多边框架和规则，处理国际假冒产品贸易问题；(3)知识产权是私有权利，未经权利人许可的使用，一般构成侵权；(4)承认各国保护知识产权的公共政策的目标，包括发展目标和技术上的目标；(5)对最不发达国家成员其国内实施法律和规章方面特别需要最大的灵活性；(6)通过多边程序解决与贸易有关的知识产权争端。

TRIPS 的基本原则：(1)成员应履行《巴黎公约》、《伯尔尼公约》、《罗马公约》和《关于集成电路的知识产权条约》；(2)国民待遇。在知识产权保护方面，每个成员给其他成员国民的待遇不应低于它给本国国民的待遇，除非《巴黎公约》、《伯尔尼公约》、《罗马公约》中已分别有的例外规定；(3)最惠国待遇。在知识产权保护上，某一成员提供其他国国民的任何利益、优惠、特权或豁免，均应立即无条件地适用于全体其他成员国民。但是司法协助协议、《伯尔尼公约》或《罗马公约》所允许的不按国民待遇，而按互惠原则，以及本协议未规定的表演者权、录音制品制作者权及广播组织权等除外。

TRIPS 的目标：应有利于促进技术的革新、技术的转让与技术的传播，以及促进生产者与技术知识使用者互利，并促进权利与义务的平衡。

TRIPS 是到目前为止世界上对知识产权保护最严格的国际条约。从长远看，它是世界大市场的一部重要的公平竞争法，对人类社会物质文明的进步和公共道德的进步有十分突出的意义。在科学技术日益发达的未来社会，所有的国家将会受益于对知识的尊重和对知识产权的保护。

四、其他组织(Other Organizations)

国际劳工组织(International Labour Organization，简称 ILO)20 世纪初录音和广播的迅速发展彻底改变了演奏者们的地位，并在该行业引起了令人不安的失业状况，于是，演奏者们开始向 ILO 寻求帮助，提出研究他们的权利的问题。从 1926 年国际音乐家联合会大会提出这些抱怨到 1961 年《罗马公约》签署这段期间，ILO 在维护表演者和演奏者利益方面起了积极作用，它支持表演者和演奏者的权利建立在劳动法基础上这种论点，因为演奏或表演首先是一种劳动成果，它的充分的经济价值使他们有权提出权利要求。ILO 为脑力劳动者开展的活动一方面涉及保护受雇作者和发明者的权利；另一方面涉及就业条件和工作条件，以及艺术家的表演被二次使用时他们应享有的权利。当然，ILO 因其目标和职能的限制，在知识产权法国际协调上的参与是极为有限。

除了 WIPO、UNESCO、WTO、ILO 等全球性政府间国际组织以外，协调知识产权国际保护的还有欧洲联盟、非洲知识产权组织等区域性政府间国际组织。

第三节 主要的知识产权国际公约
Ⅲ Main International Conventions on Intellectual Property

所谓的知识产权公约，是指各国(地区)之间为确定彼此间的权利义务而达成的规范知识产权法律关系的协议。在知识产权法的全球化过程中，国际公约扮演了举足轻重的角色。一方面，知识产权国际公约的调整内容和保护水平是知识产权法全球化进程中的国际标准；另一方面，知识产权国际公约影响甚至决定着其他条约成员的知识产权保护水平，即使对非条约成员也有指引和参照作用。

一、综合性国际公约——《保护工业产权巴黎公约》(*Paris Convention for the Protection of Industrial Property*)

During the 19th century, before the existence of any international convention in the field of industrial property, it was difficult to obtain protection for industrial property rights in the various countries of the world because of the diversity of their laws. Moreover, patent applications had to be made roughly at the same time in all countries in order to avoid a publication in one country destroying the novelty of the invention in the other countries. These practical problems created a strong desire to overcome such difficulties.

因此，在 19 世纪下半叶，随着越来越多的国家建立与完善了专利制度，以及国际技术转让许可贸易频繁，许多国家都有一个共同的愿望，即在世界范围内缔结一种保护工业产权的国际公约，以法律形式来保护各国的发明和商标，这种迫切的愿望成为《巴黎公约》产生的历史大背景。《巴黎公约》作为一个世界范围内形成的工业产权的框架已有 1 个多世纪。

The *Paris Convention* has been revised from time to time after its signature in 1883. Each of the revision conferences, starting with the Brussels Conference in 1900, ended with the adoption of a revised Act of the *Paris Convention*. With the exception of the Acts concluded at the revision conferences of Brussels (1897 and 1900) and Washington, D. C. (1911), which are no longer in force, all those earlier Acts are still of significance, although the great majority of the countries are now party to the latest Act, that of Stockholm (斯德哥尔摩) of 1967.

从 1985 年 3 月 19 日起，中国成为《巴黎公约》的成员国。在加入时，曾声明对其中第 28 条(即把有关争议提交国际法院解决)予以保留。截至 2017 年 5 月，《巴黎公约》的成员国已达到 177 个国家。

(一)工业产权的范围(The Scope of Industrial Property)

工业产权保护首先是对工业产权的界定(该公约第 1 条)。此处的工业是一个广义的概念，不仅包括狭义的与农业相对的工业，还包括农业、商业、采掘业等一切产业部门。

工业产品不仅仅局限于工业上的制成品，还包括一切天然产品。工业产权的保护对象是专利、商标、实用新型、外观设计、服务标记、厂商名称、货源标记或原产地名称，以及制止不正当竞争。对于专利，还包括巴黎联盟国家的法律所承认的各种工业专利，如输入专利、改进专利、增补专利和增补证书等。因此，《巴黎公约》保护的产权范围较广。

(二)保护工业产权的基本原则和最低要求(Basic Principles and Minimum Requirements of Industrial Property Protection)

《巴黎公约》规定了各成员国应遵守的共同原则，该原则也是对各成员国国内法提供保护的最低要求。

1. 国民待遇(National Treatment)

National treatment means that, as regards the protection of industrial property, each country party to the Paris Convention must grant the same protection to nationals of the other member countries as it grants to its own nationals.

The same national treatment must be granted to nationals(国民) of countries which are not party to the Paris Convention if they are domiciled(定居) in a member country or if they have a "real and effective" industrial or commercial establishment in such a country. However, no requirement as to domicile or establishment in the country where protection is claimed may be imposed upon nationals of member countries as a condition for benefiting from an industrial property right.

The term "national" includes both natural Persons and legal entities.

According the Article 2 "National Treatment for Nationals of Countries of the Union": However, no requirement as to domicile or establishment in the country where protection is claimed may be imposed upon nationals of countries of the Union for the enjoyment of any industrial property rights. ①

According the Article 3 "Same Treatment for Certain Categories of Persons as for Nationals of Countries of the Union": Nationals of countries outside the Union who are domiciled or who have real and effective industrial or commercial establishments in the territory of one of the countries of the Union shall be treated in the same manner as nationals of the countries of the Union. ②

From the articles 2 and 3 of this treaty, juristic and natural persons who are either national of or domiciled in a state party to the Convention shall, as regards the protection of industrial property, enjoy in all the other countries of the Union, the advantages that their respective laws grant to nationals.

这个国民待遇规定是按照《巴黎公约》建立的国际保护制度的基础之一，它不仅保障外国人的权利，而且保护他们不会受到任何歧视，这也是缔结《巴黎公约》的重要目的。对非成员国国民在成员国的"住所"，一般并不要求是法律认可的住所。但必须是较长期的住所，且是能够进行实际联系的住所。对"营业所"的要求是实际从事工商业活动的住

---

① Article 2 of *Paris Convention for the Protection of Industrial Property*.

② Article 3 of *Paris Convention for the Protection of Industrial Property*.

所。

2. 优先权(Priority)

The right of priority means that, on the basis of a regular application for an industrial property right filed by a given applicant in one of the member countries, the same applicant (or its or his successor in title) may, within a specified period of time (six or 12 months), apply for protection in all the other member countries. These later applications will then be regarded as if they had been filed on the same day as the earliest application. Hence, these later applications enjoy a priority status with respect to all applications relating to the same invention filed after the date of the first application. They also enjoy a priority status with respect to the acts accomplished after that date which would normally be apt to destroy the rights of the applicant or the patentability of his invention. The provisions concerning the right of priority are contained in Article 4 of the Convention.

确定优先权日，使申请人不必要在国内或国外就同一发明提出所有申请，因为申请人可以在 6 个月或 12 个月时间来考虑在哪些国家请求保护。《巴黎公约》的优先权原则，并不是对一切工业产权都适用。根据公约第 4 条的规定，适用优先权的仅仅是发明专利、实用新型专利、工业品外观设计专利与用于商品上的注册商标。优先权日必须是在《巴黎公约》成员国的国家中，第一次交工业产权申请案时才能确立。如果申请案提交的国家不是《巴黎公约》成员国，那么这个优先权就不成立。同时，优先权作为一种权利，可以连同专利申请权、商标注册申请权或连同专利权、商标权等一同转让。只要有关优先权的期限尚未届满，申请权或有关专有权合法受让方同样享有优先权。但此优先权必须是在权利要求书中另附一份“优先权请求书”并附有关的证明文件，包括就自己的发明或商标、在哪一个成员国、第一次递交的日期、申请号等，有的国家还要第一次申请案的复印件。

3. 临时性保护(Temporary Protection)

“Inventions, Utility Models, Industrial Designs, Marks: Temporary Protection at Certain International Exhibitions” is arranged in Article 11:

(1) The countries of the Union shall, in conformity with their domestic legislation, grant temporary protection to patentable inventions, utility models, industrial designs, and trademarks, in respect of goods exhibited at official or officially recognized international exhibitions held in the territory of any of them.

(2) Such temporary protection shall not extend the periods provided by Article 4. If, later, the right of priority is invoked, the authorities of any country may provide that the period shall start from the date of introduction of the goods into the exhibition.

(3) Each country may require, as proof of the identity of the article exhibited and of the date of its introduction, such documentary evidence as it considers necessary.

公约各成员国必须依据本国申请，对任何一个成员国举办的经官方承认的国际展览会展出的展品，可以申请专利的发明、实用新型或外观设计以及可以申请注册的商标，给予临时保护。临时保护期，对于发明，实用新型一般为 12 个月；对商标、外观设计是 6 个月。在保护期内，不允许展品以外的第三方以展品申请工业产权。如果展品所有人在临时保护期内申请了专利或商标注册，则申请案的优先权日就不是从第一次提出申请案时起算，而是从展品公开展出之日起算。临时性保护有两个条件：一是展览会必须是国际性的；二是展览会必须是官方承认的，并且临时保护的展品所有人必须取得举办国际展览会的那个成员国的有关当局的书面证明，即包括公开展出的日期和是否确属展览会展出的物品。只有符合条件的展品，才能受到临时性保护。

4. 宽限期(Grace Period)

According to the Article 5 of this convention, "Period of Grace for the Payment of Fees for the Maintenance of Rights":

(1) A period of grace of not less than six months shall be allowed for the payment of the fees prescribed for the maintenance of industrial property rights, subject, if the domestic legislation so provides, to the payment of a surcharge.

(2) The countries of the Union shall have the right to provide for the restoration of patents which have lapsed by reason of non-payment of fees.

公约第5条是对宽限期的规定，它涉及缴纳工业产权年费或续展费的期限。在多数国家中，要维持专利在有效期内的效力，必须缴纳逐年递增的专利年费。商标也一样，要维持商标专用权，必须在届满时办理续展手续并缴纳续展费。到期没有缴纳专利年费或续展费，即导致其权利的丧失。为了避免交费时由于手续或邮政上的合理延误而导致权利丧失的情况，《巴黎公约》作出宽限期的规定。要求成员国给工业产权的权利人有6个月的宽限期即维持他的工业产权。但公约中的宽限期只适用缴纳年费或续展费，不适用于其他缴费(如专利商标申请时的申请费或专利审查的审查费)。如果这些费用没有如期缴纳，则申请时必遭驳回。不过有些国家的国内法还规定了未缴费而失效后的权利恢复程序。

二、《商标国际注册马德里协定》(*Madrid Agreement Concerning the International Registration Of Marks*)

《巴黎公约》虽然也有保护商标国际注册的规定，但需要逐个国家申请，没有商标国际注册的程序，许多国家的厂商都感到履行重复注册的手续非常繁琐，要求加强这一领域的国际合作。1891年，当时已经实行商标注册制度的国家，如法国、比利时、西班牙、瑞士、突尼斯等国发起，在马德里开会，缔结了《商标国际注册马德里协定》(*Madrid Agreement Concerning the International Registration of Marks*; *Madrid Agreement for short*，简称《马德里协定》)。1892年7月生效，后经多次修订，现在适用文本是1979年斯德哥尔摩文本。据世界知识产权组织网站公布，目前加入该协定的有92个国家，中国于1989年10月4日加入该协定。

《马德里协定》向《巴黎公约》成员国开放，批准书或加入书须交WIPO总干事保存。然而由于该协定只使用法语一种工作语言，而且以先在本国注册为提请国际注册的前提，如果5年内其国内注册被取消，国际注册也随之消灭。这些使得一些国家感到难以接受，不愿加入。

为了扩大《马德里协定》的缔约方范围，特别是吸引发达国家参加，1989年6月在西班牙马德里签订了《马德里协定议定书》(*Protocol Relating to the Madrid Agreement*)，修改

《马德里协定》，补充了一些内容。《马德里协定议定书》于1996年4月1日生效，到2012年缔约方达到88个，我国于1995年12月1日成为该协定书的缔约方，《马德里协定》和《马德里协定议定书》互相补充，各国可以选择参加其中的一个或两个。

《马德里协定》和《马德里协定议定书》共同确立的商标国际注册体系，简化了注册的程序手续。凭借其程序机制的优势，该协定可使商标权利人直接向其本国或地区商标局递交一份国际注册申请书便能够使其商标在马德里联盟多个国家获得保护。由此注册的国际商标相当于该申请人在每个指定国或组织直接进行的商标注册申请或注册。如果在规定期限内(12个月或18个月)，某指定国或组织的商标局没有驳回对该商标的保护，国际商标便如同在该局直接注册的商标。鉴于注册后的各种变更或续展也可以通过同样便捷的程序进行，该协定还大大简化了对商标注册后的管理。另外商标所有人还可用同样的方式把国际注册的效力延伸到更多的马德里联盟成员国或组织。

The Madrid Protocol provides an international system for centrally filing trademark applications in its over 80 member nations. A person owning a trademark registration or application in his home country can file one Madrid application that designates any number of other member countries in which the owner wishes to register. The applicant's home Trademark Office forwards the Madrid application to the International Bureau of the World Intellectual Property Organization, which processes it, provides an international registration, publishes the mark, and forwards the application to each of the countries the applicant has designated for territorial extension of the international registration. Each designated country then has 18 months to evaluate the application based on its domestic laws and either extends the international registration or refuse extension. Registrations under the Madrid Protocol have the same scope as the registrant's domestic registration, and are dependent on the validity of the domestic registration for the first five years.

与商标国际注册的《马德里协定》在同一时间同一地点签订的还有《制裁商品来源的虚假或欺骗性标志马德里协定》(*Madrid Agreement for the Repression of False or Deceptive Indications of Source on Goods*)，这两个协定的内容完全不同，一个管理商标，一个管理原产地。根据该协定，对凡带有虚假或欺骗性产地标志、直接或间接把本协定参加国或该国的一个地方标为原产国或原产地的商品，各缔约国都有权在进口时予以没收或禁止进口，或对其进口采取其他措施和制裁。

三、《保护文学和艺术作品伯尔尼公约》(*Berne Convention for the Protection of Literary and Artistic Works*)

19世纪，西欧尤其是法国涌现出许多大文学家、大艺术家，他们创作的大量脍炙人口的作品流传到世界各地，这些国家开始相应地也就重视版权的国际保护。1878年，由雨果主持在巴黎召开了一次重要的文学大会，建立了一个国际文学艺术协会。1883年该协会将一份经过多次讨论的国际公约草案交给瑞士政府。瑞士政府于1886年9月9日在伯尔尼举行的第三次大会上予以通过，定名为《保护文学和艺术作品伯尔尼公约》(*Berne Convention for the Protection of Literary and Artistic Works*，简称《伯尔尼公约》)。《伯尔尼公约》的产生，标志着国际版权保护体系的初步形成。中国于1992年7月1日加入该公约。截至2016年9月24日，共有172个国家批准或承认这个公约的不同文本，参加了这个联盟。

The Berne Convention is the oldest international treaty in the field of copyright. It is open to all States. Instruments of accession or ratification（批准）are deposited with the Director General（总干事）of the World Intellectual Property Organization（WIPO）.

《伯尔尼公约》主要内容包括：(1)文学艺术作品，不论其表现形式如何均享受保护。(2)确立三项基本原则：一是国民待遇原则。The *Berne Convention* requires its signatories to recognize the copyright of works of authors from other signatory countries（known as members of the Berne Union）in the same way as it recognizes the copyright of its own nationals. In addition to establishing a system of equal treatment that internationalized copyright amongst signatories, the agreement also required member states to provide strong minimum standards for copyright law. ① 二是自动保护原则，即一成员国国民的作品不需要办理任何手续即可在其他成员国受到保护。三是独立保护原则，即一成员国国民的作品，在另一成员国依该国法律受到保护，不受作品在原所属国保护条件的约束。(3)作品的最短保护期限为作者在世之年加死后50年，但对于某些类别的作品，存在例外。此外，公约对文学艺术作品的各类作品所享有的专有权利作了比较详尽的规定。

The *Berne Convention* states that all works except photographic and cinematographic shall be copyrighted for at least 50 years after the author's death, but parties are free to provide longer terms. Countries under the older revisions of the treaty may choose to provide their own protection terms, and certain types of works（such as phonorecords and motion pictures）may be provided shorter terms. ②

四、《保护表演者、音像制品制作者和广播组织罗马公约》(*Rome Convention for the Protection of Performers, Producers of Phonograms and Broadcasting Organizations*)

The Rome Convention for the Protection of Performers, Producers of Phonograms and Broadcasting Organizations was accepted by members of BIRPI, the predecessor to the modern World Intellectual Property Organization, on October 26, 1961. The agreement extended copyright protection for the first time from the author of a work to the creators and owners of particular, physical manifestations of intellectual property, such as audiocassettes or DVDs.

① Berne Convention for the Protection of Literary and Artistic Works [DB/OL]. [2017-05-09]. Wikipedia, http://en.wikipedia.org/wiki/Berne_Convention_for_the_Protection_of_Literary_and_Artistic_Works.

② Berne Convention for the Protection of Literary and Artistic Works [DB/OL]. [2017-05-09]. Wikipedia, http://en.wikipedia.org/wiki/Berne_Convention_for_the_Protection_of_Literary_and_Artistic_Works.

(一)国民待遇原则(National Treatment)

The Definition of National Treatment was given by Article 2 of the Convention: "For the purposes of this Convention, national treatment shall mean the treatment accorded by the domestic law of the Contracting State in which protection is claimed:

(a) to performers who are its nationals, as regards performances taking place, broadcast, or first fixed, on its territory;

(b) to producers of phonograms who are its nationals, as regards phonograms first fixed or first published on its territory;

(c) to broadcasting organizations which have their headquarters on its territory, as regards broadcasts transmitted from transmitters situated on its territory. National treatment shall be subject to the protection specifically guaranteed, and the limitations specifically provided for, in this Convention."

任何一个成员国均应依照本国法律，给予其他成员国的表演者、录音制品录制者及广播组织，以相当于本国同类自然人及法人的待遇。但对于上述三种不同的专有权所有者，在国民待遇上作了三种不同规定。表演者依照公约享有国民待遇的条件包括：表演行为发生在其他任何一个成员国内(如发生在本国自不待言)；表演活动已被录制在受公约保护的录音制品上，表演活动虽未被录制，但在受公约保护的广播节目中广播了。录音制品录制者依照公约享有国民待遇的条件包括：录音制品录制者系其他任何一个成员国的国民(如系本国国民自不待言)，这就是所谓"国籍标准"；录音制品首次录制系在任何一个成员国进行，这是所谓"录制标准"；录音制品系在任何成员国内首先发行，这是所谓"发行标准"。广播组织依照公约享有国民待遇的条件包括：广播组织的总部设于任何一个成员国内；广播节目从任何一个成员国的发射台播放。对于录制者的条件，任何成员国均可保留不采用录制标准或不采用发行标准的权利。对于广播组织的条件，任何成员国均可声明只对总部设在某成员国并且从该国播放节目的广播组织提供国民待遇。如果某录音制品是在非成员国与成员国同时首次发行，那么也符合上述发行标准。"同时发行"即在 30 日内先后在两个以上国家发行。

(二)非自动保护原则(Doctrine of Non-automatic Protection)

If, as a condition of protecting the rights of producers of phonograms, or of performers, or both, in relation to phonograms, a Contracting State, under its domestic law, requires compliance with formalities, these shall be considered as fulfilled if all the copies in commerce of the published phonogram or their containers bear a notice consisting of the symbol (P), accompanied by the year date of the first publication, placed in such a manner as to give reasonable notice of claim of protection; and if the copies or their containers do not identify the producer or the licensee of the producer (by carrying his name, trade mark or other appropriate designation), the notice shall also include the name of the owner of the rights of the producer; and, furthermore, if the copies or their containers do not identify the principal performers, the notice shall also include the name of the person who, in the country in which the fixation was effected, owns the rights of such performers. ①

如果把表演者的演出录制下来，不仅录音制品录制者对录制品享有专有权，表演者也对它享有专有权。例如，想要复制该录音制品的第三者，不仅要取得录音制品录制者的许可，而且要取得被录制表演的表演者的许可。但录音制品录制者与表演者的这种专有权不能自动产生，而必须在录音制品上附加三种标记：录音制品录制者或表演者的英文（producer or performer）字首略语；录音制品首次发行之年；录音制品录制者与表演者的姓名。

（三）专有权内容（Exclusive Rights）

The Article 7 of this agreement specifies "Minimum Protection for Performers": The protection provided for performers by this Convention shall include the possibility of preventing: (a) the broadcasting and the communication to the public, without their consent, of their performance, except where the performance used in the broadcasting or the public communication is itself already a broadcast performance or is made from a fixation;

The Article 19 specifies that "Performers' Rights in Films": Notwithstanding anything in this Convention, once a performer has consented to the incorporation of his performance in a visual or audio-visual fixation, Article 7shall have no further application.

表演者权（performers' rights）——未经表演者许可，不得广播或向公众传播其表演实况（专为广播目的演出除外），不得录制其从未被录制过的表演实况，不得复制以其表演为内容的录音制品（公约另有规定者除外）；录音制品录制者权——未经录制者许可，不得直接或间接复制其录音制品；广播组织权——未经广播组织许可，不得转播其广播节目，不得录制其广播节目，不得复制未经其许可而制作的对其广播的录音、录像（公约另有规定者除外）。

（四）保护期（Minimum Duration of Protection）

The term of protection to be granted under this Convention shall last at least until the end of a period of twenty years computed from the end of the year in which: (a) the fixation was made—for phonograms and for performances incorporated therein; (b) the performance took place—for performances not incorporated in phonograms; (c) the broadcast took place—for broadcasts. ②

三种不同邻接权的保护期是以20年为最低限，按三者的情况分别规定的。表演者权的保护期——如果演出实况没有被录音或录像，则保护期从表演活动发生之年的年底算起20年；录音制品录制者权的保护期——从录音制品录制之年的年底算起20年；广播者权的保护期——从有关的广播节目开始播出之年的年底算起20年。在保护期内，表演者、录音制品录制者及广播组织者可以行使自己的权利，即向经其许可而利用其专有权的人收取合理报酬。当然，公约不阻止其成员国提供比20年更长的保护期。

① Article 11 of *Rome Convention for the Protection of Performers, Producers of Phonograms and Broadcasting Organizations.*

② Article 11 of *Rome Convention for the Protection of Performers, Producers of Phonograms and Broadcasting Organizations.*

(五)对邻接权的权利限制(Limitations on Neighboring Rights)

The limitations on neighboring rights are narrated in Article 15 as: "Permitted Exceptions: 1. Specific Limitations; 2. Equivalents with copyright:

Any Contracting State may, in its domestic laws and regulations, provide for exceptions to the protection guaranteed by this Convention as regards: (a) private use; (b) use of short excerpts in connection with the reporting of current events; (c) ephemeral fixation by a broadcasting organization by means of its own facilities and for its own broadcasts; (d) use solely for the purposes of teaching or scientific research." ①

公约中规定了使用邻接权所保护的演出、录音制品及广播节目时，可以不经权利所有人同意、也无须付酬的四种特殊情况：私人使用；在时事报道中有限的使用；广播组织为编排本组织的节目，利用本组织的设备暂时录制；仅仅为教学或科学研究目的而使用。此外，公约还允许成员国自行以国内立法规定颁发强制许可证条件，以防止邻接权所有人滥用自己的专有权。但颁发强制许可证不得与公约的基本原则相冲突。

(六)管理机关(Intergovernmental Committee)

Officials of the International Labor Office, the United Nations Educational, Scientific and Cultural Organization and the Bureau of the International Union for the Protection of Literary and Artistic Works, designated by the Directors—General and the Director thereof, shall constitute the Secretariat of the Committee.

公约由联合国的教科文组织、国际劳工组织及世界知识产权组织共同管理，日常事务由该公约的政府间委员会及其秘书处办理。

(七)"闭合式"公约(Closed Type)

The Rome Convention provides that in order to become a party to the Convention a State must not only be a member of the United Nations, but also a member of the Berne Union or party to the Universal Copyright Convention. Accordingly, a Contracting State ceases to be a party to the Rome Convention as from the time at which it is no longer party either to the Berne or to the Universal Copyright Convention. Because of this link with the copyright conventions, the Rome Convention is sometimes referred to as a "closed" convention from the point of view of the circle of States that may adhere to it.

五、《专利合作条约》(*Patent Cooperation Treaty*)

(一)产生的历史背景(Historical Background of Its Origin)

Under the traditional Paris Convention route, the priority of an earlier application can be claimed for applications filed subsequently in foreign countries but such later applications must be filed within 12 months of the filing date of the earlier application. This involves for the applicant

① Article 15 of *Rome Convention for the Protection of Performers, Producers of Phonograms and Broadcasting Organizations*.

the preparation and filing of patent applications for all countries in which he is seeking protection for his invention within one year of the filing of the first application. This means expenses for translation, patent attorneys in the various countries and payment of fees to the Patent Offices, all at a time when the applicant often does not know whether he is likely to obtain a patent or whether his invention is really new compared with the state of art.

通过《巴黎公约》进行国际申请，意味着每个收到专利申请的国家专利局要对所接受到的每项申请进行形式审查。当专利局对申请进行实质审查时，都必须进行检索确定发明所属领域的现有技术，并进行可专利性的实质审查。

In order to overcome some of the problems involved in the national system, in September 1966, the Executive Committee of the International (Paris) Union for the Protection of Industrial Property(国际保护工业产权联盟执行委员会) invited BIRPI (the predecessor of WIPO 世界知识产权组织的前身) to undertake urgently(紧急地) a study of solutions to reduce the duplication of the effort both for applicants and national Patent Offices. In the following years, a number of BIRPI meetings prepared drafts and a Diplomatic Conference (外交会议) held in Washington, D. C., in June 1970 adopted a treaty called the *Patent Cooperation Treaty*(《专利合作条约》). The *Patent Cooperation Treaty* or "PCT" entered into force on January 24, 1978, and became operational on June 1, 1978, with an initial 18 Contracting States. 1993 年 9 月 15 日，中国政府向世界知识产权组织递交了《专利合作条约》加入书。从 1994 年 1 月 1 日起，中国成为该条约的成员国。并按照国际规定，中国专利局成为 PCT 的受理局、国际检索单位和国际初步审查单位。

(二)缔约宗旨(Stated Purpose)

《专利合作条约》实际上是一部专利申请的程序法。缔结该条约的初衷是为了克服各国专利申请人由于法律背景、语言、申请程序以及格式上的不同而寻求一条简便快捷的途径。

As its name suggests, the Patent Cooperation Treaty is an agreement for international cooperation in the field of patents. It is often spoken of as being the most significant advance ininternational cooperation in this field since the adoption of the Paris Convention itself. It is however largely a treaty for rationalization and cooperation with regard to the filing, searching and examination of patent applications and the dissemination of the technical information contained therein. The PCT does not provide for the grant of "international patents": the task of and responsibility for granting patents remains exclusively in the hands of the Patent Offices of, or acting for, the countries where protection is sought (the "designated Offices"). The PCT does not compete with but, in fact, complements the Paris Convention. Indeed, it is a special agreement under the Paris Convention open only to States which are already party to that Convention. ①

---

① WIPO Interllectual Property Handbook: Policy, Law and Use (Second Edition) [M]. WIPO Publication, 2008: 277.

《专利合作条约》使专利国际申请制度在世界范围发挥了积极的影响，使知识产权保护的国际化迈出了极重要的第一步，因而具有重要意义：专利国际申请制度减少涉外申请过程中大量的重复劳动，克服了申请书中的语言障碍，缩短了国家间的距离；有利于了解世界上的技术动向，避免重复研究；有利于减轻专利局检索的大量工作，在国际申请中，各缔约国的专利局，特别是采取审查原则的专利局，由于可充分利用国际检索报告和国际初步审查报告，便省去了缔约国专利局为进行现有技术检索的大量工作，也减轻了审查的负担。

【英语词汇】

assembly　*n.* 大会
executive board　执行局
ILO　国际劳工组织
International Organization 国际组织
Nice Agreement　《尼斯协定》
PCT　专利合作条约
secretariat　*n.* 秘书处
UNDP　联合国开发计划署
UNESCO　联合国教科文组织
Uruguay Round　乌拉圭回合谈判
Berne Convention　《伯尔尼公约》
GATT　关税和贸易总协定
International Convention　国际公约
Madrid Agreement　《马德里协定》
Paris Convention　《巴黎公约》
Rome Convention　《罗马公约》
UNCTAD　联合国贸易与发展会议
UNEP　联合国环境计划署
UNFAO　联合国粮农组织

【英语句型】

The Agreement on Trade Related Aspects of Intellectual Property Rights (TRIPS) is an international agreement administered by the World Trade Organization (WTO) that sets down minimum standards for many forms of intellectual property (IP) regulation as applied to nationals of other WTO Members.

"set down standards for..."“为……设定了……标准”。

译文：与贸易相关的知识产权协议(TRIPS)是在世界贸易组织(WTO)管辖下对各世贸成员国设定了最低标准的国际性条约。

【阅读资料】

附录　知识产权法考试试题

Appendix　Examination Paper of Intellectual Property Law

知识产权法(A 卷)

知识产权法(B 卷)

知识产权法(A、B 卷答案)